TARTAN NOIR

TARTAN NOIR

The Definitive Guide to Scottish Crime Fiction

LEN WANNER

**FREIGHT
BOOKS**

First published 2015

Freight Books
49-53 Virginia Street
Glasgow, G1 1TS
www.freightbooks.co.uk

ISBN 978-1-910449-08-0
eISBN 978-1-910449-09-7
Typeset by Freight
Printed and bound by Bell and Bain, Glasgow

the publisher acknowledges investment from
Creative Scotland toward the publication of this book

To Chrissie and Mylo

CONTENTS

SPOILER ALERT

The following pages promise to be littered with ideas so dark and disturbing, I fear they may spoil even the purest of minds. For this, you may thank me later. For a different sort of spoiler, however, I must apologise, and I must do so in advance. Since it is not always possible to make a secret of plot twists, character deaths, and shock endings when discussing criminal drama in a critical context, and since it is not always possible to compartmentalise sensitive information and give prior warning of passages which contain it, I may, inadvertently, spoil the odd surprise. Sorry.

At the same time, however, I will do my very best not to spoil your reading pleasure by riding roughshod over any sensitive information. Instead, I hope to act as a friendly guide by clearing a safe passage to and through the literature's most relevant works. And, to demonstrate that this careful approach makes it possible to reveal a secret without ruining a book, I will reveal one now. There is only one literary form to be found in this book, and that is the novel, because although other forms, particularly the novella and the short story, do contain some excellent examples of Tartan Noir, by and large they have been neither as important to the literature's development nor as popular with its readers. Besides, so much of it has been written in novel form that, even in a book as voluminous as this one, I will have to make some difficult cuts. Aye, and a few easy ones, like cat detective mysteries. Let me reassure you that you won't come across a single one of those in the following pages, because last I heard, cats couldn't actually talk and they had absolutely nothing to do with Tartan Noir. You're welcome.

INTRODUCTION

What is Tartan Noir? At the start of a rather long book, dedicated in its entirety to this very question, you may be relieved to know that there is a short answer. Tartan Noir is a Scottish literature which began to make a name for itself under a variety of genre labels in the second half of the 20th century and which, at the beginning of the 21st, has acquired an international reputation larger than any of its contemporary Scottish literatures. It has done all of this despite a lot of confusion about what exactly the term means and what type of writing it describes, so perhaps there is no point in giving a longer answer to the above question just to remove a confusion which seems to have done the literature's commercial success precious little harm.

Then again, to say no harm at all has been done would imply that the huge success of a relatively small number of bestsellers has not narrowed public perception of the literature at large. It would also imply that the huge success of a few bestselling authors has not eclipsed a considerable quantity, and indeed quality, of writing done by authors who have largely been ignored, not only by bestseller lists, but also – and perhaps more regrettably – by posterity. Yet since both of these implications are patently false, the question 'What is Tartan Noir?' may be worth a longer answer after all. And as these introductory thoughts may have shown, another big question is worth answering with care and context: which authors and literatures are obscured when – as has become standard practice – Tartan Noir is used as a mystifying marketing label and applied rather vaguely to all dark contemporary Scottish crime fiction? In the following pages, I hope to answer both of these questions and show that the literature which generally passes for Tartan Noir is somewhat mislabelled, as it encompasses an extraordinarily broad range of styles, subjects, and sub-genres besides those associated with noir.

The best starting point for this book, then, is a short preliminary question. Why did Ian Rankin – the man who invented the label 'Tartan Noir' – choose the ambiguous word 'noir'? Or to put it another way, why did he choose the French word for 'black', a word which no longer has this literal meaning when used as a literary term? Why did he choose a word which initially described stylised, black and white melodramas in American fiction and film of the 1940s but as a literary term soon took on darker shades of meaning such as 'working class tragedy', 'transgressor fiction', and 'psycho thriller'? In short, why did Rankin choose a word which has traditionally described a literature of the margins to serve as a label for a literature which has largely been defined by mainstream art and thought?

"Well," Rankin said when I asked him, "there's no tradition of crime fiction in Scotland but there is a great tradition of quite dark, psychological, Gothic horror stories. Specifically in the '70s, I think in Glasgow, there was a move towards a kind of realistic school of writing about working class life, writing about hard men, writing about hard lives, and writing about urban experience. So it was a move away from the 'kaleyard', which was this romanticised view of Scotland. I think crime fiction tapped into that very nicely, and because there was no tradition of crime fiction in Scotland it meant a completely level playing field. Nobody had to be worried about writing in a certain tradition, and most of us weren't influenced by the English… because there was no Agatha Christie figure you didn't feel you were looking over your shoulder and you had to write a certain kind of book. So, in fact, there's a huge catholicism to Scottish crime fiction… But the balance has swung towards noir, quite dark fiction."[1]

Now, while Rankin is undoubtedly right in referring to Tartan Noir as a broad church of literary innovators, he is just as undoubtedly wrong in claiming that it was built on a 'completely level playing field' free of pioneers and trendsetters. Whether or not *he* has ever looked over his shoulder, countless compatriots of his have, in a manner of speaking, done just that by looking South to 221B Baker Street, London, where crime fiction's most illustrious, and undoubtedly

Scottish, pioneer left a physical monument to the fact that, contrary to Rankin's claim, there most certainly was a Scottish 'Agatha Christie figure'. His name, of course, was Arthur Conan Doyle, and whether or not any of his compatriots have been 'worried' about writing in his tradition, so many fictional gumshoes have followed in the footsteps of his archetypal private detective, Sherlock Holmes, that the latter has become a Scottish synonym for detective fiction which is understood, not just in Scotland, but around the world.

Further disproof of Rankin's theory has since come in the world-famous pages of John Buchan's spy thrillers, Alistair MacLean's crime novels, and Josephine Tey's detective fiction, most notably her 1951 novel *The Daughter of Time*, which in 1990 was voted number one of the 'Top 100 Crime Novels of All Time' by the UK Crime Writers Association. That list, incidentally, also includes Doyle, Buchan, and MacLean, so there would certainly seem to be a long and respectable tradition of crime fiction in Scotland, which is another way of saying that Rankin's literary history is somewhat flawed and hence fails to make sense of his genre label. After all, none of these pioneers of Tartan Noir would have been likely to call their work noir, not even if they had been au fait with the aesthetic term. Like most of today's Tartan Noirists, they favoured a mood for their writing which was far from black, so far in fact that it seems questionable whether they would even have called it noir in Rankin's vague sense of 'quite dark fiction'.

However, 'Tartan Noir' will have to do as a collective term. It is already in wide use and, due to its misleading but marketable evocation of Franco-Gaelic exoticism, it is unlikely to yield to the more exact but rather prosaic 'dark contemporary Scottish crime fiction', so the pragmatic thing for me to do in this book is to define what Tartan Noir really is and help refine the term's future use. The best way to do so, I believe, is to show that none of the writers most associated with Tartan Noir – writers like Ian Rankin, Val McDermid, Stuart MacBride, Chris Brookmyre, and Quintin Jardine – write much or any noir, while most of those who do write noir – writers like Alexander Trocchi, Hugh C. Rae, Gordon Williams, Iain Banks, and Barry Graham – are not commonly associated with Tartan Noir.

Demonstrating this in the following pages will illustrate that, while the literature's balance has indeed swung towards 'quite dark fiction', it has not swung all the way to noir.

Most Tartan Noirists, after all, have made their name at some distance from noir, be it in detective, police, or serial killer fiction, so I will discuss these three sub-genres separately in chapters one, two, and three. And seeing as Scottish Noir has mainly been written by cult writers who have been unable to make a name for their noir writing among readers of mainstream crime fiction, I will discuss this literature of the margins in the fourth and final chapter. By choosing this chapter division I do not, however, wish to suggest the existence of solid boundaries. Instead, I hope that separation signals my double intent to shed light on Tartan Noir's four main facets as well as bring out the literature's less visible connections which cut across its evident contrasts.

As for the internal chapter structure, since detective, police, serial killer, and noir fiction all have their own genre conventions and critical jargon, the introduction of each chapter will include brief histories of the respective literature along with clarifications of its key concepts. This will be followed by ten case studies, each of which will highlight at least one of the literature's defining features. And since the order of these case studies will follow the order of the novels' publication, the main part of each chapter will outline the literature's development at the end of the 20th and start of the 21st century. A short synopsis section will then draw out the features which have most distinguished the sub-genre in question, and a final, in-depth cross-examination of two novels will offer some conclusive analysis of the immense diversity as well as the surprising commonalities found in this literature.

If, by making these observations, I should succeed in sharpening the wide-angled view which I am asking you to take in the following pages, my purpose in publishing them will have been served. I do not, after all, hope to pronounce any final verdict on the 'true' identity or merit of Tartan Noir. No such verdict could be delivered upon four cross-examinations, nor even upon inclusion of 40 further case studies, and this obstacle to all final verdicts looms even larger when it comes to a literature like Scottish crime fiction, a literature so immensely diverse that one reader might justifiably object to my in- or exclusion of a particular novel while another could easily derail my attempts at composite definition by inflating the importance of a minor counter example. So in each chapter I will make my selection based, not on personal favourites or official canons, but on cultural legacy. I will try to pick the novels which have most defined the development of their sub-genres, either because their literary merit has inspired other writers to contribute to the literature's diversification across a wide range of counter-cultural movements, or because their commercial success has incentivised a degree of conformity in the literature's mainstream.

As for the countless other writers who, if not omitted, might contribute even more facets to the literature's perception, I regret not being able to include them here and hasten to add that I mean no disrespect. Unfortunately, and this may be obvious, no overview can be all-inclusive, and at this breadth it is broad enough to take in each sub-genre's range, the context of each writer's work, and the proportion of each contribution to the literature at large. Just as importantly, though, it is not broad enough to provide encyclopaedic detail, the kind that could all too easily distract from context and proportion, thus potentially disguising the literature's immense diversity. So by focusing on ten case studies and one cross-examination, I hope to demonstrate rather than distract from said diversity, and in due course this should allow me to demonstrate the literature's perhaps most definitive aspect, the fact that there are too many multi-cultural tributaries and single-minded currents in contemporary Scottish crime fiction for any mainstream to take the form new readers may expect to find, a general anti-Englishness.

Indeed, although one popular prejudice against the Scots is that they stand for nothing but against the English, as I hope to show in the following pages, very few Scottish crime writers risk a nationalist reading, let alone encourage one. Instead, there is among them a strong trend to complicate definition by nationality, which, ironically, is one of the few trends that unite the majority of Scotland's contemporary crime writers in a national literature. And this brings us to the essential difficulty in defining Tartan Noir. Not only is 'anti-English' not the right label for this literature, but there is not a single other label that would fit it any better, simply because *any* label would imply the existence of a common denominator, when in fact its many irreconcilable differences illustrate that there is no such thing. So, rather than force this hugely multi-faceted literature into some narrow theoretical framework just to make it fit the catchy label 'Tartan Noir', let me instead try to capture what can so easily escape our notice as our thoughts are increasingly crowded by boringly stereotypical and barely distinguishable marketing strategies – the literature's immense diversity.

CHAPTER ONE –
THE DETECTIVE NOVEL

Typically, detective fiction tells the story of one man's quest for truth, if not justice.

Stereotypically, the fictional detective tells his own story, that of a lone wolf who lays down the law of the jungle as he roams the mean streets of an urban waste land in search of redemption for our sins, a good man who all too often does the wrong thing, but always for the right reason. Through the lens of this 'private eye' the author lets us look at what goes on when the lights go out. He, for he too is typically a man, lets an outsider do what the police can or will not do when he looks into private indecencies of public interest. Not only does this furnish him with a narrative strategy, it also lets us see the public's indifference to the private indignities which often attend the exposure of perceived indecencies, and this soon forms our shared resolve to find a way through the thicket of clues and conspiracies. Of course, time and again the alpha male investigator loses said way among loose women and looser plots. He will even lose consciousness, repeatedly, and at times he will probably risk losing the powers of consecutive thought along with those of plot continuity. And yet he loses neither his courage nor our confidence. On the contrary, he gradually wins our trust as a professional with principles – the last of the good guys – and in the end this knight errant finds his grail, often tarnished yet always transformative.

So much for the stereotypical detective novel. Beyond this stereotype, detective fiction has long been notable for a number of serious literary merits, including the general consensus that the first form of crime fiction was a detective story, and that detective fiction is the starting point of a diverse literary heritage which has spanned some 180 years. Accordingly, the starting point of this chapter has to be 1833 and "Théorie de la Démarche" – "The Theory of the Walk". According to its author, Honoré de Balzac, this essay paved the way for a new investigative technique by expanding ground-level sociological observation with wide-angled metaphysical insight. The first to use this technique in detective fiction was Edgar Allan Poe. In a short story of 1840, titled "The Man of the Crowd", he presented the case of a curious Londoner who develops theories about criminal degeneracy as he observes crowds of strangers, and this story has since been seen as the X-ray of detective fiction.

Shadowed by the Gothic tales of the 1830s, "The Man of the Crowd" outlined literary features which Poe soon consolidated in the shape of C. Auguste Dupin, amateur detective and serial protagonist of "The Murders in the Rue Morgue" (1841), "The Mystery of Marie Rogêt" (1842), and "The Purloined Letter" (1844). These three short stories have become known as the first tales of 'ratiocination', a term Poe introduced in the second of these tales, "The Mystery of Marie Rogêt", where he used it three times to describe his detective's extraordinary detection skills with reference to his 'ratio', the Latin word for reason and computation. Ever since, these tales have shown generations of crime writers how to create tension between such classic counter concepts as brains and brawn, the hunter and the hunted, the bohemian but brilliant detective and the bureaucratic but bumbling constabulary. In the process, they have made Poe, as novelist and critic Julian Symons puts it, "the undisputed father of the detective story, although he would have been disconcerted by many of his children and grandchildren."[2]

Before moving on to some of those children and grandchildren, however, it is worth challenging the implication of this last statement, just to get the record straight in a book on Scottish crime fiction. Sherlock Holmes was *not* the first of the fictional detectives. Poe's fact-finding flâneur, lone wanderer of an alienating metropolis and grand inquisitor of an aggressive modernity, first found eminent proponents in Alexandre Dumas and Émile Gaboriau, who brought him to public attention in the tales of Messrs Jackal and Lecoq of *Les Mohicans de*

Paris (1854-59) and *L'Affaire Lerouge* (1866). At the end of the 19th and the start of the 20th century, he was further popularised by the poetry of Charles Baudelaire and the philosophy of Walter Benjamin, and yet it is Holmes who has prevailed as the most eloquent byword of the fictional detective.

By way of explaining this unique reputation, Holmes expert John Hodgson says Doyle "created a new kind of protagonist, a detective who, going beyond the mental acuteness of Poe's Dupin and the dawning professionalism of Gaboriau's Lecoq, would 'reduce this fascinating but unorganized business to something nearer to an exact science'."[3] In other words, Doyle did more for the detective story than any of his predecessors. As Hodgson reminds us here by quoting from Doyle's autobiography, Doyle reduced this fascinating but unorganized business to something nearer to an exact science by basing Holmes on his mentor in the medical faculty of Edinburgh University, Dr Joseph Bell. In doing so, he related storytelling to science.

Perhaps this goes some way towards explaining why his stories, most of which are told in the first person by Holmes's assistant Dr John H. Watson, read like descriptive accounts of experiments in detection, where the end of every adventure is followed by an explanation of every action. Yet whether or not this narrative effect was intended, Holmes's move towards 'an exact science' certainly indicates his significance in the history of crime fiction. As Lee Horsley, a leading expert in this history, states, "The evolution of a genre depends on a combination of continuity and change, and Holmes is unquestionably the first key figure from whom other writers differentiated their protagonists, only rivalled by the composite hard-boiled protagonist created by Hammett and Chandler in the early twentieth century."[4]

Yet prior to discussing those composite hard-boiled protagonist, Sam Spade and Philip Marlowe, it is worth pausing to remove the possible confusion which can attend such a personality cult. Yes, Symons is right to conclude that "part of Holmes's attraction was that, far more than any of his later rivals, he was so evidently a Nietzschean superior man. It was comforting to have such a man on one's side," if only because, "when the law cannot dispense justice, Holmes does so himself. He is a final court of appeal and the idea that such a court might exist, personified by an individual, was permanently comforting to his readers."[5] Yet literary history is full of incidents when Holmes's admirers have been a little too comfortable with the stereotype of the 'Nietzschean superior man', a stereotype which has little in common with Nietzsche's amoral artist tyrant. This complex creature, after all, was not some cartoonish superhero but the product of a thought experiment based on the philosophy of the Italian Renaissance and perhaps best understood as a Machiavellian bogeyman of the Western middle class and its pseudo-Christian value system.

As a result of removing this complexity, detectives working in the tradition of the eccentric Holmes have often had more in common with the epic Hercules. Others have gone all the way to caricature and come to resemble such camp clichés as Hercule Poirot and Lord Peter Wimsey. Yet there is a far more interesting – though far less appreciated – reason for Holmes's historical significance and enduring appeal. As Martin Priestman, an authority on classic crime fiction, puts the case, "what is far more interesting about him is the way in which he encapsulates some of the qualities of the series form itself within a fairly loose envelope of potentially contradictory traits."[6] Chief among those potentially contradictory traits is his quest for the singular cause, which repeatedly highlights his dual nature.

Holmes, who first appeared in *A Study in Scarlet* (1887) as an instinctive anti-intellectual, returned in *The Sign of Four* (1890) as an intellectual aesthete. Yet throughout two more novels and 56 short stories, he integrated the tension between these two sides of his personality in his search for single causes. So, while Holmes has become a 'Nietzschean superior man', he has earned this epithet not just for comforting his readers as a final court of appeal but also for containing his inherent contradictions. In other words, while he has become 'the first key figure from whom other writers differentiated their protagonists', key to his difference is the fact that his creator differentiated him into more than a single, static figure.

Doyle's serialisation of Holmes's adventures was, then, less the result of the character's uniqueness than of his singularity, a difference about which Doyle was very pragmatic in his autobiography: "It had struck me that a single character running through a series, if it only engaged the attention of the reader, would bind that reader to that particular magazine."[7] Doyle has indeed bound generations of readers to his series, but he has done so by giving his readers more than an engaging single character. He has also given them closure by giving explanations for everything that seemed outré, and he has given continuing life to Holmes by giving him a life outside each story. His legacy, therefore, goes beyond the entertainment value of his tales of suspense. By dramatising Holmes's dual nature over the course of a long-running series which is nominally held together by a single character, Doyle demonstrated the potential to create tension in serial crime fiction. He demonstrated that even the central character can change over the course of a series, and change several times in ways which might invite disbelief or indeed derision if dramatised in standalone stories.

One way of reassuring readers that such character inconsistencies can be psychologically sound is to remind them that, while inconsistencies of any sort tend to indicate poor writing when they occur in the span of a single story, in this case the story is situated in an overarching series and thus allows for greater flexibility of characterisation. Doyle made a habit of offering such reminders by having his investigative team repeatedly talk about their previous cases and long partnership. Such inter-textual links have since become popular genre conventions, as have Doyle's habits of proselytising on behalf of the private investigator, prioritising mystic intuition and inference over bureaucratic police procedures, and patterning serial detective fiction in harmony with a theme borrowed from baroque music: repetition with variation. It was not until these conventions started playing in concert that detective fiction took on its now familiar format and, as Priestman puts it, "it was not until the 1890s, with Sherlock Holmes, that its endless re-enactment became a fully addictive event."[8]

Doyle, then, did not just prove serial detective fiction to be sustainable. He also provided a model for others to repeat his success, and in the genre's long history, one innovation alone shares this model's immense significance: the motto 'We Never Sleep'. Taken from the emblem of the Pinkerton National Detective Agency, which had been founded in the US in 1850 by Scotsman Allan Pinkerton, this motto forever changed the way we see the Private Investigator, or PI for short. The emblem was a wide open eye, which suggested not only deep insight but also an iconic pun on the PI: 'private eye'. After World War One, this private I/eye became a regular in the pages of detective fiction, and around the same time he became 'hard-boiled', which is to say he distanced himself from the rationale of the classic detective story: that human affairs are ruled by Reason and that Reason is represented by a detective who dispassionately rights all wrongs. Developed in counterpoint to this somewhat outdated British concept, the 'hard-boiled' private detective became an American sentimentalist who differs significantly from his 'soft-boiled' ancestors.

To put it in the words of Peter Messent, an expert in 20th-century American literature, the hard-boiled PI differs "in the personal vulnerability that comes from an immersion within the violent world being investigated, in the recognition that corruption is not just confined to the criminal underclass but pervades the entire social fabric, and in the (romantic) sense of alienation and isolation from the social body that accompanies that recognition."[9] Dealing with this new set of challenges, he came to depend on qualities which set him far part from the dispassionate amateurs of Poe and Doyle, qualities which Ralph Willett, author of *Hard-Boiled Detective Fiction*, summarises as "professional skills, physical courage affirmed as masculine potency, fortitude, moral strength, a fierce desire for justice, social marginality and a degree of anti-intellectualism."[10]

Yet it was a more subtle change that was to mark the generational gap and mature these frontier characteristics into genre conventions. The hard-boiled private eye came to rely on reason only in concert with emotion, and this departure from the cold rationalism of his predecessor's puzzle-solving mentality culminated in his declaration of independence from its logical and ideological constraints.

Demonstrating this emancipation, he dispensed with the consulting detective and decided to be his own narrator, thus defining himself in his own voice from a first-person point of view. This let hard-boiled writers emphasise the 'private' identity of their private eye, so much so that he became significantly more identifiable with the private 'I' of the reader. As a result of this shift in focus, the detective could now emphasise his central role in the story along with his far more complex sensibility, and this has become a popular genre convention known as the 'hard-boiled conceit'.

Having pioneered this narrative aesthetic, Dashiell Hammett is habitually cited as the founder of the hard-boiled school. Yet his contribution to said school of writing is often confused by those who mention him in the same breath as his co-founder, Raymond Chandler, the man who popularised two of the literature's most recognisable genre conventions: lengthy passages of deep introspection and a highly wrought prose style. Hammett, on the other hand, focused on action, description, and dialogue. Thoughts and feelings he avoided almost entirely. To be clear, Hammett wrote in a spare, third-person objective style that has very little in common with Chandler's flair for poetic self-reflection and purple one-liners, and it has done far less for the development of the hard-boiled school. So it is not his style that has earned Hammett the honour of becoming known as the founder of the hard-boiled school. It is his subject.

As a former operative of the Pinkerton Agency, Hammett drew on lived experience when he selected as his central protagonist – and as that of most hard-boiled literature to come – a laconic loner. Hammett replaced the outdated bohemian dilettante of classic detective fiction with a very private investigator who lives by his own code of conduct to be tough yet true in a world that has become as confusing as it is corrupt. Admittedly, Hammett did not invent the type. A few years earlier, in 1923, Carroll John Daly had provided a prototype for this new protagonist when he introduced his PI Race Williams in the short story "Knights of the Open Palm", yet this prototype did not go into mass-production until after 1930, when Hammett published *The Maltese Falcon*. In this modern classic – a serialised novel famously adapted to film in 1941 with Humphrey Bogart in the role of PI Sam Spade – Hammett did more than refine Daly's model. He defined the hard-boiled protagonist for generations to come, so Horsley is right to conclude that, "It is Spade, of course, who has come to be seen as the archetypal hard-boiled private eye, a loner whose audacity and individualism are products of a thoroughgoing distrust of conventional social arrangements and familiar pieties."[11]

Hammett's heritage, then, is that he shaped the hard-boiled subject, the private eye. In doing so, he pushed so hard against the boundaries of a formerly rather conservative genre that they have come to accommodate a wide range of attacks on social and political establishments. In the process, so-called 'pulp fiction' has proved that it can take life and death seriously – and can therefore itself be taken seriously. Hammett was the first to prove this, and it was his way of doing so that his co-founder of the hard-boiled school recognised as an historic service to literature. As Chandler put it, "Hammett was the ace performer... Hammett gave murder back to the kind of people that commit it for reasons, not just to provide a corpse; and with the means at hand, not hand-wrought dueling pistols, curare and tropical fish."[12]

This achievement, however, should not distract from the fact that the shaping of the murder mystery – even the realistic type which has focused on the hard-boiled private eye – has been a team effort. Sure, until Chandler himself came along and changed the way the literature was written and read, Hammett was the only one to receive serious critical recognition, which explains why he was picked out of a sizeable literary movement to represent the hard-boiled school, but as class-rep he could only do so much for the private eye. As T.J. Binyon reminds us in his seminal book on the history of detective fiction, *Murder Will Out*, "if the era of Prohibition, with its lawlessness, gangsters, and corrupt police, provided the reality from which the private eye sprang, it was the pulp magazines which made him popular."[13]

According to Horsley, it was one magazine in particular which not only popularised the private eye but produced the tradition of hard-boiled writing, for "its development as a subgeneric form of crime fiction is indissolubly linked with the founding of *Black Mask* magazine in 1920... with its growing reputation for publishing fast-paced, colloquial stories, and promoting 'economy of expression' and 'authenticity in character and action'."[14] Hammett was first published in the magazine in the early 1920s, Chandler a decade later, and within no time each had made a name for himself for having conceived the true spirit of the hard-boiled private eye tradition.

Now, whichever one of these two radically different writers may have had more to do with the conception of the literature's true spirit, an ironic consequence of their collaborative parentage has been the conventional disregard for their differences. As LeRoy Panek, a leading expert in popular literature, points out, "for Chandler the concept of being hard-boiled grew to become more complex and nuanced than it had been in the hands of his predecessors... less to do with callous relationships with people and more to do with attitude. And it was decidedly more psychological than physical... their hardness comes from their ability to take punishment and bounce back, persist, and finish what they started."[15] Yet their psychological hardness also makes them strangers – even to themselves – and by granting his readers access to these internal developments, Chandler set himself far apart from Hammett and his famous avoidance of introspection. Writing at such considerable psychological depth, and indeed at such considerable aesthetic distance from his predecessors, Chandler famously made alienation a central genre convention of the hard-boiled detective story, a characteristic which has so often been mimicked that it has become something of a cliché to make one's protagonists as alienated as Chandler's are on their lonely struggles through stories of exploitation, fragmentation, and marginalisation.

Perhaps more importantly, however, Chandler established what for many, including Panek, have become essentials of the hard-boiled prose style: "non-standard diction, short declarative sentences relying on active verbs, first person narration with asides to the listener/reader, and occasional wisecracks... Most importantly Chandler made the simile a standard feature of hard-boiled style... to characterize the narrator by his range of reference and his original, shocking, or at least novel juxtapositions."[16] It is worth noting that Chandler's popularisation of this technical device went hand in hand with a topical development in the literature at large. Around the same time as PIs started using similes to make sense of an estranging world because similes allowed them to make connections through likeness, they also started taking on cases and persevering with their investigations because of their newly formed personal connections with the people involved.

To give just one example of this seismic shift in both style and psychology, Chandler's seven novel series about PI Philip Marlowe, starting with *The Big Sleep* (1939) and concluding with *Playback* (1958), charts the differences between the two types in one character. While the pre-war Marlowe typically tried to keep his distance from his case and its principals, even though he cared about both, the post-war Marlowe and the tough guys following in his footsteps typically tried to keep their distance from themselves, even as they got close to others. Yet despite such categorical differences, their dramas are heightened by the same process: their professional detachment collapses into personal entanglement. Thus, their cases have the same emotional structure. As Leonard Cassuto puts it in *Hard-Boiled Sentimentality: The Secret History of American Crime Stories*, "Chandler drew the modern blueprint for one of the ur-plots of hard-boiled crime fiction, in which the detective arrives to fix the broken family."[17]

What is more, Chandler mirrored this sentimentalism in his narrative structure, in which the detective attempts to fix or at least tie up the loose plot as he gets drawn into his client's sob story. Along the way, this cross between a family fixer and a knight-errant has become a measure of masculinity for generations of hard-boiled protagonists, an archetype monumentalised in Chandler's exhortation that "down these mean streets a man must go who is not himself mean, who is neither tarnished nor afraid. The detective in this kind of story must be such a man. He is the hero; he is everything. He must be a complete man and a common man and yet an unusual man... a man of honour... He must be the best man in his world and a good enough man for any world..."[18] Yet since these oft-quoted words have led countless imitators down the cul-de-sac of cliché, the critic and crime writer John Harvey may be right to remind you, dear reader, that you "follow old Ray down those mean streets and sumptuous sub-clauses at your peril!"[19]

What is certain is that, if you do not face this peril with sufficient attention to the complexities of the hard-boiled character, you are likely to make the same mistake as those who set Chandler's supposedly cynical tough guy in clear-cut opposition to Doyle's supposedly cerebral detection robot. That such a simplistic dialectic is indeed a mistake becomes obvious when you consider, as does John Scaggs in *Crime Fiction*, a handbook on the genre's literary history, that "the shift from the analytical certainties and reassuringly stable social order of classical detective fiction to the gritty realism of the 'mean streets' of hard-boiled fiction disguised a certain continuity, in Chandler, at any rate, with the idealistic quest for truth and justice characteristic of romance."[20]

This idealistic quest first found its way to detective fiction through the afore-mentioned tales of Poe and Doyle, and via the heraldic work of Chandler its traces have run through most detective stories written ever since. In view of this continuity, the pop culture critic Philip Simpson notes that, long after Marlowe led the way down those mean streets, most of today's fictional detectives still "embark upon quests through nightmarish worlds to solve problems of archetypal significance – in a sense, knight-errants with only their own codes of justice to guide them through a fallen world."[21]

In the hope of demonstrating how they differ in said codes of justice, and in the hope of assessing their authors' contributions to the genre, I will, in the following pages, follow a few of these errant knights as they embark upon such quests through the country which, since the days of Arthur Conan Doyle and Sherlock Holmes, may be considered the home of detective fiction – Scotland.

THE SCOTTISH DETECTIVE NOVEL

I
n Scotland, detective fiction dates back to the 1860s and the days of Edinburgh's first real-life detective, James McLevy. Famed for both his impressive clearance rate and his scientific investigative technique, which he confidently documented in a number of notebooks, McLevy became one of two models for Sherlock Holmes. The other was Dr Joseph Bell, a member of the medical faculty at the University of Edinburgh, where McLevy sought forensic advice and Doyle trained as a doctor. In 1887, Doyle introduced what turned out to be an addictive blend of the two men to the readers of *Beeton's Christmas Annual.* He called his creation a 'consulting detective' and made him the centre piece of Scotland's first detective novel, *A Study in Scarlet.*

That Holmes requires no description here, more than a century later, is evidence enough of the detective's enduring appeal to generations of readers. More noteworthy perhaps is the variety of tributes to his memory which have further increased his appeal, tributes such as John Buchan's serial character Richard Hannay. Featuring him in seven novels, most notably *The Thirty-Nine Steps* (1915) and *Greenmantle* (1916), Buchan made Hannay a soldier and occasional spy, adjusted the spirit of the character to the spirit of the times, and thus matured the amateur investigator into a professional man of action and adventure. He also shifted the genre's focus to the conflict between political and personal dramas by involving his protagonist in international affairs yet letting him tell his stories from a limited, first-person point of view. In doing so, he set the stage for the likes of Alistair MacLean, who further promoted this conflict, along with its narrative strategy, in six intricately plotted novels, of which at least *Night Without End* (1959) and *Ice Station Zebra* (1963) are master-classes in the art of integrating detective and thriller elements, yet in view of what happened in 1977, these master-classes were mere warm-up acts.

To say so in hindsight is not to diminish their literary merits, but rather to give a due sense of their proportion in the history of Scottish crime fiction. In 1977, after all, William McIlvanney redefined the literature with his landmark detective novel, *Laidlaw*, while its eponymous protagonist, Jack Laidlaw, redefined the fictional detective. The character, who has since returned in *The Papers of Tony Veitch* (1983) and *Strange Loyalties* (1991), is one of a kind, or at least he was one of a kind before generations of crime writers modelled their detectives on him. In all probability, most of these writers have done so indirectly and perhaps even unknowingly by modelling their detectives on a far more famous colleague of Laidlaw's, Ian Rankin's John Rebus. Yet as Rankin himself is quick to admit, he owes a lot to McIlvanney:

"McIlvanney was very important to me personally because he was a literary novelist, you know. He'd won the Whitbread Prize for fuck's sake, and then suddenly he's writing gritty urban crime novels set in Glasgow… it was important to me that a serious writer was writing crime fiction."[22]

Rankin has since blurbed the reissued paperback version of *Laidlaw* to add, "It's doubtful I would be a crime writer without the influence of McIlvanney's *Laidlaw*." And as I will show in the following round-up of 10 novels, which together span and define the modern era of Scottish detective fiction, *Laidlaw* has influenced not just Rankin's writing career but also his characterisation of Rebus. That is to say, McIlvanney has influenced the work of most modern Scottish detective writers. He legitimised their chosen genre by treating it as a literature worthy of 'serious' writers. He put a character at the heart of this literature who may now strike many as a cliché but who was then a true original: the Scottish drinker with a detection problem. And he profoundly influenced Rankin's work, which has since made his attitude to detective fiction as popular as his archetype of the fictional detective, Jack Laidlaw.

William McIlvanney – *Laidlaw*

So let's start with *Laidlaw*. Almost four decades after its publication, it is almost impossible to overstate this novel's significance, for it is proof of the fact that McIlvanney was – and is – more than the pioneer of a new era in Scottish detective fiction. It is also proof of the fact that Andrew Pepper, an authority on 20th century crime fiction, was right when he recently pointed out that "the variety and scope of what we might call hard-boiled writing has too often been overlooked in favor of the canonization of its chief practitioners."[23] McIlvanney was – and is – better known for his writing outside the genre of crime fiction, presumably because versatility is often deemed a division rather than an addition of assets, so his due fame, the routine repetition of praise, has been delayed by the variety of his writing. I say delayed rather than denied because ever since the recent republication of his collected novels, including such modern classics as *Docherty* and *The Kiln*, his services to literature have been lauded with the solemn ardour of the late convert, while his afore-mentioned influence on Scottish crime fiction has earned him the unofficial title 'godfather of Tartan Noir'.

Now, in case this belated celebration of McIlvanney as the man behind Tartan Noir – arguably Scotland's biggest literary movement of the past half-century – should strike some as a bit of a grandiose reception for an old and fairly short novel, it is worth noting that in 1977, *Laidlaw* was more than just another portrait of the detective as a cynic. And despite having inspired a lot of more or less artful imitation in the intervening years, it remains more than just another one of those old-familiar portraits. Yes, it bears evident traces of the American hard-boiled tradition, but *Laidlaw* is the Scottish precedent of a living original, a story about a distinct and dynamic personality suspended in what McIlvanney eloquently calls "that careful balance between pessimism, the assumed defeat of contrived expectations, and hope, the discovery of unexpected possibilities."[24] It is the introduction of Chandler's 'unusual man' to Scotland, where his 'search of a hidden truth' leads Laidlaw through an investigation of his cultural Calvinism to a mind- and genre-expanding discovery.

As he says about criminality – and about our social arrangements which allow some of us to think we have nothing to do with it – "we're all accessories. It's just that in specific cases some are more directly involved than others."[25]

In this case, Laidlaw comes to understand the disheartening pragmatism of our justice system, namely that "the Court will keep only what matters, the way in which the person became an event."[26] On an impulse of defiance which is as stubborn as it is compassionate, Laidlaw lets himself get more directly involved to keep the people at the heart of his investigation in his heart's memory, refusing out of superior veracity to forget the victim, the bereaved, and the fact that murder, though the end of devastation for the dead, can lead to the undoing of lives that have yet to be lived. As the genre critic George Grella says about this type of public servant, "No matter what it may cost him, the detective follows his moral code [which] often exacts severe personal sacrifice."[27]

To be more specific, Laidlaw's moral code exacts severe personal sacrifice as he tries to deal with the judgmental distance from his colleagues, the attritional digs from his friends, and the inevitable divorce from his wife. Understandably enough, the latter looms largest in his mind, for even incidental remarks have the irresistible power to entrench the two of them in habitual enemy positions from which they exchange harsh words across a disagreement that is as central to their marriage as it is insurmountable, a disagreement on the value and dignity of other people's lives. It is in one of these exchanges that Laidlaw sets himself as far apart from his wife as from his equally insensitive colleagues as he tells her honestly, though rather abrasively, that "Somebody is fucking dead. That may be a nuisance to you. But it's a fucking sight worse for them."[28]

Laidlaw is a man of contradictions, an unfaithful believer in fidelity who finds faith in his desk drawer, where he keeps his cache of the hard stuff, only in his case the hard stuff is not some seasoned single malt but a literary blend of Kierkegaard, Camus, and Unamuno. He is indeed an unusual man, yet perhaps most so in the fact that, although he is often afraid that he might lose the courage of his doubts, he somehow always manages to hold on to it. And while his polarising personality might make some disagree that he is 'the best man in his world and a good enough man for any world', few will disagree that he has become an inspiration for countless Scottish writers, an inspiration not to fall into the genre trap and write about detectives who happen to be human beings, but to look beyond their protagonists' plot function and write about them as human beings who happen to be detectives.

With *Laidlaw*, then, the hard-boiled detective landed in Scotland and hit the ground running, an image McIlvanney introduces as the novel's leitmotif even in its opening lines: "Running was a strange thing… Running was a dangerous thing. It was a billboard advertising panic, a neon sign spelling guilt."[29] Losing no time to depart from the orderly progression of classic detective fiction, McIlvanney tells us in the opening scene that the speaker of these lines is the murderer, a man running through the darkness of Glasgow to escape not his pursuers but his guilt, so from the get-go we know that we are reading not a 'whodunit' but a 'whydunit'. And by way of disorienting readers accustomed to the literature's neat moral categories, Laidlaw's introduction in scene two suggests that there is a lot more common ground between the admittedly guilty and the apparently innocent than readers of detective fiction were until then used to seeing. After all, Laidlaw creates a strong associative link between himself and the criminal from the previous scene when he picks up his running motif and admits that, far from feeling safe in the sense of moral enlightenment traditionally accorded to fictional detectives, "he remembered nights when the terror of darkness had driven him through to his parents' room. He must have run for miles on that bed."[30]

Back in the present, we learn that Laidlaw has a sidekick named Harkness, yet while this may suggest that the child's fear has become the adult's friend, it may also suggest that darkness is never far from his side, metaphorically or not. The latter can be read as subtle symbolism of the novel's central theme, Laidlaw's charge that we are all to one degree or another accessories to what goes on when the lights go out. As he soon discovers, some will go to extreme lengths to ensure that their connections to certain dark deeds remain hidden in darkness, and so the rest of the novel is about Laidlaw's sustained attempt at measuring these extreme lengths and limiting the damage which those who go to them can do, not only to individuals, but to entire communities. This being a crime novel, his daring efforts create increasingly dramatic interference from the murderer's network of undesirables, yet despite a tenacious legion of dangers and distractions, Laidlaw's focus stays on the novel's overriding question whether this murder is really the result of a love story gone bad. The answer he finally finds is as honest as it is affecting: "I don't know. But what I do know is that more folk than two were present at that murder. And what charges do you bring against the others?"[31]

'The others' come from all classes, so when Laidlaw brings his charges against the city of Glasgow, he brings them against a microcosm of humanity. Perhaps it is this universal validity of his charges that has guaranteed the novel's lasting impact on Scottish detective and crime fiction. Perhaps it is the deeply understood nature of the people he addresses with his two main charges that has done so, charge one being that we abominate in others the faults and failures that are most manifestly our own, charge two that we then allow ourselves, with a mind-blowing lack of shame and shrewdness, to be astonished by them. Or perhaps *Laidlaw* is still read and revered because its detective, unlike so many of his colleagues, avoids facile finger-pointing and instead admits that writing people's faults and failures off as monstrosities is "the tax we pay for the unreality we choose to live in. It's a fear of ourselves."[32] Since most of McIlvanney's protagonists are partially blinded by this fear, they see the world not as it is but as they are, and eventually all these twisted perspectives form a kaleidoscopic discourse on individual hurt and structural violence. Yet this intellectual discourse also resonates on a deeper, visceral level, for it is reflected in the structure of the story where no single viewpoint gives unity to the violence, and so the many emotionally charged perspectives create a sharp 360 degree view of a dangerous city and its divided society.

Ian Rankin – *Knots & Crosses*

Building on this design of the detective as a questioner in whose consciousness the meanings of other people's lives emerge, Ian Rankin based his detective in Edinburgh. Starting in 1987 with the publication of *Knots & Crosses*, he has documented its changing social and political lives in a series of 19 novels featuring one of the world's most famous fictional detectives, John Rebus. Ageing in real time, Rebus initially retired in 2007's *Exit Music* but returned to work in 2012's *Standing in Another Man's Grave*. In the course of this career, which by the standards of real detectives and indeed by those of their fictional counterparts has been exceptionally long, Rebus has shown that Rankin's work is influenced in equal measure by William McIlvanney and James Ellroy.

Like those grand masters of Tartan and LA Noir, Rankin portrays the dynamics of urban change through the prism of a city's police work. And like them, he does so in the awareness that this shift in narrative perspective from the alienated private detective to the professional police detective constitutes what Josh Cohen, an expert in modern literary theory, calls "a critique of the romanticised and historically inaccurate figuration of crime as existential conflict between alienated individual and urban modernity."[33] Yet despite this implicit critique, Rankin characterises Rebus as an alienated individual locked into an existential conflict with urban modernity. So Brian Diemert, an authority on the history of genre fiction, is right to observe that "the Rebus novels are clearly tied to the traditions of American hard-boiled fiction and film-noir."[34]

To clarify how far back these ties go, Rankin lets Rebus describe himself as "one of the old school… a one-hundred percent policeman's policeman, that's me."[35] In other words, Rankin makes him a sarcastic sceptic of institutional authority and thus makes it clear that he conceived Rebus as a typically – some might say stereotypically – Scottish cousin of the American hard-boiled private eye. A little later, Rankin removes all doubt as to Rebus's position on the family tree of hard-boiled literature. With confidence bordering on impertinence, he places him on its Scottish branch, right beside McIlvanney's Jack Laidlaw, by letting it be known that Rebus is neighbours with a certain Jock Laidlaw, "an old man... with a stick... his bottom false-teeth had been lost or forgotten about... an old trooper."[36]

Now, some may read this description as Rankin's tongue-in-cheek attempt to belittle or even besmirch McIlvanney's legacy. Yet perhaps it is better read as a young writer's harmless – if rather charmless – attempt to mark his territory. Not only is the latter reading consistent with Rankin's characterisation of Rebus as a man who "isn't exactly friendly with anybody."[37] It is also consistent with Rebus's history of competitive machismo, having "trained for the SAS and come out top of his class."[38] Indeed, it is even consistent with his backstory, for when the disciplinarian ethos of his previous employer, the army, pushed Rebus into a mental breakdown, he decided to quit and start working for another disciplinarian institution, the police, and much like his competitive nature, this masochistic decision demonstrates that Rebus is not merely scratching at Laidlaw's image. He is also made in it.

See, like the 'old trooper', this young upstart is a man of contradictions, a contrarian determined to go his own way in an authoritarian institution built on team work. Indeed, so numerous are their commonalities that Gill Plain, an expert in 20th century crime fiction, might as well be talking about Laidlaw when she says about Rebus that, "He is a hard-drinking obsessive loner, who has difficulty sustaining relationships. He is distrustful of institutional structures and is inclined to privilege his private morality over public law – a tendency which inevitably sets him in conflict with authority."[39] So it should come as no surprise that such a conflict with authority arises within the opening pages of his debut and that Rebus resolves it less like a typical policeman than like an old trooper. Upon learning that a superior officer has taken him off a case, he decides – as one suspects Laidlaw would do in the same situation – "Well, sod him then. I'll find the bastard anyway."[40]

As for his 'difficulty sustaining relationships', in *Knots & Crosses* Rankin anchored Rebus and his future series in the only intimate relationship he has been able and willing to sustain, his relationship with the city of Edinburgh, the city to which he emigrated from Fife 15 years earlier and which he now describes as "a schizophrenic city, the place of Jekyll & Hyde sure enough, the city of Deacon Brodie, of fur coats and no knickers..."[41] Stripping back the many layers of her genteel appearance, Rankin turns Edinburgh into both setting and symbol of his social and political discourse. Time after time, he sends Rebus on reconnaissance tours around its Old and New Town, and as the detective follows in the footsteps of Poe's flâneur, he never misses an opportunity to discuss the city's duality. Yet what sets Rebus apart from more pedestrian tour guides is that he frequently extrapolates from the sharp contrasts he observes on the surface of the city's architecture to a deeper contemplation of the two distinct personalities which he believes reside within people as well as places, and it is suggestive of the series to come that his debut is about his discovery of what he calls "the self that lurked behind his everyday consciousness."[42]

Rebus finally makes this discovery when he realises that the anonymous letters he has been receiving were sent by the 'Edinburgh Strangler', a child-murderer who plays on the pun of noughts and crosses to fashion string knots and match crosses into cryptic clues only Rebus can decipher. Until then, however, Rankin presents Rebus as a potential suspect and sender of said letters by giving him violent out-of-body experiences and framing them with references to Robert Louis Stevenson's *Strange Case of Dr Jekyll and Mr Hyde*. In one such episode, for instance, Rebus almost strangles a woman during intercourse, and thus suspicion gradually arises that he might suffer from a mental illness akin to Dr Jekyll's dissociative identity disorder – and that he might therefore be the murderer without being aware of it. Yet the case, and thus the meaning of the title, is a little more complicated, for when Rebus undergoes hypnosis to access suppressed memories, he discovers that, while he is not the 'Edinburgh Strangler', he is as inextricably tied up in the murderer's fate as the knots in the novel's title suggest.

As it turns out, the two have a shared history of violence and trauma, a history which ties them to one another in much the same way as it ties them to their psychological problems. Rankin reinforces these ties by giving the two similar surnames, describing them both as "slightly soiled"[43], and making Rebus narrate his flashback to their shared history in the first person. Together, these measures gradually strengthen the suspicion that, whatever it may be that created their ties, it is as far beyond their control as is one's name, it has left a somewhat humiliating mark on them, and it has made Rebus intimately familiar with the pressure that has shaped the murderer's mind. Yet by gradually shifting our suspicion from Rebus to his 'frienemy', Rankin simultaneously strengthens the suspicion that he wants us to look below the surface of their apparent similarities.

Looking below that surface, we see not only that the strain of Rebus's fraternal relationships is symbolic of his struggle with the very concept of brotherhood, be it in the army or in the police. We also see how this sensitivity is related to the appeal of the Rebus series as a whole. Detective fiction such as this, Pepper observes in his essay 'The Hard-Boiled Genre', "deconstructs the hard-boiled persona to reveal the... detective as anxious, wounded, and internally divided, and shows the violence of both the detective and killer to be projections of these insecurities."[44] In short, Rankin entered Scotland's social and political discourse by starting a series which has let millions see what McIlvanney's *Laidlaw* had shown him: that the 'baddy' does not have to be the only one with two faces.

Philip Kerr – *March Violets*

In 1989, so only two years later, Philip Kerr started a series which has had a similarly lasting impact on detective fiction the world over. Just when McIlvanney and Rankin had finally brought the genre up to date in Scotland, Kerr set the clock back by setting his debut, *March Violets*, in the Germany of 1936. There, he has found enough material to let Bernie Gunther, his PI protagonist, spend another eight novels investigating the country's military past while taking the internationally bestselling series through the Second World War all the way up to the Cold War. As I will show at the end of this chapter, in a comparative reading of two historical detective novels set in Scotland, Kerr's influence has been felt keenly in this country, too. Yet a fact rarely noted – and one all too easily ignored in view of his seemingly native skill at bringing Germany's history to life – is that *this country* is his home country. Kerr was born in Edinburgh, Scotland, so despite the foreign setting of his Bernie Gunther series, there is good reason to discuss its lasting impact on the genre here.

Starting Gunther's journey through war-torn Germany in *March Violets*, Kerr has indicated which course the hard-boiled PI might have taken if Chandler, upon leaving London, had not gone west to Los Angeles but east to Berlin. Much like Marlowe, Gunther typically gets hired when family members or their murderers go missing. As he puts it with Marlowe's characteristic nonchalance, "Trying to find them is a large part of my business."[45] And like Marlowe, he makes sure that business is good by working for rather questionable clients without asking them too many questions. When moral conflicts do arise, he settles them with a blend of wry honesty and sober pragmatism, as when he senses his client's capacity for violence and muses, "I hoped he wasn't planning some private little execution, because I didn't feel up to wrestling with my conscience, especially when there was a lot of money involved."[46] Much like his transatlantic contemporary, then, PI Bernie Gunther is more than meets the eye. His talk of self-preservation is as loud as that of the period, yet his walk down Germany's mean streets follows a quiet, less popular sense of purpose. As he states his case, "I am naturally disposed to be obstructive to authority,"[47] "I'm not a National Socialist,"[48] "I'm not on anyone's side, and the only thing I'm trying to get is the truth."[49]

So much for the commonalities between Gunther and Marlowe. Yet while the latter, whose name in early short stories was Malory, aspires to the Arthurian ideals popularised by his namesake Sir Malory, the etymological roots of Gunther's name suggest that he is cast in sharp contrast to the classic private eye/knight errant. So it comes as no surprise when, true to the German stereotype of the grounded goal getter, Gunther does not let some higher sense of honour get in the way of his financial reward, loyal though he may seem to his paymaster. As he readily admits, "It's not that I'm the honourable type, protecting my client's reputation, and all that crap. It's just that I'm on a pretty substantial recovery fee."[50] Unlike Marlowe, then, Gunther refuses to close the case when he discovers that the crime he was hired to investigate has been kept in his client's family for almost as long as their money. Upon learning this, he does not go home but instead follows the money trail all the way to the junction at which family affairs turn into affairs of state. So, while both writers see the state as the family writ large, Chandler generally backs away from family drama before Marlowe can draw any critical comparisons between the crimes of individuals and those of institutions. In *March Violets*, on the other hand, Kerr lets Gunther close in on a criminal family as he gradually peels back its many layers of intrigue and finds ample space for the drawing of precisely such critical comparisons.

That this can be a largely dramatic process, one in need of few discursive asides, becomes evident within a few pages. In quick succession, Gunther is hired by two clients with the same name to work the same case from two angles. First, he is hired to investigate the death of a woman by a certain Hermann Six, the woman's grieving father who also happens to be a rich industrialist. Then, he is hired to find the thief of her diamonds by a certain Hermann Goering, a family friend who also happens to be the real-life founder of the Gestapo, the secret police of Nazi Germany. Contrary to the latter Hermann's assurances, however, he is not motivated by the compassion found in extended families when he puts the significant state power he wields in the service of a private – yet powerful – citizen. As Gunther eventually learns, both Hermanns have invested in him to gain political control, yet rather than surprise him, it merely confirms his long-held belief that "Corruption in one form or another is the most distinctive feature of life under National Socialism."[51]

That said, what sets Gunther apart from other private eyes of the time, most notably the Marlowe of the pre-war period, is not so much that Gunther works for two clients whose private agendas he fails to see. What really sets him apart is that he does the work of two critics by contextualising an individual's crimes of rapacity in the corruption of the regime. That, and the fact that Kerr illustrates the effects of institutionalised corruption in the individual setbacks his PI suffers when he becomes an outcast. As Susan Rowland, an expert in literary theory, puts it, "the *processes* of the detecting narrative are beset by failure, vulnerability, evidence of social unfairness and of the impermeability of modernity to reason."[52] In other words, unlike pre-war Marlowe, Gunther fails to remain aloof, and so he fails to contain the world's moral disorder within a cute one-liner. All he can do is criticise it from the outside, for after he falls in love and finds that his lady friend has been made to disappear, he falls foul of the Nazi Party and ends up in Dachau's concentration camp.

Ironically, Gunther becomes the odd one out even though he tries to make sense of his strange new world with Marlowe's old trick, the simile. Yet while Marlowe usually succeeds in clarifying his world by comparing the strange to the familiar, Gunther succeeds only in codifying his by comparing the new to the obscure, i.e. curiosities that are very much of the period, such as the incidental factoid that "Joey Goebbels has a problem finding his size in shoes."[53] Psychologically, however, such obscurantism clarifies something else. Kerr's PI is stuck in his longing for a simpler Germany, a time of "carefree philosophies,"[54] which ended when Hitler passed his Enabling Act in March 1933. So Gunther's odd way of relating to his country indicates his refusal to be assimilated as one of its March Violets, a loaded term for latecomers to the Nazi Party. And when he finally escapes Dachau and its threat of assimilation or death, he escapes with a lesson about the legacy of individuals who defy institutions: most failures of conformity are sooner or later seen as triumphs of conscience.

Christopher Brookmyre – *Quite Ugly One Morning*

Perhaps the most influential and innovative Scottish writer to have taken up this theme in contemporary detective fiction is Christopher Brookmyre. Yet rather than do so with the genre-typical wryness which goes all the way back to po-faced Chandler, Brookmyre has repeatedly written about failures of conformity and triumphs of conscience with an unusual – and usually charming – blend of eloquent rants and cheeky grins. This, and the fact that he has successfully carried off a heavily anti-establishment agenda in a traditionally conservative genre, has led to frequent comparisons between his work and that of a different American cult writer, one whose politics and readers tend to sit far to the left of Chandler's. The writer in question is Carl Hiaasen, whose eco-satires indeed have some striking commonalities with Brookmyre's early work, yet over the years critics and promoters have made so much of these commonalities that the Hiaasen comparison is at risk of eclipsing the perhaps more important – though certainly less noted – influence of yet another American cult writer, the dark but outrageously funny singer-songwriter Warren Zevon.

Evidence of this can be found as early as in the title of Brookmyre's debut, *Quite Ugly One Morning*. Published in 1996, the novel takes said title from a song off Zevon's 1991 album *Mr. Bad Example*, which would seem to have two implications: one, the novel's villain, a grotesque Tory caricature called Stephen Lime, is meant to be read as Mr. Bad Example, as he is indirectly named after Zevon, who also went by the name of Stephen Lyme. And two, the novel's title is meant to be read with a view to Zevon's signature macabre outlook, so 'quite ugly one morning' does not suggest that the story will focus on some tough guy who wakes up one morning with a face full of bruises and a hard-boiled attitude which lets him get on with the day as though it were only 'quite ugly'. Contrary to such genre-typical machismo, the reference to Zevon suggests that the title is best read as a sarcastic comment on the state of the nation as captured in this novel: Britain's harsh awakening from Thatcherism and the political, social, and cultural hangover which made the country's future look more than just 'quite ugly'.

This, then, is Brookmyre's wakeup call. Yet it is also his introduction of Jack Parlabane, investigative journalist and serial protagonist of five novels to date. Looking back at this first appearance in the knowledge of Parlabane's later success as a serial protagonist, we do of course know that he will somehow make it out of the novel alive, but for the duration of his debut it seems like he may have met his match.

As Horsley puts it, "the nauseating, xenophobic, frighteningly right-wing Stephen Lime has hatched a scheme to kill off long-stay geriatric patients to facilitate the closure of a hospital."[55] Trying to take over the National Health Service before the police or Parlabane can stop him, this cartoon super-villain has delegated the assassination of an inconvenient doctor to Darren Mortlake, his clumsy henchman who is so closely modelled on Hiaasen's 'Chemo' from *Skin Tight* that he has caught his bad luck along with his terminal stupidity. So much for the premise, and so much for Brookmyre's skill in hammering home serious political critique while flirting with farce.

This rare skill is probably best – and certainly most memorably – demonstrated in chapter one of *Quite Ugly One Morning*. Doing full justice to the title's literal meaning, Brookmyre describes a crime scene so farcically nauseating that even a police officer loses control of his bodily functions as the chapter reaches its earthy climax. Yet this scatological opening does more than set the tone of the novel to come. It also gives us the measure of the man who remains serious in the face of this farce. Parlabane recognises the pile of human waste as a symptom of Britain's political malady, and to remedy it he promptly reinvents himself as a PI. From then on, he follows in the footsteps of Douglas Adams's Ford Prefect, cheerfully wandering into enormously dangerous situations and effortlessly making them far worse. Along the way, this anti-authoritarian one-man-army pursues a private investigation into the country's post-Thatcher management failure, state-sanctioned manufacture of consent, and numbers-first mentality which puts financial profit above human life. What is more, Brookmyre makes Parlabane do all of this jetlagged after only just returning to Glasgow from LA, birthplace of the hard-boiled private eye. In other words, Brookmyre uses Parlabane to radicalise the genre.

In this case, "Parlabane had raised the stakes,"[56] as Brookmyre puts it, by targeting white-collar criminals. And by making him do so, Brookmyre has raised uncomfortable questions about our mass-complicity in abiding a social and political system which allows such crimes to happen with alarming frequency and, all too often, with even more alarming impunity. Admittedly, his subversive rants are often more memorable than his serious writing. Yet whether he ridicules career politicians for their arguably harmless infatuation with state-of-the-art commodities or reprimands them for their embezzlement of government funds – which he shows suggests is anything but harmless – as Horsley concludes, "consumer greed acts as a metaphor for moral bankruptcy... The parable of spectacularly greedy consumption sustained by large-scale human sacrifices is supported by satiric vignettes of the massive Lime in his luxurious bath."[57]

Incidentally, it is also in a bath scene that S. Lime reveals just how telling his name is. Giving physical shape to the slime that is his political philosophy, he arrogantly reviews his position in the grand scheme of things just after having "farted contentedly to himself. He was not, he was convinced, fat. Poor people were fat. Stupid people were fat. He was a man of imposing stature."[58] Showing Lime in this moment of unguarded self-righteousness, Brookmyre reveals the naked truth behind his 'imposing stature' and makes it painfully obvious that even public servants can be experts at hiding their criminality behind false narratives of respectability. And as Lime's example suggests, at least some of them do so with what Parlabane calls "meaningless wank-language."[59]

Yet a novel does not radicalise a genre simply by exposing the obesity of naked self-interest, not even when that novel is a worst-case scenario of entrepreneurial ruthlessness and establishment cover-ups. What makes *Quite Ugly One Morning* radicalise detective fiction is that Brookmyre situates his dystopian plot in a period of optimism prior to New Labour, a zero hour which the Pulitzer Prize winner Michael Chabon has called "that difficult fulcrum between innocence and experience, romance and disillusion, adventure and satire... between a time when outrage was a moral position and a time when it has become a way of life."[60] In other words, Brookmyre writes with a masterfully controlled outrage that is not a fanciful pose but a firm moral position in which he refuses to forgive the British bourgeoisie for its centuries of social and political engineering because it has left the lion's share of power and privilege in the hands of tiny elites and, according to Parlabane's verdict, turned the UK into a failed state.

Paul Johnston – *Body Politic*

One year later, in 1997, Paul Johnston published a novel set in an independent city state of the 2020s where the notion of the UK as a failed state defines political philosophy as much as it does daily life. The city state in question is Edinburgh, and its recent secession from the UK was the result of an ideological fragmentation which Johnston predicted would occur around the turn of the century and which proved, at least in part, to be dauntingly prescient. Two decades later, he picks up the action in a dystopian Scotland in which his alternate history has led to a police state based on platonic principles of social and political engineering, a state which prides itself on its zero murder rate until it suddenly has to deal with the appearance of several mutilated corpses. This, then, is the state of internal conflict in which *Body Politic* is set.

Beyond the novel's heady premise, Johnston's elaborate efforts at building a fictional universe for his dystopian thought experiment are underpinned by his narrator's extensive philosophical commentary, so the Sunday Times were right, at least in part, to say that *Body Politic* reads like "Plato's *Republic* with a body count." The part they were right about is the novel's lengthy exposition, which reads, to be less grandiose, like an introductory sketch of classical political philosophy, with the odd corpse thrown in to make sure the pages – and stomachs – keep turning. In its dramatic parts, however, *Body Politic* reads like a cross between a science fiction satire and a hard-boiled detective novel in which a wise-cracking custodian of civil liberties takes on a moribund socialist idyll which has degenerated into an inhumane big brother state. As a whole, then, *Body Politic* allows two rather distinct readings.

In one reading, *Body Politic* is an intellectual puzzle which tries to arrange hard-boiled genre conventions such as wry investigators and red herrings around a dramatic adaptation of familiar Platonic and Orwellian ideas about authoritarian governance. In the other reading, *Body Politic* is a physical metaphor on the gradual debilitation of democracy, as revealed by Johnston's narrator in the future city state of

Edinburgh, and as remembered by those in power in pre-independent Scotland. The reason why *Body Politic* accommodates both of these readings is that it appropriates rather genre-untypical elements of political and philosophical literature, such as abstract theorising and Socratic dialogue. And the reason it can do this without losing the plot is that, as the crime critic Andrew Pepper puts it, "hard-boiled writing's flexibility and elasticity allow for such appropriation – so long as its structuring tension is kept alive."[61]

Johnston keeps this all-important structuring tension alive by creating a scenario in which the success of his high profile investigation depends on a man who seems inherently unqualified for the job. Persistent though he is, this man is so obviously and irremediably at odds with his society that even his name marks him out as an outsider who will struggle to get the necessary support from the city's tightknit police network. Quintilian 'Quint' Dalrymple, who has since appeared in four more novels, was demoted prior to this investigation for refusing to toe the party line. Yet while this demotion at first makes him seem too far removed from the centre of power to get anywhere in this case, it soon puts him in the unique position to investigate a crime which officially no longer exists. Unlike more accomplished and better known police detectives, he can act as a private investigator and go unnoticed when, with clandestine help from the party's inner circle, he steps outside the law to deal with a lawbreaker whose very existence the government has to hide from the public.

It is worth noting, however, that Johnston does not condone subversion per se, not even in an authoritarian regime. What he does is dramatise the moral difference between his two transgressors, and in doing so he enters into an international discourse on civil disobedience which, having almost exhausted itself over the previous centuries, started raging with renewed vehemence shortly after the turn of the century, i.e. shortly after the publication of this timely novel. Quint, who acts in accordance with the true meaning of 'civil disobedience', defies certain laws to demonstrate their injustice by accepting the consequences of breaking them. The murderer, who acts in accordance with a popular misinterpretation of 'civil disobedience', defies the law as an institution to demonstrate that it protects an unjust society, on which grounds this dissenter claims immunity.

To bring this moral difference to dramatic life, Johnston makes both of his dissenters commit increasingly serious acts of civil disobedience, all of which put them or others in ever greater danger. And the more outrageous the murderer's acts become, the more obvious becomes the reason why Quint rejects the murderer's philosophy along with that of the state, which he is only reluctantly trying to protect as the lesser of two evils. This increasingly obvious reason is that the murderer is only resorting to outrageous acts in response to the similarly outrageous authoritarianism of the social and political system, and this moral predicament is the central theme of *Body Politic*. As philosopher and psychoanalyst Slavoj Žižek puts it, "the sad fact that opposition to the system cannot articulate itself in the guise of a realistic alternative, or at least a meaningful utopian project, but only take the shape of a meaningless outburst, is a grave illustration of our predicament."[62]

Now, lest it should seem far-fetched to say that Johnston and Žižek are talking about the same predicament even though Johnston is talking about a fictional one which has yet to happen, let me bring in a third cultural critic to clarify a general point about the literary tradition in which *Body Politic* was conceived. Literature such as this is an example of what Horsley calls "science fiction as extrapolation. The element of fantasy consists entirely of an extension of… counter-cultural aggression."[63] So, when Quint walks down the mean streets of Johnston's future Edinburgh, he is not wandering off into some fairy-tale fantasy but merely continuing down the road on which we are currently travelling as we move towards the kinds of economic disparities and political turbulences which lead to internal conflict in *Body Politic*. And when it becomes obvious that both Quint and the murderer step outside the system because they deem it unfit for purpose, another parallel between Žižek's present predicament and Johnston's future one becomes obvious, and again Horsley clarifies it nicely. In times of crisis, be they present or future, "official irregularity and the abuse of authority almost wholly supplant any legitimate procedure."[64]

That this is often necessary raises philosophical questions about the conflict between individual conscience and ideological compromise, and in Johnston's novel the most arresting of these questions arises from the afore-mentioned body metaphor. In this metaphor, the savage mutilation of a physical body represents the dark fate of the body politic, the political entity that is Edinburgh. Johnston places this mutilated body in the hands of a certain Citizen Haigh, the manager of a crematorium who seems to personify the combined evils of John George Haigh, the Acid Bath murderer, and Field Marshal Douglas Haig, the Butcher of the Somme. In these hellish final moments, the corpse's last act on earth is that it represents the violent death of Plato's organisational principle according to which different parts of the body work in health and harmony, as do different parts of society.

At this point, Quint concludes his investigation of the body politic and belatedly diagnoses its sickness to be chronic corruption. All that is now left for him to do is ask rhetorically, "quis custodiet ipsos custodes?"[65] Who will guard the guards themselves? Yet as the afore-quoted academic Pepper points out in response to the apathy with which most people respond to this catch 22, "civil society cannot sustain itself in the absence of a strong, functioning state and, in the final analysis, the hard-boiled operative must act in the interest of the state and the law."[66] Quint does exactly that, even though he discovers that the murderer is a likeminded conscientious objector to both the state and the law. So, when he decides to protect the very system to which he objects, he is at pains to point out that he shares the murderer's grounds of objection, not the means. Doing so, he refuses to join the conservatives of the genre in suggesting that robust enforcement of the status quo is the only – or indeed the best – solution to problems of civil disobedience. Instead, he tries to enforce said status quo selectively while suggesting, with an acute sense of irony, that it is often an unnecessary cause of such disobedience, rather than a necessary answer to it.

Louise Welsh – *The Cutting Room*

Shifting focus from structural to sexual violence, Louise Welsh pushed the hard-boiled operative even further out of his traditional comfort zone in *The Cutting Room*, published in 2002. So genre-untypical is Rilke, her accidental PI, that he is not only a promiscuous homosexual but also a professed ex-junkie. When we first meet him, he is working as a small-time house clearer, yet when he discovers a rich client's collection of dirty books and dirtier eight-by-tens, he gets the queasy feeling that he may have hit the big time, so he reluctantly turns private eye and starts looking below the surface probity of Glasgow's high society, a surface which remains hard to crack but suddenly seems a lot less glossy. After all, the dated photographs depict what looks like the sexual torture and murder of a young woman among the soft furnishings of an aristocratic hard-core pornography ring, and seeing as voyeurism is an occupational hazard for private eyes, it is hardly surprising that Rilke takes a closer look.

What is surprising is that all this leads to a lot more discomfort than usually comes with secret acts of voyeurism and their involuntary discovery. As might be expected, this type of discomfort does follow Rilke's sporadic accounts of masochistic pornography, but a more troubling kind of discomfort, and a much rarer one at that, comes with the growing awareness that the genre has a long and controversial record of casual misogyny. As Rilke keeps investigating what he suspects are snuff images, he gradually ascertains that the photographs depict the female victim in helpless poses which still speak eloquently of gendered exploitation, long after her male abusers permanently silenced her. Yet rather than take this in his stride, or at least hide behind the typical hard-boiled facade, he shows some arguably 'unmanly' signs of how deeply troubled he is by such exploitation, the predatory nature of which is perhaps most obvious when Welsh contrasts it against Rilke's own aggressive yet consensual sexual exploits. In doing so, she sees to it that one of the genre's most controversial and yet common gender stereotypes becomes impossible to ignore.

Writers of detective fiction have traditionally been far from troubled, and often positively comfortable, to depict women as silenced objects of male desire and abuse. Breaking with this tradition, *The Cutting Room* makes things a lot less comfortable for its readers, for in the literary striptease that is detective fiction, the novel marks a sharp contrast to the photographs. It is about tease, rather than strip. Indeed, like Rilke, we are never given full exposure of the case and its principals but repeatedly tantalised by the sense of things happening just out of sight. And like Rilke, our sense of being teased increases at the thought of deliberately being kept out of the picture, though in our case this is not the work of anonymous perverts who are trying to hide their dirty secret. It is the effect of Welsh's episodic style, which similarly lets us catch glimpses here and there but never gives us the whole story.

What makes this episodic style even more appropriate in this context is best explained by Fredric Jameson, an eminent authority on cultural theory: "the detective's journey is episodic because of the fragmentary, atomistic nature of the society he moves through."[67] Rilke exposes this dark and often dangerous side of Glasgow society as he takes us deep into his social circle, noting that "if you like a bit of rough and have drowned your fear and your conscience, this is the place to come."[68] Central to this place, and central to this novel, is a crowded bar and a telling episode in which Rilke questions an informant. Again, there is a sense of things happening just out of sight, yet this time, we get a chance to catch a glimpse of the story's hidden truth. As Rilke momentarily takes his eyes off his informant, he catches a glimpse of a seemingly glamorous transvestite, yet when she suddenly grins at a camera and exposes her nicotine-stained teeth and receded gums, we see that nobody can be taken for who or what they seem to be.

Having gained this surprising insight, Rilke starts questioning other people's true identities and motives, yet since each further glimpse of the truth is as partial as the above, Welsh delays his discovery that, much like her Glasgow, *The Cutting Room* is all about "petty respectability up front, intricate cruelties behind closed doors."[69] So it is with a certain irony that Rilke gets shown door after door before he eventually discovers that the culprit has been hiding in plain sight all along, and in hindsight this raises two uncomfortable questions: one, what else did he – and what else did we – miss prior to this late discovery? And two, who else was complicit in the cover-up of what turns out to be the tip of the iceberg, the cold business of people trafficking which mostly happens out of sight?

Since answering these questions would pierce the story's tremendous tension, while adding nothing by way of critical insight, the only thing worth adding here is how Welsh manages to further increase said tension. After the above bar scene, Rilke switches his investigative strategy. He finally stops wasting time by listening to people's cover stories and starts paying more attention to how they perform their parts. Doing so, he sees that this is a world in which actions are more important than words as nothing anyone says can be taken for granted. And since this late insight potentially discredits the very findings that have brought him to this point and directed his suspicion, it significantly increases the novel's dramatic tension.

As for the afore-mentioned gender tension, that tension increases steadily as Welsh lets her male narrator look at the subject of *The Cutting Room* – the many ways in which people use those weaker than themselves – through a feminist filter. Gradually, she focuses Rilke's – and indeed our own – suspicion on male predators, and this gendered perspective soon focuses our combined efforts on seeing behind every man's public mask; or almost every one, for as Rilke grows more confident in his ability to probe other men's intimate sense of self, Welsh lets him have sex and thus demonstrates how little we ought to trust our perception of powerful men. Admittedly, Rilke is not powerful in the obvious sense of controlling a lot of financial, political, or social capital, but as narrator he has power over our perception of events, of other people, and even of himself. So, when we witness him having his afore-mentioned rough sex – during which he, too, uses another person weaker than himself – we see that even this sensitive man's public persona hides an unexpected penchant for masochism and a stereotypical yet equally unexpected male, sexual aggressiveness.

That said, and though its expression may seem sudden, this critical feminist commentary has echoed through Rilke's narrative voice all along. As Professor of Communication and Culture James Naremore says, this voice "isn't quite the voice of Reason… because it has less to do with solving puzzles than with exposing various kinds of falsehood or naïveté… It is more like the voice of Male Experience, and it usually speaks with brutal frankness after a period of reticence or silent knowingness."[70] Perhaps the most revealing example of this comes at the end of Rilke's sex scene, when he rolls off his one-night-stand and recites, "the after dream of the reveller on opium – the bitter lapse into everyday life – the hideous dropping off of the veil."[71]

As brutal in his need as he is in his honesty, Rilke lets us see that he is not a nice man, and yet he tries long and hard to be the best man in his world. Indeed, even though he is strongly encouraged to "drop the Philip Marlowe impersonation,"[72] he follows in the footsteps of Chandler's hard-boiled macho until he gets his man. When he does so, however, the solution to the mystery of the woman in the pornographic photographs seems less important to Rilke, and indeed to Welsh, than the novel's composite image of 21st century Glasgow and its modern man.

Perhaps unsurprisingly, this image is best captured in yet another bar scene in which Rilke finds himself, as so often, in a hostile crowd of alpha males. Scanning the bar, he notices the ossified head of a bison mounted on the wall above the men, and like the afore-mentioned Philip Marlowe, the genre's revered figurehead, it seems oddly out of place in the 21st century, never mind in a Glasgow bar. When Rilke sees that the crowd is nonetheless jostling for the best place under the dated macho totem, he wearily leaves the bar to be his own man, and it is in this quiet act of defiance that Welsh demonstrates how Chandler's hard-boiled original can avoid ossification. All he has to do is move with the times, and in this case, that means moving out of the macho's comfort zone.

Denise Mina – *The Field of Blood*

Taking this feminist agenda one step further, Denise Mina has not only pushed the hard-boiled operative further out of the macho's comfort zone by casting an unusually flustered, unusually free-spirited, and unusually female character for the role. Mina has also furthered the genre's flexibility. Prior to the publication of *The Field of Blood* in 2004, the Scottish detective novel had traditionally treated sadism as a predominantly psychological phenomenon, yet in the mind of this young woman, Mina finally gave the marginalised social element of sadism its due equality of status.

Set in 1981, the novel introduces said young woman, Paddy Meehan, as an eighteen-year-old gofer who has only just started working for a national broadsheet. Paddy has since smashed the glass ceiling of newspaper journalism in two sequels, yet in this debut she is still the young pretender, self-conscious in her girlishness, self-satisfied in her feminism, and self-loathing in her dieting. Despite these typical traits of adolescence, however, it seems unlikely that she would sit comfortably among typical girl sleuths like Nancy Drew, because Paddy's amateur efforts at private investigation are not motivated by a lust for juvenile adventure. They are motivated by a loss of youthful innocence. Paddy cannot afford to play games or depend on others if she wants to see justice done, be it in her career or in this case, so those amateur efforts in and beyond the newsroom can be read as a criticism of the pressures suffered by ambitious women who, in the early 1980s, started making their way in a man's world.

Mina broadens this criticism by making Paddy's experience an illustration of the fact that those pressures are not limited to a woman's professional life. Paddy also comes up against them – and just as frustratingly so – in her private life. The reason for this dual pressure is that her independence of thought and action cannot stop at the conventional pieties of her religious family and friends once it has assailed those of her patriarchal bosses. So although she keeps her atheism in the closet and even tries to camouflage it with her loud and proud careerism, her Catholic community knows as well as her colleagues that she bridles against their combined pressure to accept her place. At least in part, then, it is an expression of their shared resentment and bruised egos that, when they feel betrayed by Paddy, they both instantly ostracise her.

Her colleagues feel betrayed when she refuses to write a potentially lucrative story about a high-profile murder case even though she has exclusive inside knowledge. And her community feels betrayed when one of Paddy's colleagues writes the story instead of her, because this colleague names a member of Paddy's extended family as a suspect and in doing so suggests that Paddy sold out and passed on her inside knowledge. Like most women of her time, then, Paddy refused her thirty pieces of silver only to be rewarded for her integrity with isolation, and if the bitter irony of this reward is not obvious, please consider the novel's title. "The Field of Blood" is a biblical reference to Judas Iscariot's cardinal betrayal and his reward of iniquity. Yet unlike Judas, Paddy is falsely suspected of betrayal, and what makes this bitterly ironic is that she refused to betray her community's implicit trust in her confidentiality only to be betrayed by the person in whom she herself confided.

Interestingly, Mina does not make this person an easy target of feminist outrage by casting some insensitive male bully in the role of office Judas. Instead, she casts one of Paddy's few female colleagues, somebody Paddy assumed would understand the pressure she is under, not reinforce it by abusing her trust for a meagre professional advancement which comes at the high price of making another woman seem like a sell-out and a push-over. Thus, Mina's subtle casting decision does not cheapen the novel's feminist agenda by playing to facile gender stereotypes. Instead, it indicates the complexity of workplace dynamics when women are vastly outnumbered as well as the cut-throat competitiveness among those women when they feel they have to step on each other to reach the top.

Despite this frustrating situation, however, Paddy does not join the ranks of the genre's many cynics. Instead, she puts her betrayal into perspective by concluding, "We're all heartbroken idealists. That's what no-one gets about journalists: only true romantics get jaded."[73] Admittedly, such remarks do suggest that Paddy speaks with no more emotional maturity or historical relevance than a typical eighteen-year-old sentimentalist stuck in eighteenth-century woman's fiction, but Mina's social realism rescues her from both gender and genre stereotypes. It does so because Mina – unlike so many of her literary ancestors, and indeed many of her contemporaries – clearly appreciates a critical point previously made by the crime critic Messent: "the romantic individualism commonly associated with the private eye, and the related sense of alienation from her or his surrounding environment, is a falsification of the actual nature of her or his social role and position."[74] And this is perhaps most obvious in the fact that *The Field of Blood* can be read as one woman's conflict with conformity.

In this reading, Paddy is a romantic in the true yet lately rather uncommon sense. Yes, she is deeply heartbroken about her betrayal, and even more so about her community's loss of faith in her, and such emotional reactions certainly fit today's most common definition of 'romantic', but her subsequent actions do not. After all, neither does she become apathetic nor does she whinge about her bruised romantic ideals. Instead, she investigates the afore-mentioned murder at great personal risk, trumps every mundane second thought with an inspired sixth sense, and defies official orders to do so. In other words, she reasserts the true romantic's ideal of animated being by practising the virtues of impulse, intuition, and insubordination. And what makes this reassertion doubly romantic is her double objective. One part of Paddy decides to go down this dangerous road because she wishes to redeem herself by way of self-sacrifice. Yet it is another part of her that decides to keep going down that road when the danger of doing so becomes real, and this part takes over as Paddy enters into the spirit of self-abnegation. At this romantic turning point she realises that, caring deeply about the victim, she cares little that there is no other way to prevent a miscarriage of justice than to put herself in its way.

It is also at this turning point that her double objective, to quote Scaggs once again, "makes explicit the sort of divided identity that often characterises the figure of the private eye, and which manifests itself in the figure of the *alter ego*."[75] Paddy sees a lot of herself in the real-life Paddy Meehan, a middle-aged man who comes into this story as an unfortunate character, wrongly convicted of criminal charges, and pardoned late in life after a journalist's campaign brings attention to his innocence. Worried that she is doomed to repeat her namesake's long struggle to restore his reputation, the young Paddy tries to help him as much in sympathy as in the superstitious hope of warding off his fate by selflessly helping him change it. Yet when her objective becomes truly selfless and she tries to restore the reputation of the ten-year-old murder suspect in her family, it becomes obvious that her alter ego is not her namesake but the journalist who put his own reputation at risk because he believed in the old Paddy's innocence.

This journalist is Ludovic Kennedy, named after the real-life journalist famous for re-examining such cases as the Lindbergh kidnapping. Like him, the young Paddy eventually informs public opinion and even influences the police investigation by re-examining the murder case and re-constructing an alternative version of events. Yet unlike her alter ego, she cannot prove innocence. All she can do is partially restore the ruined reputation of the official suspect, and since her story is about adventure as much as it is about mystery and romance, she can only accomplish this by personally confronting her own suspect. As John G. Cawelti explains in his seminal work *Adventure, Mystery, and Romance: Formula Stories as Art and Popular Culture*, "the hard-boiled detective sets out to investigate a crime but invariably finds that he must go beyond the solution to some kind of personal choice or action… to define his own concept of morality and justice, frequently in conflict with the social authority of the police."[76] In *The Field of Blood*, the hard-boiled detective does so by smashing her head against – and ultimately through – a wall that has been put between her and her double objective, a wall made of social conditions and gender expectations.

Ray Banks – *Saturday's Child*

In *Saturday's Child*, published in 2006, Ray Banks created a crossover between this tradition of urban social realism and American and English traditions of hard-boiled pulp fiction. And by doing so in an atmosphere of near constant anxiety, he pushed the contemporary Scottish detective novel to its noir frontier. *Saturday's Child* is the first of four novels about Cal Innes, reluctant private eye and mob enforcer, and its claim to fame – as yet widely ignored – is that it redefines male metropolitan dysfunctionality. In doing so, it rescues from oblivion all that is worth remembering about Dashiell Hammett's Sam Spade and Ted Lewis's Jack Carter. Like Hammett, Banks pits a morally ill-defined character against the corruption of a society split into decadence and depression. And like Lewis, he lets his tarnished anti-hero snoop around unofficial centres of power, slowly drawing out the insidious chauvinism of class difference which festers at the heart of the novel's social crisis.

Notwithstanding such extensive commonalities, however, there is a critical difference between Banks and these earlier greats of hard-boiled realism. Unlike them, Banks lets his protagonist acknowledge the anachronism and indeed the absurdity of an amateur private detective who drinks his way to the bottom of his case at a time of highly professional and tightly regulated law enforcement. In his own eyes, Cal is "The drink-shakes private dick, a walking, talking cliché. I should be shot for crimes against reality."[77] In other words, he is self-critical and thus, despite being self-appointed, a useful judge of his time, place, and peers. This may explain why, instead of granting Cal's wish and killing him off early, Banks makes him endure his growing self-loathing. Cal's endurance, as he takes the PI's maladjustment to its miserable yet psychologically sound conclusion, gives Banks not only a subversive and seemingly trustworthy mouthpiece but also plenty of time to use it for critical commentary on everything from genre clichés to social problems, as when he finds that "Private investigators have steel in their pocket and iron in their spit. Me, I've got shit in my pants and blood in my mouth."[78]

Put less euphemistically, Cal is tarnished and afraid, and he is self-aware enough to see both of these genre taboos in himself. Yet what is even more unusual for a hard-boiled *private* eye is that Cal makes sure that we see them, too. Painting several images as self-deprecating and darkly comical as the above, he gradually reveals the source of his shame and fear: the physical and psychological abuse he suffered at the hands of violent men before and, perhaps even more problematically, after he was released from prison. As Cal has had to learn the hard way, having weaknesses in prison hurts, but what seems to hurt even more, or at least more lastingly, is that "no matter how open-minded people say they are, you mention either mental illness or prison and they start looking for the nearest exit."[79] As Cal's experience soon proves, this awkward restlessness is certainly a fair assessment of the effect he has on most of his peers. Yet Cal's conception as a traumatised, impotent ex-convict has a second effect on the reading experience, and one that is a good bit more radical, because by raising questions about his psychological stability, it challenges what Messent calls "the sense of individual autonomy, objectivity, and authority on which the detective genre has tended traditionally to rely."[80]

At the same time, Banks distorts our view of these genre conventions by letting two narrators take turns to tell two very different sides of the same story. Cal, the private investigator, and Mo, the career criminal, look at the case which has brought them together from moral standpoints which could hardly be further apart, and since each one's perspective is somewhat skewed in its own favour, it throws a shadow of doubt on the other one's autonomy, objectivity, and authority. Together, then, they challenge the unity of the single voice from which the detective novel tends to derive its clear moral direction. And as though that were not disorienting enough, Mo narrates in the past tense while Cal does so in the present tense, which is to say that Cal does so without the authority typically associated with the past tense, since the immediacy of the present tense denies both him and his readers the distance which typically creates a secure position for judgment.

Without this temporal distance to the story, Cal often seems to have too little time to plan his actions carefully enough, and as the plot speeds up, he becomes ever more anxious and amateurish in his increasingly reactive attempts to control this disorienting case. So it may be his vague desire for support and stability which makes Cal call Mo's father 'Uncle' Morris and thus tie himself to Mo as a fictive cousin. What is certain is that, with or without such tenuous links between the two rival narrators, their story is a family saga reminiscent of the Old Testament. Not only has Cal grudgingly done time for Mo, but when he is now hired by Morris to track down a casino dealer, Mo bridles against his father's order to steer clear of Cal and eventually obstructs his investigation, ostensibly to beat his 'cousin' to his father's respect. Meanwhile, Cal is distracted by personal issues, such as his biological brother's drug addiction, so he is slow to discover that Mo is not trying to locate the casino dealer for his father's sake but for the sake of the child he fathered with the dealer's partner, an elusive woman who turns out to be a sixteen-year-old girl – and his sister.

From the start, then, there is rather a lot of bad blood between the two 'cousins', and in time their rivalry becomes so violent, it, too, is reminiscent of the Old Testament. This brings us to the novel's supreme irony. It is the frequent transgression on both sides of this biblical rivalry that infuses the novel with a pervasive amorality, and eventually this amorality makes the detective and the criminal similarly hard to judge. See, even though *Saturday's Child*, as Pepper might put it, "focuses primarily on the investigation rather than perpetration of crime… this distinction is often blurred to the point where it is difficult to tell law enforcer and law breaker apart."[81] In their own ways, both Cal and Mo are law breakers, yet both of them are far more complex individuals than this categorical term suggests. As Banks subtly demonstrates in their many internal monologues, the structures of violence in which they have grown up, and which they have to varying degrees internalised, have turned them both into victims afraid and resentful of life.

Given this gradual emergence of their unexpected commonalities, it is perhaps the novel's most remarkable distinction that Cal's and Mo's narratives are nonetheless easy to tell apart. The main reason for this, aside from the obvious clash of characters, is that they both draw on large arsenals of demotic idiosyncrasies and thus tell their stories in clearly distinct voices. This – perhaps surprisingly for those who believe that literature is better without 'bad language' – has the intellectually valuable effect of diversifying the novel's socio-political agenda, as does the fact that Banks lets a delinquent from Scotland play detective in England. Having chased Mo around the tourist-free parts of both Manchester and Newcastle, Cal finally comes face to face with him in a social context so dire, it suggests Cal might be right when he calls it "the great British public, otherwise known as It's None Of My Fucking Business."[82] What all this comes down to, then, is that Saturday's child has to work hard just to keep living. Yet as I hope to have shown, his struggle is worth the effort, if only because it demonstrates the many difficulties in discussing Britain's social, cultural, and political problems, particularly the fact that, while crime is always deplorable, sometimes it is also a criticism of the causes which it is respectable not to discuss.

Tony Black – *Paying For It*

Continuing this subversive trend in *Paying For It*, published in 2008, Tony Black demonstrated how the world's false standards can cause the warping of character. Distilling the styles and subjects of Irvine Welsh and Ken Bruen into this first of four novels about Gus Dury, Black directed the PI's subversive energy at a national attitude which had grown conformist under the rule of social and economic elites chiefly concerned with their own preservation. Indeed, Gus spends the best part of the novel butting heads with Scotland's Minister of Immigration, Alisdair Cardownie, whom he regards as an apt personification of these social and economic elites, not least when he describes him as a "slack-jowled, in-bred son of privilege."[83]

Seeing as this unfortunate appearance hides an even more unfortunate attitude – a big-headed dismissal of all those less privileged than himself – some may find it satisfying in a moral as well as a visual sense when Gus reveals in one of his many flashbacks that he once literally butted heads with the MSP. At the height of his success as a journalist, Gus head-butted Cardownie live on national television. He has since paid a high price for this privilege by losing his job, his purpose, his home, his wife, and, whenever possible, his sobriety. What he has not lost, however, is the strong head that got him into all of this trouble, so when we first meet him here, he is drinking his way around Edinburgh as a "saloon bar Socrates."[84] And as he ploughs a seemingly inexhaustible effort into his seemingly never-ending pub crawl, we realise that he is not drinking to forget but to find a way of dealing with a number of deaths, namely the murder of a friend's son, the passing of his own father, and a quiet death he is almost alone in mourning – the suicide of Scotland's culture.

Feeling like a stranger in his own land, Gus soon starts sympathising with people who, though for more practical reasons, feel the same. When he finds out about a deal between Cardownie and Benny Zalinskas, a Lithuanian people trafficker, Gus rages against the involuntary prostitution forced on the trafficked foreigners, yet as he walks down the mean streets of multicultural Scotland, his own country's eagerness to sell herself strikes him as similarly obscene. Since this sordid eagerness is most visible in the commercialisation of her ancient cultural identity for the quick cash of international tourists with an insatiable appetite for Scottish clichés, Gus never misses an opportunity to criticise that "Tartan shops blasted teuchter music at every turn."[85] So, rather than base this story about power and exploitation on an imperialist platform or write from a nationalistic point of view to enforce a categorical division between 'them' and 'us', Black ensures that there is, as Horsley puts it, "no secure position within the text constituting a moral high ground."[86]

Yet even for readers who are blind in the right eye, Black undermines any delusion that his white, male, and native private eye is speaking from a moral high ground. Far from it, he made Gus an alcoholic whose debauchery must leave every reader in doubt whether any two sentences are spoken by the same man or alternately by Gus Sober and Gus Drunk. In time, this debauchery lets us share Gus's acute sense of disorientation, and this in turn lets us share the belief of the writer and critic Michael Chabon that "a quest is often, among other things, an extended bout of inspired madness."[87] By way of intensifying this sense of disorientation and madness, Gus repeatedly starts and stalls his quest as it careers along a twisted narrative arc of loosely connected scenes in which his fitfully lucid mind fastens not on any moral high ground, but on a hard-boiled article of faith – that the femme fatale has a finger in every fly. Fortunately, Gus is not "fuckstruck,"[88] so he sees through the dangerous temptress and realises that she is involved in Cardownie's and Zalinskas's criminal affairs. And by letting Gus use her to expose the two criminals, Black not only inverts the private investigator slash femme fatale dynamic. He also implies that at the heart of modernity's decadence is the dirty affair between respectability and crime.

So, in *Paying For It*, as in all of Gus's cases and indeed most of Scotland's detective novels, it is the ability to subvert expectations which enables the hard-boiled investigator to survive in a hazardous environment. Yet since Gus is conceived in the spirit of Welsh's and Bruen's outsiders, he has grave doubts that his environment is ultimately worth the effort, and since he is the type of outsider who embraces such doubts, his apparent failure to fit in can be read as another form of subversion, another attack on the current mainstream and its collective pretensions. As he puts it, "I just didn't buy into this new lifestyle thing. I aimed for an anti-lifestyle."[89] His idea of such an 'anti-lifestyle' is to do all the good bad things life has to offer, yet after doing so for a while he becomes anti-social to the extreme and so addicted to his poisons of choice that it seems like he could give Welsh's Mark Renton and Bruen's Jack Taylor a run for their drug money.

Yet what makes his resemblance to those cult drop-outs even more striking is that, like them, Gus has the necessary combination of moral integrity and aggressive indignation to give every phony the finger – including himself. Paradoxical though it may sound, he subjects his own behaviour to the same scrutiny as that of others. It just takes him a while to spot the hypocrisy of preaching accountability and altruism while drinking his way into an early grave and paying for it with the money of a man who is deeply invested in his survival, not just because he sees Gus as his last remaining hope to find closure after the loss of his son, but also because he loves him like a son. Yet when Gus does finally spot this hypocrisy, he sobers up as much from self-disgust as from self-discipline. So, like Renton and Taylor, he differs notably from the generic hard-boiled protagonist who can say "the hell with it" and at the same time, as the pop culture critic Cawelti observes, "retain the world's most important benefits – self-esteem, popularity, and respect."[90] Gus, like Renton and Taylor, is too honest in his self-assessment to enjoy any of the above.

This brutal honesty is perhaps most clearly visible when he opposes the presumptions of his peers with the reality of himself, "a perfectly unreconstructed example of maledom… My career was washed up. I had a serious alcohol problem and, on top of everything else, I'd lost most of my top row of teeth."[91] As this example of his 'anti-lifestyle' and its dangerous fallout suggests, the distance at which he keeps himself even from his family and friends is certainly a responsible safety measure. Yet as he admits, it is also a measure of his proud alienation and thus of his disinterest in collective identity: "I watched the pinstriped yuppies power walking towards fifty-grand-a-year, superannuation and medical benefits – would need to come with a crate load of Prozac to get me interested."[92]

Most days, just leaving the house triggers similarly subversive rants on his social anxieties about addiction and unemployment, yet it is safe to conclude that Gus chafes against all things false, not just pinstriped yuppies. While he is in routine conflict with modern life and at pains to keep himself at a curmudgeonly remove, his distaste for falsity and unfairness forces him to work in the sewers of his society when he realises that they harbour crimes as filthy as people trafficking. So, while his Socialist rawness festers in the novel's air of realism, his "urge for justice and revenge"[93] feeds on what Horsley calls "the tendency of others to sell out to a plausible but corrupt system and to put the demands of tame conformity above truth and justice."[94] As a result, *Paying For It* keeps the promise of its title. Gus makes the right people pay for their criminal parts in the plausible but corrupt system of involuntary prostitution, and Black recasts the hard-boiled private investigator as a hard-up conscientious objector to all those who let criminals get off scot-free just because they put the demands of tame conformity above truth and justice.

Peter May – *The Blackhouse*

Perhaps the most celebrated writer to have continued this subversive trend in the present decade is Peter May. His bestselling Lewis trilogy has had an impact on the on-going re-direction of the Scottish detective novel that is as yet immeasurable, but already it has led to a massive shift in the genre's reputation around the world. It has done so by following an introverted PI to the Outer Hebrides on a 'journey back in crime', a journey which starts in *The Blackhouse*, published in 2011 as the trilogy's first instalment. In this hybrid novel, May brings together genre conventions of the 18th century Gothic, the 19th century sentimental, and the 20th century coming-of-age novel with those of an ageless literature: travel writing. The result is a vast literary and geographic space in which his PI nonetheless feels acutely claustrophobic as he investigates the novel's most arresting theme, the imprisonment of the individual in a shameful privacy.

When we first meet him, Fin Macleod is taking leave from his job with Lothian and Borders Police to investigate a hanging in his fictional home town of Crobost on the Isle of Lewis. By way of reacquainting him with the place and its people, May illustrates in long descriptive passages how the frontier mentality and mind-bending vastness of the Outer Hebrides turn the professional detective into a private eye whose focus is on the private 'I' at the centre of his investigation. In the process, Fin comes to realise that although he has finally managed to escape the trappings of urban police bureaucracy, he cannot avoid the old trap of island kinship dynamics. Having never found closure in his mainland exile, he is forced to revisit the events and emotions of his childhood. And when the islanders keep closing their doors on him, he resigns himself to the bitter fact that, in order to solve the local murder mystery, he has to unlock the cloistered mentality of island life, which means he must once again face the inward-looking disciplinarianism of a place he both loves for being his home and loathes for being the last bastion of fundamentalist Calvinism, a complicated place which is a far cry from the island idyll romanticised in tourist brochures.

As Fin describes it, life on Lewis is a "sad existence... strangled by a society still in the grips of a joyless religion. An economy on the slide, unemployment high. Alcoholism rife, a suicide rate well above the national average."[95] Yet it is not just the place that asks us to look beyond generic images of life in the Scottish isles. The novel, too, is far from typical of mainstream Tartan Noir, and this is true in a topical as well as in a technical sense.

What makes *The Blackhouse* untypical in a topical sense is the fact that the murder which initiates proceedings soon proves to be incidental. Within only a few days of Fin's arrival, the suspense of his early investigative work gives way to a sensitive exploration of the guilt issues of his friends and the sins of their fathers. And what makes the novel untypical in a technical sense is the fact that the narrative arc parallels this double distraction from the murder mystery. As soon as May is done with his exposition, he radically departs from the novel's detective strand to spend its remainder skipping back and forth between two strands which run at a great distance from the genre's typical narrative strategies: one, the third-person account of Fin's adult struggle to make sense of the social tensions and cultural practices of island life. And two, Fin's first-person flashbacks to his youthful struggle to fit in with island culture, a struggle that ended during a fatal gannet-culling ritual on the fictional island of An Sgeir.

In the end, it is to this barren basalt stack in the Atlantic that Fin must return as the two narratives dramatically collide, Fin having discovered that he has a teenage son and that this son's life is presently in danger on An Sgeir because of a traumatic episode from Fin's own adolescence. Now, it is only after a lengthy exploration of this adolescence and its many raw emotions that Fin can access this long repressed memory, so for quite a while it seems as though the novel were drifting irretrievably beyond the boundaries of detective fiction, but when Fin does finally access his repressed memory, sentiment suddenly gives way to suspense, the prose is energised by Fin's powerful force of feeling, and as it tells of Fin's desperate rescue attempt it races towards a crashing climax, driven by the wild rage of a father whose son is about to relive his traumatic fate. Along the way,

Fin's physical journey takes him out to sea in the middle of a biblical thunderstorm, so we see him brave these elemental forces both in- and outside himself, and this does more than symbolise his long and arduous emotional journey. It also signals the novel's late turn to the Gothic and proves earlier indications that *The Blackhouse* is a family drama riding on the engine of detective fiction.

In short, the investigative journey to the cause of repression extends the family drama's ethical range. It throws questions of communal responsibility into sharp relief, as it dramatises Fin's journey towards acceptance of the traumatising fact that he suffered what he calls "abuse the like of which no child should ever have to suffer."[96] This not only makes him a vehicle of compassion but also creates a contrast between him and those who are beyond atonement, for while Fin takes action to save his son from similar abuse, those who could and should have intervened on Fin's behalf again remain passive. Now as then they are silenced, be it by their wish or by their need to fit in, so when Fin realises that both this wish and this need stem from the fact that repressive religious dogma and strict social codes still govern island life, he understands that those who may not freely discuss one topic are timid upon all topics.

Understanding this timidity, however, does not make him any more forgiving. On the contrary, it makes him a vocal advocate of honesty, an advocate whose admission of his own faults eventually shames a few of the silent bystanders into an acknowledgement of their moral complicity. As for all those who remain standoffish, they too reveal an important aspect of island life by showing that lifelong conformity can make people immune to honesty, even when it is contracted by someone with whom they are in frequent contact. And by registering this, Fin proves that the eminent cultural theorist Fredric Jameson is right in saying that "the honesty of the detective can be understood as an organ of perception, a membrane which, irritated, serves to indicate in its sensitivity the nature of the world around it."[97] Yet Fin also proves a more important point, namely that even the strongest organ of perception can be impaired by the human frailty of wanting to ignore or forget suffering. After all, while he resents his peers for doing so, he knows that, until recently, his selective amnesia made him just as dishonest, so he has to ask himself, "How could he not have remembered?"[98]

The answer is that, unlike those who choose to forget their dark past so as to appease their conscience, Fin forgot his because he was abused as a child and later repressed every memory associated with his abuse so he could function as an adult. Hence, he certainly understands the human frailty of wanting to ignore or forget suffering, but his understanding yet again fails to make him any more forgiving, especially of those who ignore or forget only the suffering of others. What Fin ignored and forgot for so many years was his own suffering, and while this certainly serves as a convenient plot device, creating suspense by keeping the dark secret even from its bearer, this convenient side effect is not as significant as what his selective amnesia reveals about his character. It shows that Fin directs his efforts at piecing together his fragmented and partially obscured past, not because he is self-absorbed, but because it is his only way of getting to the dark secret which binds him to the island community, the dark secret which is also the only key to a full understanding of what has so tragically changed this community that one of them has turned to murder.

In time, these sensitive social studies show that it is fair to say of Fin what Ross Macdonald, the man who famously redefined the private eye some 60 years previously, said of his PI Lew Archer: "While he is a man of action, his actions are largely directed to putting together the stories of other people's lives and discovering their significance. He is less a doer than a questioner, a consciousness in which the meanings of other lives emerge."[99] Creating Fin in this image, May demonstrates that the hard-boiled investigator can within one story personify the two central topics of detective fiction – the loss of the abused and the lonesomeness of the disabused. Fin has lost not only years of his life to abuse and amnesia but also his sense of identity, for the latter was rooted entirely in place and community, and after being sorely disabused of his delusions about both, he has become a nomadic loner and a stranger to himself. Fin, then, really is a 'private' eye, and when he takes a critical look at a place and community which seem to have turned selective amnesia into a cultural condition, he reflects a strong tendency among hard-boiled investigators of Scottish detective fiction – the tendency to raise hard questions about the terms of communal life and then turn to the self for even harder answers.

THE ROUNDUP

Now, if these observations have not suggested that Scottish detective fiction is a homogenous national literature, then I have done my job. An honest overview of the authors' many different subjects, styles, and sensibilities cannot but create a sense of literary fragmentation, for their writing creates neither a panoramic view of some Scottish genre building project nor the sense that any aesthetic tradition has been co-opted from abroad. Instead, it creates a mosaic of disparate genre conventions, variously appropriated from American, European, and other domestic literatures to paint pictures of social, cultural, and political significance on regional, national, and global canvasses. This, of course, is not to say that literary heterogeneity makes a sense of fragmentation inevitable. What makes it inevitable in Scotland's case is the lack of a cogent design in the mosaic, because this lack shows that contemporary Scottish detective fiction is not the coordinated effort of any one school of art – neither do its writers work on a shared syllabus nor do they draw on a common set of influences.

Sure, they engage with one another. They do so indirectly every time they engage with their country's social, cultural, or political situation, because through such individual engagements they enter into a larger national discourse with one another, and indeed with all those who explore aspects of Scotland's sizeable diaspora whether they write in response to domestic or foreign influences. What is more, as I hope to have shown in the previous pages, they also engage directly with one another, be it by developing the ideas and innovations of their literary ancestors or by subverting their inherited genre conventions. And, of course, they also engage with one another by using – and in some cases by abusing – the same overly-familiar genre clichés, such as the afore-mentioned divorced drinker with a detection problem. Yet since such clichés are hardly unique to Scottish detective fiction, let alone definitive, it would be a waste of time to discuss them here only to demonstrate once again what others have already demonstrated beyond these pages, namely that detective fiction from Scotland is not just written by innovators. Much like detective fiction from anywhere else, it is also written by countless imitators.

Yet what is unusual about contemporary Scottish detective fiction is that most of its writers – as I hope to have shown in this representative sample – have not made a habit of buying into genre conventions. Certainly, as in most developed countries, the divorced drinker with a detection problem has made it to the status of genre convention in Scotland. Indeed, via William McIlvanney's Jack Laidlaw and his internationally bestselling tribute, Ian Rankin's John Rebus, he has even made it to the top flight of the country's hard-boiled PIs. But like these detectives, their creators tend to avoid the standard practices of their chosen profession. They tend to pick and mix not only their topics but also their techniques from a variety of social sciences and literary traditions, and almost always, they do so by looking beyond Scottish borders. As a result, there is in this literature no obvious mainstream and among its writers neither a widespread negative identification with any unifying anti-foreign sentiment nor a widespread positive identification with any one literary tradition.

Admittedly, there is a Scottish author whose considerable national and international success can create the assumption that whatever else Scots have recently contributed to the genre, it must surely be the legacy of this author. After all, Scotland is a small country and this author is a big deal at home as well as abroad, where he has dominated bestseller lists for decades and thus defined a lot of people's reading in the genre. Chances are, then, that most readers who come to Scottish detective fiction will do so via the writings or screen adaptations of this author, in which case their first impression of Scottish detective fiction will confirm this assumption of an obvious mainstream. The author in question, of course, is Ian Rankin. Yet as even the genre sample on display in this chapter demonstrates in its considerable diversity, not even Rankin's successful Rebus series represents a majority movement in Scottish detective fiction.

As for the country's many cult writers, neither has Chris Brookmyre's considerable success with Jack Parlabane led to a wave of investigative journalists pursuing socialist vendettas against white-collar criminals, nor has Louise Welsh's equally considerable success with Rilke led to a counter-cultural surge of gay Philip Marlowes pushing feminist agendas on upper-class misogynists. What majority movement there is in contemporary Scottish detective fiction is the essence of these two examples – a strong trend towards the left. Yet even in this trend there are too many multi-cultural tributaries and single-minded currents for any mainstream to take the form one might expect to find – a fervent anti-Englishness. A popular prejudice, after all, suggests that the Scottish stand for nothing but against the English, and if this prejudice were founded in fact, even such knee-jerk anti-Englishness would certainly destabilise my argument of there being in Scotland no widespread negative identification with any unifying anti-foreign sentiment.

Yet as eight out of the above ten examples have clearly shown, this prejudice is not founded in fact. As for the two writers in this chapter who do risk a potentially nationalist reading, when Tony Black does so by creating a composite image of villainy from two foreign criminals, one of whom is the epitome of English imperialism, he instantly complicates a nationalist reading with two plot twists: one, Gus Dury's discovery of police corruption moves the novel's focus from foreign criminals to Scottish cover-ups, and two, the surprise solution of the novel's murder mystery hinges not on simple finger-pointing at foreigners but on a complicated admission of complicity on the Scottish side of a boundary which Black suggests is far too blurred and unstable to mark a moral difference between 'them' and 'us'.

The other author who risks a potentially nationalist reading, but who in fact undermines the very idea of national superiority, and thus the basis of any anti-foreign sentiment, is Ray Banks. After all, he sends a Scottish PI after English criminals and in doing so may seem to court anti-English readers, but he also makes Cal Innes the polar opposite of a nationalist, and indeed of any other type of chauvinist. Cal is a displaced Scot who not only lives and works in England but also went to prison there and, somewhere along the way, absorbed Englishness to such a significant extent that he articulates his national observations as a cultural hybrid who has seen enough crime on both sides of the geographical border between Scotland and England to know that it is no moral boundary between 'them' and 'us'.

Besides, the fact that Banks draws on English as well as American literary influences in his writing is a further celebration of this anti-nationalist spirit and its concrete manifestation, the cultural hybrid. And by virtue of being and writing about a Scot who demonstrates this open-mindedness in an English setting, he not only makes it zero out of ten for those who would believe that there is room in Scottish detective fiction for the cliché of the anti-English Scot. He also demonstrates that contemporaries of Scottish detective fiction can be as distant from one another as they are diverse, and this brings me back to my previous point about the literature's mainstream. As Banks indicates by being and writing about a cultural hybrid, there is in this literature no widespread positive identification with any one literary tradition, no concerted effort at building the genre around nationalist tenets or define it against foreign canons, and that makes it difficult to see what gathers its writers into a national mainstream nonetheless.

Ironically, it is this widespread disinterest in nationalist definition which connects them in an identifiably Scottish literature. Even as they go their separate ways in terms of their influences, politics, and styles, they tend to make their private investigators go on a shared journey, a journey of restoration from a crime on the social periphery through the fall of a self-destructive society to its collapsing centre, the family. So, while theirs is no typical community of writers, they nonetheless have a topical commonality in their writing. The difficulty in defining it, as I hope to have shown, is that the literature's diversity acts as a disguise. It cannot, however, act as disproof, for in the final analysis its diversity is a symptom of its commonality. Admittedly, this seems counter-intuitive, yet despite all their diversity, the novels in this chapter have not demonstrated any irreconcilable differences in ideology between any of their writers. On the contrary, they have demonstrated that all of them look back to the domestic ideology of an earlier time, regardless of whether they set their stories in this time.

The time in question dates back to the peace process that ended World War Two, and even Paul Johnston has one eye on the domestic ideology which started to define the West in this period. Even though he lets his private eye look into future affairs of state as he examines the body politic of a prospective Scotland in the 21st century, his views reflect a well-familiar, libertarian notion of personal autonomy and an equally well-familiar belief that the best kind of society is the family writ large. What is more, as Quint Dalrymple goes further in his examination, he starts probing the organisational principles of Johnston's future society – an authoritarian distortion of the organic post-war model – and as he does so, he starts looking back even further to the social models of the period's ideological precursors: the Scottish Enlightenment and Platonic philosophy.

In the other nine cases, the private eyes are similarly retrospective in their ideologies. In each case, the detective takes a stand against a community which takes little to no care of its weak and vulnerable – a community which idly stands by as the disenfranchised, the dissenting, or the merely different are reduced to victims afraid and resentful of life. Every one of these detectives offers at least one such victim the kind of support which, nowadays, is typically reserved for family relations. And whether they do so pro bono or for a modest charge, their localised work tends to benefit the wider community, so it is fair to say that contemporary Scottish detective fiction allows at least two generalisations: one, it suggests that society worked better when capitalist self-interest was weaker and family values were stronger. And two, the notion of the individual agent who combines anarchic ingenuity with moral integrity has become a vital fantasy in our age of faceless multi-national profiteering and zero public accountability.

As for the huge diversity of cultural and political identities which have come to characterise these detectives, it is worth remembering that they are all reflections of Scotland's recent search for an independent identity amid its ever-increasing multiculturalism. Perhaps this explains why Scottish detective fiction has featured so many new archetypes in the past few decades, everything from the philosopher of the mean streets to the feminist with a mean streak – and often within one character.

On a more prosaic note, it is, of course, also true that some writers of contemporary detective fiction look back to the domestic ideology of an earlier time simply because it allows them to preserve the private investigator as a plausible protagonist. In other words, it allows them to dispel the suspicion – strong though it has become in our time of multi-faceted police work and inter-agency collaboration – that the last time an amateur PI solved a murder mystery was never. What is more, as the PIs in this chapter have shown by being retrospective without being anachronistic, they have somehow made us overlook the fact that this generation has had rather few occasions to witness in the pages of detective fiction what we know to be relevant developments in actual detection. The secret of this success, to risk another generalisation, has been their unbureaucratic flair. While other crime fiction has foregrounded the process and progress of policing to ensure that its well-connected agents work more or less realistically within the justice system, detective fiction has instead foregrounded its lone investigator's flair: the individual manner that lets him or her act radically with extra-systemic freedom.

Now, it is possible that the writers in this chapter have simply foregrounded this extra-systemic freedom because they, too, do their best work sui generis. Fact is, though, that they have made it possible, and indeed popular, to disregard that the private eye's limited perspective and marginal position ought to seriously decrease his or her power to detect and contain serious criminal activity, the kind which draws the largest audience in both life and literature. What is more, they have increased the credibility of their PIs along with the relevance of the entire profession. And they have done so by making it seem self-evident that, when crimes are committed by, in, or against families, private investigators are likelier than police officers to be trusted and assisted in their investigations by the members of said families, the very people who are statistically most likely to be involved in the crimes.

Hence, these PIs have been highly successful figures of literature, even in the heyday of information technologies and mass-market police dramas, a time when one may be forgiven for assuming that amateur detectives were only ever going to be successful as museum pieces. Modern media, after all, have seen to it that even readers with limited exposure will suspect that they are more up to date with procedures of investigation and problems of jurisdiction than are most fictional PIs. Yet despite the seemingly insurmountable obstacles which our suspicious times have placed in the way of the literature's lasting success, all the writers in this chapter have found ways to dispel the suspicion that amateur PIs are – and for quite some time have been – past their sell-by date.

Admittedly, the most successful of these writers have done so by sending their PIs back in time to periods in which neither information technologies nor TV cops would have made them look dated, because when we look back to the 1930s, we do not expect the likes of Philip Kerr's Bernie Gunther to be up to date with today's investigative protocols. And as the example of Denise Mina's Paddy Meehan shows, PIs can seem just as credible and relevant when they are sent back to times as recent as the 1980s. So it seems that, looking back to *any* time in which PIs had more legal room to manoeuvre than they have now, we let them sidestep today's many obstacles to plausibility, whereas their colleagues working in the present day must demonstrate considerable skill in navigating around these obstacles before many of us take them seriously.

For instance, today's PIs cannot simply wander around any crime scene they fancy. Their access, unrestricted though it may be in family affairs, is often restricted to those same family affairs, so we expect them to earn their right to any further access, as in Peter May's case. When we grant his Fin Macleod the historical PI's licence to ignore present-day protocols and act like a police detective as he investigates an entire community, even though his case is set in the present day, we do so only because May navigates around modern obstacles to plausibility by posting his PI to the Outer Hebrides – which is essentially a journey back in time.

Then again, perhaps the case is more straightforward. Perhaps contemporary writers of historical detective fiction send their PIs on this journey back in time, not to escape our present-day expectations, but to embrace our long-distance relationship with the past, now that a general interest in history has been rekindled. After all, this interest is perhaps greatest among the literature's main readership – the baby boomers and their parents – so allow me to remind you how fascinated these generations are with the mounds of historical rubble which buried their sense of self in the war-torn, death-ridden tragedies of the 20th century. Perhaps some of the continent's most popular writers of detective fiction are reflecting this fascination, indeed perhaps they are even reflecting a fear that we are condemned by the crimes of our ancestors and thus not wholly masters of our own destiny, when they set their investigations in and around the wars of the last century.

Yet whichever reasons these writers may have for looking back to events or ideologies of the past, they do so from a Scottish vantage point which lies halfway between American machismo and European tribalism. As I hope to show in the final section of this chapter, even on the rare occasion that they lament a loss of self in stories about the loss of Empire, their stories are still best read as family dramas in which a lone, hard-boiled investigator seeks to rebuild the world – one case and community at a time. To subsume this transatlantic, hard-boiled humanism in American or Anglo literary traditions would thus be misleading. Self-effacing introspection, after all, is more in fashion with Scottish writers than square-jawed idealism or stiff-upper-lip imperialism, whether they investigate past or present crimes.

THE FINAL CROSS-EXAMINATION: CRAIG RUSSELL & GORDON FERRIS – *LENNOX & THE HANGING SHED*

Arguably, nothing has affected the course of contemporary detective fiction in quite the same way as the fact that, back when the prototype of the hard-boiled private eye started walking down those infamous 'mean streets' of America, he saw himself – and was seen by his clients – as a free agent. Indeed, so trend-setting was Raymond Chandler's Philip Marlowe in this regard that, even in faraway Scotland, the vast majority of PIs have since followed his lead and looked at themselves in the same way as their clients have looked at them – as free agents. Seeing as this trend seems to be continuing, it is worth pointing out that this image of free agency is as misleading now as it was then, and there are two reasons for this.

One, like Marlowe, most PIs of contemporary Scottish detective fiction pledge their loyalty to the job rather than to the client, and yet they let their personal involvement with other people's problems get in the way of their personal gain. Thus, they are committed less to free agency than to family-centred community – to bringing people together wherever they can. In other words, like the American prototype, Scottish PIs let their actions contradict the hard-boiled ideals of free agency and self-sufficiency. The key difference is that Marlowe stuck to the mean streets, so he merely got cornered every now and then by half-hearted attacks of longing and self-doubt, and though these feelings certainly provided a second challenge to his ideals of free agency and self-sufficiency, that challenge was as strong as it was sporadic.

Meanwhile, Scottish PIs tend to contradict these hard-boiled ideals as they walk among the mean mounds of Europe's historical rubble, the countless disasters of the war-torn, death-ridden 20th century which not so much corners their sense of self as makes them feel that it has been buried. After all, they tend to have a sharp eye for traces of this history, traces which provide a multi-generational measure of the world's disorder, and so it is retrospection rather than introspection that brings us to reason number two for their limited free agency: the sense that they are condemned by the crimes of their ancestors and thus not wholly masters of their own destiny. And what this twice limited free agency suggests is that contemporary Scottish detective fiction is proto-American in its embrace of the literature's first principles, yet in its deeply entrenched self-analysis it is retro-European.

The two writers who perhaps best represent this transatlantic blend are Craig Russell and Gordon Ferris. Their novels *Lennox* (2009) and *The Hanging Shed* (2010) mark the beginnings of two series about World War Two veterans, hard men who have limped out of foreign trenches onto the mean streets of Glasgow, where they nonetheless find occasional glimpses of purity in the city's underworld and bring a quaint chivalry to their often dirty work. Incidentally, and in spite of the novels' Scottish setting, this knightly spirit brings us to the proto-American aspect of the two series, accurately described by the genre historian Lee Horsley: "In series such as these," she says, "the honourable ghost of Marlowe is often near at hand, encouraging the nobler possibilities within the hard-boiled tradition, bringing to the fore the moral integrity, the compassion and the tough-sentimental view of life that infuse the investigative narrative with a redemptive potential."[100]

Yet at the same time, these Scottish PIs are also retro-European. While Marlowe, the model of hard-shelled masculinity, cultivated his tough sentimentality in the United States to defy the era's sad spectacle of broken men and fragmented families, Russell's PI Lennox and Ferris's PI Brodie fought in Europe, where they became tough to camouflage an equally sad but distinctly European sentiment. They became tough to camouflage their guilt at having managed to win a world war yet failed to build a better world. So, while they often sound like their American contemporaries in their anti-bourgeois tough talk, these Scots are rarely confident enough in their moral superiority to echo the Americans' frequent battle cry to rescue the proletariat from the crimes and corruption of their social 'betters'. Having only just left the site of the century's worst moral mud bath, Lennox and Brodie both feel far too tarnished to follow Marlowe's lead and fight crime as 'the best man in his world'. Indeed, so tarnished do they both feel, that they are reluctant even to return home, be that home in Canada or Kilmarnock, so they settle in a city which offers space for self-analysis, self-deprecation, and, hopefully, self-improvement.

That both should do so in Glasgow is perhaps more than a coincidence. When the war ended, millions of men were released into unemployment, and this social reorganisation suspended more than domestic hierarchies. It also suspended the British class system. So, for about a decade, it was possible in Britain to see the American dream of self-improvement by force of willpower as more than a voluntaristic cliché, and Glasgow, which at that time was still the second city of the Empire, was both a place where it was possible to think big and a microcosm of Britain's momentary Americanisation. In short, when the war ended, Glasgow briefly became a space in which Scottish PIs could suspend disbelief in an American myth, the typical hard-boiled myth of the self-made man who beats the odds of his low social standing by taking down the high and mighty.

Both as an historical and as a geographical space, then, post-war Glasgow accommodates the detective genre's big idea of overcoming social and official barriers along with the larger implication that 'the sky is the limit'. Of course, this American platitude would strike many as being sorely out of place in today's Scotland, but as both Russell and Ferris are at pains to remind us, both Lennox and Brodie inhabit a far less rigid Scotland in which even the unconnected and untrained can deploy Marlowe's extraordinary anti-authoritarianism as a standard tool of the trade in what the cultural critic Philip Simpson calls "the service of a strong individual code of ethics rooted in frontier mythology and owing little to the liberal dictions of modern culture."[101] As a result, their post-war Glasgow can be read as the Wild West of Scotland, where men of tarnished conscience

71

set forth to rebuild the world amid the chaos of social, cultural, and political restructuring.

Yet as so often among Scottish crime writers, a striking similarity draws attention to a surprising difference. Against the backdrop of Britain's collective and often compulsive effort at restoring the rank and respect it enjoyed prior to the war, it is surely a striking similarity that when Lennox and Brodie rebuild their corner of Scotland, neither of them does so to restore the old orders of Kingdom and Empire. On the contrary, disgusted with the enormous sacrifices that have once again been extracted by this moribund social institution, both of these veterans do so first and foremost to redeem themselves, and yet, even as they embark upon their remarkably similar redemption campaigns, their seemingly shared moral horizon draws attention to a surprising difference. While Lennox seeks only to redeem himself, Brodie further seeks to redeem a man who has lost his humanity in the court of public opinion and a woman who has lost her confidence in the court of law. Symbolically, then, and in his small way, Brodie seeks to redeem an era which has lost its innocence, while Lennox seeks only to redeem an individual who has lost his, and this difference in moral attitude is where the gap between them is greatest.

On one side of this gap, Brodie's evangelical attitude proves the writer and critic Ross Macdonald right in saying that "The detective-as-redeemer is a backward step in the direction of sentimental romance, and an over-simplified world of good guys and bad guys."[102] On the other side, Lennox's often failed attempts at being the change he wishes to see in the world prove that Macdonald's generalisation is itself over-simplified. Sure enough, Lennox rarely succeeds in effecting any significant moral change, never mind the one he hoped for, but he always defies the tidy moral categories of the sentimental romanticist, acknowledging out of superior veracity that he has been, and continues to be, both a good and a bad guy. So, far from settling in a cosy narrow-mindedness, his uneasy attitude keeps shifting from one doubt to another and thus shows that there is clearly room in the detective-as-redeemer concept for Russell's broader ideological agenda. In other words, while Brodie is perfectly at ease in his role as "avenging angel,"[103] Lennox is never at ease, so thoroughly convinced is he that "no one is who you think they are."[104]

At second glance, then, this gap in moral attitude reveals another surprise. Not only does it indicate what unexpected diversity there is even among two PIs who, at first glance, could hardly seem more alike. It also indicates that the best way to investigate the diversity of the literature at large is to look at some of the other differences which at first may seem to be similarities. Doing so should clarify that we are not just looking at two examples of Scottish detective fiction but also at one example of pastiche noir vis-à-vis one example of the western novel – proof, in short, that at the very points at which *Lennox* and *The Hanging Shed* seem to be making contact with one another, they are in fact marking contrasts, not only between one another but also between two rather divergent literary forms which nonetheless converge in one, broad genre: detective fiction.

First off, both Russell and Ferris make direct reference to their seemingly shared literary tradition. It is even at the same stage of each story, and almost on the same page, that each writer turns his private eye into a cowboy. Russell marks this moment by letting Lennox answer the question why he is going beyond the call of duty with a cowboy's characteristic blend of hard pragmatism and easy humour: "You're my client... Or maybe it's just that I've watched too many Westerns. It's my turn to be the good guy."[105] Similarly, when Brodie is asked to be the good guy without "turning Glasgow into the Scottish Wild West,"[106] he responds like a West Coast John Wayne. Bothering with neither an answer nor a pause, he simply locks and loads his guns.

Yet while both seem equally prepared, perhaps even impatient, to answer yet another unexpected call to arms, they could hardly be less alike in their attitudes when they do strike out as one-man-armies. Brodie soon becomes sentimental and launches a pro bono appeal case to save an old friend and confessed murderer from death by hanging, even though the accused man ended their friendship many years ago when he cuckolded Brodie and left *him* hanging. In sharp contrast, Lennox does not get sentimental. He gets paid, in this case by a man who, in a striking synchronicity of genre conventions, is concerned that he is being cuckolded. And then he gets paid again, this time by Glasgow's three main gang lords who, perhaps not all that surprisingly, are just as concerned that they are being cuckolded by a fourth.

Meanwhile, and with the typical stridency of the macho gunslinger, Brodie single-handedly takes the fight to "a stronghold of nationalism and the Irish Republican Army," seemingly untroubled by the fact that "the British Army were given a hard enough time of it over the last three hundred years." His only concession to the outlandish size of the challenge is that he asks himself the question most readers will by now be asking themselves: "Why would one man fare any better?" With the same stridency as above, however, he neither admits the absurdity of his plan to face countless enemies alone, and on their home turf, nor does he see any reason to be afraid in view of such overwhelming odds. Instead, he responds as though the mere question were an insult to his evident competence and courage: "This was what I was trained for. It's what I'm good at." And he remains this strident when he puts his frontier philosophy into action, first by going "off to find the OK Corral," and then by getting the better of all those baddies, "guns blazing."[107]

In contrast, Lennox is so far from strident, he does not even trust received distinctions between goodies and baddies. In his book, everybody is a bit of both, so after telling his client that it is his turn to be the good guy, he tells his readers that "I laughed bitterly at my own joke."[108] And with this bitter laugh, he resigns himself to his apparent fate, a fate which sees him work case after case of missing persons and mistaken identities as he follows dangerous leads through the thick fog of a depressingly colourless Glasgow, a pastiche version of film noir's doom and gloom. And he remains on the pastiche side of noir, for after being left to die, guts bleeding, Lennox makes a speedy and full recovery only to take his cynical revenge and quip, "Funny thing is, I always considered myself too cynical to go in for revenge."[109] So, while both PIs may seem to bring the mentality of the Wild West to the frontier of the peace process, only Brodie sees organised crime as a deadly serious business. Lennox sees it as a dark joke.

Yet before we take a closer look at the different personality types reflected in the differing views of these two private eyes, I believe my observation that their views differ so deeply on organised crime – a major social issue of the period – raises a prior question. How does each of them make us look at the post-war period? At first glance, both seem to focus on its fears, not just because they both suffer from battle fatigue, but also because they understand that the unifying force of any age is its fears. Yet while Brodie indicts organised crime as the post-war period's source of general anxiety, Lennox interprets it as a sign of specific anxieties. The historical contrast, then, is this. Brodie discovers organised crime in bed with organised religion, which makes us look at the post-war period as a time when neither law nor life was holy. Disgusted by this institutionalisation of moral corruption, Brodie responds with a western hero's lethal mix of righteous indignation and impromptu vigilantism. After confronting a priest about his sins and convincing him to confess that he "colluded in rape, torture, murder, perjury and perverting the course of justice," he controls "an almost uncontrollable impulse to give him his wish. To tarnish the white with his own tainted blood."[110] Then, to contain the threat that such organised crime might return to Glasgow and once again tarnish his town, he kills every male member of the syndicate which committed the above obscenities.

In contrast, Lennox discovers that three up-and-coming entrepreneurs are not only in bed with one another but also in competition for the controlling stake of the city's underworld, which makes us look at the post-war period as a time when big business became too big for the law. Watching this process at close quarters, Lennox realises that the unofficial and thus unregulated economies, which have burgeoned since the end of the war, have also created massive anxieties about the recent peace accords and their promised stability, be it by triggering frequent turf and gang wars or by making it bloody obvious that the old checks and balances are no longer operational. Disconcerted by this normalisation of criminal proceedings – and increasingly so by his participation in this process – Lennox plays the new system with a laconic mix of self-preservation and self-loathing. And since he frequently comments on how bemused he is by this behaviour, it soon feels like he is consciously parodying the amoral, angst-driven pragmatism of the noir anti-hero.

In contrast to Brodie, then, Lennox ends up with mixed feelings about his unscrupulous conduct, if only because he is "uncomfortable about how things had gone. After all of this was over," he muses, "I would need to operate in this town."[111] To be more specific, because his unscrupulous conduct has got a lot of innocent people killed, it seems unlikely that he will get another job, never mind another chance to redeem himself. So, unlike Brodie, Lennox makes us look at the post-war period as a time when a single man could be consumed by organised crime and was more likely to contribute to its collateral damage than contain it. And since he remains realistic even in his resentment, he faces the noir fact that he is not, as he puts it, "the only casualty. As I lay in the dark feeling sorry for myself I heard the soft, muffled sound of a woman sobbing. From Mrs White's flat."[112]

This domestic scene is worth a moment's pause. In one room of a shared solitude lies Lennox, one of a legion of scarred soldiers, and with an expanding sense of bereavement he is listening to his landlady, one of the period's countless walking wounded who is grieving next door to him for the husband whom she fears has joined the ranks of the fallen. As this quiet image of her muffled sobbing sinks in, her family name 'White' speaks volumes about the many nameless losers of every war, the tragically innocent who have never worn a uniform, whose loved ones have sacrificed their lives for king and country, and whose unnegotiable fate it is, nevertheless, to suffer in solitude as they grapple with an overwhelming sense of loss. Contemplating this in the dark, Lennox seems acutely uncomfortable in the new and unexpected role he is suddenly playing. Saddled with survivor's guilt, he appreciates that, while he is reluctant to embrace the period's patriarchal ethos, he is now the man of the house. And as he tries to figure out how it could have come to that, the novel's background story gestures back to a time before the war had destroyed families and denied them closure.

In contrast, and in the uncomplicated fashion of a frontier man,

Brodie simply takes the place of his landlady's dead father by moving into his house, wearing his clothes, and taking his guns. Then he takes his daughter, too, so even though the lady misses her father and the clothes are too big for Brodie, they find happiness by "pretending to be lovers."[113] And this brings us to the afore-mentioned issue of differing personality types, even though at first glance the two PIs may seem to be one of a kind. After all, both have chosen lodgings which reflect Horsley's observation that, "What we see in novels of this kind is a softening of the protagonist by allying him with others, often with a larger surrogate family that represents those marginalised by the dominant society."[114] Not only are both aware of becoming more soft-hearted, they are also both aware, and proud it seems, of becoming more soft-hearted while remaining hard-nosed. As Lennox puts it, "I'm contrary that way, but when someone tries to warn me off with a beating, I tend to get stubborn."[115] And Brodie seems to echo this stereotypical PI sentiment, "I don't respond well to other folk yanking my strings, especially vermin."[116]

Their differing personality types, however, soon become evident as we read on and realise that, at 34, Brodie still brags about this touchiness, saying in all macho seriousness that "It's a failing of mine, but not something I'm working on."[117] Meanwhile, at 35, Lennox seems more than just a year older when he quips that "It's what makes me an interesting and complex person."[118] The most evident difference, then, is that while Brodie has a western hero's big head along with his small regard for all those who get on the wrong side of him, Lennox has a knack to hit the nail on the head. This, along with his ability to call his assessments into doubt with a heavy dose of self-deprecating humour, parodies the noirist's lack of self-knowledge along with his inability to assess anything reliably.

As for the thoughts and actions which are perhaps most profoundly affected by this difference in personality type, they all have to do with the two men's courtships. Indeed, while both lust after an unavailable woman, each of whom incidentally is called Fiona, Brodie is given to self-righteous reminiscences about her "great betrayal that gnawed at me still." And by focusing on this "girl who'd speared my open heart,"[119] he adapts a pre-war sentimental ideology to his post-war frontier narrative. Then he beds Sam, a woman with a man's name, as if to prove his hyper-masculinity. After all, by "pounding in sweet assault and battery,"[120] as he puts it, he proves a point previously made by the cultural critic Cassuto, namely that "This new sentimental man is no woman in drag. Instead, his aggression protects sentimental virtues. His violence defends the home and makes sentimental domesticity possible."[121] True to type, then, Brodie is all about protection and procreation.

In contrast to this sentimentalist, Lennox is "a cynical fuck."[122] Though sympathetic, he goes about his business with "the direct, no-nonsense disregard for finesse that has made Scotsmen the envy of every Latin lover."[123] And although he does so with a number of such witty one-liners, his business is a singular and serious one. Born in Scotland but reared in Canada, Lennox becomes the favourite freelancer of the three afore-mentioned, up-and-coming entrepreneurs known as "the Three Kings: the triumvirate of Glasgow crime bosses who controlled almost everything that went on in the city."[124] So, while Brodie chooses to be a homemaker, Lennox is chosen as a peacekeeper. And while Brodie starts a gang war, Lennox prevents one, though at similar risk to his own safety, which suggests two alternative ways of reading the two PIs: Brodie as a sentimental reimagining of the Lone Ranger, and Lennox as a sobering remembrance of Lester B. Pearson, the Canadian pioneer of modern peacekeeping. In this reading, the two PIs differ not only in intellectual maturity but also in moral outlook.

As in most detective novels, both of these qualities are reflected in the outcome of the PI's adventure. So, while Brodie and Lennox both seem to have completed their missions successfully at novel's end, a comparison reveals that not every successful mission makes for a happy end. Brodie for one follows the lead of so many confident frontiersmen when, having come to Glasgow with a crippling sense of inadequacy, he leaves it morally restored "to take off into the westering sun in a fine yacht."[125] Meanwhile, Lennox stays "to prove that I could still do the right thing even after all the shit I'd been through."[126] To Lennox, doing the right thing means keeping the peace, not executing some fiery brand of summary justice and then turning his back on the structural violence that breached the peace in the first place and could do so again at any moment. So, if his novel's end is also to be classed as happy, it can be done so only in a bittersweet sense.

Sweet, because when Lennox reaches said end, there is a moment's relief that, for now, he has saved Glasgow from descending into another war, this one internal. Bitter, because even as he contemplates this moment's relief, the city is still teetering on the brink of gang warfare, and as he contemplates the remedial action he has taken, the brutality of it makes him feel lastingly bad. "Bad for me. And not because of the trouble it could bring. I felt bad because I had enjoyed it. Because that was who I had become. Post-war me."[127] Facing this post-war self, Lennox recognises one of noir's great ironies: when wrongs are righted with ever greater brutality, the gap between what people do and what they claim to believe in eventually grows wide enough to put redemption, the very thing for which they are aiming, beyond their reach.

At the end of *Lennox*, this gap is as wide as the Atlantic. Despite his success as a peacekeeper in Scotland, he cannot make peace with his past precisely because of the sacrifices he has made for this success, so as he closes his case, he feels that he is further than ever he was from the prospect of going home to Canada. Unlike Brodie, then, whose detachment from the bad guys places him so close to the frontier morality of the western hero that he plays with the notion of setting off to America as he looks "out into the wide open Atlantic,"[128] Lennox fails to make his longed-for journey of redemption. He ends up where he started out, with no choice but to stay in Scotland, and arguably worse off because he fears that this is unlikely to change any time soon.

These, then, are some of the stark contrasts between the differing personalities and prospects of these two PIs, and what makes them even starker is that they are plain to see in their differing narrative strategies. While Brodie illustrates the steady increase in his control of the investigation with his increasingly linear storytelling, Lennox reveals right at the start of his story that he will have no control of the outcome, for he tells it in the form of a novel-length flashback, "with a hole in my side."[129] From this noir opening onwards, it is hard to forget that whatever control he will momentarily gain, he won't, ultimately, be able to control his investigation sufficiently to prevent that hole in his side. Lennox is at all times bound for the misfortune which has already happened to him, and by narrating 30 of 31 chapters with a supposedly fatal wound, he pushes noir's penchant for pre-determination to the point of pastiche, which brings us to perhaps the most surprising point of difference between these two PIs.

While *Lennox* and *The Hanging Shed* both pay tribute to *The Long Goodbye* by Raymond Chandler, ultimately only one of the two Scottish PIs can be read as a tribute to the novel's main protagonist, the classic American PI, Philip Marlowe. Sure, both Brodie and Lennox are throwbacks to Marlowe's era of brave macho men who set out on archetypal quests to save damsels in distress and fix fragmented families. And both Ferris and Russell make their post-war knights-errant tip their Fedoras at *The Long Goodbye*. Ferris, for instance, establishes an associative link between Chandler's narrator and his own before he even starts telling his story simply by choosing for his novel's epigraph a quote from *The Long Goodbye*. In other words, he allies Brodie to Marlowe in the spirit of defiance which the latter had famously expressed in the words "I'll take the big sordid dirty crowded city."[130]

Russell, meanwhile, sets his novel in 1953, the year in which *The Long Goodbye* was published and Marlowe, the long-time cynic, finally became a sentimentalist. In 1953, after all, Marlowe finally took a case because he wanted to help a friend who he believed had been falsely accused of murder. Yet as I hope to have shown, this character profile does not fit Lennox. It fits Brodie, for it is Brodie who takes a case because he wants to help a friend who he believes has been falsely accused of murder, and it is Brodie who forgives his friend's betrayal, again like the sentimental post-war Marlowe. Lennox, meanwhile, would seem to be a throwback to an earlier version of Marlowe, namely the cynical pre-war Marlowe, for he, too, neither forgets nor forgives. Yet given his name and the fact that he makes his first appearance in 1953, it seems more likely that Lennox is modelled on Paul Marston, Marlowe's friend and murder suspect who reinvents himself in *The Long Goodbye* as one Terry Lennox.

Besides, like Chandler's Lennox, Russell's Lennox is a veteran of World War Two who tries to reinvent himself abroad. Like Chandler's Lennox, Russell's Lennox is visibly changed because he undergoes plastic surgery. And like Chandler's Lennox, Russell's Lennox wears his facial scars as signs of an inescapable past. Wherever he goes, they remind him of the man he is desperate to leave behind, and yet they also remind him that ever since he first faced violence, he has met with both the respect of men and the favour of women, both of which he rather welcomes, so perhaps his scars are best read as symbols of noir's existential crisis. In such a reading, they symbolise the part of him which, in spite of his best efforts, he cannot kill because it is the very part of him which, in all its violence and vanity, keeps him alive. And what pushes this noir impasse to the point of pastiche is that his scarred face looks like it will never get beyond the half-way point on its journey to recovery, so whenever he catches even the faintest glimpse of his reflection, his evidently arrested development forces him to face some overwhelming odds, namely that he will spend the rest of his life in- and externally scarred – at once ashamed and proud of it – and thus never more than half-way to redemption.

This, at long last, is the point at which the gap between *Lennox* and *The Hanging Shed* is the greatest. And it is at this point – a potentially misleading one at which it might look as though no single genre could contain two such vastly diverse novels – that I should like to make a final observation about their many commonalities and contrasts so as to situate this cross-examination in the wider context of Scottish detective fiction. Seeing as these two hard-boiled private eyes share everything from the source novel which gave imaginative life to their characters and the setting which hosts their investigations into organised crime, all the way to the Christian name and aching unavailability of their heartthrobs, Lennox and Brodie are the closest that Scottish PIs come to one another and indeed the closest any Scottish PI comes to the traditional, Chandlerian definition of the private investigator. Indeed, the case for their commonality is stronger still, because both of them do what Liahna K. Babener, an authority on Chandler, says of his characters. They "discard their old selves, and invent new ones."[131]

And yet, as I hope to have shown, it would be misleading to set these commonalities above their contrasts. Sure, Lennox and Brodie are a lot like Chandler's self-inventors in that they pick reinvention as a path to redemption, but they are unlike any of them in that they do so as they walk among the mean mounds of Europe's historical rubble, the countless disasters of the war-torn, death-ridden forties and fifties which have buried their sense of self under layers of guilt and trauma largely unknown to their colleagues across the Atlantic. And while both of them may seem like American PIs in their hard-shelled masculinity, they are thoroughly European at heart, for they harness their underlying ideal of family-centred community to an obvious European frustration that they are not wholly masters of their own destiny, now that the war has made them feel their dependence on outside help. Hence, both Russell and Ferris are proto-American in their appreciation of the literature's first principles, yet in their self-analysis they are retro-European, and it seems to me that it is in their markedly contrasting versions of this transatlantic blend that they best represent the diversity of Scottish detective fiction.

CHAPTER TWO –
THE POLICE NOVEL

Typically, police novels start out as stories about how cops work on the job, yet they soon turn out to be stories about how the job works on cops.

Stereotypically, they are about skilled workaholics who, in highly dramatic circumstances, are forced to push the boundaries of law enforcement so as to serve or protect several innocent victims of serious crime, all of whom are instantly forgotten as soon as the first mystery or action element kicks in. This happens when a cop is mystified by a detail which has escaped his colleagues' notice or attacked by a criminal who has targeted him personally. Determined to do something about this, the cop starts a compulsive and at least fitfully collaborative process of investigation, evidence gathering, and suspect interrogation, all of which soon demonstrates that he or she is not only a seasoned professional but also a civil servant, for most of these procedures require access to official support networks and government authorities.

Despite all of this, however, the cop spends a lot of time failing to catch the criminal, and this failure takes centre stage for two reasons: one, most police novels are 'howdhecatchems', not 'whodunits', and every time the cop fails to catch 'em, more of our attention is focused on how he or she will succeed in the end, this ultimate triumph of cop over criminal being one of the genre's most reliable promises. And two, it is in the failure to catch the criminal that we get to know the cop, for every time the cop fails, he or she has to deal with yet another critical news or progress report along with yet another attack from rivals or regrets. Worse still are the incompetent performances of the cop's inferiors and the inflexible directives of his or her superiors, which is why the cop, who is often working multiple cases, is eventually tempted to break protocol by meeting force with force, and so grows the tension in the narrative arc, in the chain of command, and in the cop's moral fibre. All along, we read in anticipation of the moment and manner in which at least one of them snaps – only to be reassured by the novel's resolution that, even if the cop does snap, the police will survive to fight another day.

This is why I prefer the term 'police novel' to such alternatives as 'cop novel' and 'police procedural'. The term 'cop novel' suggests that the sub-genre under investigation is all about the police officer, singular, when in fact it is an ensemble piece about police *work*, involving as it does a squad of cops whose interactions with one another foreground the institutional dynamics of policing, even when the story focuses on a single cop. Similarly misleading, the term 'police procedural' suggests that the fiction pays close attention to all the real procedures of policing, including the ways in which police officers perform routine jobs such as going from door to door and filing reports, when in fact the literature would be unreadable if it did not take poetic license with such prosaic procedures. So, what restricts the usefulness of both of these terms is that they are themselves too restrictive, the best example being that 'cop novel' is associated with an old school approach to policing which leaves no room for the literature's ever more frequent excursions into such modern sciences as profiling and forensics. Similarly restrictive, 'police procedural' is associated with a narrative structure which, as Messent puts it in *Criminal Proceedings: The Contemporary American Crime Novel*, organises "criminal act, detection, and solution in orderly sequence."[132]

In contrast, the term 'police novel' restricts the sub-genre neither in its style nor in its structure but in something which gives a better sense of what this literature is about, namely its subject. All it says is that a novel thus named is about the police, and while some readers may assume that the police is of literary interest only because they investigate crime, the term 'police novel' – unlike 'cop novel' or 'police procedural' – does not restrict our sense of the literature to this basic assumption. On the contrary, it leaves room for stories about those who come into sustained contact with the police, not because they investigate crime, but because they perpetrate it. What is more, the term 'police novel' even leaves room for those who write or read about the police, not as a squad of cops or a set of procedures, but as a social or political institution. To put it in Messent's words, the police novel accommodates "many types – novels of detection, thrillers, psychological and/or sociological novels, narratives reliant on gothic effects, and so on – but all focus on crime and police work."[133]

Perhaps the first question to answer, then, is how the police novel has become such a diverse sub-genre of crime fiction. Answer: police work is the most visible performance of state power and by far the most dramatic. As a result, its perception is more diverse than that of private crime fighting, and so is its dramatisation. Yet before diversity of perception led to diversity of production, it led to centuries of no production, seven centuries to be precise. This takes us back to the 13th century when, in continental Europe, the two earliest precedents of the modern police were formed in Spain and France. The 'Hermandades' of Spain were brotherhoods, municipal defence leagues which functioned as civil police forces, while the 'Maréchaussée' of France was the Marshalcy, an army outfit which functioned as a military police force. In England, meanwhile, the Statute of Winchester of 1285 regulated policing until Sir Robert Peel introduced the Metropolitan Police Act of 1829 which established the Metropolitan Police of London. Yet although this first modern police force could look back on a European history of six centuries, and although the English were already familiar enough with their police officers to call them 'bobbies' in honour of Sir Robert, it took another century for the police to command its own literature.

The reason for this long delay is that it took this long to change people's perception of police work. Initially perceived as a use of force which serves a private agenda, police work had to come a long way before it was commonly perceived as a system of law enforcement which serves the public interest. And just before it got to the end of this long journey, the likes of Edgar Allan Poe and Arthur Conan Doyle made police work out to be a plodding form of bureaucracy, fit only to serve as a foil to the investigative brilliance of the private detective. Hence, the literary historian Binyon concludes, "the policeman did not become an important figure in the detective story until the 1920s."[134] And even after this long delayed change of perception, it was not until "the late 1940s," as the crime fiction historian Panek remembers, that "radio shows like *Broadway Is My Beat*, *The Man from Homicide*, and *The Line Up* introduced radio audiences to dramas that combined sordid crime, petty criminals, real surroundings, police procedure, and hard-boiled cops, the principal ingredients of the police procedural novel."[135]

Around the same time, so-called 'semi-documentaries' did much the same thing for television audiences. Typically filmed on location and with the co-operation of the investigating law enforcement agency, films like *T-Men* (1947), *The Naked City* (1948), and *Border Incident* (1949) fictionalised real cases, thus depicting police work more realistically than contemporary detective stories, and when writers like Ed McBain, John Creasy, and Elizabeth Linington saw that police films were becoming more popular than detective films on account of this investigative realism, they saw an historic opportunity: the most profitable way to innovate the crime novel would be to include this element. When they did just that, they set the police novel on the path to becoming one of the literature's bestselling sub-genres of the late 20th and early 21st century.

Of course, Horsley is right to remind us, "The private eye is by no means out of a job, but narratives focusing on one man's isolated, stubborn assertion of individualistic masculine agency have receded in importance in comparison to narratives involving the teamwork of official detection."[136] At the same time, there have been some seismic shifts in the investigative protocols of the past few decades which have made the private eye's isolated, stubborn assertion of individualistic masculine agency seem rather unrealistic, and this has finally led to a changing of the guard in crime fiction. As the genre historian Martin Priestman observes in his essay 'Post-War British Crime Fiction', "In the more-than half-century since the Second World War, a growing demand for a semblance of realism has been met by giving the main detective roles to the only people actually empowered to investigate serious crime: the police."[137]

Needless to say, perhaps, this new realism has not reduced the literature's readership to cops and clerks, even though cops and clerks would seem to be uniquely qualified to read novels which focus on what the police *really* do for the most part of their professional lives, namely paper work. One reason this has not happened is that, in the more than half-century since the Second World War, hard-boiled writers like Joseph Wambaugh, James Ellroy, and Michael Connelly have shown generations of police novelists that literary realism can be something other than literal realism. They have shown that – when the police novel focuses on the real, moral dilemmas of policing – it can be realistic in a sense which is arguably more significant in cultural terms than faithfulness to the reportage of real, procedural detail.

Ever since, the police novel has typically done so by looking at crime and its containment through the eyes of police officers, plural. The result is a composite view which typically takes in more than even the best private eye can, be it because a typical police novel has more vantage points than a typical detective novel or because at least one of these vantage points is typically more central to the investigation than the PI's typically rather compromised point of view. And since this composite view typically makes the efforts of the police more informed than those of a PI, or at least appear that way, the police novel's shift in narrative perspective constitutes a critique of the private eye, whose marginal position and limited perspective have reduced him or her to a figure of ineffectuality bordering on irrelevance, at least with regard to current representations of criminal activity and its containment.

Beyond this critique, it is worth adding that the police novel's shift in narrative perspective has not just been a shift from one private investigator to several police officers. In most cases, it has also been a shift from the first to the third person. Hence, says the literary theorist Cohen, it also "constitutes a critique of the romanticised and historically inaccurate figuration of crime as existential conflict between alienated individual and urban modernity."[138] Although in most cases, police novelists have retained the considerable dramatic potential of this conflict by keeping the narrative focus on individual detectives who navigate through an alienating modernity or, as the cultural critic Simpson calls it, "the hazards of a fallen, corrupt environment, guided only by an inner compass of besieged idealism and an individual code of ethics."[139] So, not that much has changed after all.

What *has* changed is that police officers, at least those in modern Scottish literature, are often less alienated from the rest of society than are private investigators, and the fact that they enjoy more public respect is only one reason for this social and psychological difference. Another reason is that police novels, as Panek points out in a frank essay on the form, "drag into public view that the police must deal with the sickest, stupidest, most perverse and depraved parts of modern life."[140] Yet at the same time, police novels demonstrate that most police officers, unlike most private investigators, do not have to deal with those depressing and often dangerous parts of modern life all by themselves. They are part of a bigger community, much as they are part of a bigger story, and the literature's shift in narrative perspective is a constant reminder of this.

Another reminder, though by no means constant, is the literature's institutional and systemic context. Typically, the police novel has two main settings – the home and the workplace – and whenever it switches from the private to the professional sphere it reminds us that the protagonist is part of a state apparatus. This system of power, as Panek puts it, "does not reward merit because it does not understand it. Upper echelon officers are, almost universally, anti-professional political brown nosers, boot-licking junior executives, or bird-brained efficiency experts."[141] And the inner workings of this system are usually plain to see, because police novels are almost universally about lower echelon officers who, although they resent this power structure for rotting from the top down, nevertheless reinforce it whenever they close a case, restore the peace, and thus make themselves tools of state authority. Perhaps more conflicting still is the fact that, simply by representing this authority, they implicitly agree to being associated with its collective agency and identity. And what this association means is that even when a police novel does not explicitly address issues surrounding the executive force of state power, its representation of a few officers' conduct can nevertheless be read as a comment on it. As Messent concludes in *The Crime Fiction Handbook*, "The strength and importance of modern police fiction, then, lie in its institutional and systemic context – its representation of policing as a central part of a larger state apparatus."[142]

Writing within this context, police novelists tend to pick between two camps and stick to one of them over the course of their careers. In one camp are those who focus on the investigative efforts of a single officer, typically an individualist, and in the other camp are those who focus on several officers, typically operating as a team. Of course, all police novelists try to shift their readers' attention from policing as the kind of abstract idea, which works best in the background of a PI story, to specific police officers who personify law enforcement and foreground the workings of state power. Yet some police novelists do so by focusing our attention on police officers who try to stand *apart* from this power. Others do so by focusing our attention on officers who try to be *a part* of it. And each focus indicates the author's position in the literature's discourse on individual rights and communal responsibilities.

It does so because individualists tend to focus on individual rights, teamsters on communal responsibilities, and police novelists on one or the other, depending on whether they believe rights or responsibilities to be more at risk of being overlooked by the law. To be clear, when they focus on individualists they tend to assuage concerns about *absolute* state power, whereas when they focus on teamsters they tend to assuage concerns about *restricted* state power. In the case of those first concerns about absolute state power, it is worth noting that individualists represent an alternative sense of justice, even when they enforce the law, and that they are sure to demonstrate their belief that the system they represent is flawed, even when they are not seen to act on this belief. After all, they map the system's moral fault-lines by pointing out their individual sense of right and wrong, and with every line they add to this map they illustrate that their individualism is unlike that of a PI, because police officers who decide to go their own way cannot do so with a PI's extra-systemic freedom.

First, police officers have to decide whether their fealty is to their official superior or to some other superior veracity, i.e. whether or not their conscience trumps their agency's code of conduct and its collective wisdom. Then, they have to find a way to follow through on that decision while remaining within the system, so the PI's straightforward individualism gives way to what Messent calls "a more problematic vision of individual detectives operating through systemic procedures."[143] Thus, rather than recreate the private eye's one-way focus on some independent investigation, individualists in uniform create "a three-way focus: first, on individual law enforcers and the policing communities to which they belong; second, on the exercise of state power and bureaucracy (the way society is policed); and third, on the general health, or lack of it, of the social system thus represented."[144] In short, when police novelists focus on individualists, they tend to avoid the loner romance commonly associated with PIs, even when they demonstrate that police officers, too, can assuage concerns about absolute state power.

As for those opposite concerns about restricted state power, in that case it is worth noting that teamsters represent implicit subordination to the system, even when they do not enforce the law. Even when they fail or refuse to execute official justice, they do not put themselves above their team and, by extension, above the state. On the contrary, they are sure to demonstrate their belief that the police must be above doubt, that its cause must be larger than anyone's ego, and that its sphere of influence must have no bounds. Often, they act on this belief because they see the police as their family, a family of shared purpose and respect, and more often still they behave as if even the law had no right to impose a limit on their loyalty. Thus, the ensemble police novel can usually be read as a study in police culture which, according to Charles J. Rzepka, co-editor of the definitive *Companion to Crime Fiction*, is usually a study of the interplay between "hierarchical authority, individual agency, trust, and teamwork."[145]

In other words, teamsters not only challenge the individualists' claim to autonomy. They also tend to avoid the loner romance commonly associated with PIs, and they do both of these things for the same reason. As Messent points out, "the relationship between the detective's role and the agency of the state is necessarily foregrounded."[146] Even when the ensemble police novel tells its story from a street level view – a view which typically focuses on lower echelon officers – it still lets us see that the teamsters among them typically view themselves as the human face of state power. In this representative role, they can assuage concerns about restricted state power by showing that the executive force of this power can see off any threat to the safety and stability of the state and its citizens, as long as those teamsters retain their absolute dedication to the team, the job, and the public – in that order.

In short, the police novel typically tells the story of how a bureaucrat, individually or in a team, fights crime. However, it cannot focus on the procedures without foregrounding the problems of the police, for as the story is bound to show, the choices bureaucrats make are charged with moral controversy. Sure, finding themselves at odds with official policy, cops can choose from a menu of official options: loyalty, voice, or exit. Yet if the cops in this story were to exit the agency, the story would become that of a private investigator, and if they were to voice complaints rather than investigate crimes, it would soon become a tract, so the protagonist of a police novel typically chooses between loyalty and the appearance of loyalty. Sooner or later, though, said protagonist will have to meet our demand for drama, at which point he or she has to choose from a menu of unofficial options: self-sacrifice, vigilantism, or violence. So, in the end, the criminal drama, as well as the critical dimension of the police novel, comes down to the stress of making and living with one's choices, and it is the apparent diversity of these choices which brings us to the literature's perhaps most surprising genre convention.

Even though one cop's choices may be in stark contrast to those of a second, and even though both may be in even starker contrast to those of a third, each lot is typically determined by one of only three ethics. As Professor of Political Science William T. Gormley concludes, a police novelist typically chooses from a menu of only "three roles: the moralist, the pragmatist, and the rogue. Each role corresponds to a distinctive ethical profile. Rogues, for example, disobey orders, lie, break the law, ignore lesser crimes, and use excessive force. Moralists obey orders, tell the truth, uphold the law, and exercise restraint in difficult situations. Pragmatists fall somewhere in between; reluctant to disobey orders or to lie, they nevertheless do so under certain circumstances."[147] So, perhaps the most revealing way to read the following police novels is to look for an answer to the question every police novel asks: can this crime make us welcome a world in which individual bureaucrats habitually break the law, righteously enforce it without exception, or conveniently interpret it as nothing more binding than a loose set of suggestions?

THE SCOTTISH POLICE NOVEL

I n Scotland, police novels have for several decades now commanded a broader audience than perhaps any other literature. An obvious reason for this success is that they have inspired an unrivalled number of television crime dramas. Yet while adaptation and imitation have no doubt been beneficial to the genre's reputation, and while they have created the convenient side-effect that some of the novels discussed in the following chapter will already seem familiar and thus not require lengthy introduction, they have also created a certain risk. The risk is that images from a TV show – or simply *the* image of the police as seen on TV, which has become virtually impossible to ignore as countless unrealistic TV shows have stylised it like a neon mosaic of stereotypes – will distort perception of the literature.

For instance, readers who come to Ian Rankin's Rebus series after seeing *Rebus* on TV are likely to picture the detective as one of two actors, depending on whom they saw in the TV show: John Hannah played John Rebus from 2000 to 2001, and Ken Stott played him from 2006 to 2007. Besides, even the views of readers who can see past an actor's personality and performance are likely to be somewhat distorted, if not by the TV show's depiction of its host country, then perhaps by a host of scriptwriters and directors who, over the course of four seasons, distorted Rankin's vision to fit a novel's storytelling into an episode's runtime of 90 minutes. Either way, a viewer-turned-reader is likely to look at a novel through the lens of the TV show based on it, even when that show has little in common with the source material.

As for the risk of TV shows not just distorting or reducing but creating false expectations about the people, places, and plots of a written police series, see *Wire in the Blood*. Not only are those who have already seen the TV show likely to read Val McDermid's original series with a rather too functional Robson Green in mind, the actor who played the lead role of clinical psychologist and mentally unstable Dr Tony Hill from 2002 to 2008. After watching the man work his magic for six seasons, the same readers are also likely to have Dr Hill's modern-day Sherlock Holmes methods in mind when they read McDermid's stories about team based police work. And after seeing this work staged in real locations around West Yorkshire, any viewer-turned-reader is likely to picture those real places when reading about the novels' main setting, the fictional English town of Bradfield. But the most glaring interference in perception must surely be the TV show's frequent departures from McDermid's plots. Time and again, the show rewrites everything but the protagonists' names, which is to say it repeatedly creates false expectations about the novels upon which it is nominally based.

In other words, there is a considerable risk that some readers will picture the police as portrayed on TV when, in the following pages, I take a look at some of Scotland's contemporary police novels, and this is not just a risk with Scottish readers. Many German readers, for instance, are likely to be aware that the public broadcaster ARD has recently screened two adaptations of Scottish police novels, Craig Russell's *Wolfsfährte* in 2010 and the sequel *Blutadler* in 2012. So there will not only be those who bring preconceived ideas and false expectations based on a translated adaptation to their reading of these novels. There will also be those who talk about the novels without even having read them, and when they go on to talk about the Scottish police novel at large, their understanding is at least in part defined by a foreign televisual distortion.

Of course, this is just as likely to happen in the English-speaking world, where people who have yet to see any of the above will still be discussing the Scottish police novel with a TV show in mind, a show which, arguably, is not even based on a book: *Taggart*. Written for television by Glenn Chandler, the show's pilot season is suspiciously reminiscent of *Laidlaw*, an earlier novel by William McIlvanney, yet whether or not the Glasgow-set TV series stems from an uncredited literary source, it has lastingly affected the way in which most English language readers approach Scottish police novels, including

McIlvanney's supposed original. After all, the show has now been on air since 1983, which makes it the UK's longest-running police drama and a byword in most discussions of the Scottish police novel. So, at the risk of disappointing those who expect the following discussion to focus on writers who have attracted TV attention, I will try to see beyond televisual distortions of the literature's perception by instead focusing on those who have most affected the police novel's literary genre conventions.

M.C. Beaton – *Death of a Gossip*

Perhaps the earliest example of how a TV police drama has given a false reputation to its source text – and indeed to the Scottish police novel at large – is *Hamish Macbeth*. Starring Robert Carlyle, the TV series is loosely based on M.C. Beaton's long series of murder mysteries. However, so loosely is the show based on the books that it bears relation to them only with regard to Hamish and his Highland precinct, and to those only in name. In its 20 episodes, broadcast by BBC Scotland between 1995 and 1997, *Hamish Macbeth* tells a series of tall tales about a little village constable who solves mysteries with the help of the clairvoyant and otherwise superstitious, and this surrealism is enhanced by the director's decision to underscore the already soft-boiled plots with the soft Gaelic music of John Lunn and countless soft focus shots of a misty Plockton and Kyle of Lochalsh. Unsurprisingly, this makes Hamish's hometown of Lochdubh, a fictional village in the Scottish Highlands, seem more like a romantic ad campaign for a fairy-tale Caledonia than a recognisable adaptation of what Marion Chesney, writing as M.C. Beaton, has depicted in 29 novels to date.

Starting with *Death of a Gossip*, published in 1985, Beaton has not so much contributed to this romanticising of rural Scotland as coquetted with the Kailyard tradition of Scottish literature. The novel, much like most of its sequels, opens with a domestic scene in which rural Scotland is as yet untroubled by the realities of place and people. John and Heather Cartwright, joint owners of the local fishing school, are merrily discussing John's routine anxiety about meeting his new pupils, all of whom are soon introduced by full name, social type, and telling detail. Among the likes of a sheltered secretary, a "Pretty, wholesome-looking girl; slight Liverpool accent, wrong clothes," and a retired army major, a hothead with a "Small grey moustache in a thin, lined face; weak petulant mouth; brand-new fishing clothes," we meet the unassuming village constable, Hamish Macbeth, patiently studying the "crossword and whistling through his teeth in an irritating way."[148]

So far, so familiar, yet suddenly a violent death occurs amid the diverting high jinks in the lochs of the bonny Highlands. Lady Jane Winters, the title's gossip, is found swimming with the fishes. As Hamish soon discovers, the late scandalmonger used to work as a gossip columnist and had infiltrated the fishing class incognito, dead set on writing about the trip "to prove that the sort of people who went on these holidays were social climbers who deserved to be cut down to size."[149] Yet setting herself up for an even greater fall, she had informed all of her potential victims that she had found evidence of their false pretences, and it is in the following investigation of these claims that Beaton cunningly undermines the Kailyard form. Making Hamish check each suspect's alleged motive, she sketches a series of social aspirations and private indiscretions which – though at first it seems as inconsequential as the parochial gossip of Kailyard stories – eventually tells its own story about the dangerous jealousies of a community divided by class.

At the same time, *Death of a Gossip* can also be read as a country house mystery, tongue-in-cheek yet cosy. The country house in this case is the Lochdubh Hotel, where Hamish stages the grand finale when he reinvents himself as a pastiche version of Hercule Poirot, assembling his suspects in the lounge and solving the murder mystery with his little grey cells. Parodying the form even further, he hardly gets any police work done in the seven days prior to this classic denouement, so much time does he spend playing the bumbling village bobby in order to placate the "big brass,"[150] three homicide detectives who want him out of sight as they make the big catch.

Yet in contrast to their exaggerated officiousness, Hamish is far more concerned with keeping the peace than he is with enforcing the law, so he prefers to do his work behind the scenes, all the more so when his suspects start seeking his private counsel.

Some ask him how to clear a loved one of suspicion. Others are only interested in convincing him of their own innocence, but they all appeal to the pragmatist and family man in Hamish, and they are all right to do so. As a bachelor who is supporting his aged parents as well as his six younger siblings, Hamish is not only pragmatic but, after near lifelong conditioning, instinctively supportive of anyone who has vulnerable dependants. By way of illustrating this, Beaton includes an otherwise pointless scene in which Hamish lets off a small-time poacher because, as he puts it, "Angus has the wife and three children and it would not be right to take their useless father away from them to prison."[151]

Of course, it would be just as wrong to write Hamish off as a useless policeman. Only a few pages later Beaton balances this sentimental scene with one in which Hamish blackmails a boy's mother to give up her son, because she has repeatedly failed to take care of her family. Speaking and acting as a conscientious guardian of the vulnerable, he shows that he is deeply dedicated to the spirit of the law – if not the letter – by telling the boy's mother in a rather menacing tone that "You are going to leave Charlie here to stay with his aunt and I suggest you go back home and see one o' thae head doctors. You'll drive the bairn mad with all your hysterics. If you don't do what I say… I'll bring mair scandal down on your head than you ever could hae imagined."[152]

Fighting fire with fire – or gossip with gossip as the case may be – Hamish does not, however, stoop to the level of the murderer. He merely uses the threat of emotional violence, and he does so only to take care of the pastoral duties of his profession. In the final analysis, he is reluctant to break the rules of said profession, so when he can see no other way to look after his community, he breaks them resourcefully, rather than remorselessly. Rewarding this considered pragmatism, Beaton not only lets him catch the fisher killer like a level-headed professional when the big brass is up shit creek without a paddle. She also lets him get a confession in the cunning manner of a classic Golden Age detective, which is to say that she proves once and for all that the Scottish police novel can be read in more ways than TV audiences are led to believe by schmaltz-fest adaptations such as *Hamish Macbeth*.

William McIlvanney – *Strange Loyalties*

As for the darker type of police novel which most readers will associate with Tartan Noir, the type which Ian Rankin has turned into an international bestseller, the type which is best read as a detective novel in uniform – that type may never have been written were it not for William McIlvanney and his *Strange Loyalties*, published in 1991. Since the novel's central protagonist had already made a name for himself in *Laidlaw* (1977) and *The Papers of Tony Veitch* (1983), this may come as some surprise. Yet after those two prequels had made significant contributions to the development of both the Scottish detective novel and the Scottish noir novel, the first sign of this third novel's impact on a third sub-genre, the Scottish police novel, comes as early as in the first chapter, when the narrator announces, "It was a death I had to investigate, not for police reasons, though perhaps with police methods. Investigator, investigate thyself."[153]

Investigating himself here is Jack Laidlaw, a seasoned detective inspector who has just learned that, sadly, he has been right all along to suspect that life in the police, and indeed life in Glasgow, always has more bad news in store. What he has just learned is that his brother, seemingly of sound mind, has stepped in front of a car and died. As early as in the first chapter, then, McIlvanney defies two long-established genre conventions by opting for a first person narrative perspective and opening with a suicide, rather than a murder. And as each of the following chapters confirms, such defiance is as definitive of McIlvanney's narrative strategy as it is of Laidlaw's investigative strategy, so Messent would have a strong case if he were to apply his measure of hard-boiled individualists to both of these men for being "romantic in their emphasis on an individual conscience, a sense of morality and agency functioning independently of the institutional matrix."[154]

Laidlaw is the quintessential individualist and as such Scottish crime fiction's original rogue detective, its first official bad ass with a good heart. So, if at first he seems like so many of today's fictional detectives – a divorced drinker with the superficial manners of the down-and-out and the deep refinement of the debonair – it is worth taking a second look at him. Unlike most of his colleagues, Laidlaw plays the urban maverick of the factotum one-liner with a singular honesty of commitment. Whether he talks about himself or others, he speaks a hard and yet poetic truth. Talking about divorce, for instance, he says, "Sunday: the day of the child, the new agnostic sabbath when all over the western world diffident fathers turned up to catch a glimpse of the only things they still believed in from their marriage."[155] Talking about drinking, he says, "I headed for the drink, even though that was a defensive reflex that clicked on an empty cartridge."[156] And talking about feeling down-and-out, he says, "I was a middle-aged detective who liked to try and read philosophy, like someone studying holiday brochures in the poorhouse."[157]

Unfortunately, the context of these one-liners is too long to quote here, and in its absence I know of only two ways to capture its rare flavour of mind. You can either stop reading here and dip into the novel for a taste of it, or you can read on and take my word for it that he speaks these lines with something rarely found in police novels, something so rare in fact that he sets himself far apart from the many stereotypical tough talkers of American and English police novels. Where they distance themselves from what they say and do with American wryness or English sarcasm, Laidlaw embraces the hard-boiled worldview in a manner which is as Scottish as the man himself. He faces everybody, including himself, with the confidence of his doubts, and this rare ability to be honest without triggering a wry or sarcastic response, even from hard-boiled readers, means that he can deliver the above one-liners in a police novel without turning it into a morality tale.

Just how remarkable this achievement is should be obvious when you consider that the two stories of *Strange Loyalties* are driven mainly by the restlessness of private guilt and the anticipation of poetic justice. The first story is about a hit-and-run accident which happened many years ago when Jack Laidlaw's brother Scott and three of Scott's university friends killed a stranger. The second story is about a second hit-and-run accident which happened only a few weeks ago when Scott Laidlaw was killed by a stranger. As Jack Laidlaw investigates the first accident to understand why the second was not an accident at all, it becomes evident that the novel's first story is about the strange loyalties of four estranged friends whose shared crime has changed all four of them beyond recognition – one into a moral idiot who feels vindicated simply because he has not been found out, another into a hypocrite who feels empowered because he has made a career of avoiding the law, yet another into a man of charity who gives because he feels guilty, and Scott Laidlaw into a suicide who takes his life because he cannot kill his idealism.

As Jack Laidlaw meets the men whose pact of silence drove his brother to suicide, it becomes evident that the second story is about Jack's own strange loyalties, about the way in which he settles the conflict between his loyalty to his brother and his loyalty to his ideal of forgiveness when he finds out which of the four men drove the murder weapon and forced the rest to take the truth of their communal crime to their graves. On his way to this discovery, however, Jack realises that "In our haste to get to the places to which our personal and pragmatic loyalties lead us, we often trample to death the deeper loyalties that define us all – loyalty to the truth and loyalty to the ideals our nature professes."[158] Realising this, Jack also realises that anybody can be crushed by "the power of guilt,"[159] even a man like Scott, whose moral constitution is the strongest in the novel and whose name is an invitation to read his personal debilitation as a symptom of a national disease. Seeing how guilt left even his morally upstanding brother with nothing but self-contempt – and thus ill-equipped to challenge immorality in others – Jack gets off his high horse and decides not to go after the driver, even when the latter is finally identified by one of the four men whose hit-and-run crime sent Scott down the road to perdition.

Both Laidlaws, then, come to the conclusion that they share in a guilt which defies such neat categories as driver, passenger, and victim. As one of Scott's accomplices puts it, "We were all driving."[160] And as McIlvanney indicates by capturing his perhaps most recurrent theme – moral complicity – in this symbolic image of multiple drivers, he conceived *Strange Loyalties* as a moving meditation on the limits of the law. With that in mind, it is as inevitable as it is anticlimactic that both Laidlaws should decide not to bring their case to court, because following standard protocol would exact a high price of those who have already suffered enough, as Jack concludes when he speaks not just on Scott's but on all Scots' behalf, "What would we achieve? The resurrected pain of an unknown man's family, the damaged lives of a lot of innocent relatives who didn't even know the perpetrators when it happened... This guilt was not absolvable. All I could do was take my share of it. I took the secret into myself. But I would live with it on my own terms... It gave me a proper fear of who I was."[161] With this resounding call to self-awareness and accountability ends yet another McIlvanney novel about shared guilt, and like the collective self-investigation of the previous two novels, this ending suggests that the Laidlaw trilogy should be read as though it were titled *Scotland, Investigate Thyself.*

Val McDermid – *The Wire in the Blood*

In contrast, the next case allows no such national reading, even though it gave its title to a TV show which has introduced millions of foreign viewers to Tartan Noir. *The Wire in the Blood*, published in 1997, is the second instalment of Val McDermid's internationally bestselling series of police novels. Like the rest of the series, it is set in and around West Yorkshire where a largely English force of police officers investigates an Englishman whose crimes fall within the remit of one of England's Major Incident Teams, led by Detective Chief Inspector Carol Jordan and "Dr Tony Hill, BSc (London), DPhil (Oxon), the profiler's profiler, author of the definitive British textbook on serial offenders."[162] Dr Hill is now in charge of the new National Offender Profiling Task Force in Leeds, and were it not for DCI Jordan, whose unconnected investigation of serial arson in Seaford puts her firmly in charge of the subplot, the novel might have been a 'psycho thriller'. Even as it stands, with its descriptions of choreographed violence and its elevation of a psychotic villain to cult status, it has rather little in common with the typical Scottish police novel and rather a lot with the American psycho thriller popularised by Thomas Harris.

For instance, the novel's psychotic villain is one Jacko Vance, a man of such strong charisma and superlative deviance he could be the lovechild of Hannibal Lecter and Jimmy Savile. When this deeply disturbed man is identified as the serial killer of seven teenaged girls, the case duly moves into psycho-analysis, and in line with the psycho thriller definition offered by the cultural critic Simpson, psycho-analysis is from then on "harnessed to the relentless forward momentum of a narrative designed to generate suspense."[163] Yet by way of bringing the story back into the jurisdiction of the police novel, McDermid introduces a second narrative strategy in her sub-plot, where she merely gives us clues to the identity and motive of the serial arsonist. So, as she makes us work backwards from clues to culprit, she creates the suspense of a 'whodunit' in her sub-plot while in her main plot she goes back and forth between the interiorised voices of the serial killer, victims, and profilers, letting us know who does what and why so as to create the suspense of a 'howdhecatchem'.

Using these two narrative strategies in tandem, she gradually creates a gendered dissonance between the squad's two investigative strategies. As the suspense slowly builds in each investigation, the interruption of one by the other becomes increasingly irritating, and the more irritated we become, the more sensitive we are to the competing investigative strategies and their implicit gender politics. Thus, as the increasingly hectic storyline of Tony's chase is halted time and again by updates on Carol's stakeouts, our initial irritation with her comparative slowness is followed by a new, ever-increasing irritation: the woman is only slow to make progress because she is neglecting *her* work to assist the man in *his*. Though in fairness to

Tony, he in turn takes time off *his* case to work on a profile for Carol's serial arsonist, and it is this profile which allows Carol to close *her* case. In short, Carol gets her man with the help of a man, whereas Tony has to wait for *The Retribution* (2011) to get his man and thus equal the woman's success.

What this contrast comes down to is a feminist critique of institutionalised gender inequalities. And this critique is reinforced every time McDermid rewards the initiative and insubordination of an act-utilitarian, a protagonist who acts in disregard of convention when this allows him or her to solve a case or help others do so. In McDermid's police force, one such convention is "traditional Yorkshire male chauvinism"[164] and Carol's initiative reaps instant rewards after she acts in disregard of said convention by suspending a male detective whose chauvinism got one of his female colleagues killed. The man in question was the woman's only backup on a fatal stakeout but went to the pub without telling her because she was "Not one of the lads."[165] When Carol discovers this, she is disgusted by both his prejudice and his lack of professionalism, so like a good act-utilitarian, she makes sure that this bigoted amateur does not remain one of the lads, whereupon the arsonist is caught in the next stakeout.

Another convention in McDermid's police force is homophobia, and this one, too, is unfortunately left unchallenged until it is too late for anyone, including her act-utilitarians, to save a victim of emotional violence from becoming a victim of physical violence. Tony's most capable officer, indeed the only one who manages to identify the serial killer, is a lesbian, and like the other female murder victim, she pays for her otherness with her life. Then, much like in the case of her colleague's murder, the crime is analysed by a lead investigator and used as a platform on which to impress upon every subordinate that the best investigative work is done in defiance of institutionalised gender inequalities. The implicitly criticised alternative is that those who feel increasingly ignored and isolated can only do their job on the kind of desperate solo run that takes them out into the open where, without the support and protection of a close-knit team, they soon join the growing list of casualties. And as if to emphasise that such criticism is closely aligned to a feminist agenda, both of these casualties are women, and both of them are killed by men.

Indeed, as Adrienne Gavin puts it in her essay 'Feminist Crime Fiction and Female Sleuths', "The central concern of feminist crime fiction remains violence against women. Women are victims: captured, raped, murdered, butchered and in the hands of forensic detectives dissected into evidence. In emphasizing violence against women, feminist detective fiction makes a gendered protest. It also implies a gendered question: if even the detective figure is violated and attacked, is justice possible?"[166] In this case, the answer is yes. For all its focus on violent crime, *The Wire in the Blood* represents a centred world, a world in which men may occasionally abuse or even kill women, but in which not even endemic chauvinism and homophobia can erode the lead investigators' moral high ground. And since we have it on the good authority of Jacko Vance that "People like him were so rare it was almost an argument for the existence of God,"[167] McDermid's world remains morally clear-cut from start to finish.

Stuart MacBride – *Cold Granite*

In sharp contrast, Stuart MacBride's world does not even start out morally clear-cut. As we can see in *Cold Granite*, published in 2005 as the first in an on-going series of novels about the team around Detective Sergeant Logan McRae, his world is messy on both sides of the law. And by letting us see that not even a superior's rousing appeal to professional responsibility can contain the moral transgressions of said team, MacBride reflects what Messent calls "a greater awareness of the pressures, stress points and failings of the social system it represents."[168]

Perhaps surprisingly, MacBride lets us see this moral grey area with greater clarity than most by making Logan the quintessential moralist. Logan is the type of police man who obeys orders, tells the truth, upholds the law, and exercises restraint at all times. As such, he serves as a foil for his fellow officers who frequently break these rules of conduct, never more so than when their department is over-worked, under-staffed, and under media scrutiny, all of which is the case within hours of Logan's return to work. After a year's sick leave, he is barely in the door of Grampian Police HQ in Aberdeen when the corpse of a three year old murder victim is found, the "BBC and ITV, with their cameras and serious-faced presenters," start channelling public outrage, and Logan finds himself in charge of the investigation as "the rest of Aberdeen's CID were either off on a training course or off getting pissed at someone's retirement bash," and the detective inspector, "who was supposed to be easing Logan back into the swing of things, was busy getting his head stitched back together after someone had tried to take it off with a kitchen knife."[169]

To make matters worse, another young boy soon goes missing, another body is found in a council tip, and the police are as convinced as the press that a paedophile serial killer is at large in Aberdeen. Then sensitive information is suddenly reported by a local paper and public opinion turns against the police, who almost uniformly turn on Logan as the suspected leak, yet even in these stressful and ignominious circumstances, he proves himself to be a true moralist and team player. Even after he is relieved of his command and reproved by his superiors, he is interested not in regaining his power but in removing the suspicion that he must be lacking in loyalty, and he would rather do so by demonstrating said loyalty than by deferring to a sympathetic superior who offers to "have a word with the troops. Let them know you're not a rat."[170] Logan, after all, is motivated neither by the promise of official endorsement nor by the payment of lip service. He is motivated by his duty, the duty to stick to the side he picked when he signed up for the job, and while this lets him solve the case, it also lets MacBride calculate the cost of such absolute moralism: "Another case solved. Another life ruined."[171]

See, what Logan does not consider until too late is who else has to pay for his principles, and this is why the moral dimension of *Cold Granite* is far from clear-cut. MacBride leaves it to the reader to decide whether Logan is right, morally rather than legally, to close the case when he can. He also leaves it to the reader to decide whether the life Logan ruins by doing so is that of the criminal he arrests or rather his own. The fact that said criminal is plagued enough by his guilt to make a voluntary confession does suggest that the criminal's life is the one ruined, but Logan has made far greater sacrifices than self-indictment, so there is also a case to be made for an alternative reading in which this glum final verdict is about Logan's life. Either way, MacBride makes police work in general, and Logan's in particular, seem like something Panek calls "an unrewarding, soul-destroying alternation of boredom, coping with the ludicrous and trivial, coming to terms with the morbid and depraved, and facing rare moments of absolutely terrifying physical danger."[172] And as the above example of dark ambiguity reveals, he does so with writing that hides the cunning of its craft.

Perhaps this is why, on second reading, *Cold Granite* is reminiscent of *Grey Granite* in more than title and location. Like Lewis Grassic Gibbon, MacBride writes in a knowing and often mocking tone about those who live in and around Aberdeen, as when he first describes them en masse: "Everyone looked murderous and inbred. When the sun shone they would cast off their thick woollens, unscrew their faces, and smile. But in winter the whole city looked like a casting call for *Deliverance*."[173] In the previous lines, however, he suggests an alternative reading when he describes how "A minority trudged along, wrapped up in waterproof jackets, hoods up, umbrellas clutched tight against the icy wind. The rest just stomped along getting soaked to the skin."[174] Not only do these lines create a strong sense of place, people, and precipitation. They also create a strong sense of the defiance MacBride respects in east-coast Scots, a defiance which he, just like Gibbon before him, contrasts against the ill-effects of urban life in a community which becomes so fragmented that we neither notice nor care when principles – or indeed people – fall through the cracks.

I say 'we' because both Logan, *Cold Granite*'s team-playing policeman, and Ewan, *Grey Granite*'s left-wing political activist, personify our communal responsibility for such social and moral fragmentation. Both novels represent a mix of social groups and both indicate their debilitating lack of cohesion by juxtaposing multiple disconnected plotlines, both of which effectively implies that we as a society are as fragmented as their narratives. In both cases, the result is a sense of disorientation, but for a technical reason this sense is greater in *Cold Granite*. MacBride uses a lot less exposition, a lot less than Gibbon and a lot less than most crime writers. Indeed, so tantalisingly little does this modernist write by way of introduction and backstory that *Cold Granite*, despite being the first novel in a series, makes us wonder how much of the protagonists' backstories we have missed, and this niggling uncertainty, more than anything else, rules out any clear-cut moral judgment.

Craig Russell – *Blood Eagle*

Setting his sights beyond Scottish borders, Craig Russell also looks at the dangers and difficulties of forming judgments, just in a different moral morass. To those who have read *Blood Eagle*, a novel published in 2006 as the first in an on-going series about Kriminalhauptkommissar Jan Fabel, this may come as a surprise. After all, Russell here seems to tell that familiar, age-old story about the dark forces of evil, the eventual triumph of good, and the enormous value of clear-cut definitions, so the only thing which is not clear-cut about this novel would seem to be that it is not set in Nazi Germany and yet published in Britain, where interest in Germany is still largely limited to the times and crimes of the Third Reich. *Blood Eagle* is set in present-day Germany, Hamburg to be exact, and it tells the story of a modern-day ideologue and would-be mass murderer. The first indication, then, that things are not as morally clear-cut as they may initially appear to be is that a publisher believed there to be a sizeable British readership for a modern take on a quintessentially German cautionary tale, the one about the dangers of received wisdom and wilful gullibility about the need for violence in the service of some esoteric, Germanic identity complex.

This is evident even in the novel's opening pages, as they contain a transcript of a cryptic email which has been sent to Fabel by one 'Son of Sven', a self-confessed murderer who is writing to say that he will keep killing to continue his "sacred act" in the name of some "sacred duty" on Germany's "sacred soil."[175] Soon, we learn that the sender is actually serious, that he is supported by a secret society, and that he believes his duty to be sacred because he sees himself as an instrument of divine ethnic cleansing. In the course of these revelations, then, it becomes obvious that what seemed to start out as a serial killer novel is in fact a police novel about Fabel's team effort to stop the outbreak of ethnic genocide by the ancient Nordic ritual known as the 'blood eagle': victims have their backs cut open, their ribs broken at the spine, and their lungs pulled out through the wounds to resemble blood-stained wings, all because, as the megalomaniac über-Viking predicts, "in time, we will take our places next to Odin… but first sacrifices have to be made."[176]

At first, these sacrifices seem to be what *Blood Eagle* is all about. Not only do they give the novel its title. They also take on the entire genre in the competition for the most heinous crime committed to paper. Yet Russell never writes about such surface violence without revealing the false reasoning behind it, as when he has an historian reveal why the murderer has developed this modus operandi: "Every time he kills in this manner he is making a reference… he has reached into the darkness of the past to pull out a fragment that makes sense of his present. It would be remarkable if it weren't so obscene."[177] Ironically, *Blood Eagle* is remarkable precisely because it is so obscene, because it tells a horror story about what happens when ideologues instrumentalise T.S. Eliot's historical sense. As Russell's fictional historian explains, "History is shaped by our present, not the other way around. We have spent the last two centuries reinventing our past… The fact is there is no German race."[178] Yet as this story shows, one of the greatest obscenities in human history is that it is full of those who will invent a racial identity only to kill for it.

In this case, John MacSwain, an impressionable man of mixed heritage, falls prey to Vasyl Vitrenko, a testosterone-fuelled killing machine of mythic heritage. Formerly a colonel in the Ukrainian army, Vitrenko is now the cultish leader of a paramilitary death squad which he has formed by propagating his "philosophy of the 'eternal soldier'" and brainwashing his followers into believing that, regardless of their nationalities, their shared bloodline flows all the way back to

"The Kievan Rus. The founders of Kiev and Novgorod and who gave their name to Russia." If, at first, this genealogy does not seem to explain why the murderers are determined to restore the supremacy of some Nordic-Germanic super race, rather than that of a Slavic race, Fabel eventually solves this potential mystery when he learns that the Kievan Rus "weren't Slavs... They were Swedes. Swedish Vikings..."[179] Eradicating some imaginary racial weakness on the strength of this sketchy genealogy, MacSwain is convinced that he is enforcing a higher law, and as if to prove this point he creates a 'blood eagle' while impersonating a police officer. Then he demonstrates his utter disrespect for our legal order, rather than his racial one, by killing actual police officers.

In one such case, MacSwain articulates this motivation when he lectures his victim on the merits of Vitrenko's perhaps most tenuous kinship study, which he believes links him to Fabel. This study, apparently, shows "that Herr Fabel and I share the same mix of blood. That we are both half German, half Scottish. That we have both chosen our place. That is why Herr Fabel has been chosen for me as an opponent."[180] And that, finally, is why Herr Fabel was chosen as the central protagonist for this novel. Not only does his mixed heritage allow him to understand and frequently comment on a European Union which in 2003, the year in which this story is set, is ten years old, i.e. a European Union which is going through puberty and having trouble deciding what it wants to be when it grows up. Fabel's degree in history also allows him to discuss the differences between Europe past and present. And his name tells its own cautionary tale about the dangers of being too literal in our reading of the stories which seem to tell us who and what we are, stories such as those told by writers of crime fiction.

Today, Russell seems to imply, crime stories can function in the same way in which fables have functioned for millennia. They can caution us about the dangers of disobeying moral imperatives. Yet as *Blood Eagle* demonstrates, there are also dangers in reading cautionary tales without differentiating between imperatives and narratives. Ideologues like the aptly named MacSwain, for instance, will butcher narratives for swinish moral imperatives without asking why, when, where, and by whom these narratives were created. Yet as *Blood Eagle* demonstrates, there is also a danger that moralists like Fabel will get distracted by unnecessarily scrupulous attempts to ask and answer all of those questions, attempts to read all of the narratives right, and attempts to always decode the letter of the law before acting in its spirit. Weighing up all of these dangers, Russell, a former police officer, seems to conclude that moralism is nonetheless indispensable, just as long as it is informed. Hence, Fabel does not close the case because he sticks to superior, unquestionable moral laws, but because he is a stickler for the two chief principles of any good cop: rules and research.

Caro Ramsay – *Dark Water*

Back in Scotland, Glasgow to be exact, no such professionalism encumbers the cowboy methods of Caro Ramsay's two cops, DI Colin Anderson and DS Freddie Costello. A case in point is *Dark Water*, published in 2010, which shows that, had *they* shown just a little more respect for the rules and done just a little more research, this third novel in their on-going series might have been a short story. This, after all, is a story about a none-too-subtle revenge killer, who is granted open access to case officers as well as progress reports, both of which is against the rules, and given a background check that cannot honestly be called research. Yet while this lack of professionalism may simply be read as a minor piece of character development, it also tells a separate story of major significance, a cautionary tale about a risk which most police officers acknowledge but few police novelists address: human error.

Working out of Glasgow's soon to be demolished Partickhill police station, Anderson and Costello are only too aware that the very survival of their careers depends on their success in this high profile murder inquiry. Ten years ago, an alleged rapist was acquitted. Now his case is reopened because he is found dead and his corpse is found to have sustained the very injuries he was accused of inflicting on the earlier victim. Then the injuries are found again, this time on the mentally disabled sister of an ageing Glaswegian beauty queen, and as the investigation rapidly turns into a media spectacle, we see police politics come into conflict with police procedures. We see policy makers and press spokesmen try to placate the press by calling for progress at all costs, and we see Anderson and Costello respond by working overtime, until said costs become incalculable. Suffering from stress and sleep deprivation, they are distracted enough to make mistakes, waste time by suspecting the innocent, and risk lives by trusting the guilty, while all along their sense of being hounded by the media, of having their every step and – more distressingly still – their every misstep scrutinised, makes them ever more absent-minded and accident-prone.

Meanwhile, their paranoia is personified by a photographer who follows them around for a publicity project, captures the stagnation of their investigation in the immobility of his photographs, and makes it impossible for anyone to ignore the frustrating fact that it is the development of their inquiry that is arrested, not the killer. The killer, by the way, is called 'Mr Click', and thus the symbolism continues. His name was chosen by the press because his blindfolded victims remember him making an ominous clicking sound, and as the police search for him by sound, rather than sight, the fog around wintry Glasgow thickens as much as the plot. See, the killer has been trying in vain to kill Costello, as we know from his regular interior monologues, and he finally comes face to face with the detective when she gets lost in the fog. At the same time, incidentally, an elusive albatross gets lost in the same fog where he finally comes within reach of his pursuers, and it is by way of such overt symbolism that we are invited to see Costello as a bird which may have to pay with its life for having been blown off course, i.e. for having disregarded the rules and done too little research.

Without spoiling the ending, it is safe to spell out what all of this symbolism has already indicated, namely that it is as Gothic as the rest of the novel. Yet before we get to this Gothic ending, it is worth pointing out that *Dark Water* has dark family secrets and a cast of characters who are haunted by sins of the past. It has a labyrinthine plot and an atmosphere of foreboding in the face of an indomitable nature. It has a naïve heroine and a pathologically narcissistic villain. It has Innocence and Guilt. All that is missing from the Gothic novel formula is an incestuous relationship which leads to the proverbial Fall, and then it has that, too. A seemingly innocent flirtation turns out to be a budding sexual relationship between a brother and a sister, and it is the imminent consummation of this relationship which finally leads to said fall from grace, a proverbial fall which, in keeping with the rest of the novel's overt symbolism, is symbolised by a literal fall into a winter's lake of – you guessed it – dark water.

Rounding off this Gothic theme is the fact that the fallen woman and those whom she drags down with her see neither the proverbial nor the literal fall coming because they fail to see themselves for what they are. As Anderson freely admits, "it was much easier being here and dealing with someone else's nightmares than having to face your own."[181] Gothic to the last, Ramsay makes these distracting nightmares almost cartoonishly daemonic by revealing that her villain is a rare freak of nature, a man so inhuman that Costello can only think to attribute his sadistic impulses to a dangerous birth defect. And while she concedes that "lots of people have birth defects," she insists that "millions of people aren't born pathological narcissists, and that's the big issue."[182] In the end, she concludes, the fact that this man has killed for pleasure makes it all very simple. The big issue, as far as she is concerned, is not that this man was born into a broken family which finally broke him, or that he was born with a manageable but tragically ignored medical condition. The big issue, she believes, is that he was born bad, which is to say that his innate depravity trumps every social and medical cause of his crimes. And the fact that nobody takes issue with this conservative idea suggests that, as far as Ramsay is concerned, there is no reason to complicate our analysis of sadistic crimes beyond the moral categories of 'good' and 'bad'.

Anderson and Costello, then, are simple moralists. They see the killer's cruelty as something to be condemned, contained, and consigned to what the crime critic Messent calls "the realm of pure evil and individual moral monstrosity." Doing so, Messent continues, "is 'a way of isolating it from all social, political or economic causes, and 'explaining' it as freakish and psychopathic exception to all that we know to be normal."[183] In other words, it is a way of calling a criminal 'bad' without criticising or even questioning the context which helps create such badness, and that, according to the philosopher and psychoanalyst Žižek, "is an ideological operation par excellence, a mystification which collaborates in rendering invisible the fundamental forms of social violence."[184] So, without spoiling the ending, it is safe to say that *Dark Water* offers a dark resting place for such liberal ideas as the search for explanations and extenuating circumstances in a criminal's environment. Ramsay's criminals are simply bad. Case closed.

Quintin Jardine – *A Rush of Blood*

In contrast to such hard moralism, the criminal underworld policed by Quintin Jardine's super-cop Bob Skinner is downright soft-boiled. Skinner is a highflyer who had already flown by the time Jardine landed his debut, *Skinner's Rules*, in 1993, and he has since starred in a series of 23 police novels, all of which are perhaps best read as soap operas. Published in 2010, *A Rush of Blood* is book 20 in the series, and as if to mark the special occasion, Skinner has finally arrived at the top. He is now the Chief Constable of what Jardine so coyly avoids calling Lothian and Borders Police that it is clearly just that, and despite Skinner's coyness about turning 50, he is clearly still the man in charge, the man of action, the man about town, in short, the Man. As he puts it mannishly, "I've got a team around me that's pretty much hand-picked, and I can do the job the way I want to, spreading myself around without getting tied down by paperwork and meetings."[185]

In this case, as in every prior case, doing the job his way means that he leaves the menial, procedural stuff to his team of loyal experts and instead focuses on following his wayward impulses, be it because he likes to spread himself around, or because he cannot delegate. Either way, his adamant insistence to do things his way typically turns

113

out to be a secret strength, rather than a managerial weakness, as we see when he eventually takes the entire case into his own, strong hands and closes it with sheer force of character. Even before he does so, though, we see that Skinner is simply a compulsive individualist who sees himself as a bit of a rogue. When the suicide of an infamous Lithuanian businessman known as Tommy Zale coincides with the closing of an infamous ring of massage parlours around the Scottish capital, Skinner's subordinates are looking to close the case because they fail to see how these events are connected. Skinner, however, has his own ideas, and with his intuitive understanding of criminal networks he keeps the investigation on track until said events are traced back to the infamous McCullough clan. At this point, Skinner calls a private meeting of clan chiefs and cautions Grandpa McCullough that, like him, he calls the shots in his clan with impunity and is ready to get his hands dirty when the job calls for it.

Before the job can call for such a long-anticipated climax, however, the meeting is over and another cop reassures us that Skinner's hard man act was enough to make even this hardened criminal toe the line without any recourse to violence. And for those of us who ever doubted it, he adds that 'Big Bob' is still on the side of the angels: "I watched the two of you in there and I thought, thank God one of them's on our side of the fence, otherwise we'd all be fucked."[186] Since the eye witness delivering this verdict is a senior policeman, there seems to be no need to worry about the morality of what just happened. And yet, since this verdict is delivered in chapter 88 of 90, Jardine himself seems to worry that without this late reminder, some of us may look at Skinner's tactical roguishness and fail to see his moral righteousness, not that such on oversight is likely, seeing as moral certainty runs through the entire story like a sky high fence, clearly separating the goodies from the baddies.

This, incidentally, is why *A Rush of Blood* is best read as a soap opera. So sensitive is this novel to the fact that subtlety is scorned by readers eager for spectacle that it combines strong, simple emotions with large, unmistakable manifestations. And for those who prefer to have everything spelled out for them, Jardine provides enough expositional dialogue to ensure that we are A, never in doubt about the place of each protagonist in this ensemble piece and B, always up to date in the many private and professional melodramas which have given this series its enduring appeal. Skinner, we soon learn, works in Edinburgh but lives in Gullane, East Lothian, with his wife Aileen, the former First Minister of Scotland. She has recently been demoted to lead the Scottish opposition, whereas Skinner has recently been promoted to lead the capital's police force. "Brian Mackie's the perfect deputy… and Maggie Rose is settling in as well as I knew she would as assistant chief."[187] In this routine manner, the usual suspects are namechecked and changes in their circumstances noted.

Next, they all get to work as if the police were their very own start-up family business. Skinner even gets to work with his daughter, who has only recently been promoted to partner in some big Edinburgh law firm but already gets to represent as big a client as Tommy Zale's widow. And with all this family feeling taking over the narrative mood, it is perhaps not surprising that this police patriarch does not comment on the social context of his case, be it when he leads his team to a ring of human traffickers or when he discusses their crimes and capture with friends and family. Such avoidance of social commentary, after all, is par for the course in Jardine's type of police novel. As Messent explains in his essay 'The Police Novel', "the type of police novel focusing on the team, an 'extended family' who follow a set of day-by-day procedural routines, is less likely to question the dominant social system than those novels featuring one or two individual protagonists… The only real subject of critique here has to do with the institutional arrangements governing police life."[188]

At least indirectly, then, novels like *A Rush of Blood* cast a vote of confidence in the efficacy of the law and suggest unquestioning approval of the social order it protects. They do not raise questions about such overarching themes as social justice or structural violence, and this, as Messent rightly concludes, "suggests the dangers inherent in such an approach – in too close a commitment to the ground-level cop point of view."[189] Jardine provides no outside angle which could put some kind of critical perspective on the self-congratulatory picture his cops give us of their conduct. Instead, he makes us see things through the eyes of his cops, and they all more or less look up to Big Bob in hero worship, because he gets the job done, every time. Thus, Skinner is soap opera's acme of fulfilment, a man so respected and resourceful that he can afford to act like a cowboy even though he is the Chief Constable, and in typical soap operatic fashion, it is this success story which provides the novel's resolution, not the potential criticism that Skinner's management style is a reactionary argument for a police system in which bullies get results without getting tied down by due process – or as he calls it, paperwork and meetings.

Karen Campbell – *Proof of Life*

In contrast, Karen Campbell's policewoman, Anna Cameron, is an advertisement for accountability. Perhaps attention to the reality of police work is not surprising in her case, considering that Campbell worked as a police officer before she started writing about others. But what surely *is* surprising is that, as a crime writer, she has not made her case for accountability by making her lead officer a paragon of due process. On the contrary, she has made Anna the kind of cop who puts her own advancement above accountability, be it in her professional or in her private life. And it is by documenting the unintended consequences of such arrogance that Campbell turns Anna into such a mess that her entire life story can be read as a cautionary tale about the risks of getting results without getting tied down by paperwork and meetings.

Perhaps the best example of this is *Proof of Life*, published in 2011. In this closing novel of the Cameron quartet, a cold case dating back to Anna's debut in *The Twilight Time* suddenly throws her long-sought, quiet domesticity into disarray, yet following the habit of a lifetime, Anna asks for neither the support nor the sympathy of her team. Instead, the habitual individualist goes it alone, and since the official avenues seem to lead nowhere, she soon goes rogue. First she abuses the power of her position as Chief Inspector to access confiscated drug money in an attempt to pay off her blackmailer. And when this fails, she tries to bury their shared past once and for all by killing the man. Yet in a rare complication of the genre's central hunter/hunted dynamic, Anna is going through pregnancy, which on a symbolic level suggests the inescapability of the past and on a practical level makes it hard for her to walk, never mind outrun the man when he, in turn, decides to go after her and her family.

By the time he has followed her home, framed her for a revenge murder, and nearly killed her partner and step-daughter, she is so desperate to get him off her back that she has become a danger to herself and others. And what this turnaround of the afore-mentioned hunter/hunted dynamic illustrates is that, as Panek, one of the leading theorists of the police novel, puts it, "The mental or moral fervour of criminal investigation can follow an officer home, but, more insidiously, the aftershocks of physical terror creep into the individual's whole consciousness."[190] So what happens next will come as no surprise to CID officers, though to readers of conventional police novels it might do just that. Unlike most fictional cops, Anna neither manages to make a violent felon toe the line simply by acting the big man, nor does she make him toe the line by due process of law. She does not make him toe the line at all, because this is not the Wild West where cowboys and criminals risk their lives to restore their honour. This is the West of Scotland where Anna's rogue mission fails so spectacularly that it constitutes a worst case scenario of zero accountability.

Setting the scene for the novel's explosive combination of indefatigable commitment and unintended consequences is a terrorist attack on Glasgow airport in June 2007. After a burning car crashes through the main doors, a fire breaks out, a conveniently placed camera crew records Anna's spontaneous attempt at containing the bomb threat, and the policeman who pulled the driver out of the burning car "catches Anna's eye, half smiles, ashamed at all the fuss. His hands are red and burned, and that is his job. Damping fire with his hands and saving the life of a man who would kill thousands, that is his job, the one he's paid to do every day. It is a reflex not to recoil."[191] A little later, Campbell dramatises this same reflex in a case of civil discontent, when a peaceful protest suddenly erupts into panic and several protesters suffer the unintended consequences of human error, this time committed by police officers, "the men and women who were equally panicked, who were sheepdogs herding sheep. They did not mean to bite."[192]

Between these two reflexes, both of which are shown from a cop's point of view, the full spectrum of Campbell's perspective on policing is visible. In the indefatigable commitment of that first reflex it is plain to see that she does not want to glorify police work, only show that it does not need glorifying. And in the unintended consequences of that second reflex it is equally plain to see that she does not want to excuse police violence, only show that it needs to be seen in context and proportion. As Campbell demonstrates in each case, there is a difference, morally. And this difference is evident throughout, because although she writes about a rogue cop, she nonetheless offers a balanced view of the short time in which police officers have to make far-reaching judgment calls, the high pressure under which they routinely discharge their duty, and the occasional, low moments in which even good cops can do bad things.

It is, then, in the context of several sobering tributes to social and psychological realism that Campbell throws overboard the police novel's perhaps most unrealistic genre convention. Unlike most conventional police novelists, she neither ignores nor inflates the importance of a simple-minded and all too easily sensationalised breed of police officer – the renegade who gets carried away when the riot gear comes on. Such individuals are reprehensible, Campbell suggests in passing, but they are by no means representative of the typical man or woman in uniform, not in Glasgow anyway, so she gives them minor roles and without much fanfare reveals them to be pseudo-militants who lead from the rear, "all bluster and so much front it made you wonder what they were suppressing."[193] Having thus situated *Proof of Life* in the tradition of the humanist police novel, she then swiftly moves, as the feminist critic Gavin might put it, "away from hard-boiled, streetwise toughness and places the detective's psychology and human and social issues at its core."[194] Around this she layers sub-plot upon sub-plot, slowly but steadily bringing together three stories which initially seem to have little to do with one another and even less with a police novel, yet which finally collide in an unexpected and literally explosive conclusion.

Alex Gray – *A Pound of Flesh*

Avoiding social and psychological realism almost entirely, Alex Gray has instead relied on genre conventions of mystery and romance fiction in her on-going series about Glasgow heartthrob, William Lorimer. Add to this her female characters' audible palpitations whenever Lorimer enters the scene and it should come as no surprise that each of his gallant adventures in crime fighting reads like a sentimental novel from the 19th century. Perhaps the best example of this is the ninth in the series, *A Pound of Flesh*, published in 2012. Lorimer, now in his late thirties, has just been promoted to Detective Superintendent, and well he deserves it. After all, as his many lady admirers hasten to remind us, he has long been "an intellectual whose honesty, loyalty and deep desire to right society's wrongs were his greatest strengths." Better still, "the strength of his physique was more than matched by a different sort of power; those unsmiling eyes and that granite jaw came from a man whose experience of life had hardened him into a formidable opponent of the worst sort of criminal." And yet "he cared, he really cared about the victims of crime," so much so that every woman he meets seems to ask herself: "Who wouldn't be charmed by a big, bonny lad like Lorimer?"[195]

That, of course, is a rhetorical question. Not one of Gray's protagonists seems either able or willing to answer it, not even with a polite suggestion that some of us might fail to be charmed by Lorimer's holier than thou comportment, his patriarchal chauvinism, or perhaps his grandfatherly domesticity. This is really rather surprising, given that, far from today's often prurient portrayal of intimate acts and thoughts, Gray's bonny lad displays such puritanical coyness in all matters of love and lust that he seems to have been conceived as a somewhat prudish mother-in-law's ideal of companionable wholesomeness. Yet whether or not a younger and more liberal readership is charmed by any of the above, the fact that he has appeared in 12 books – and counting – implies that at least some of us have now witnessed "the flowering of the male domestic detective," as the cultural critic Cassuto observes in his seminal genre study, *Hard-Boiled Sentimentality*. This domesticated detective, he continues, "now acts out versions of all of the cardinal sentimental virtues that the early hard-boiled writers originally posed against… family loyalty, temperance, religious faith, community ties, and hard work."[196] Indeed, Lorimer has eyes only for his wife, never swears or loses his temper, quotes scripture in times of crisis, and always acts like the guardian of the family writ large, even "getting up in the middle of a bleak January night." After all, "Hadn't the shepherd left all his flock to go and rescue one lost sheep?"[197]

This question, of course, is also rhetorical, but this one has two implications: one, Lorimer feels duty-bound to play the role of the policeman-father who protects a Christian ideal of family with emotional sensitivity and personal sacrifice, as did the Father in heaven according to St Matthew's Gospel, chapter 18, verses 12 to 14, as referenced in the novel's epigraph. And implication number two of Lorimer's rescue mission is that the moral shepherd plays a vital role in 21st century Glasgow, a role last played by the house-bound mother of the 19th century sentimental novel, and if today's Glasgow seems like an unlikely time and place for such a renaissance, it is worth noting that Gray does not really write about today's Glasgow. What she writes about instead is a sentimental projection of dated and bucolic community values onto the city's modern topography, and in this fictional Glasgow there is deep respect bordering on outright reverence for a moral shepherd like Lorimer, a man who is both able and willing to single-handedly rescue a black sheep, return it to its all-white, middle-class flock, and reinforce the good old social ties which keep flocks together by binding those in need to their missionary benefactors.

The black sheep, in this case, is a prostitute, but she is only black in the sense of being tarnished. Ethnic diversity is reserved for the criminal, an Eastern European who is not only responsible for the killing of several white prostitutes. As Gray implies, he is also responsible for the killing of several white men, including Scotland's Deputy First Minister, for while the foreigner did not kill those men himself, he corrupted the Scot who did, a previously law-abiding man who only turns into a vigilante when the police fail to follow up on their only reported clues, namely that the prostitute-killer drives a white Mercedes and picks up his female victims in Glasgow's red-light district. So it is only in the hope of doing his civic duty and helping justice on its way that the Scot stops every driver who fits that profile and kills him.

In Gray's book, then, the Scottish killer is morally superior to the foreign one, and should this not already be clear from the above implications, it becomes impossible to ignore when Lorimer explicitly states that picking up prostitutes and paying for sex are "nefarious activities."[198] Besides, we are repeatedly reminded, the Scottish vigilante only kills those nefarious men because the police are too busy investigating the murder of the politician to stop that of further prostitutes. Correction: *most* of them are too busy; Lorimer is not. Moralist that he is, he objects when the prostitute murders have to take a back seat, because "Lorimer was a man capable of feeling great pity for murder victims... and would treat these poor, vulnerable women with as much compassion as any other girl who had been brutalised."[199] This character reference comes with the professional authority of his psychologist sidekick, Dr Solomon Brightman, so it should come as no surprise when Lorimer starts pulling secret night shifts around Glasgow's red-light district, heroically moonlighting as a private investigator in the belief that he can rescue these poor, vulnerable women – the afore-mentioned black sheep – from the predators whose lechery he sees as the root cause of prostitution. After all, he says to himself, it all starts with "early abuse at the hands of a father or father figure, then a decision to go on the game and earn money for the sexual favours that had already been stolen from them for nothing."[200]

So far, so specious, but this pop psychology becomes even more controversial when he concludes that "It was hardly surprising, given

121

the way that so many of Glasgow's prostitutes had been treated, that they had become lesbians."[201] According to this arch-conservative, nature does not determine sexual orientation. Abuse does. Women are attracted to other women, and they end up selling sex, because they have been abused by men. And yet, in defiance of this questionable rationale, nature does determine the sexual deviance of the prostitute-killer. So, when he is finally identified, he is simply written off as a monster – a moral degenerate who was born evil – which explains why any discussion of crime's social causes is, as the crime critic Peter Messent might put it, "largely stifled here by its consignment to the category of the monstrous moral exception to the general rule."[202]

Denise Mina – *Gods and Beasts*

It is only fitting, then, that such conservative writing is itself a moral exception to the general rule, at least as far as the Scottish police novel is concerned. Even in novels set in the same crime-ridden city, it is rare for writers to duck complex social, cultural, and political questions by reducing them to the personal, let alone the monstrous moral exception. Perhaps the most compelling, and indeed the most recent, example of this is Denise Mina's on-going series of novels about the many complicated friends, foes, and factions which surround her equally complicated DS Alex Morrow. And perhaps the most insightful example of this exemplary series is *Gods and Beasts*, published in 2012.

In this third instalment, Mina once again creates a multi-faceted view of Glasgow's many divided societies by telling a multiplicity of stories from a multiplicity of viewpoints. As indicated by the title reference to Aristotle's *Politics*,[203] the novel focuses on people who are either unable to live in one of the city's societies or so self-sufficient that they can live outside of them all. According to Aristotle, such people are either gods or beasts, but in Mina's book they are all sympathetic human beings and their stories of social activism and estrangement raise three searching questions about the nature of human community: one, what determines our social obligations?

Two, how do we deal with anti-social elements? And three, how do we take care of our social obligations when anti-social elements threaten our immediate communities, or indeed ourselves?

In search of answers to these perennial questions, Mina's three main protagonists make their way through a tribal Glasgow, while the collateral damage of a seemingly random act of violence gradually exposes hidden connections in their class-divided community. The act in question is a man's murder in a busy post office, where his dying struggle to put his last instructions into words is set against a background of confused people silently clutching parcels. And since this scene would appear to symbolise the breakdown of communication, it is rather poignant that all three of the novel's main protagonists strike out to answer the above questions by and for themselves.

What they learn along the way is this: Martin Pavel, a private philanthropist who witnesses the post office murder and wants to help the victim's family, learns that it is not enough to throw money at a social problem because, if that is all you do, "you learn nothing… it's the practice, the effort that teaches you courage and honesty and humility."[204] Kenny Gallagher, the "potential future leader of the Labour Party," learns that those who sell out to anti-social money men, while pretending to stand up for victims of social inequality, can get away with "self-interest masquerading as something noble."[205] And Alex Morrow, a police detective who returns from maternity leave to lead the murder inquiry, learns that "You have to participate in your community," not just police it, if you want to live in "an ethically healthy environment as much as a physically healthy one."[206]

At first, their stories are barely related, yet the connections between them gradually become stronger, as does the sense that connection itself is the novel's main subject. So, even though our attention is initially directed at such themes as quiet philanthropy, social inequality, and early maternity – themes which are typically developed in the private rather than in the public sphere – the ever-strengthening connections between Mina's characters eventually draw us towards her subtle discourse on Glasgow's social and political system. And as their attempts at understanding the power dynamics of their community take them deeper and deeper into the underworld of organised crime, they raise uncomfortable questions about its parallels in the overworld of social politics.

These parallels are perhaps most obvious when DS Morrow interrogates a career politician in Kenny Gallagher and a career criminal in Danny McGrath and realises that she is dealing with "one on each side of the 'they' divide."[207] And while each man's success says a lot about the rewards of secretly crossing that 'they' divide, her inverted commas say even more about the false morality of said divide and its shaming connotations. Is it surprising that a policewoman should possess such a sensitive moral compass, a woman who has chosen the very profession in which people are paid to enforce this 'they' divide? Given the internal inquiry Morrow had to face prior to this case, the answer would at first seem to be a clear yes, but then Mina reminds us of three facts which police novelists often let us forget in order to sustain the comforting illusion of a clear-cut divide between cops and criminals.

First, she reminds us that *her* cop cannot sit comfortably on the side of the supposed 'goodies' because, like any real person, she has personal connections which, whether she likes it or not, span this impersonal divide. Many of these connections, after all, are inherited from the community in which she spent her formative years and the family into which she was born. Thus, at least some of her connections to so-called 'baddies' – as for instance those to Danny McGrath, her half-brother – are so intrinsic to her sense of self that she cannot simply cut them. She can deny the risk of contagion but not the fact that suspicion "was serious enough to prompt an investigation into her entire career." To her relief, she hastens to add, "The depth of the inquiry had left her the most trusted, vetted DS in Glasgow and put the shame of her past behind her."[208] Yet despite the positive outcome, the experience has left her highly sensitive to the shaming connotations of this 'they' divide and its implicit fallacy that 'they' are all categorically different from 'us'.

This brings us to the second reason for her sensitive moral compass,

Scotland's high degree of social mobility. As somebody who has spent a lifetime transitioning from one social and professional class to another, Morrow knows that there are several halfway houses and that each of them makes a nonsense of the assumption that there are categorical moral differences. In other words, having seen Scotland's high degree of social mobility up close, and having experienced it herself, Morrow knows that there is no shortage of Kennies and Dannies, people whom some would regard as criminals by choice and others as victims of circumstance. And having been misjudged herself, she also knows that there is no shortage of Morrows either, people who are sensitive to the injustice of categorical judgment because they can see that 'they' are all individuals whose conduct has to be judged in context, not in contempt of the 'other'.

This, then, brings us to the third reason for her sensitive moral compass. Morrow is a woman, and like most women she knows all about the shaming connotations of being referred to as 'they'. So, although the realist in her can appreciate that anonymity is an incalculable advantage for a cop – just like it is for a criminal – the moralist in her cannot abide the implied sexism, and it is in defiance of such sexism that Mina makes her cop more than just successful at her job. She also makes her central to the narrative. As a result, Mina's feminist critique of power displacement is anchored in the very structure of her novel, and this, in conjunction with Morrow's insistence on probing every layer of the city's power structure, makes it rather hard to ignore the story's central question: who really runs Glasgow? In fact, the only thing harder to ignore is the implication of its open end: as in real life, figure it out for yourself.

THE ROUNDUP

Someone like Denise Mina's DS Alex Morrow – a woman who is in the police but not of the police – is a good example of an important fact, a fact which to those who have skipped the previous case studies and come straight to this summary section might come as some surprise. Contrary to the impression created by the genre's best known maverick, Ian Rankin's DI John Rebus, the Scottish police novel is not all about men who have a hard time identifying with institutional authority. As Morrow's example shows, it can also be about *women* who have a hard time identifying with institutional authority. And as her example further shows, it can also be about people who set aside their problems with institutional authority to get a better view of the benefits attached to police work, such as the knowledge that they are helping others and simultaneously giving themselves a good chance of staying on the straight and narrow.

So, at least in some cases, the police can play a thoroughly positive role in the Scottish police novel, for not only does it give someone like Morrow a professional identity preferable to what lies in store if she were to go into her family business and become a law breaker, but by giving her the professional identity of law enforcer, it also gives her the personal satisfaction of turning from a barely tolerated individualist into a well-liked team player. And in making this transformation, Morrow shows that someone like her is a good example of the often ignored fact that the Scottish police novel is not all about rogue cops who embrace their individualism in the anarchic spirit of Rankin's infamous Inspector Rebus.

I say 'someone' like Morrow is a good example of all this because, as the ten police detectives in the previous pages have shown, she is by no means the only one. Of course, there are also those who, like Rebus, could pass for private detectives wary of the establishment they embody, but there are quite a few more who, like Morrow, respect official policy, protocol, and professionalism. In fact, if we take Rebus out of the picture, as I have done above, it becomes evident that, contrary to the national stereotype, the Scottish police novel is less about rogues than it is about moralists. Only three out of these ten reputed authors write about rogue officers who routinely lie, disobey orders, break the law, ignore lesser crimes, or use excessive force. And out of these three, only McIlvanney writes about a cop who gets results by doing so. Jardine's cop may pose as a rogue, but he only gets results because his obedient subordinates solve the case for him, and Campbell's cop, who only goes rogue under duress, does not get results at all.

This is hardly a ringing endorsement of anti-authoritarianism, the less so since only two out of the remaining seven authors write about cops who will break at least a small rule for a big reward, i.e. pragmatists. And out of these two, only Beaton's one is not reluctant to do so, but that is not because he is some anarchist. On the contrary, far from wishing to endanger the status quo, he wants nothing more than to protect it, so when his good work invites the double threats of promotion and relocation from his cushy set-up, he breaks a few small rules just so his superiors will take his case away from him. And when they do just that, he is quite happy to let them take his credit as well, so he is barely even reprimanded, never mind mistaken for an anti-authoritarian.

As for the only other example of pragmatism, the kind propagated by McDermid's cops, that one is perhaps even further from anti-authoritarianism. So reluctant are her cops to defy authority that they only do so when the consequences of complying with the rules are morally reprehensible. And since such act-utilitarianism is a form of pragmatic moralism, not anti-authoritarianism, her example has less in common with the above-mentioned authors than it does with the remaining five – MacBride, Russell, Ramsay, Gray, and Mina – all of whom write about cops who obey orders, tell the truth, uphold the law, and exercise restraint in difficult situations, i.e. classic moralists. The conclusion this suggests is that the contemporary Scottish police novel, contrary to the historical reputation of the ever-rebellious Scot, is rather more concerned with moralism than it is with anti-authoritarianism.

What is more, even though Rankin has given the dated image of the anarchic Scot a new lease of life, rather few of his peers have kept this image alive by writing about anarchic cops. In fact, McIlvanney is alone in doing so, and he remains in a small minority even when the definition of 'anarchist' is stretched so far as to include any individualist who would rather not be restrained by official policies and protocols, i.e. armchair anarchists like those of Beaton and Jardine, who appreciate their autonomy but do not risk upsetting the order of things, because they are comfortable with their place in the police's institutional command structure. A good counter-example would seem to be Campbell's cop, who fights her own battle at great risk to the people around her and thus makes it four out of ten for the individualists, but although her unilateral defiance of official protocol initially empowers her to defend herself against dangerous anti-social elements, she ultimately loses this battle because she cuts herself out of the institutional command structure, so her example is a rather ambiguous endorsement of anarchic individualism.

The final blow to this stereotype, then, is not the marginal majority that six out of ten Scottish police novels are about team players but that nine out of ten are about cops who are deeply concerned about their place in the police. While several of them may seem like they could not care less about their relations with their colleagues, never mind their career prospects, McIlvanney's Laidlaw is the only one who is ultimately untroubled by the prospect of jeopardising his belonging to the police. In contrast, even the country's reputedly most roguish cop, Rankin's Rebus, is more often than not well-nigh obsessively concerned about his continued belonging to this state apparatus, the more so the more roguish he seems.

Yet before I try to reveal the workings of this often hidden psychology in a closer reading of *Resurrection Men*, let me repeat the definition of a rogue cop to make a final observation about the roguish reputation which is so frequently, and alas often falsely, accorded to the lead detectives of Scottish police novels. A rogue cop routinely lies, disobeys orders, breaks the law, ignores lesser crimes, or uses excessive force, whereas in nine out of ten cases, the lead detective of a Scottish police novel is far too aware, and usually appreciative, of his or her status of employment and place in the police to do any of the above routinely. Instead, he or she routinely champions a few libertarian values like the primacy of individual judgment and civil liberties, yet ultimately these are trumped by official protocols and office politics.

This is not to say that the majority of these police officers thrive on collaboration. On the contrary, although most of them at least partially respect official protocols and at least occasionally get involved in office politics, they are not fully committed to shaping policy, and as a result of this half-in-half-out attitude to collaboration, the slow progress they make within a team structure is typically followed by a breakthrough when they act on their own initiative. What this comes down to is an implicit endorsement of individualism – even by authors who are explicit in their casting of team players – and this endorsement finds further expression in the authors' decision to do their own thing, too. Thus, despite frequent assurances by publishers that they have found 'the new Ian Rankin', i.e. somebody who writes and should therefore sell like him, they have done no such thing and are unlikely to do any time soon. After all, while there are certainly similarities between individual Scottish police novelists, there are not enough of them to create a sense of unity, for they seem negligible when set against their many differences in subject and style.

For instance, both McIlvanney and Rankin have pushed the genre boundaries of the police novel in similar directions, yet so different are their subjects and styles that, while both have written documents of social history, McIlvanney's novels can also be read as novels of ideas, Rankin's on the other hand as human geographies, as I will try to show in the following pages. Mina's novels, meanwhile, can be read as both, so they certainly go a long way towards closing the generic gap between McIlvanney and Rankin, but since her novels can also be read as feminist literature, a gap remains. And these divisions continue even within the feminist faction of the Scottish police novel, for while there are points of contact in the politics of writers like Mina,

Campbell, and McDermid, their novels are nonetheless separated by large generic gaps. Certainly, each of them foregrounds the fact that the experience of her female protagonists has, to a large extent, been shaped by her gender, but they explore this experience in very different aesthetic terms: Mina in those of the literary traditions just mentioned, Campbell in those of women's writing, and McDermid in those of the psycho thriller. Then, of course, there are writers who, on the other side of yet another aesthetic and generic gap, address this very theme of fragmentation, writers like MacBride and Russell who manage to write about the same problem of social and psychological fragmentation yet do so in a modernist fragment on the one side and a modern-day fable on the other.

Completing this mosaic of Scotland's police fiction are the many authors whose work provides a marked contrast to this so-called 'gritty' writing, 'gritty' having become a buzzword in discussions of all Tartan Noir ever since McIlvanney gave crime back to the kind of Scots who commit it for reasons, not just to provide a corpse; and with the means at hand, not hand-wrought dueling pistols, curare and tropical fish. Yet while the writing on the other side of that 'gritty' divide is all far from realistic, and often feels rather dated in its depiction of policing, any such appearance of a mainstream is marred by further aesthetic and generic gaps. Indeed, judging by the above evidence of Beaton's Kailyard country house mystery, Jardine's cowboy soap opera, Gray's old-fashioned sentimental novel, and Ramsay's symbolist Gothic novel, the Scottish police novel is divided, and ultimately defined, by aesthetic and generic gaps on either side of the 'gritty' divide.

Any attempt to define the literature more cohesively would come with the false implication that there is a common denominator sizeable enough to span the above gaps, for, as I have tried to show, no such common denominator exists among Scottish police novelists. For instance, they share neither a widespread positive identification with any one literary tradition nor a widespread negative identification with any unifying anti-foreign sentiment. Instead of collaborating on any joint genre-building projects, they pick and mix their topics as well as their techniques. So, while there are certainly those whose considerable critical or commercial success can create the first impression of a national mainstream, the diversity on offer in this chapter should demonstrate that no single writer, nor even a particular style of writing, represents a significant majority movement in the Scottish police novel.

In fact, the only significant majority movement in this sub-genre has nothing to do with style and everything to do with a strong trend towards Scottish settings and casts: local crimes for local cops. Within this geographical self-consciousness, however, there are too many single-minded currents and multi-cultural tributaries for a mainstream to take the form new readers may expect to find: a fervent anti-Englishness. So although the popular prejudice against the Scots, should you need to be reminded, is that they stand for nothing but against the English, those who actually do so are few and far between. When Beaton casts a stereotypically English bully as her murder victim, she is one of only three writers in this entire chapter who risk a nationalist reading, and even in this, by Scottish standards exceptional case, two other casting decisions invalidate any such reading: one, in the role of the murderer she casts neither an English-hating Scot nor any other nationalist whose crime could be celebrated by chauvinistic readers as a valiant expression of anti-imperialism. And two, in the role of the apprehending officer she casts an individualist, a simple village bobby, not his three senior officers who make every mistake in the book, and such institutional incompetence ultimately invalidates any nationalist reading.

As for the other two writers who risk such a reading, Russell does so by casting two foreign bullies as murderers. Rather than channel any anti-foreign sentiment against these protagonists, however, he makes *them* the xenophobes. Then he promptly invalidates their negative ethos by demonstrating its central fallacy, the fact that blanket hatreds like xenophobia and racism are easily undermined by migration histories and kinship studies, because such hatreds are all based on unstable and revisionist assumptions about inherent geographic or genetic superiority. And what gives this demonstration a special resonance is that it is not articulated by some sanctimonious native but by another foreign protagonist, a man who speaks with personal experience when he maps out the daft and dangerous route from wilfully defined nationality to violent nationalism.

This, then, brings us to the third writer who risks a nationalist reading – and the only one who actively encourages it. Not only does Gray cast a foreigner in the role of murderer. She also reduces this Eastern European to a beast of inhuman evil, the mysterious and monstrous other, whereas on the other side of a clear moral and national divide, she as good as deifies her lead detective, a white Scot. But such racial and national chauvinism, as I have tried to show, is a rare exception in the Scottish police novel, where nine out of ten writers either ignore anti-foreign sentiments or invalidate them. So it is Russell rather than Gray who represents the literature's dominant stance on the question of national differences when he emphasises that Scots have more in common with the foreigners around them than might set them apart.

Of course, the fact that he makes this anti-nationalist point in a foreign setting means that Russell is more of an internationalist than most of his compatriots. Yet nonetheless his point marks a strong tendency among Scottish police novelists, a tendency to complicate attempts at defining the literature nationally, and this, ironically, is one tendency which unites most of them in a national literature. The other is a tendency to write in detail about the powers, the politics, the professional hazards, the ethical problems, and especially the personal sacrifices of policing, in short, everything but its procedures. Indeed, every one of the police novels in this chapter is sketchy at best when it comes to police procedures, and the obvious problem – that books about bureaucrats would otherwise be unreadable – does not seem to be the main reason for this dearth of procedural detail. The main reason would seem to be that every one of these writers would rather foreground the individual than the institutional.

Doing so, they have made it possible, and even popular, to disregard the fact that their fictional cops rarely bother with the bureaucratic stuff which real cops cannot avoid in the fight against serious criminal activity, the kind which draws the largest audience in literature as in life. What makes this remarkable is that they have done so in the heyday of whistleblowing, information technology, and television crime drama, i.e. at a time when most readers of crime fiction are almost inevitably better informed about the reality of crime fighting than are most of these fictional cops. Yet even in our clued-up times, the writers in this chapter have persuaded millions of readers to disregard, or at least deprioritise, the fact that their police officers really ought to show a little more concern, not just for the procedures of policing, but also for its rules and regulations.

As I hope to have shown in the above ten cases, surprisingly few of them have done so by writing about notorious mavericks like Rankin's Rebus, a supposed rogue whose charisma alone stops his colleagues, and perhaps even his readers, from questioning his methods. On the contrary, most of them have done so by making their cops adept at finding various legal grey areas in which to accommodate independent and often unofficial action. As a result, their writing is far more diverse and at odds with genre convention than the reputation which Rankin has given the Scottish police novel – a reputation so false it does not even fit his own writing, as I hope to show in the final section of this chapter.

THE FINAL CROSS-EXAMINATION: IAN RANKIN & IAN RANKIN – *RESURRECTION MEN & THE COMPLAINTS*

I n any consideration of Tartan Noir, Ian Rankin must stand alone, and he must do so for two reasons: one, in the last two decades, his increasingly recognisable name has been mentioned in connection with countless Scottish crime novels besides his own, so much so that 'Ian Rankin' has become a literary reference point, a seal of approval, and a genre label of sorts. Yet as those will agree who have heard his name without having read any of his books or seen any of their TV adaptations, Rankin has become well-known without being known well. So, to make sure that his larger than life reputation, a kind of friendly caricature, does not hide his writing like a disguise, we have to set aside what we know about his work by association, and the best way to do this is to focus on his work alone.

Besides, since every second emergent crime novelist from Scotland seems to be billed as 'the new Ian Rankin', the man's reputation is at risk of hiding not just his own work but also that of his compatriots, and this brings us to reason number two for why, in the following, I will focus exclusively on Rankin's work. Rankin was famously crowned 'the King of Tartan Noir' by a man who should have known better, the leading US noirist James Ellroy, though as Ranking admitted in a recent interview, "'Tartan Noir' is a term that I'm confident I invented but I gave it to James Ellroy... I was explaining to him that I was a crime writer as well and wrote about Edinburgh and the darker side of Scottish life. I said, 'You could call it Tartan Noir.' He laughed and signed the book to 'the King of Tartan Noir'. So then I pretended that he'd invented it."[209] And on the basis of this pretence, Ellroy's naïve flattery has for decades now been mistaken for fact. Countless readers and even critics seem to think that Rankin is, if not the King, then at least an accomplished representative of Tartan Noir, so even if his are the only Scottish crime novels they know, his false reputation allows them to think that they know something about Tartan Noir. Unfortunately, however, they are all wrong. Rankin is not the King of Tartan Noir, he does not represent Scottish noirists, and there is a simple reason for both. Rankin does not write noir, not Tartan, not any.

What Rankin writes are mainstream police novels, based on the far from noir premise that the system works and that it is a good thing, really. Sure, it has a few minor flaws, but although his cops have to bend the odd rule, at times even break one to preserve order in Edinburgh, preserve it they most certainly do. And although theses occasional rule breakers have a few minor flaws of their own, they overcome them all like the heroes they are. To anyone who has read any real noir – which is discussed in the final chapter of this book – these are sure signs that Rankin does not write in this literary tradition. Suffice it to say here that, if Rankin wrote noir, his cops would neither bend nor break any rules to preserve order, because there would be no order. If Rankin wrote noir, his heroes would not have any flaws, because he would have no heroes, just protagonists. And as I hope to show in my reading of *Resurrection Men* (2001) and *The Complaints* (2009), even in the two novels in which he casts his two serial cops in the darkest light, Rankin relies too heavily on the ethics and aesthetics of reform to be called a noirist.

Indeed, as both of these examples show, John Rebus and Malcolm Fox are far from noir even when they go a little further than usual in order to right the world's wrongs. Even when they pursue an arrest a little too ardently and end up at the edge of Rankin's moral universe, the farthest-reaching consequence of their slightly shady methods is temporary suspension with full pay. The social abyss, it seems, is reserved for the odd suspect and only glimpsed in passing when a cop briefly skirts it to rendezvous with an informant. In such scenes, Rankin is rather sketchy on the details of urban blight, economic stratification, and structural violence, so while his novels offer the occasional glimpse of the third world that hides in the shadow of the first, they never linger there for long enough to be seen as noir. And while they stand out from more conservative police novels by showing that the police is itself in need of policing, they are not subversive enough to tell the inconvenient truth about criminality, namely that it is less about greed, grudges, and genetics than it is about poor decision making born of poor education and poverty itself. So, not even at its darkest is Rankin's writing noir, and since that rules out his being the King of Tartan Noir, it suggests that a more sensible way of reading his significant contribution to Scottish literature is in the tradition of the police novel.

Doing so without looking through the prism of his much-vaunted noirishness, it should be possible to see what novels such as *Resurrection Men* and *The Complaints* really show us about Rankin's writing, namely that his reputation does not fit it and that it fails to do so for a simple reason: his writing is far less at odds with genre convention than his reputation. Perhaps the most obvious proof of this is that in Rebus, he is reputedly writing about an exceptionally roguish individualist, in Fox about an exceptionally moralistic team player, and neither of these types could be read as a representative police officer, neither in Scotland nor anywhere else. Yet as a close reading of *Resurrection Men* and *The Complaints* should reveal, neither Rebus nor Fox are what they would have others – or indeed themselves – believe. Far from being polar opposites and rare extremes, they are gradually morphing conflations of the above types. And for instance in the United States, that conflation of conservative moral righteousness and subversive anti-authoritarianism is rather a common sight, at least among fictional cops.

Thus, it is possible to agree with the literary critic Patrick Anderson when he notes a strong kinship between Rankin's Rebus and US author Michael Connelly's famous ex-cop. As Anderson puts it, "I think of Rankin's Inspector John Rebus as Harry Bosch's dissolute Scottish cousin: middle-aged, overweight, alcoholic, gruff, a loner, a chain smoker, an enemy of all authority."[210] And this familial association between Rebus and Bosch remains strong even in a case like *Resurrection Men*, which clearly demonstrates that Rebus has at least one defining trait which he does not share with his American cousin. Rebus has a somewhat providential fear of being 'found out', not so much for anything he has done as for who he is. This fear clouds just about every thought like an existential migraine, a heady blend of his acute self-consciousness and his much-accursed cultural heritage, Calvinism.

Of course, Rebus is just as familiar with the common fear that a specific criminal offence will be found out, a fear based not on some fantasies of providence but on the realities of probability. This fear takes possession of him when he is asked to infiltrate a posse of rogue cops, because he has reason to believe that the assignment is a setup for him to prove in the company of other supposedly corrupt cops that his superiors are right to suspect him of a related breach of protocol. And it is in order to manage this fear that he accepts the undercover assignment after just a moment's hesitation, because, as he sees it, his willingness to investigate corrupt cops will either prove that *he* is not the kind of cop who could have committed this breach of protocol or at least that he is *no longer* the kind of cop who could do so. Either way, he hopes, going undercover will put him above the suspicion of his superiors by reassuring them that, whatever he may or may not have done in the past, he is morally superior to his corrupt colleagues.

Privately, however, Rebus is plagued by that providential fear, the fear that he is not above suspicion after all, that he may not be what he would have himself and others believe, and that the day must surely come when the truth of his nature will finally be found out. So his second, deeper motivation for accepting this assignment is to play the role of righteous cop a little longer and thus postpone his inevitable reckoning. And it is this deeper motivation which brings us to the central irony of this character's life. Time and again, Rebus goes beyond the call of duty because, as well as being stubborn, he is haunted by that providential fear and the compulsion it induces to score a few moral points which might count in his favour when his real nature – his *rogue* nature – is found out. Yet time and again, he has no real reason to fear such a reckoning. Time and again, his bosses are quite happy to take him back into the fold, and they do so not because he makes amends, but because he was never really a rogue to begin with. Sure, Rebus occasionally goes further than the moralists around him, but in contrast to real rogues like the afore-mentioned Bosch, he always makes sure to stay within moral boundaries which, if pressed, he feels he could justify to a lenient superior. So his drive to get the job done is ultimately checked by his desire to stay in the job.

Similarly, Rankin's more recent creation, Inspector Malcolm Fox, turns out not to be the moral type he initially appears to be. Starting out as a classic moralist and thus as the apparent antithesis to Rebus – a polite, sociable, teetotal non-smoker and friend of authority – Fox, too, has a transformative experience while investigating corrupt cops. Having joined the internal affairs department – 'the complaints' – in the belief that moral transgression is simply not in his nature and that those who justify moral transgression as a means of getting the job done should simply not be in the police, he turns around at the first sign of moral conflict and crosses a moral line precisely to get the job done. Instead of continuing a surveillance operation as instructed, he puts his own sense of right and wrong above an official directive by breaking cover with the suspect when he comes to doubt the integrity of his investigation. So, like Rebus, Fox becomes a pragmatist when he tries to do the right thing, morally, rather than legally.

Perhaps surprisingly, given these two men's contrasting reputations, this shared turn to pragmatism is foregrounded twice, once by the stories of these two novels and then again by their narrative structures. As the crime critic Messent points out in his reading of *The Naming of the Dead*, "It is clear from both the structure and particular content of the novel and from the emphasis on Rebus's marginality that the reader is expected to question the ways in which official authority systems work."[211] Messent could have said the same thing about *Resurrection Men*, since the novel raises that same question on the same two levels. On the structural level it does so because it is divided into two halting inquiries, the slow progress of which is slowed down even further by Rankin's narrative strategy and the frustrating timing with which he interrupts one inquiry whenever it finally seems to be picking up a bit of pace, only to report yet another setback in the second inquiry. This narrative strategy allows us to share Rebus's growing frustration with the causes of his setbacks, such as the sell-outs in his own ranks and the scandal that sensitive information keeps leaking to suspects who keep evading arrest. And the strong emphasis Rankin places on such frustration on the content level, where Rebus, the would-be rogue, turns into a whistle-blower to fight endemic corruption, suggests that the reader is expected to question, not only the ways in which official authority systems work, but also, and perhaps more rigorously, the ways in which they do *not* work.

This distinction is further clarified by means of an engineering analogy in *The Complaints*. In an early conversation with his father, Fox is warned, "Machinery… it's not to be trusted."[212] Though he initially dismisses the old man's words as automatic reflexes to a world rendered untrustworthy by the speaker's general scepticism, rather than by any particular flaw in its mechanisms, Fox eventually picks up on both his father's sentiment and the symbol in which he chooses to express it, when he concludes: "The police force consisted of a series of connected mechanisms, any one of which could be tampered with, or become misaligned, or need patching up."[213] What gives these words a particular poignancy is that the mechanism which has been tampered with and which now needs patching up is Fox himself. Having been suspended from duty because of a false murder charge, the formerly 'whiter than white' internal investigator suddenly finds himself in the compromising position of having to go against his natural instinct and work outside the police apparatus, not just to repair his tarnished reputation, but to find the real murderer and thus facilitate the continued working of the justice system.

Both Rebus and Fox, then, heroically overcome the limitations of their nature to preserve moral order. Yet the fact that they are both marginalised in the process and have to step outside the system to fix it suggests that there are several questions we are expected to ask ourselves in each case and that those questions are as follows: should we applaud civil servants who try to fix a structurally flawed justice system with extra-systemic methods, even if they have failed to pass muster with a professional standards unit? Should we concern ourselves more with their motives than with their methods? Should our support of their methods depend on the success of their missions? Should we simply trust in the benign nature of their missions and believe that negative outcomes are failures in good faith, because to scrutinise their every method would be to limit their scope of action and increase the risk of failure? And to raise the underlying question, a question Professor Gormley asked in a recent issue of the *Public Administration Review*, "At what point does the appearance of corruption become indistinguishable from corruption itself? These cases force us to confront the limits of honesty and the dangers of deception."[214]

What makes this question of quasi-corruption especially pressing here is that Rebus and Fox only manage to close their cases because they resort to force – or do they only appear to become as corrupt as the criminals they investigate? In Rebus's case, it initially appears as though this time he might actually be going rogue, but when he is sent back to training college it turns out that he is only playing the part of corrupt cop to convince the squad of vigilantes he is trying to infiltrate that he is one of them. Later, however, he seems to cast considerable doubt on this reassurance that his bad guy act serves a greater good, for he resorts to force in a case which is seemingly unconnected to his undercover work. In what seems to be an act of aggressive self-preservation, he physically assaults a man and threatens him that, "this town ain't big enough for the both of us. I see you here again after tonight, you're dead meat. Understood?"[215]

In fairness to Rebus, his tough talk sounds a bit hammy because, as previous cases have shown, acting the tough guy is not his true calling. In this case, however, part of him appears to take to the act with a vengeance, so when one of the vigilantes dares him "to shut that door… sort things out here and now," he no longer seems to be in control of himself. "Rebus's fingers were around the door-handle. He didn't know what was about to happen, but started pushing the door closed anyway…"[216] In the end, he does not close that door, though he does temporarily close a door on official protocol in order to close the case, but since he once again acquits himself heroically in the eleventh hour, when he single-handedly foils the corrupt officers' dastardly plan and even manages to reform one of them, he is officially reinstated, which is to say that he is implicitly recommended to the reader's favourable judgment.

In a similar case of quasi-corruption, Fox, too, makes tactical use of force to close an otherwise career-ending case, and again it seems like one of Rankin's male investigators is taking advantage of a cause greater than his own ego to indulge his petty chauvinism. First, he floors one of the liaising Complaints and Conduct officers who are investigating him, and then he adds insult to injury: "I'm not sorry for what I did… I just didn't expect him to go down like a sack of spuds."[217] Much like Rebus, then, Fox seems to have trouble reigning in his bravado. Once he picks up the criminals' scent, he is no longer the cop who thought of himself as, "A bear of a man… Slow but steady, and only occasionally to be feared."[218] Instead, he proves himself to be as sly as the predator whose name he shares, for not only does he trap his prey, but he ultimately escapes punishment for his breach of protocol. Better still, since he acquits himself heroically in the eleventh hour, when he foils the criminals' dastardly plan and even manages to reform a presumed deviant, all thanks to his calculated risks to career and health, he is officially reinstated. That is to say he, too, is implicitly recommended to the reader's favourable judgment.

Both of these cases, then, reiterate one of the police novel's central questions: can exceptional circumstances excuse the threat, and indeed the use, of physical violence? In Rebus's case, Rankin's answer seems to be yes, but then his DI Gray, "the Glasgow Rebus,"[219] threatens the criminal whom Rebus had earlier kicked out of town, telling him that "we're the lowest of the low, the absolute fucking zero as far as the Scottish police force goes… We could kick your teeth down your throat, and when they came to tell us off, we'd be laughing and slapping our thighs… See what I'm saying?"[220] What he is saying is that some cops get away with murder, not because their superiors think they are squeaky clean, but because somebody has to do the dirty work. And what Rankin is saying is that a police officer's character is the all-important circumstance in determining whether dirty work, such as the threat or use of physical violence, is excusable. After all, when Gray and his gang do it, Rebus punishes them in a way which suggests that they will never work for the police again. Yet when Rebus does it himself, he goes back to his job without missing a beat, which suggests that *his* behaviour *is* excusable.

Excusable, of course, does not mean that he gets off Scot-free. Since Rankin's moral universe is ultimately a conservative one, some kind of payment is exacted from everyone who gets their hands dirty, or at least from all those who get carried away in the process, and since Rebus has on occasion done both, he has to pay for his minor immoralities with a major, if momentary, sense of guilt about his "grubby motives and a spirit grown corrupt."[221] This sense of guilt, incidentally, is shared by Fox, who is less vocal in his self-flagellation but just as conflicted about resorting to force, and so it comes as no surprise that both of them eventually wonder whether theirs is a quest for moral justice or for personal vindication.

However, while the similar way in which they speak about police corruption implies a shared despondency, the two cops differ significantly in their attitudes to dealing with it. Rebus "wondered whether it really mattered one way or the other. A few grand... even a few hundred grand... pocketed with no comebacks, no harm done."[222] Similarly, Fox "wondered: did it bother him that the world wasn't entirely fair? That justice was seldom sufficient? There would always be people ready to pocket a wad of banknotes in exchange for a favour." Yet while Rebus spends the remainder of *Resurrection Men* seeking ways to justify his own moral compromises – even as he condemns them in cops like Gray – Fox spends the remainder of *The Complaints* seeking ways to bring compromised cops like Rebus to justice. So, while Rebus is on a quest for personal vindication, Fox is on a quest for moral justice, and whereas Rebus fails to remove all doubt about his fallibility, Fox succeeds.

Yet lest this obvious contrast distract from a more subtle, ideological difference between the two cops, it is worth noting that Rebus would strongly disagree with Fox's definition of success. For Rebus, failure such as his – i.e. the failure to disprove one's fallibility

– is the only true success. As his partner and protégé Siobhan Clarke says, "he relished the idea of his own fallibility. He was only human, and if proving it meant enduring pain and defeat, he would welcome both. Did that mean he had a martyr complex?"[223] Assuming that she is not using the word 'martyr' in its original sense – i.e. a man of god, called to witness for his religious belief – but rather in its now predominant sense – i.e. a man so committed to his secular cause that he will risk his life – then the answer is yes, Rebus has a martyr complex. He is determined to build a solid case against his squad of corrupt cops, and since doing so depends on him getting a confession, which in turn depends on him gaining their confidence, he cajoles them, provokes them, divides them, invites them into his home, and repeatedly puts himself at their mercy, despite their suspicions against him. By the end of the novel, his survival is nothing short of a miracle.

Meanwhile, Fox makes damn sure that he is never in need of such a miracle, and his reason for doing so is what sets him so far apart from Rebus. As he puts it, "Crucifixion's not high on my wish list."[224] In other words, Fox has no martyr complex, and this categorical difference between him and Rebus is encapsulated – how could it not be, given Rankin's famous flair for pop-culture references – in a passing reference to one of Scotland's most famous celebrities. When, early on in *Resurrection Men*, Rebus and his squad of corrupt cops do a walking tour of Edinburgh, he is asked by one of those corrupt cops whether he believes that the notorious Knox is "everything that makes us what we are." Glibly, Rebus replies "Which Knox?"[225] Of course, the context makes it obvious that his questioner is referring to John Knox, the Scottish clergyman who led the Protestant Reformation. At the same time, however, Rebus's counter question makes it obvious that there was another, lesser known Knox who, at least in Rebus's view, might also be seen as their spiritual forefather. This other Knox, internal evidence suggests, is Robert Knox, the Scottish pioneer of anatomy who illegally purchased corpses from grave robbers – so-called 'resurrection men' – to advance his scientific research. So what Rebus may be hinting at here is that what really characterises 'us' – i.e. him and his squad of corrupt cops – is their kinship with a coldblooded pragmatist, a man capable of burying his finer sensibilities to 'get the job done'.

This, then, is the defining moral difference between Rankin's serial cops. Given each man's moral stance, it seems fair to say that Fox stands nearer *John* Knox, Rebus nearer *Robert* Knox, and perhaps the clearest manifestation of this difference is where each of them stands on the subject of Edinburgh. Rebus may be ambivalent in the afore-mentioned scene, where Gray defines his adoptive city as "Knoxland,"[226] but having moved to Edinburgh from his native Cardenden, Fife, he has lived in the city centre for decades. And having studied the place with the outsider's keen attention to detail, he has seen enough of its dark underbelly to tacitly agree with Gray that, "When it comes to Edinburgh, sir, John knows where the bodies are buried."[227] In other words, Rebus regards present-day Edinburgh as a grave monument to its past, and he sees himself reflected in its darkness and duality because, like him, parts of the city embrace its horrible history even as others try to escape it.

In contrast, Fox was born and raised in Edinburgh, and like most people who grow up on a tourist site, he is not particularly interested in the past on which it is built. Instead, he is interested in what gives shape to its present distress, in this case speculative property development. So when a local property developer goes missing and his debts are found to be as high as his tower blocks, Fox agrees with another local businessman's criticism: "Buy a parcel of land, sit on it for a year and then sell at a profit... Money from thin air, that's what it seems like. And nobody asks any questions because that might break the spell."[228] Ironically, this indignant businessman has himself been making money from thin air by sitting on the city council and taking bribes from the very developer he is now criticising, and when Fox starts asking questions, the spell indeed breaks. Yet more ironic still is the fact that Fox only gets to the councillor because he outsmarts his beautiful yet naïve wife, a woman who is so much younger than the councillor that she does not have enough life experience to counter Fox's request for access to her husband with her own request for an arrest warrant. In short, Fox only gets to the councillor because the man has treated his marriage in the same morally corrupt way in which he has treated Edinburgh – as a vanity regeneration project.

Thus, while Rankin sees to it that the more conservative reader's demand for poetic justice is met, he also has a keen eye for the social injustice which has led to some of the most significant transformations of Edinburgh past and present. And since the moral views of Rebus and Fox are reflected in the frequent comments they pass on these transformations, we can see in their contrasting descriptions of Edinburgh – their shared city – where each of them stands on the divisive issue of moral compromise. Rebus seems to see Edinburgh as a series of crime scenes, a tightly woven network of shady deals and hidden agendas of which he himself occasionally cannot help but be a part. In contrast, Fox seems to see the city as a place to live, a largely benign space surrounded by a few corrupted fringe elements from which he can usually stand well apart. So, while the literary theorist Cohen is right to observe that stories like these are often "underpinned by a confluence of explosive political and economic interests," and while Rankin's leading men occasionally have to contend with what Cohen calls "crisis-ridden masculine identities… intricately bound up with this destabilising experience of urban transformation,"[229] both Rebus and Fox manage to close their cases. More importantly still, they are both brimming with courage and competence, and despite the close contact they often have with supposedly toxic, anti-social elements, they always manage to avoid lasting contamination, which is to say that, contrary to the popular belief that Scotland's fictional police forces are staffed by rebellious anti-heroes, not even their most famous cops can be diagnosed as such.

Instead, they seem to be suffering from an uneasy compulsion to reassure themselves and their readers that some good greater than their own gratification will come from revealing the false cover stories which corrupt police officers and public officials tell in order to conceal the fact that they are no more than gangsters in legitimised positions of power. And perhaps the most revealing thing about Rankin's writing is that this greater good never turns out to be some liberal delusion but an at least intermittent return to social stability. Accordingly, both novels end on a genre-typical note of patrician reassurance. Yes, they concede, there may be occasions on which social justice is not best served by those in power, but the weak are certainly better off for being protected by the likes of Rankin's leading men. And while there would seem to be room for only one of Rebus's kind in any one police department, his heroics guarantee that he, much like the more accommodating Fox, never really has to worry about his place in the police.

On the contrary, despite their breaches of protocol, both men end up being more firmly installed in their departments than perhaps ever before, and it is this reward of the subversive which, ironically, makes these books so conservative. Even though both Rebus and Fox have bent and broken the odd rule by the time they close their cases, they are both rewarded because their superiors have the extraordinary magnanimity to respect the fact that, once again, their rule-breaking ultimately served the interests of the state. As they see it, Rebus only asked for "a favour" from "the east coast's biggest gangster" because his usual policy of condemning criminals, rather than collaborating with them, would in all probability not have been effective enough to stop a corrupt cop from getting away with murder, which is to say it might have indirectly damaged more innocent people. Likewise, Fox's superiors appreciate that he only blackmailed a corrupt cop because his usual policy of granting "No favours"[230] to criminals would in all probability not have been effective enough to lead to the man's resignation, which is to say it might have indirectly damaged both the police and the people he hoped to protect.

In the end, then, it is not just Rebus who turns out to be a heroic if "unstable custodian of the law,"[231] as Rankin expert Gill Plain calls him. Fox, too, qualifies for that doubtful accolade, despite his introduction as a moralist who is above all doubt. And what they both show with their shared strategy of guarding the law by conflating a streak of subversive anti-authoritarianism with a strong habit of conservative moral righteousness is that Rankin's writing is less at odds with convention in this traditionally so conservative genre than his reputation would have us believe.

CHAPTER THREE –
THE SERIAL KILLER NOVEL

T ypically, the serial killer novel is about a large-scale, last-ditch attempt at apprehending a man who has escaped police detectives, psychological profilers, and forensic scientists, even though he has committed multiple homicide and courted media attention as a result of being deeply shamed and/or highly abused as a child.

Stereotypically, the serial killer novel is structured into three parts. In part one, the lead investigator discovers the serial killer's crimes to date. Soon, he or she has reconnoitred the latest crime scene, researched the post-mortem examinations of all known victims, and recognised the killer's pattern. Thus, the investigator – and with him or her the reader – realises early in the narrative that the killer is fiendishly crafty and sadistically cruel. Then, in part two, the writer reveals the killer's background, gradually letting the reader see how the man came to be the monster. At the same time, incidentally, the reader comes to see that the investigator is also troubled, if not tortured, by some combination of a lonely personal life and the related stress of thinking like a serial killer in order to catch this particular serial killer. Finally, in part three, the killer strikes again. Having taunted the police as well as terrified the public – typically by inflicting signature injuries on his victims and signalling his intention to kill again – he kidnaps a young woman.

Here, the game of 'catch up' finally turns into a game of 'catch me if you can', as the investigator stops researching the killer's past and starts racing to the killer's suddenly known hideout. Too impatient, or too involved in the case to wait for backup, he runs the risk of becoming yet another victim in what soon turns into a frantic attempt to rescue the young woman before the killer can start his torture and murder ritual all over again. Yet even as he gets himself into a potentially lethal standoff with the killer, he single-handedly saves the kidnapped woman from certain death, and in a last-minute dispensation of poetic justice, the killer dies in the standoff. Since he does so before he can be questioned, neither the investigator's conscience nor the story's happy end is troubled by thoughts of how much pain and grief have been caused by all this killing, and in place of any cerebral reflection on the mental or social circumstances which can create serial killers, a visceral relief that the threat of this particular killer has been contained provides the story's resolution.

Now, even to those who have barely read any crime fiction, large parts of this pattern should be familiar. These days, every second crime novel seems to be a serial killer novel, and every second serial killer novel seems to include most, if not all, of the above elements. No other sub-genre of crime fiction has inspired a deeper faith in a single narrative formula, and no other formula has matched its singular commercial success, so it should come as no surprise that just about every crime writer who has tried to break into the bestseller lists of the past two decades has written at least one serial killer novel. What might come as a surprise, however, is that few have written more than one, presumably because they have found it to be a confining sub-genre, but before we concern ourselves with the particulars of this confinement, it is worth noting what makes this sub-genre so popular.

According to Professor of Philosophy Sara Waller and Professor of Cognitive Science William E. Deal, "Serial killers hold a fascination in the popular imagination far disproportionate to their actual social significance."[232] One reason for this is that there are far more serial killers in fiction than there are in fact. Reading about them with far greater frequency in novels than we do in the papers, we think about them far more than is really necessary, given the rather small threat they pose to society in the real world. Another reason for this disproportionate fascination is that the countless serial killers who so brazenly flaunt their sadism and sophistication in the realm of fiction tend to be sensationalised and often rather stylised versions of a select few real-life serial killers, infamous individuals who are already far more fascinating than the average real-life serial killer.

Some critics, such as Martin Priestman, view this distortion of reality with concern, warning that serial killer novels may "come to be read as accurately reflecting an unstoppable trend in 'real' crime, so that the fiction-led mass-fear of the serial murderer becomes the lens through which attitudes to actual debates about crime and punishment are shaped."[233] In theory, this is certainly an intelligent observation, yet for an obvious, practical reason it reflects too little faith in the reader's intelligence. Fictional serial killers can be read as more than just examples of an unstoppable trend in real crime. They can also be read as embodiments – albeit enlarged ones – of our own anti-social impulses, epitomes of our on-going repression of women, and evidence of our widespread 'wound culture' – a phenomenon which Mark Seltzer, an expert in cultural and media studies, defines as "the public fascination with torn and open bodies and torn and opened persons, a collective gathering around shock, trauma, and the wound."[234] What is more, in some cases fictional serial killers can even be read as evangelists of a right-wing disciplinarian ethos, given that some of them act as righteous agents of punishment in a dissolute world of left-wing permissiveness. Yet in most cases, as the cultural critic Cassuto puts it, the fictional serial killer can be read as an exemplification of our "collective anxiety about the presence of the mentally ill in middle-class space."[235]

This calls for a clarification. Writers who cast their serial killers in the role of 'sicko' or 'psycho' – i.e. in the role of an individual which barely qualifies as a human being and must be terminated because its dangerous mental illness cannot be cured – such writers position themselves on the detractor's side of the literature's central debate on the efficacy of psychotherapy. On the other side of that debate are writers who make their serial killers stand in for people with dangerous but treatable mental illnesses – i.e. for human beings who commit just as horrendous crimes as the afore-mentioned sickos and psychos but who could, if caught, learn how to control or even be cured of the personality disorder which so gravely impairs their capacity for compassion and remorse that they can kill and kill again.

To be clear, then, there are two types of writers in this sub-genre. One type appeals to readers with a fascination for bogymen, criminals who have been turned into caricatures by ill-informed generalisation or ill-willed demonisation. The other type appeals to readers with a fascination for the dangerously disturbed, criminals who are afflicted by a potentially dehumanising mental illness yet are seen to have at least a vestige of human connection with the rest of society.

That said, whether or not serial killers are written with any sympathy, they are predominantly treated as case studies of mental illness. The operative question, after all, tends to be 'How did he become this?' – not 'Why did he do this?'. And this question arose out of what Cassuto calls "the historical dialogue about mental illness during the second half of the twentieth century."[236] To briefly summarise Cassuto's point, in the late 1950s social activism started changing America's mental health debate. Attacking fundamental presumptions of psychiatry, it soon changed both government policy and public perception of the mentally ill. The result was a popular demand for legal reform, so in 1963, President John F. Kennedy signed an act into law which led to a lasting reduction of federal support for inpatient treatment of mental illness: the Community Mental Health Act.

Through six administrations, this act led to a redirection of the anti-psychiatry movement towards the government's economic goals. Costs were cut as cheaper outpatient community health centres replaced the old state mental hospitals, and this downsizing continued for two decades until President Ronald Reagan finally consolidated what little federal aid remained for the treatment of mental illness into block grants to individual states. So, by the early 1980s, the government had not only delegated its responsibility to distribute mental health care but also deprived its state authorities of the necessary resources to adequately deal with said responsibility in its place. After all, these economic measures had led to an ever-accelerating deinstitutionalisation throughout the entire country, and this, in turn, had led to a ground-breaking shift in the public's attitude towards the mentally ill, because as more mental patients were released into the community, mental illness became more visible. As a result, more people got scared of such high-profile illnesses as psychopathy, and thus more serial killer novels got written.

Besides, as Professor of Clinical Psychiatry Richard A. Friedman puts it, the "violent mental patient makes people feel safer by displacing and limiting the threat of violence to a small, defined group."[237] Perhaps surprisingly, the violent mental patient can also make people feel joyful, because when we discover that multiple murders were committed by a single individual, the positive feeling of relief co-occurs so closely with the negative feeling of fear that we can control and even enjoy the negative feeling by reassuring ourselves that it causes the positive feeling. As Eric Dietrich and Tara Fox Hall explain in their essay 'The Allure of the Serial Killer', "What is actually alluring is the *idea* of the serial killer, but only when that idea is contemplated from a certain, specific, safe reference frame that allows *both* the positive and the negative emotions associated with serial killers to be experienced at the same time."[238] In other words, reading a book or watching a movie about a serial killer might trigger the kind of negative feeling which will co-activate a positive one. Finding out that your neighbour is a serial killer probably won't. Chances are, if you enjoy what Priestman calls "all the horror and apparent randomness of the violence lurking somewhere 'out there',"[239] you do so only when it is safe to assume that 'out there' does not mean 'next door'.

But back to the history lesson: since 1988, this complicated allure of the fictional serial killer has often been attributed to the work of one man, Thomas Harris. In 1988, after all, Harris gave the world Hannibal Lecter, the cannibalistic serial killer of *The Silence of the Lambs*. One testament to the immense and almost immediate impact of this novel is that only three years later, in 1991, Jonathan Demme directed Anthony Hopkins in his seminal film adaptation of the novel, and although Hopkins was only on screen for little more than 16 minutes, his fascinating blend of cruelty and charisma won him an Academy Award and made Hannibal 'the Cannibal' Lecter a cultural icon the world over. So it is perhaps not surprising that the character's infamy has often let his fans forget that he had important precursors in both fiction and film.

As Lee Horsley, an authority on crime fiction and the historical imagination, remembers, "In the mid-1950s, Patricia Highsmith and Jim Thompson created some of the most powerful portrayals of the 'abnormally normal' multiple murderer."[240] And at the end of that decade, in 1959, Robert Bloch created perhaps the most powerful of them all in his suspense novel, *Psycho*. The titular psycho, Norman Bates, is a transvestite serial killer whose first name can be read as a pun on the protagonist's ability to seem 'normal' despite his violent, dissociative identity disorder. Norman Bates – who like Hannibal Lecter is loosely based on the American real-life murderer and body snatcher Ed Gein (1906-1984) – is a sympathetic character until Bloch reveals that he killed his mother, keeps her corpse in his house, habitually assumes her identity, and stabs people to death while 'Mother' gradually takes control of him in a terrifying escalation of violence which became world famous when Alfred Hitchcock adapted it to the screen in 1960.

Five years later, no less a cultural barometer than Truman Capote indicated the degree to which the serial killer had taken hold of the public imagination. Then at the height of his fame, and at the centre of contemporary pop culture, Capote chose the infamous case of Perry Smith and Richard Hickock as the subject of what he called the world's first 'nonfiction novel', *In Cold Blood*. Published in 1965 as an attempt to at once rationalise and dramatise a case of quadruple murder which had gone largely unnoticed since its perpetration in 1959, the story instantly reached a nationwide audience and brought the concept of serial murder squarely into the country's cultural discourse, though the term 'serial murder' was not widely used until the following year, when the critic John Brophy introduced it in his study, *The Meaning of Murder*.

As for today's standard term 'serial killer', that goes back to 1979, when criminologist and FBI agent Robert K. Ressler started the Criminal Personality Research Project. Not only did this project establish the Bureau as the official authority on the subject of the serial killer, it also established 'serial killer' as the authoritative term in US political and public policy circles. What is more, within just a decade this term gained a cultural currency of international validity as the afore-mentioned Hannibal Lecter established himself as the unofficial authority on the subject of the serial killer – and as its world-famous personification. So Cassuto is probably right to conclude that we should acknowledge Hannibal's creator, Thomas Harris, "as perhaps the most influential American crime writer since Dashiell Hammett... Though he clearly did not invent the serial killer story, Harris thus stands as the Henry Ford of the genre, the man who enabled its mass production."[241]

If this economic analogy seems a little insensitive, given that it focuses attention on the literature's impressive commercial potential and thus might distract from the stark fact that the serial killer novel revolves around the most loathsome of criminals, it is worth noting the form's central paradox. Though the term 'serial killer novel' suggests that such a novel is all about a serial killer and his loathsome crime – serial killing – it is not unusual for such a protagonist to spend as little as one seventh of the story time on stage, as does Hannibal Lecter in *The Silence of the Lambs*. Most serial killer novels concentrate not on the literature's presumed topic – the violent dissolution of the 'abnormal' mind – but on the 'normal' world and its resilient cohesion, which most authors sentimentalise beyond recognition only to suggest that this non-existent idyll is seriously threatened by the dangerous outsider. And by letting us spend rather little time in the company of the serial killer, most of these authors encourage us to identify with the investigator and the victim, which not only allows us to indulge a desire for imaginary retaliation against threats to society but, since the victim is typically female, also allows the male readers among us to indulge an emotionality which may otherwise seem embarrassing.

In most cases, this sympathetic embrace of the poor victims is steadily reinforced. On the one hand, we get to see how members of the bereaved community move closer together on account of their rich social bonds, bonds which tie us to an acute awareness of the victims' disempowering absence from the narrative. On the other hand, we become ever more repulsed by the serial killer, be it because we are told again and again about his old reputation or because we see new evidence that he is indeed an anti-social and aggressive loner who shares his exploits with no one, derives pleasure from preying on the community, and commits acts as heinous as torture, cannibalism, and murder, all of which indicates the extreme degree to which these characters are alienated from social existence. Of course, it also implies the need for an explanation, and the most convenient one by far has been to label serial killers as monsters – a rare breed of killing machine.

Less convenient is the fact that this is no explanation at all. It is an excuse, implying as it does that the killer is not human and can therefore not be explained to human beings. His cruelty, so the reasoning goes, trumps any medical explanation for his conduct, yet fortunately this is not a problem, so the reasoning goes on, since there is not much to explain anyway. Serial killers are simply evil. Less fortunate for proponents of such reasoning is the fact that machines are not sentient, so they cannot be evil. From this logical fallacy arises the need for a more intelligent explanation, and those who acknowledge this need tend to address it by labelling serial killers as psychopaths, but what is a psychopath? Are all psychopaths the same? And if not, which types of psychopath tend to feature in serial killer novels?

According to psychologist and criminal justice expert Richard Gray, "in psychopaths, the *amygdala*, the brain's centre of emotion, is damaged. This means that they are not only indifferent to the feelings of others but the normal processes of learning, including conditioned fear and conditioned pleasure, are defective… they are unable to learn the kinds of felt associations that create a sense of right and wrong, the moral restraints that prevent us from living out our own fantasies and perversions." Thus, their disorder is defined by "two factors. The first factor accounts for their lack of empathy, remorselessness, and callous indifference to human suffering, and is shaped largely by genetics. Up to 60 percent of this trait is inherited. The second factor, which is associated with their irresponsibility, impulsivity, and anti-social behaviour, has a strong environmental component."[242] In short, few of them are simply crazy, yet despite the extensive taxonomic literature, only four types of psychopath tend to feature in serial killer novels: the hedonistic, the visionary, the mission-oriented, and the power-oriented serial killer.

This, then, brings us to my earlier observation about the sub-genre's confinement. Not only do most writers working within this sub-genre confine their choice of serial killer to one of these four types. They also tend to separate the killer from the deed so as to defer our disgust enough to keep us reading. Whether they write about the hedonistic type – which kills out of lust or for the thrill of it – the visionary type – which kills in the service of some imagined voice or vision – the mission-oriented type – which kills to eliminate a specific kind of person – or the power-oriented type – which kills to exercise control or power over another person – for the most part, they tend to confine their narrative treatment of serial killing to an expert's analysis of such facts as numbers of killings, times between killings, and reasons for killings. Most of the actual killing happens off-stage. And unlike the vast majority of real-life serial killing, which victimises those on the social margins, most fictional serial killing happens in the middle class. There, victims can be relied upon as powerful vehicles of sympathetic identification for most readers, but for most writers it is a confined space, because few middle-class readers want to think too long and hard about the implications of living next door to a violent psychopath.

Hence, even writers who base their stories on the serial-killer-next-door scenario confine their killer to a so-called 'frame', a cognitive science concept which influences our perception by presenting facts in a certain context. According to Professor of Cognitive Science William E. Deal, "fiction writers change our view of their characters by framing them in certain contexts and giving us some facts and not others," the reason being that "Our judgments of moral responsibility are not just a matter of rational thought, but of how the frames through which we view the world impact our emotional responses."[243] Taking full advantage of this opportunity to influence our moral judgments, most writers of serial killer fiction will hint at certain telling details of the killer's modus operandi while covering up others, thus titillating

157

us with voyeuristic glimpses of the killer's psychopathology which, eventually, should create one of two typical reader responses.

The typical liberal response is compassion. This response is based on a pathological, disease-oriented view of individual cruelty, yet despite its initial sympathetic impulse, this response can and often does lead to an eventual rejection of the serial killer on the grounds that he or she is too sick to be 'one of us'. As for the typical conservative response, condemnation, that, too, starts with a sympathetic impulse, as it is based on a Christian belief in evil, and Christianity's community-oriented view of sin is predicated on the principle of embracing the sinner. However, despite its initial sympathetic impulse, this response, too, can and often does lead to an eventual rejection of the serial killer on the grounds that he is irredeemably depraved. Hence, Cassuto concludes, "Serial killer stories nearly always end with the death of the murderer because there's no hope for him, and no pity. In other words, no fellow feeling."[244] And this brings us to the final, perhaps most confining feature of the serial killer novel: its violence.

As the 19th-century philosopher Henry Longueville Mansel reasoned, "It is necessary to be near a mine to be blown up by its explosion; and a tale which aims at electrifying the nerves of the reader is never thoroughly effective unless the scene be laid in our own days and among the people we are in the habit of meeting."[245] At the end of the 20th century, cultural historian Jacques Barzun revisited this controversial topic only to conclude that, over the years, "the explosive devices have changed surprisingly little. The dose of shock has merely been increased to keep up with the inflation of all effects."[246] And now, at the beginning of the 21st century, the question of violence in literature seems to have lost its controversy, at least if you ask the literary critic Patrick Anderson. "Why all this violence? Why not? Ours is a violent species and this is a violent age. Our writers have grown bolder about holding up a mirror to our darker impulses. And readers have grown more willing to accept – and in some cases be titillated by – these horrors."[247]

That said, while the general inflation of 'these horrors' has been met with a general increase in the reader's willingness to countenance them, it has led to a potential problem in serial killer fiction. There, the horrors have become so dire that the heroic investigators have with increasing frequency and ferociousness reached a point at which they feel forced to dispense with due process of law and instead exact a form of frontier justice. At that point, the crime fighter tends to justify extreme violence or even murder to contain the threat of the serial killer, and if the same crime fighter features in more than one story, then this way of dealing with the general inflation of 'these horrors' will typically lead to a morally highly ambiguous point, the point at which he has killed enough serial killers to qualify as one.

That, of course, is not the frame in which most readers wish to see a representative of law and order, so most writers frame their violence as a containment strategy for dealing with the criminally insane. As for the violence perpetrated by the typical serial killer – the epitome of the criminally insane – most writers confine it to short sections with little plot or character development – sections which are easily skimmed or skipped altogether – because most readers do not read to be surfeited with violence. On the contrary, most readers are still disgusted when confronted with the details of mental or physical violence, and while disgust can cause broad popular agreement, it can also cause moral paralysis and a reluctance to keep reading. Hence, most writers of serial killer fiction make short work of the ultimate violence – murder – and focus far less on the act than on the motive and containment of the murderer. In doing so, they avoid the risk of consigning their readers to a disgusted misanthropy and instead afford them the emotional distance of a medical case study, and in most cases this narrative strategy shifts focus from the literature's inherent question how you, a human being, can enjoy reading about somebody who kills other human beings, one after another. The question foregrounded instead is a lot less personal and thus a lot more palatable: how can another human being, seemingly inconspicuous, turn out to be a serial killer?

THE SCOTTISH SERIAL KILLER NOVEL

I n Scotland, the reputation of the serial killer novel has recently been dominated by two writers, Val McDermid and Stuart MacBride, and yet in Scotland, perhaps more than anywhere else, the writing in this form has a long history of lurid diversity. What is more, for a country of only five million inhabitants, Scotland has produced and suffered a surprisingly high number of serial killers. For a full account, read Michael Newton's *Encyclopedia of Serial Killers*, first published in 2000, though for a sense of context it is probably enough to note that Scotland's reported history of serial killing dates back to the mid-14th century, when Andrew Christie, a butcher from Perth, made his name as a notorious cannibal and, so legend has it, the country's first serial killer. During a famine, he is said to have led ambushes on 30 mountain travellers, earning his nickname 'Christy Cleek' by pulling the horsemen out of their saddles with a 'cleke' – a large iron hook fastened to a long pole – and even centuries later, the mere mention of this nickname is said to have been enough to inspire fear in Scottish children.

Meanwhile, his story had inspired the legend of another cannibal, that of Alexander 'Sawney' Bean. 'Sawney' is a Lowland Scots diminutive of Alexander, but in the 16th century the English started using the name as a collective term of derision for all the people of Scotland because it was widely believed that Alexander Bean, Scottish chief of a 48-member clan, had killed over 1,000 people, most of whom were allegedly English. Eventually, James VI had Sawney Bean executed, but his name remained a stain on his countrymen's reputation even into the 19th century. Then, in 1828, two Irish immigrants became synonymous with Scotland's history of macabre crime as they became the country's most infamous serial killers. William Burke and William Hare first made a name for themselves as grave robbers in Edinburgh, disinterring fresh cadavers and selling them to Dr Robert Knox for dissection in his anatomy lectures, but when demand increased, they supplied even fresher cadavers by 'burking' at least 16 people in what became known as the West Port murders. 'Burking' was the name given to their murder method of smothering the victim while compressing its chest so as not to damage the body, and one measure of the men's lasting place in the national memory, besides various museum exhibitions and movie adaptations of their work, is the fact that the word 'burking' has remained in the popular vernacular, now meaning to suppress something quietly.

The next Scottish serial killer to gain notoriety was Dr Thomas Neill Cream, the Lambeth Poisoner who, after claiming at least five victims, claimed at his hanging in 1892 that he was Jack the Ripper. Given that Dr Cream was serving a prison sentence at the time of the Ripper's Whitechapel murders, this late claim to fame is rather questionable, yet nevertheless the man's infamy by association has long outlived him. The same, incidentally, is true of Peter Manuel, the Beast of Birkenshaw who was convicted of nine counts of murder and died on the gallows of Glasgow's Barlinnie Prison in 1958. Admittedly, Manuel did not stake a claim to another killer's reputation, but ever since the movie *Manhunter* was released in 1986, his memory has lived on in at least one incarnation of Hannibal Lecter, seeing as the Scottish actor Brian Cox played Hannibal with Manuel in mind. So, what even this brief glance at Scotland's most notorious serial killers suggests is that the number and variety of their fictional counterparts should come as no surprise.

Frederic Lindsay – *Jill Rips*

What might come as a surprise, though, is the fact that the first of these fictional serial killers to appear on screen was, unlike all of the above, a woman. In 1999, Kristi Angus played the role of Jill the Ripper – a female serial killer – in the movie adaptation of Frederic Lindsay's novel, *Jill Rips*. Yet unlike the movie, which is set in 1977, the novel is set in 1987, the year of its publication, and with this later setting in mind the story's feminist premise makes a lot of sense, in a macabre sort of way. After all, the story is based on the premise that it has been exactly one hundred years since Jack the Ripper famously started killing prostitutes in 1887. Now, to mark the centenary, someone is signing public murder confessions as Jill, "someone who had it in not for the prostitutes but for their clients... A woman who hated what men did to women, the way men exploited them... A twentieth-century crime just as the Ripper's belonged so well to the nineteenth. Women's lib instead of Victorian exploitation and hypocrisy."[248]

As Deborah Cameron, a Professor of Communication, and Elizabeth Frazer, a Professor of Politics, put it in their seminal study, *The Lust to Kill: A Feminist Investigation of Sexual Murder*, the sex killer provides "a self-conscious role or identity for individuals to take up and define their acts by."[249] Accordingly, the savage mutilations and serial murders committed by Jill the Ripper, which invert the gender dynamics of those committed by Jack the Ripper, can be read as a gendered, violent protest against the dominant theory of the time which held that only men commit such crimes. As Elizabeth and Harold Schechter agree in their essay 'Killing with Kindness: Nature, Nurture, and the Female Serial Killer', this theory that serial murder is a male crime is based on a sexist prejudice which still "cuts across political lines, being shared by social reactionaries (who persist in seeing women as the 'weaker sex'), middle-class liberals (who idealise women as less prone to violence), and radical feminists (who tend to see their sex as morally superior to the male)"... Hence, the Schechters add, "the female serial killer is commonly denied, or merely ignored, as something of a conceptual impossibility."[250]

There is, of course, another reason for this common ignorance, an historical assumption which is patently false and yet rarely contested. As the cultural critic Camille Paglia puts it, "There is no female Jack the Ripper."[251] If you accept as historical fact the nonsense that no woman has ever committed crimes as contemptible as those of Jack the Ripper – though for all we know Jack the Ripper himself might have been a woman – then you do not have to be a social reactionary, middle-class liberal, or radical feminist to deny or ignore the female serial killer as a conceptual impossibility. You just have to be ill-informed. And if you agree with Paglia's implication that, unlike Jack the Ripper, no woman is synonymous with serial murder – though the names of women like Myra Hindley and Rose West bring to mind some of the worst serial murders known to man – then your belief in gender stereotypes is evidently strong enough to believe that no woman is as infamous as Jack the Ripper because women – as a sex – are simply incapable of committing such crimes.

If, however, you are neither ill-informed nor simple-minded, you are likely to appreciate the point which Lindsay is making in *Jill Rips* by casting a woman in the role of serial killer and showing how many men fall into the killer's honey trap because, in their inability to conceive of such a thing as a female serial killer, they ignore even the most obvious evidence that they are flirting with just that. So, not only does their violent demise prove the sexists wrong. It also shows how dangerous such sexism can be, and it reminds us that the danger of sexism cuts both ways.

As Lindsay's male victims learn all too late, it is dangerously sexist to believe that women are incapable of killing men, and as Lindsay's male investigator learns with almost the same fatal delay, it is also dangerously sexist to ignore the voice of female experience which says that these crimes "matter more because it's men who are being killed."[252] Those are the words of a feminist who says them partly to criticise the male investigator and partly to caution him, and as it turns out they articulate the very resentment which drives the female serial killer. Yet with an unconscious poignancy, the male investigator makes the common and dangerous mistake of dismissing the feminist because he would rather indulge the egalitarian gender politics of his personal idealism: "You're talking rubbish… It doesn't matter whether it's men or women. It makes no difference."[253] Not to him, perhaps, but it makes a dramatic difference to the serial killer, a woman who kills men to stage a violent protest against a chauvinistic society in which the death of a man matters more than that of a woman, and when he ignores this pervasive culture of chauvinism, he puts himself at personal risk.

The other thing that makes a dramatic difference, as mentioned above, is that Lindsay sets this novel in 1980s Glasgow, and this difference to the movie is significant enough to deserve a second mention. In the 1980s, Glasgow was a city of mass unemployment and widespread urban decay as coal mines, steel works, engine factories, and other heavy industries were going out of business. Towards the end of the decade, however, the city was entering an economic and cultural recovery. And in 1987, the year of *Jill Rips*, it was at a peculiar midway point between post-industrial depression and private enterprise anxiety on account of its burgeoning financial services sector. Thus, the Glasgow of 1987 is the ideal time and place for a story about a depressed private investigator anxiously navigating his way through a world of career criminals, callous entrepreneurs, and corrupt officials.

This private investigator is Murray Wilson, one of the last honest men in town. When less honest men start turning up violently murdered by what appears to be a sex killer, Murray gets hired by perhaps the least honest man in Scotland to find the psychopath who is giving symbolic shape to the era's cutthroat spirit. This psychopath soon identifies herself as 'Jill the Ripper', and as Jill cuts and kills one man after another, the scene of her crimes, a certain Moirhill, seems ever more aptly named. Not only does this fictional suburb of Glasgow sound like *Noir*hill, but it also seems like the physical and metaphysical definition of noir, with its anonymous tenements where personifications of failure live and die amid strangers. As for the second part of the place name, Moir*hill* also seems an apt name for the place, as Murray's search for support among the suburb's sadists and cynics is an uphill battle, one in which he not only gets beaten up by company men but also broken down by a femme fatale who, to depress him even further, is the unavailable wife of his brother.

Despite such in- and external challenges, however, Murray proves to be the right man for the job when he turns out to be as hard-working as he is soft-hearted. "Not the best in the world, but I know my trade. I trace, I snoop, I find out, the way someone else makes chairs or wires a circuit. If a man has nothing else, he can hold to his trade.

I'm a good tradesman..."[254] Hold to his trade is what Murray does, and in doing so, Lindsay seems to be saying, he is also holding to the values of Glasgow's manufacturing past. Despite being surrounded by progressive advocates of private enterprise – read: greedy chancers like his little brother Malcolm who is fast losing his way among loose women and shady investments – Murray embraces what in this social and economic context appears to be a rather dated community spirit. He puts the feelings and interests of others first.

Much to his material disadvantage, this last year's man ignores every opportunity for personal advancement. Rather than hold to account the many corrupt members of his community whose cover-up of the serial killer's hidden agenda makes his job both difficult and dangerous, he persistently holds to his trade and tries to stop the killer from dealing a lethal blow to the city's already crumbling social edifice. Yet just when his good work seems to be paying off, he realises that the police and media have colluded to compose an all too tidy account of an all too messy killing spree, while conveniently washing their hands off their all too sordid complicity. Outraged, he decides that busting a hole into this stitch up – this massive network of corruption which is gradually being woven into the social and economic fabric of his city – is worth getting his own hands dirty. This he does with a final act of self-loathing which is so dramatic it concretises the novel's ubiquitous atmosphere of existential dread. He singlehandedly carries the heavy burden of his decision whether to help the authorities punish the serial killer or whether to help the serial killer punish an arguably even greater criminal, the monster which created her and made countless other women afraid and resentful of men.

Philip Kerr – *A Philosophical Investigation*

Perhaps surprisingly, the same timeless moral dilemma is at the centre of Philip Kerr's *A Philosophical Investigation*, published in 1992. Even though the story is set in a futuristic and radically different cultural context, and even though the character making the controversial utilitarian decision is not the investigator but the killer, this story, too, draws its dramatic potential from the controversy that one man may be willing to commit a hugely troubling crime for the greater good. Yet what sets Kerr's novel apart from Lindsay's, and indeed from most serial killer novels, is that his utilitarian criminal makes an enormous intellectual effort to shoulder the burden of proof that his crimes, horrific though they may be, do serve the greater good. That and the fact that he barely makes any effort at all to convey a sense of the emotional weight of said burden.

In the circumstances, this does make sense, given that the killer suffers not only from a critical congestion of untapped intelligence but also from a dangerous genetic defect, an incurable neurological condition which leaves him prey to one raw, irrepressible instinct: aggression. However, by giving the killer these characteristics along with the room to work them out where other authors typically develop their supporting cast, Kerr reduces most of his other protagonists to bit players with generic defects, such as star investigator Isadora 'Jake' Jakowicz, Chief Inspector of the Metropolitan Police London. Smart, sexy, and single, Jake is successful in an environment dominated by men: law enforcement. Yet Kerr offers little by way of explanation for this supposedly exceptional success, so we are left to suspect that it must have something to do with the banal fact that Jake goes by a male name. That or the occasional suggestion that she is driven by obscure father issues to seek the approval of men in a job which seems somehow to have taught her how to channel her general hatred of men: a detective job in the department of 'gynocide'.

Such character sketches, however, are rarely drawn from what we see Kerr's characters do. For instance, we are told early on that Jake has father issues and hates men, but within mere moments of meeting her, and within mere moments of her having established the fact that she has built her formidable professional reputation on her high clearance rate in murder cases involving female victims, she is asked to lead an investigation into a serial killer of men. A little while later, we learn that she quite likes the male killer, and eventually she is the only one left to empathise and side with him against those who would have him executed for reasons of political expedience, so throughout the case, her alleged misandry remains as much of a mystery as her appointment to said case. Since even central characters remain cyphers and their motivation subject to speculation, all we can do is speculate that her superiors have identified this case as a hot potato and appointed Jake as the fall guy.

What makes this case so controversial is that the killer is not only a significant threat to a sizeable demographic but also a secret product of a psychological experiment condoned and conducted by the state. Hence, the killer is nicknamed 'the Lombroso Killer', after Cesare Lombroso, the 19th-century criminologist and founder of criminal anthropology, who is here presented as the intellectual father of this new initiative in offender profiling. The year is 2013, the setting a dystopian London on the edge of a crime-ridden European Community, and the Lombroso mental health test the first generation of a national census which tries to record the number and identities of potential murderers in the UK's male society with a view to containing and curing these born killers before they succumb to their predatory nature. Unfortunately for some of them, and unfortunately for the government which sanctioned this census, a man codenamed Ludwig Wittgenstein sees in his positive test result a call to arms, rather than a call for therapy. So, with both the determination and the brutality of a military operation, he breaks into the programme's database, identifies loose cannons like himself, and starts killing those other potential killers, all in the belief that he is performing a vital – if violent – civil service.

This being one of Kerr's early novels, the serious business of murder is offset by a touch of dark comedy which some may see as light relief. In his mission to protect society from men like him, Wittgenstein is targeting men whose codenames are picked from "the current Penguin Classic catalogue."[255] Thus, he is targeting the very shapers of the Western intellectual tradition whose 'thought crimes' the real Ludwig Wittgenstein, i.e. the influential 20th-century philosopher, aimed to eradicate in his seminal work of intellectual subversion, *Philosophical Investigations*. Yet since the fictional Wittgenstein takes this battle of the wits to a physical level by shooting in the head those of whose mental state he disapproves, he raises three very serious questions of his own. One: are the predators he kills a greater threat to the public than he is? Two: would we welcome pre-crime policing in the real world? And three: would we consent to having a protective assassin like the fictional Wittgenstein on the government payroll? Each of these questions relates to social contract theories in general, yet by dramatising what can happen when a person, or indeed a government, justifies illegal actions on the basis of hypothetical consent, Kerr encourages us to apply Wittgenstein's utilitarianism to a specific analogue in the real world: our implicit endorsement of government-sanctioned 'black-ops', i.e. covert military operatives who, without court orders, capture or kill hostiles suspected of having the intention to harm innocent people.

A version of this scenario plays out in Kerr's techno-philosophical thriller when state authorities impede Jake's investigation, first to ensure that Wittgenstein is not arrested before he has done the government's dirty work, and then to drive him to suicide so as to save the cost of its new age capital punishment, punitive coma. Indirectly, then, the government is acting as a serial killer, and unlike Wittgenstein, it does so chiefly for reasons of convenience, not conscience. As Jake puts it, "So what, if someone decided to kill a few potential psychos? It would save her the time and trouble of catching them. Not to mention the lives of all the innocent women they might eventually kill."[256] Since Jake utters these words early in the novel, and thus long before the public discourse is dominated by far more severe deprecations of Wittgenstein and his fellow 'psychos', you might still be sufficiently sensitive to the civil and human rights of so-called 'psychos' to find this statement remarkable for its blasé tone. And what you might find even more remarkable is the Freudian slip in the last sentence of said statement.

When Jake adds 'Not to mention the lives of all the innocent women they might eventually kill' to her reasons for condoning Wittgenstein's murder of 'a few potential psychos', the words 'not to mention' can, of course, be read in their idiomatic sense. Accordingly, they might signal that the saving of innocent lives is so obviously a reason to condone Wittgenstein's pre-crime assassinations that those innocent lives need not be mentioned. Yet as the rest of the novel will demonstrate, the words in question can also be read as a Freudian slip. So little mention is made of the many innocent victims in this story – including the many men who are killed by Wittgenstein before they have committed any crime of their own – that the words 'not to mention' might just reveal the unconscious attitudes of Jake and the authorities she represents. For them, it would seem, the innocent are an afterthought, either not mentioned at all or only after the bureaucrats and cynics have had their say on the apparently bigger question of how much time and trouble can be saved by letting someone without an official mandate assassinate potentially murderous – but de facto innocent – members of the public. For Wittgenstein, on the other hand, the innocent come first, and to an extent, Jake realises, this makes him morally superior to the state.

Why, then, does Jake eventually agree with her superiors that they must try to stop this moral crusader, even though he is working for the greater good and doing so pro bono? And why does she disagree with them when they suggest that driving him to suicide is the best way to do so? Jake changes her mind because, despite the fact that one of his twelve victims turns out to be a serial killer of six innocent women, and despite the fact that Wittgenstein killed the man to prevent an even greater loss of life, she comes to the conclusion that even his utilitarian rationale does not give him the right to take the law into his own hands. As she tells him, "it's not your position to make such a choice. It sets a bad example in society."[257] A little while later, she realises that this very argument against vigilante justice is also an argument against the death penalty, and this brings us to the second question: why does Jake disagree with the highest ranking officers in the police when they decide that Wittgenstein must be driven to suicide? She disagrees, and even defies them, because she believes that the judiciary, not the executive part of the government, is in the 'position to make such a choice'. As she puts it, "he's still got some rights. There is still a proper way of doing things... I want a proper trial."[258]

Meanwhile, her superiors try to sabotage her efforts with a strategy borrowed from the 18th-century philosopher Immanuel Kant. Speaking to Wittgenstein, they challenge his utilitarianism with Kant's categorical imperative, which dictates retributive killing for the killing of innocent people. As Kant argues in *Philosophy of Law*, "This ought to be done in order that every one may realise the desert of his deeds, and that bloodguiltiness may not remain upon the people; for otherwise they might all be regarded as participators in the murder as a public violation of justice."[259] In other words, Wittgenstein ought to apply to himself the moral rule upon which he has been acting so consistently – the rule to kill those who pose mortal threats to society. In his own case, however, he rejects this rationale and refuses to kill the mortal threat to society – himself. So, without spoiling the ending by revealing Wittgenstein's ultimate fate, it is safe to say that, with it being decided in court, order is restored.

Ian Rankin – *Black and Blue*

In stark contrast, no such genre-typical restoration of order will reassure the reader of *Black and Blue*, published in 1997 as Ian Rankin's eighth Inspector Rebus novel. Not only is the killer not caught and guilt not absolved but, more unconventionally still, the novel is neither about the crime of serial killing nor is it about the categorisation of serial killers, at least not as much as it is about the state of the nation. The two serial killers, Rankin seems to be suggesting, are merely symptoms of a greater malady in a bruised Scotland which dominates every part of this novel, including its title. Taken from an album by the Rolling Stones, 'Black and Blue' reflects the cultural and political tones of this novel as well as its two central themes: oil and cops. What is more, it also foreshadows that these two themes will become entangled, as indeed they do when Rankin starts mapping out four far-ranging plot strands and merges them until Rebus's investigation encompasses Scotland from Edinburgh all the way to Shetland, so even a cursory glance should reveal that this is no typical serial killer novel.

Having said that, it does open in rather typical fashion, when Rebus follows up on a violent death and finds evidence of a notorious serial killer's modus operandi. Yet as soon as he realises that he is on the trail of a copycat killer, a certain Johnny Bible, Rebus starts researching the real case which seems to have inspired this copycat, and with that, the novel shifts focus from sensational fiction to social history. The real case, after all, goes back to the late 1960s, when a man known only as 'Bible John' put the fear of God into Glasgow by killing three young women and creating his own folklore by eerily quoting scripture to a lucky survivor. After that, he suddenly stopped and is believed to have eluded capture to this day, although since the publication of *Black and Blue*, it has been suggested that Bible John was just another pseudonym of Peter Tobin, the infamous Glaswegian serial killer who, upon his conviction of three unrelated murders in 2009, claimed to have killed as many as 48 women. In 1997, however, Bible John was as anonymous as he was mysterious – Scotland's answer to Jack the Ripper – so Rankin brought him out of retirement and into *Black and Blue*.

There, he mounts his own investigation into the Johnny Bible killings, though unlike Rebus, he does not do so because he objects to the immorality of his fellow citizens being killed. He does so because he is outraged that 'The Upstart', as he calls him, has the impertinence to copy his MO and thus tarnish his legacy. Worse still, Johnny Bible is revering false idols. Not content to be known merely as Johnny Bible, he is also calling himself by the name of another real-life Scottish serial killer, Peter Manuel, the so-called 'Beast of Birkenshaw', who in the 1950s killed at least three times as many victims as Bible John did in the following decade. To punish this insult and put an end to the ruin of his reputation, Bible John poses as a cop and, in full awareness of the irony that he should do so as a man of secular law and order, he hunts down Johnny Bible.

A perhaps even deeper irony, of which Bible John is also fully aware, is that his participation in the hunt for Johnny Bible puts him on the same side as the novel's third John, John Rebus. Yet if the fact that they all share the same Christian name suggests a genre-typical reason for Rebus to enter into the race – ego-driven competition – it may come as a surprise to discover that Rebus has a reason which is as untypical of the genre as it is of him, a sudden sense of responsibility for the course of cultural history. As Rankin puts it, "Bible John meant the end of the sixties for Scotland; he'd soured the end of one decade and the beginning of another. For a lot of people, he'd all but killed whatever dribble of peace and love had reached this far north. Rebus didn't want the twentieth century to end the same way. He wanted Johnny Bible caught."[260] And if the fact that he races to catch him suggests a genre-typical outcome – arrest and analysis – the end of the race may come as an even greater surprise than its circuitous course and unusual team formation.

Without giving this surprise away, it is safe to say that the novel's ending puts the final nail into the coffin of any lingering suspicion that this was ever meant to be read as a typical serial killer novel. Instead, *Black and Blue* seems to be conceived as a gothic frontier narrative about guilt and machismo. It is only when Rebus crosses an official boundary to access the criminal network of an imprisoned hard man that he gets a lead on Johnny Bible. And it is only when he follows this lead across Scotland's internal borders of the mind that Rankin hits his stride and starts doing what readers the world over have since come to expect from him. He starts delineating the thoughts and feelings of his central protagonist in critical counterpoint to his environment by tracing the moral fault lines of his country's cultural, social, and psychological landscapes.

In her critical study *Ian Rankin's Black and Blue*, this led Gill Plain to conclude that Rankin is "fundamentally concerned with borders and boundaries – the points at which law and social structures unravel to be replaced not by chaos, but violent and threatening mirror images of themselves... Rankin pits this criminal system against the embattled forces of the law."[261] So embattled is Rebus in this case that he is hard pressed to defend himself against charges of corruption in two separate investigations, one led by a superior with a personal grievance and the other filmed for a TV show, thus making it even harder for him to hide behind the vague claim that he is merely following standard protocol as he investigates two suspicious suicides. And since one of them is his former mentor, the other a man who was falsely convicted because Rebus perjured himself to cover the dirty tracks of this mentor, it is only a matter of time until the sins of the past catch up with him.

When they do, the tables are turned and Rebus's own protégée remarks despondently that there is "Too much history around here." Yet rather than join in the lament that the long memory of the Scots makes it hard to focus on the country's present problems because past misdemeanours rarely remain in the past, Rebus replies with a loaded rhetorical question which suggests that he embraces this long memory as part of his love-hate relationship with his country and its people: "What else have the Scots got?"[262] According to the Gospel of Bible John and Johnny Bible, the answer is guilt and machismo. Yet whereas both of them act all macho in the arrogant belief that they can easily escape their guilt, Rebus proves on several occasions that, even though he often seems to fit the same description, he is in fact acting all Presbyterian in the similarly arrogant – but perhaps less aggressive – belief that guilt is a Scotsman's birthright.

One such occasion is his response to the double suicide mentioned above, a response in which he also proves that *his* machismo, unlike that of the other two Johns, is really a form of heroic masochism and thus an insecure man's coping mechanism. Rather than feel emasculated when his body, his career, and his ego all take savage beatings, he embraces them as due punishment for his part in those suicides and feels empowered by the thought that this embrace proves both his manly endurance of pain and his even manlier endeavour to redeem the sins of the world through his suffering. Thus, Plain concludes, "Rebus's heroic masochism represents a significant feature of one of the novel's central concerns – the pressures surrounding contemporary masculinity."[263] And since Rebus spends most of his time testing the boundaries of male camaraderie, competitiveness, and conscience, Plain believes that, "ultimately, Rankin is less interested in whodunit, or even particularly in why they did it, than in what it means to live in a society in which such crimes are possible."[264] By

Rebus's own verdict, his investigation of these crimes ends somewhere "north of hell,"[265] and judging by his general attitude to the state of the nation at the turn of the century, that 'somewhere' is a version of purgatory. This, of course, may well be too fanciful a reading of Rebus's worldview and Rankin's moral outlook, but if it is not, then this novel's title might just have another meaning. It might just mean that there is no such thing as a clear conscience in *Black and Blue*.

Douglas Lindsay – *The Long Midnight of Barney Thomson*

A similarly purgatorial atmosphere can be found in Douglas Lindsay's *The Long Midnight of Barney Thomson*, published in 1999, but there the similarities end. Lindsay's novel is an unusual genre-hybrid, a serial killer satire crossed with something perhaps best described as a barbershop noir death junky thriller. It is also the first in an on-going series of 'Barney books' – seven novels, four novellas, and one collection of short stories to date – which can be read either as daft sendups of genre clichés or as deft illustrations of attribution biases, but more about that later.

First, let me introduce the main protagonist of these 'Barney books', the Glaswegian barber Barney Thomson whose darkly comical antics have elevated Lindsay to cult status in the Scottish literary scene. Barney is difficult to describe, not only because he has moments of side-splitting humour and nerve-shredding adventure, and others in which he could bore for Scotland, but also because most of his character traits have changed dramatically in the course of the series. In fact, the only one which seems to have survived all the trimming and remodelling he has undergone in the past 15 years, and the one which puts him a cut above the genre's typically rather excitable serial protagonist, is his laissez-faire attitude. Barney is a quiet sceptic who looks at life with a raised eyebrow. Having spent the best part of his adult life looking at the backs of male heads, which seem to have been filled with an irrepressible need to air their most inane thoughts right in front of him, he has come to the conclusion that barbery is about more than cutting hair. It is about providing an all-round service for head and soul in what must be one of the last remaining male protectorates in the developed West of Scotland, a homo-social sanctuary where men of all backgrounds come together to cultivate their prejudices, pontificate on such pressing issues of the day as the on-going plight of Partick Thistle Football Club, and generally talk pish.

Unfortunately, however, Barney has two left feet when it comes to these far-ranging pastoral duties. Not only does he hate football, but he cannot keep up with the two other barbers in the shop whose dizzying speed and agility in the daily discussion of the beautiful game and its bearing on world politics has put him so far off *his* game that, by the time we meet him, he has developed a reputation for leaving nothing beautiful on and in the heads of his customers. Shunned even by the most faithful of his regulars, and stunned by his follicular disasters, he hits rock bottom when he is suddenly and unceremoniously relegated from what he believes to be the Champions League of barbery, the chair in the window. And this is where the comedy of manners, which dominates the opening pages of Barney's debut, suddenly and unceremoniously gives way to a comedy of murders, as Barney is dead set on getting his chair back, by whatever means necessary: "Murder! Why not? They deserved it. You should never humiliate your colleagues in front of the customers. Wasn't that one of the first things they taught you in Barber School?"[266]

Incriminating as this may sound, though, Barney has no serious intention of killing his colleagues. It is merely an accident when he ends up doing just that. And when he bags and bins the bodies, it is only to remove the police's inevitable suspicion at the fact that he should be the sole survivor of this accident. What he does not foresee is that by removing the bodies, he is leaving the police with no evidence of his innocence and a lot of time to follow the only remaining lead, him. This they promptly do, though not just because he fits the profile of the barber killer. They also have him in the frame for several murders committed by another Glaswegian serial killer. And if your mouth is already watering at the thought of this Quentin Tarantino blend of bad decisions, burlesque dialogue, and baroque violence, you will be pleased to know that Lindsay refines this recipe for macabre tragicomedy by adding a few surprise ingredients. First, he makes this other serial killer butcher young men, then he reveals that this killer is a cannibal who cooks the corpses for an unsuspecting houseguest, and with a stomach-turning flair for the grotesque he lets it be known that this cannibalism includes a distasteful form of catering, as each victim's family is posted a package of leftovers. The biggest surprise, however, is neither the cannibalism nor the catering. The biggest surprise is the foul aftertaste which kicks in late – but with a rarely matched power to linger – when Lindsay reveals that our sympathetic anti-hero Barney was the unsuspecting houseguest and his octogenarian mother the cook.

Among the countless genre clichés caricatured in the confection of these contrived crimes are the contrived crimes themselves, the kinky sex killer, the clueless spouse, the connoisseur of cannibalism, and the conclusion which somehow makes sense of all these clichés. Take for instance the crimes. One lot of them is committed by Barney, a ridiculously inept man, the other by his mother, a seriously infirm woman. Barney seems to have the worst luck in the world, as he never really wants to hurt anybody and yet repeatedly finds himself in the wrong place at the wrong time and with the wrong utensil at hand to prevent the many accidental deaths that occur around him. As for his mother, the woman is 84 and yet somehow manages to slaughter a series of nubile toy boys after appealing to them in a lonely hearts column and seducing them with the promise of casual sex. And when she cooks them, she is so far from being a connoisseur, Barney gags at the mere smell of this culinary atrocity.

Meanwhile, Barney's wife misses every one of the myriad clues that she has married into a family of serial killers. She even misses Barney's confession, so religiously does she adhere to her daily regimen of soap operas. And when Barney is finally caught by the police, he is as surprised as anyone with even the slightest knowledge of serial killer fiction must be when he does not get his genre-typical comeuppance. Yet still more untypical than the fact that Barney somehow survives his police encounter is the final shootout in which the investigating officers suddenly all kill one another. And perhaps the best measure of Lindsay's deconstruction of genre conventions is his decision to give this closing scene the title 'Reservoir Frogs'. Not only does this title acknowledge his afore-mentioned debt to Tarantino and such cult classics of self-satirising pop art as *Reservoir Dogs*. It also reminds those of us who have seen the movie that it is possible to recoil from certain criminal protagonists while rooting for others who have committed the very same crime – just like most of us would want nothing to do with Barney's mother yet are likely to hope that Barney himself will escape punishment, even though both are proven serial killers – and this brings us to the afore-mentioned attribution biases.

Attribution biases are distortions in the process of event evaluation. They determine our decision whether an event is a good or a bad thing, whether it is the result of an action or an accident, and who, if anybody, is responsible. In most serial killer cases, these biases work against the killer, but not because people object to killing per se, nor because they object to those doing the killing, but because something in this case disgusts them. As Mark Alfano, an expert in moral psychology, explains, "when people feel the emotion of disgust they are more inclined to describe someone's actions as blameworthy or punishable – even if the disgust is wholly irrelevant to the person being judged."[267] Lindsay illustrates this in two cases. In the first one, Barney decides that his mother is blameworthy, not when he realises that she has killed several innocent young men, but when he remembers how disgusting her flat smelled when she cooked them. And this memory suddenly makes him inclined to believe that she may be blameworthy for countless other crimes besides those recent killings: "All those strange jams and wines and pies she'd made all her life; what had been in those? … Everything he could remember her doing, and he had over forty years of a dominated life to look back upon, was now shrouded in suspicion, every act potentially barbaric."[268] Even his father's fatal heart attack now seems like it may have been his mother's doing.

Meanwhile, the police arrive at the same general suspicion that she must be one of those "sick people out there." And like Barney, they arrive at this suspicion not so much because she has proven herself capable of some truly depraved crimes, but because they are disgusted to learn that, before she killed and cannibalised her victims, she seduced them with "eastern lovemaking." Of course, they admit, seducing men who are sixty years younger than herself "isn't as sick as lopping someone's napper off and mailing it to their mother,"[269] but it is precisely the thought of her exotic sex life that makes the investigating officers think of her as a dangerous deviant. So, at least in this case, the verdicts that her murders are a bad thing, that they could not have been accidents, and that they are blameworthy as well as punishable are determined by disgust at situational details which are wholly irrelevant to the charge of murder.

In Barney's case on the other hand, Lindsay illustrates that attribution biases can also work in favour of a criminal. Barney's guilt, after all, is as certain as that of his infamous predecessor Sweeney Todd, and like that other barber-turned-serial killer, Barney seems to premeditate his crimes, as when he indulges a murder fantasy after being humiliated in front of his customers. Yet in spite of such incriminating evidence, Lindsay manages to predispose his readers towards an interpretation of Barney's murders as pitiable accidents rather than punishable actions, and this is where attribution biases work in his favour. Lindsay predisposes his readers to this interpretation by presenting Barney as a victim, a man who has been dominated by his mother for more than 40 years. So, from when we first meet him "on a freezing cold, dank, sodden day in March,"[270] we are likely to develop a favourable bias which will allow us to believe that his morbid deeds are accidents and that blame is to be attributed to his domineering mother, not because we know this for a fact, but because he seems disarmingly angsty, whereas she seems disgustingly aggressive. As a result, *The Long Midnight of Barney Thomson* can be read either as a dark comedy about the genre clichés of serial killer fiction or as a cautionary tale about the unconscious – and often unconscionable – ways in which we attribute blame even in matters of life and death.

Campbell Armstrong – *Butcher*

This latter reading brings us to Campbell Armstrong's *Butcher*, another Glasgow-set investigation into the dangers of attribution biases. *Butcher* was published in 2006 as the fourth and final novel about Detective Lou Perlman, and like *The Long Midnight of Barney Thomson*, it features protagonists on both sides of the law who badly misjudge one another and put people's lives at grave risk because they focus on overt behaviours, rather than on underlying personality traits and pathological conditions.

Genre-typically, this has the gravest consequences when an event evaluation is distorted by repulsion. When Perlman evaluates the threat of Dr Dorcus Dysart, whom he will later identify as a serial killer, he is deeply repulsed by the man's repeated lying, his reckless disregard for others and self, and his total lack of remorse. Yet rather than investigate further when he discovers these behavioural deficits, Perlman makes the fatal mistake of which experts in moral psychology like Chris Keegan warn us, namely that "we may end up missing the grounding reasons for our repulsion towards certain behaviours because we never acknowledge the deep-seated human traits that are being violated."[271] Perlman misses the grounding reason for his repulsion because he acknowledges only Dysart's superficial behavioural deficits, not the deep-seated human trait that is being violated – the ability to feel for other people, to see them as more than bodies from which he can harvest organs. All Perlman sees is an awkward loner with a stutter who lives in a house rumoured to be haunted, a mausoleum full of mementoes of his late parents: "OK, mildly eccentric, maybe a touch morbid, but a long way from criminal."[272] And since this 'eccentricity', as Perlman puts it euphemistically, repels so many people around him, Perlman is dismayed at the injustice of their attribution biases, and in an effort to do better, morally, he decides to rise above his own repulsion.

In effect, however, he simply looks away from the cause of his repulsion. So, like the many disgusted detractors who keep their distance from Dysart, and whom Perlman repeatedly criticises for failing to see past their biases when looking at his 'eccentricities', Perlman fails to see that the man's nervous stutter, his mechanical use of repetitive speech patterns, and his humourless inability to be anything but literal are all signs of an impaired communicative rationality. Perhaps the best example of this impairment is a conversation between Dysart and a customer of his, a trafficker of human organs. In this awkward exchange, Dysart refers to the organs he has harvested from his victims as 'parts'. The trafficker laughs, because he misinterprets this literal description as a technical joke, and Dysart is left dumbfounded because he cannot see "what was so funny about parts."[273]

Seeing as this is his typical response when the direction of a conversation or the mood of a person suddenly changes, people as sensitive as Perlman should instantly see that Dysart can neither take another person's perspective nor respond to an emotional stimulus without first rationalising it and parsing a response. Yet just when Perlman is about to take a closer look at these symptoms of psychopathy, he sees how enthusiastic Dysart's guard dogs are in the company of their owner. On the strength of the popular attribution bias that an animal's enthusiasm is attributable to its owner's empathy with its needs, rather than to more prosaic reasons like the animal's lack of exercise, Perlman decides that Dysart must be capable of empathy and can therefore not suffer from psychopathy. Instead, he decides, this friend of animals must just be incapable of dealing with human beings, which would suggest that he suffers from some relatively harmless Anti-Social Personality Disorder.

Such confusion, of course, is common enough. As Keegan notes, "ASPD manifests through behaviours like repeated lying, reckless disregard for others and self, and lack of remorse, while psychopathy manifests through personality traits like lack of empathy. The difference is that ASPD is strictly about how we act, whereas psychopathy is about inherent and entrenched reasons or conditions for one's actions."[274] Yet as Perlman ruefully admits when he looks back at his many awkward encounters with Dysart and realises that the man is in fact a dangerous psychopath – not some harmless 'daftie' as he falsely assumed – the difficulty in distinguishing between these two disorders is not an acceptable excuse for a detective's failure to look beyond a suspect's 'eccentric' actions to the entrenched reasons for those actions. Had he done so, he might have seen Dysart's coldness in response to reports that his dogs had viciously attacked local children as evidence that he is capable of dissociating himself from other people's pain, which is what makes serial killing possible in the first place. Perlman might even have prevented some of those killings.

Seeing as *Butcher* closes on Perlman's realisation of these tragically missed opportunities, it makes sense both psychologically and dramatically that the novel's resolution is provided by Perlman's regret at having failed Dysart's victims, rather than by the genre-typical revelation why the killer selected, tortured, killed, and mutilated his victims. That Dysart killed people to earn money from the sale of their organs, and that he had no scruples to do so because his traumatic childhood desensitised him, is revealed with such anti-climactic timing and undramatic nonchalance that most readers are likely to care as little about the reasons for Dysart's violence as Perlman does. Besides, as Jerry Piven, an expert in the psychology of death, reminds us, Dysart's reasons are hardly surprising. "Psychological studies continually show that violence is often the result of protracted shaming, coercion, neglect, and abuse of children."[275] And as Dysart reminds us in several interior monologues, he, like most serial killers, ran the gauntlet of all these terrors throughout a long and inescapable childhood.

Armstrong, then, makes these potentially shocking revelations without the usual suspense and sensationalism. As a result, Dysart's backstory takes a backseat. Instead of placing flashbacks to the childhood which shaped the killer at the forefront of the novel, Armstrong focuses attention on the social issues which are presently shaping Glasgow's children. So, when Perlman says "Inflict pain, you always get some of it back,"[276] he seems to be referring to more than the pain which was inflicted upon Dysart in the shape of shaming, coercion, neglect, and abuse, and which Dysart is now giving back in the shape of serial murder. Perlman seems to be referring to victims of structural violence, specifically to the children he sees in Glasgow's ghettos, where many of them are going through a similar childhood as Dysart's and some of them get caught in a lifelong cycle of pain. "These were the city's children, brought up in doomed housing, failed by parents and teachers and priests, and all those useless theorists and planners of civic order, shrinks, sociologists and politicians."[277]

The further into the novel we advance, the fuller Armstrong's Glasgow seems to be of these failed children. Time and again, his protagonists leave the safety of their homes only to be accosted by gangs of thuggish children who roam the city's crime-ridden council estates. And the further Perlman advances in his investigation, the more he fears that his home town is not just full of children who are being failed by their elders, but also full of the failing adults these children so often become. One tragic example of these failing adults is Dr Ben Tartakower, a former surgeon who is now hanging out on the fringes of Glasgow, and indeed of this novel, as an 'eccentric' recluse with a ferret and an apostolic following of feral children. Like Dysart, Tartakower is a victim turned victimiser, and like in Dysart's case, Perlman sees only a benign fantasy version of the real man. Yet while in Dysart's case he was guilty of an attribution bias, he is now guilty of proactive interference, a psychological process in which, as Piven puts it, "Our perceptual schemas funnel whatever we 'see' into pre-existing patterns and categories... So we believe we see, but we react to our own fantasies and then believe that's the way things really *are*."[278] Inevitably, then, the case gradually falls apart as Perlman contemplates not the genre-typical mystery of how to catch the killer, but the many mysteries of temperament which have so often blinded him and broken others.

Christopher Brookmyre – *A Snowball in Hell*

Contemplating those same mysteries – though at the opposite end of the literature's aesthetic spectrum – is the comical cast of Christopher Brookmyre's *A Snowball in Hell*, published in 2008. Brookmyre's forte is social satire, and in this case the target of his Wildean wit is our turn-of-the-century celebrity culture. This he obliterates with a scattergun of ridicule, his weapon of choice in most of the genre-bending books published under the name 'Christopher', as opposed to the tamer PI novels published under the name 'Chris'. Here, this scattergun is perhaps most competently – and certainly most controversially – wielded by Simon Darcourt, the former terrorist-for-hire who shot to notoriety in 2001's *A Big Boy did it and Ran Away*.

Having returned as a militant campaigner for cultural reform, Darcourt is trying to solve – or at least make as many people as possible think about – the mysteries of temperament which have created and kept alive our current celebrity culture. Yet since old habits die hard, the campaign trail soon turns into a trail of corpses. As early as on page five, Darcourt signals his deadly intent in his private reality show, aired on the Internet and cynically titled "I'm a Celebrity and I'm Never Getting out of Here."[279] Having abducted and incarcerated a celebrated producer of vacuous pop music and similarly vacuous performers – a perhaps rather unfriendly caricature of Simon Cowell – Darcourt soon makes a cautionary example of him by broadcasting his execution online. Having thus gained the attention of both the police and the wider public, he rapidly escalates the violence, first by incarcerating a selection of the late producer's celebrated performers, and then by forcing them to compete in a televised karaoke show in which their miming performances are judged and their oxygen supplies regulated by public vote, until the losers literally run out of airtime.

Any attempt to trace or terminate the broadcast, so the police are told, will be penalised with the murder of all surviving contestants, so it is decided that the show must go on. And since the viewing figures are soon in the millions, as Darcourt predicted they would be, it is difficult to simply dismiss his argument that our spectacle obsessed society has a voracious appetite for even the very lowest forms of vicarious adventure – voyeuristic atrocity – and, at least in certain sections, violent attacks on its own members. As he puts it, "That's why I've never exactly been inclined to hang my head in shame any time the newspapers called me a monster. I *was* a monster. I am a monster. But let's not pretend for a second that they anything but loved me for it."[280] As in most of Brookmyre's writing, this false moralism is the over-arching subject of scorn. In this case, he makes a mockery of it by triggering a hysterical media circus with Darcourt's announcement that his karaoke death-match will be decided by the amount of news coverage each contestant receives. True to Darcourt's prediction, the tabloids cover the story extensively, and true to his charge of false moralism, they do so under the pretext of civic duty while courting readers with increasingly mawkish sentimentality and maladroit sensationalism, until the column inches can be measured in miles.

Meanwhile, DI Angelique de Xavia, who is leading the official inquiry, is secretly recruited by an anonymous blackmailer who orders her to deliver Darcourt to him before the police make their arrest. Seeing no way out of this evident conflict of interests, de Xavia secretly recruits a professional illusionist – Zal Innez, last seen in 2003's *The Sacred Art of Stealing* – and from here on in, very little is what it appears to be. That goes not only for a number of unusually surprising plot twists, which it would be a shame to reveal here, but also for Darcourt. Sure, he is a brilliant, manipulative, and ultimately remorseless serial killer, and as Andrew Terjesen, an expert in moral psychology, points out, "The idea of the brilliant, manipulative, and ultimately remorseless serial killer is not unusual in serial-killer fiction,"[281] but Darcourt is unusual in a different sense. Unlike most serial killers, he is difficult to judge, at least he is for me, and perhaps I should speak only for myself in this exceptionally controversial case. See, despite the hard fact that Darcourt has killed more than 400 people, and despite the even harder fact that he shows no sign of remorse, every wannabe celebrity he kills makes it more difficult for me to judge him, because every rabble-rousing soap-box rant he offers by way of justification makes it more difficult to pretend that I anything but love him for it.

This, of course, is both an irresponsible endorsement of a hate preacher and a harmless exercise in wish fulfillment, given that Darcourt exists only in fiction, but it is also a fair expression of the moral conflict Brookmyre engenders with his narrative strategy.

Telling large sections of the story in Darcourt's voice, he not only makes me relate to his worldview, at least in this fictional context and solely for the sake of argument, but he also makes me relate to Darcourt's criticism of his victims, because in contrast to their rabid, right-wing histrionics or their rehearsed, pop-culture platitudes, his rants seem rather reasonable. Having said that, I am well aware that other readers will find ample room for disagreement in Darcourt's foul-mouthed definition of the categorical contrast between him and his victims, i.e. their inexcusable lack of cultural sophistication and common decency which he believes is undermining civilisation. Yet the left-wing readers whom Brookmyre has made a career of courting are unlikely to fault his criticism of the "fat, sweaty, pish-stained, prematurely middle-aged arseholes seeking the cheap route to notoriety and populist approval by acting the keyboard hardman in a tabloid,"[282] or even the "eager little slut-monkeys... only interested in locating the path of least resistance between themselves and the cover of *Heat* magazine."[283]

What those left-wing readers *are* likely to see as a fault, though, is Darcourt's method of criticism. By going beyond verbal castigating to violent killing of undesirables, he moves even further towards fascism than such retrograde culture assassins as the fat, sweaty, pish-stained, prematurely middle-aged keyboard hardman. And this finally brings us to the genre-typical question: why does Darcourt kill people? According to Darcourt himself, he first crossed that moral boundary because, "like the Victorian gentleman-amateur, I played for the love of the game." Yet later in life, he seems to have developed a social conscience, for he adds that, "though I can't truthfully present the common good as a central motive, it does feature as an auxiliary beneficiary."[284] In other words, even though he now kills eager little slut-monkeys and anyone who aids or abets the spread of celebrity culture, he is still not a mission-oriented serial killer, for his main motive is not the killing of certain people but the killing itself.

Darcourt, then, is one of those unusual serial killers who kill for the thrill, the hedonistic type whose main beneficiary is his sense of self. As he admits, "I did what I did because it electrified me every moment I was awake..."[285] Yet while most would identify this as sadistic self-gratification, Darcourt seems to see it as heroic egoism. Then again, it is only normal for a Sadean hero to see it that way. As David Schmid observes in his essay 'A Philosophy of Serial Killing', "One of the keys to understanding the psychology and behaviour of the Sadean hero is to appreciate the importance of his egoism... Sadean heroes always evaluate conventional morality through the prism of self-interest." The other key, Schmid adds, is to appreciate their eager self-justification. "At the slightest provocation, they will pause in the midst of their debauches and undertake the most exhaustive (and repetitive) explanation of why they are entirely justified in their chosen course of action..."[286] Without acknowledging these contradictions in his nature, Darcourt is at all times true to them, and it is his dual obsession with his afore-mentioned politics of terror on the one hand and his Sadean polemics in justifying them on the other which explains how such a radical social critic can be at once terribly offensive and troublingly convincing.

Craig Robertson – *Random*

Even more troubling is the thought that this moral conflict between condemning and condoning the crimes of a serial killer may not depend on such a divisive cultural context, that it may be possible to be sympathetic to a serial killer for a single mitigating factor – a personal cause. This is the thought experiment at the heart of *Random*, Craig Robertson's debut novel published in 2010. Robertson's killer is not concerned with the culture around him, not even with the culture of careless driving which led to the accidental death of his daughter. All he is concerned with is that particular case, and all he wants is revenge to take the edge off his hurt, not some miracle remedy to cure the underlying social malaise.

So what he decides to do is kill the man who knocked down his only child and got away with it by blaming the girl's casual traffic behaviour, the difficult driving conditions, the critical response time, in short, anything but his own carelessness. Yet rather than simply kill the man and risk being caught with both means and motive, he takes great care to go after him under the mantle of anonymity by selecting five strangers at random – hence the title – and killing all six of his victims with extreme violence and a signature wound – hence the police's misdirection. Too busy looking for a sadistic serial killer, they do not look twice at the sad man whose murder motive accounts for only one of six victims. Thus, he is left to complete his mission – and in the process conflict his readers – by framing himself as a victim while victimising five people who have done nothing to warrant their deaths.

How could anyone be morally conflicted rather than simply outraged at reading this? Well, despite the fact that the killer describes each murder in detail, from his strategic stalking all the way through his clinical MO, despite the fact that he shows no signs of empathy or regret while pursuing his mission, and despite the fact that he deliberately makes each victim suffer a "grotesque, undignified death,"[287] Robertson nevertheless makes it possible to empathise with the man, at least to a certain extent. By telling the story from his point of view, he makes us look at the killer's native Glasgow through eyes which are unable to cry at the relentless pain, anger, and depression he feels when he realises that, bereaved of a loved one, "you can find a reason to kill anyone if you look hard enough."[288] Besides, unlike most serial killers, he does not find his reason to kill by looking hard at his victims, but by looking hard at himself.

Sure, as the mission-oriented type of serial killer he is like a lot of fictional serial killers, but unlike most of their missions, his is not defined by some psychopathological drive to eliminate a certain type of person. It is defined by a grief-stricken and overwhelming desire for revenge against *one* person. And as the expert in death psychology, Jerry Piven, points out, this instrumentalisation of murder shows that, "as selfish and depraved as people might be, murder is not just an instinct or some sinister lurking force waiting to erupt. It reflects the need for control in the wake of helplessness and vulnerability."[289] So, although his violence appears to be psychopathological, this appearance is in fact a deliberate deception and his violence a temporary effect of post-traumatic dissociation. We know this because, as our narrator, he shares with us his plan to deceive the police, and once this deception has allowed him to accomplish his violent mission, his compassion kicks in and he is struck down by his conscience. Realising that "A man who wants to scream out his darkest secret to the world will never know peace,"[290] he repents and contemplates suicide as his only remaining path to peace.

Of course, neither his pain nor his self-imposed death penalty will absolve him in the eyes of every reader, let alone in the eyes of all the bereaved. Most of us will consider murder to be an inexcusable form of grief management, especially when, as in this case, it is so profoundly selfish that, while his wife manages her grief by channelling it into an anti-drink-and-drive campaign to improve road safety and thus benefit people she does not know, he kills people he does not know to benefit himself. And while she is in dire need of his emotional support, he distances himself from her emotionally to pursue his private revenge mission. But perhaps most selfish of all is his guilt management, for although he turns it into a long-term project which consumes most of his spare time and all of his emotional energy, he does not consider the effect it will have on his wife.

Understandably enough, he cannot let his wife know that the guilt he is trying to manage is more complicated than hers, that he is not just feeling guilty for having been unable to protect his daughter, but also for having been unable to stop himself from killing other innocent people. So it is perhaps in the spirit of sincerity that, even though she repeatedly reaches out to him in her naïve need, he does not let her try to make him feel better. Yet even if it is a sign of sincerity, it is nonetheless a sign of selfishness that he does not even try to convince her that she *could* make him feel better, for by denying her even this harmless delusion, he also denies her the comfort of believing that, despite the loss of her only child, she may yet gain a new sense of emotional purpose. Instead, he tries to resolve his emotional conflict by and for himself, and when he fails to do so, he also fails her. His contingency plan, after all, is suicide, and in making that plan he does not have a lot of time for thoughts of collateral damage, such as the emotional devastation his wife is bound to feel when she learns that, having already lost her only child, she has now also lost her only husband and thus probably the only real hope she ever had of overcoming her grief.

As he is quick to clarify, however, neither his selfishness nor his serial killing is "evil or any such pish, just uncontrollable obsessions. There is a lot of rubbish talked about evil when it comes to serial killers. Numbers mess with people's moral outrage."[291] To refute some of this 'rubbish' and stifle some of our moral outrage, he cautions us that "We are all more than we seem, even to ourselves. We are all capable of much more than we or others might think. None of us can be sure of who we are or what we are, far less of what we might do."[292] Worse still, he adds with mixed feelings of rage and regret, "one outrageous fucking horrible life-changing, mind-wrecking, drive-you-fucking-crazy happening"[293] is enough to turn an average person with no history of violence into a sadistic serial killer with a skewed and self-deceiving moral code. In his case, it is the careless nature of his daughter's death which convinces him that he is right to avenge her by killing her attacker – right in a moral if not in a legal sense – and that he is justified – again in a moral if not in a legal sense – to use whatever means necessary to accomplish this mission, even if that involves killing other people and cutting off their little fingers to give the police false clues, which, incidentally, is how he earns his nickname: the Cutter.

The crux of his moral conflict, then, is that committing five decoy murders is not really about doing right by his daughter. As he eventually realises, it is really about avoiding the consequences of his moral crusade: suspicion, arrest, and imprisonment. Yet while this unconscious motive may seem morally repugnant, a quick glance at a few cases of real-life serial killers will show that it is far from rare. As Susan Amper observes in her essay 'Dexter's Dark World: The Serial Killer as Superhero', even a quick glance at other *fictional* serial killers, including such box office hits as Jeff Lindsay's Dexter Morgan, will show that self-preservation is nowadays often a strong motivating factor in a serial killer's moral crusade, as it "reflects very well the ethics of the day. If earlier ages emphasised obligations to others – called people to duty, to meeting their obligations to God, family, country, community – today people are more called on to work out *their* problems."[294] Some of us, then, are likely to share the Cutter's ethics and thus easily excuse his self-centredness, if not his serial killing. We might even find it hard to empathise with the Cutter's victims because his narrative perspective makes us focus on his own sense of victimhood. What is almost certain, however, is that the unease we feel at seeing how easily one person can destroy another, followed so closely by his desire for self-destruction, will cause a moral conflict rarely found in serial killer fiction.

Lin Anderson – *Picture Her Dead*

In stark contrast, Lin Anderson leaves room for neither mixed feelings nor moral conflicts amid the scientific certainty her main protagonist displays in *Picture Her Dead*, published in 2011. This is the eighth case of Dr Rhona Macleod, a forensic scientist who, once again, turns out to be the only hope Strathclyde Police have of solving a murder mystery which, once again, has rather little to do with forensic science. Yet despite the fact that the investigative procedures required to solve this mystery lie well beyond her remit, Rhona, once again, becomes indispensable to an increasingly amateurish police investigation.

Not only does she lend her professional expertise to the official CSI team when a decomposed corpse is found in a derelict Glasgow cinema during a search for the disappeared photographer Jude Evans. Rhona also gives freely of her limited spare time – and indeed of her similarly limited sleuthing talent – to an unofficial team of dilettante private detectives, a team consisting of herself and a certain Liam Hope, an anxious young man who happens to be both her son and Jude's friend. So far, so cosy. Yet rather than focus on the conflict of interest which arises from the obvious fact that Rhona is both professionally and personally involved in the case, Anderson focuses on her collection of forensic data. In other words, she focuses on what the cultural critic Cassuto describes as the type of "careful forensic research that gives scientific authority to procedural serial killer narrative."[295]

Accordingly, Rhona's personal life is confined to a few paragraphs, sentimental vignettes which seem to be inserted into the main narrative at random and do rather little by way of character development while taking a lot of time to draw out a few sketchy sub-plots, be it the one about her half-hearted effort to enrich her impoverished relationship with her estranged son, or the one about her absent-minded attempt to protect a former lover from an infamous gangster. In fact, the only thing these asides do, and do so repeatedly, is prove that Rhona is indeed, as she self-pityingly puts it, "a mother who was incapable of sustaining any relationship, with a lover or a son."[296] Yet as we soon see, such emotional incapability is evidently not what this scientist cares about, for neither does she mention it beyond the odd throwaway remark, nor does it trouble her enough to distract her from her life- and novel-defining work.

Meanwhile, Anderson reinforces this clinical atmosphere, in which forensic fact is prioritised over fellow feeling, by making even fewer and scanter revelations about the personal lives of Jude and her killer. The female victim is relevant, not as a once living person, but only as a permanently passive body. Before she is found, she is the object of an adventurous search, and after she is found, she is the object of Rhona's forensic study. Similarly, the male killer is objectified throughout the investigation. Even though he is still alive, he is largely removed from the narrative, and even when he makes a brief appearance, he is only relevant as a passive link in a long chain of evidence, a chain which connects Jude's murder to the corpse found in the cinema and a snuff film recorded at the ancestral seat of Lord Dalrymple, where three men died prior to this case and in sadomasochistic circumstances which are deemed to be as suspicious as those at the cinema.

For the most part, then, attention favours the dead. The narrative focus is on analysis, not empathy; categorisation, not understanding. This is especially clear in the reduction of the killer's stage time to brief cameos during which he is interrogated about his method, rather than his motive, because what this reduction reflects is a diminished interest in an understanding of murderous impulses. What matters to

Rhona is how he killed the girl, not why he felt compelled to do so, and this scientific rationale sets the killer far apart from our human community, because it foregrounds actions to which most of us strongly object rather than anxieties to which some of us may relate, at least to an extent. We do eventually learn why he killed the girl, but the explanation is as technical and contrived as the prior investigation. Rather than make us understand why he got involved with Lord Dalrymple's secret society of sex killers and how he feels about having covered up their crimes, Anderson offers a short explanation of the society's MO, which ties up her loose plots in a few short newspaper clippings by connecting Jude's murder with that of the body found in the cinema and three prior sex killings. So, all we learn about the character of Jude's killer is that he has a questionable appetite for sadistic sex and an even more questionable taste in friends.

As for his most questionable friend, the sadist who killed the other four victims, he "died before being brought to court."[297] Here, as in most conservative crime fiction, the death of the criminal is offered in place of a comment on the mental or social circumstances which can create such criminals. Thus, relief that the threat of this particular criminal has been contained provides the story's resolution, while the demonising portrayal of his sadism suggests that there is no need to think about him or his sexual deviance beyond novel's end. All we need to know is that he was a power-oriented serial killer who killed because he was truly evil, and Rhona has good reason not to dwell on this mysterious motive. As she puts it, "Most people never encountered true evil. And that's how it should be."[298] So, when professionals like her do encounter it, they neither waste their time analysing it nor burden other people with attempts at explaining a degree of deviance which is so otherworldly that it ultimately defies human understanding.

Admittedly, such reasoning is rather common in serial killer fiction, but not all readers are likely to accept that a killer's deviance can be explained by calling him or her evil. In fact, some readers strongly object to this so-called 'explanation' because, as Peter Messent puts it in an essay on the logic of contemporary crime fiction,

"To consign crime to the realm of pure evil and individual moral monstrosity is a way of isolating it from all social, political or economic causes, and 'explaining' it as freakish and psychopathic exception to all that we know to be normal."[299] In other words, the popular 'evil rationale' is not an explanation but an emotive categorisation. And as the expert in the psychology of death, Jerry Piven, warns us, "One surefire way to remain a complete ignoramus is to lump people into rigid, cumbersome, ridiculously simplistic categories, stereotypes, or psychiatric diagnoses. Doing so may provide a nice feeling of certainty and understanding, it may make you feel smart, and it may make you less afraid, but it is actually a method that makes a virtue out of refusing to think."[300]

In this case, of course, as in a lot of serial fiction, refusing to think saves the author the effort and embarrassment of having to explain another piece of lazy thinking: the continuity error. Refusing to think – or preferring to forget – makes it possible for Rhona to ignore the many clues which point towards a killer whom she has already studied in forensic detail in a previous case. Only when it conveniently allows her to create the novel's single plot twist does Anderson fix this continuity error by tacitly acknowledging that she has been recycling old material. At this point, Rhona surprises herself along with the less attentive reader by suddenly noticing "A violent sexual death, a leather collar, asphyxiation. Trademarks she recognised from the rent-boy case… the similarities with the current case seemed apparent. She couldn't believe she hadn't thought of it before, but it was a depressing truth that she saw so much violence day to day that she preferred to forget the details of each case once it seemed to be over."[301] Perhaps this is why the novel ends in the above-mentioned series of newspaper clippings – to explain the case to readers with similar memory loss.

G.J. Moffat – *Protection*

Another example of a Scottish serial killer novel in which highly expositional storytelling meets a deeply evil killer is *Protection*, written by G.J. Moffat and published in 2012 as the fourth case of lawyer-turned-bodyguard Logan Finch. Yet while Moffat's ethics and aesthetics may at first glance appear to be similarly simplistic as Anderson's, a second glance should show that a subtler mind is at work here.

Let's start with the more obvious difference, the novel's aesthetics. Moffat repeatedly interrupts his main plot with transcripts of an official Interpol correspondence, transcripts which tell of dramatic developments in one of the agency's top confidential investigations. Like so many writers of serial killer fiction, Moffat makes these dramatic developments happen offstage, which is to say that he tells rather than shows us a lot of the story's critical information. Now, in most cases, this narrative strategy guarantees that such allegedly dramatic developments seem anything but dramatic. Instead, they tend to seem both disruptive and distracting, rather like a theatre director would if he or she were to abruptly halt the drama, step in front of the audience, and declaim what has been happening *off*stage even though it should be obvious from the actors' performance *on*stage. So it seems safe to say that these expositional sections would soon become tedious, were it not for the fact that, in this case, they have a rare and rather surprising cumulative effect.

Each of these confidential memoranda is a failure report in the agency's ongoing mission to apprehend an assassin, codenamed subject Eve, who has been hired to kill a high-profile target, codenamed subject Night. Meanwhile, the target, who soon turns out to be an international celebrity by name of Chase Black, has hired Logan's team for his personal protection as he tours the UK to promote a bestselling book about his experience of going to court on multiple murder charges, appealing his life sentence, and gaining release from prison in the US. Yet undermining this official verdict is a subplot in which police are following new leads in Black's case and gradually arriving at the conviction that his initial sentence was not a miscarriage of justice after all. Before they do so, however, there is reasonable doubt as to whether Black is the victimiser or the victim, so when all those Interpol memoranda report failure after failure to apprehend his assassin, the possibility that an innocent man may soon be murdered by a serial killer for hire looms larger in Logan's mind – and presumably in that of most readers – than the genre-typical certainty that the serial killer will soon die at the hands of poetic justice. In short, these memos make it possible to sympathise with a man suspected of being a serial killer.

I say 'possible', rather than 'inevitable', because while these memos create the intuitive sympathy one feels for the target of an assassin, Moffat gradually creates the instinctive antipathy one feels against Machiavellian schemers. He does this by providing glimpses of Black's ruthless and manipulative nature, and he times these brief moments of revelation so that Logan is present on several occasions when Black's alienating darkness is visible through the cracks of his resplendent public persona. Thus, it soon becomes possible to see not only Black's sympathetic side, the side illuminated by the above memos, but also his secret, psychopathological self, and this double vision creates a moral conflict rarely seen in serial killer fiction. At various stages in the novel, it is possible to look at this case from an unusually liberal point of view, applauding those who side with Black on the basis that he is innocent until proven guilty. Yet at other stages, it is possible to look at it from the genre-typically conservative point of view, applauding those who go after him in the belief that he is evil, i.e. that he was born guilty and therefore deserves to be punished without an official verdict.

What makes this novel most unusual, however, is that it acknowledges the fact that it is possible to go back and forth between these opposite moral positions, as Logan does on several occasions. Initially taken in by Black's public show of innocence, he is increasingly troubled by the man's questionable behaviour behind closed doors, yet despite the fact that he frequently sees the public mask slip, he is easily reassured by the odd friendly gesture and an even odder bromantic moment where the two share a hotel room for a private heart-to-heart, a bearing of souls which is so strictly heterosexual that the room barely seems big enough to contain all the strained macho posturing. Moving from such intimate moments to others in which he is stunned by Black's insensitivity, Logan goes back and forth between the strong desire to protect his client and the daunting sense that he deserves to be punished.

As Logan puts it, "We get paid to put ourselves in harm's way for our clients. We volunteer to do it and we get trained to ensure we are as good as we can be."[302] Having said that, however, he does worry that his client may not be as good as he claims to be, and when every last person whom Logan trusts has lost trust in Black, he does start listening to the persistent rumour that his new friend has killed five entire families. It is in this period of doubt that he has his heart-to-heart with Black, and it is a measure of Logan's moral and emotional conflict that, when he quizzes the suspected serial killer on what he fears may be a dangerous talent for calculating hypocrisy, and Black lies to his face that he "did not kill all those people,"[303] Logan believes him. He believes that Black's international serial killer reputation, so pruriently played upon by the press during his book tour, reveals not the man's evil nature but the media's ill-natured demonisation of people for profit. Yet while there is an uncomfortable truth in this assessment of certain media outlets and their more salacious reporting practices in both the US and the UK, Logan's belief in Black reveals two far more uncomfortable truths about the nature of human perception – truths which are central, not just to this novel, but to serial killer fiction at large.

One, it shows that, as Professor of Criminal Justice Richard Gray observes, "humans tend to believe confident narratives over coherent narratives."[304] And two, it shows that humans tend to think in stereotypes. Logan thinks Black is trustworthy because, for one, Black confidently says so, and two, Black is not the stereotypical psychopath which Logan so vividly has in mind. Because of this psychological double whammy, Logan spends a lot of time ignoring the fact that Black only seems normal when he consciously and charismatically disguises his hedonistic appetite for violent murder, i.e. when his human side provides a cover for his inhuman side. And the fact that this disguise can deceive even a lawyer turned bodyguard – i.e. someone who has spent the best part of his professional life within touching distance of liars and posers – this undeniable fact shows what makes this novel, and serial killer fiction in general, both deeply disturbing and highly successful: the implication that anyone could be a serial killer.

Just how disturbing this implication is becomes apparent when subject Eve, the above-mentioned serial killer for hire, turns out to be the typical girl next door. Not only does this revelation imply that anyone could be a serial killer, even – whisper it – a woman. More disturbingly still, it also shows what can happen when this possibility is ignored. Black, after all, has bought himself all the protection he wants and armed himself with every defence mechanism in the book – from cognitive dissonance to cocky cynicism – yet when Eve plays on the stereotype of the weak and willing airhead, she puts on just the right performance for the ignorant macho in him to gain his trust, and with it admission to his inner circle. So, because her human side provides a cover for her inhuman side with just the right combination of sexy confidence and seeming compliance, she manages to get close enough to her target and familiar enough with his protection to take a shot at him.

Now, since this shooting scene is not the novel's grand finale, and since *Protection* is a typical serial killer novel in the sense that the killer is alive at the time of said grand finale, I am not ruining the ending by revealing that Eve does not kill Black when she takes that shot. Yet perhaps surprisingly, the man's survival offers no reassurance to readers who would like to believe that women simply do not have the balls, brains, bad manners, and so on – insert gender bias here – to do such unladylike things as shoot and kill men. Instead, the man's survival may well be the most disturbing aspect of this sudden and genre-untypical escalation of female on male violence, as he survives, not because his attacker acts on some weak female impulse and misses on purpose, but because his bodyguard acts on a basic human instinct and shoves another human being out of the line of fire, and while this near miss may offer some relief that a potentially innocent life has been saved, it leaves no room for any pretence that Black and his bodyguards were right to assume that one always recognises a potential killer. As the shot shows, this woman is without a doubt a potential killer, she just got unlucky, and everyone who treated her as a harmless harlot got it wrong, disturbingly so.

Another explanation for why Black's survival of this assassination attempt may be even more disturbing than the attack itself is that it leads directly to an even greater escalation of violence. Had Black died in Eve's first attack, she would not have launched a second one from closer range, Black would not have seen it coming, and he would not have been able to resort to anything as disturbing as the coldblooded violence he used when defending himself and executing his attacker. What is more, Logan would not have been forced to witness this slaughter, he would not have been forced to ask himself whether Black really killed in self-defence, and he would not have been forced to rely on his impaired judgment in the knowledge that getting it wrong would have disturbing consequence. Yet since Logan helped Black survive both assassination attempts and put him in the position to kill a person in the process, he has to live with the thought that, whether or not he now attempts to apprehend Black himself, he is already directly responsible for the survival of a potential serial killer and indirectly for the murder of yet another victim.

In the end – and this is where you might want to skip to the next section if you do not want to read about said end here – Logan misses both his moment and his man because he defers this vital decision for too long. The reason he does so is that Moffat, unlike most writers of serial (killer) fiction, insists on character consistency. As throughout the build-up to this climax, he makes Logan strain under the burden of flawed perception, as discussed above. So, when Logan reviews Black's case in those final moments, he sees what he wants to see. Even though he has seen a suspected serial killer skilfully stab another human being to death, and even though he was surprised that Black did "not try to rationalise the killing more than he had," like "any normal person would have done – sought to exonerate themselves by giving elaborate details,"[305] Logan does not see Black as a serial killer. He sees him as an insensitive but ultimately innocent victim of media demonisation on the one hand and mental illness on the other, and he makes sense of the man's instinctive violence by persuading himself that it was purely *reactive*, an automatic reaction to an acute threat. This interpretation allows Logan to agree with the general consensus that Black suffers from Anti-Social Personality Disorder, not violent psychopathy which, unlike ASPD, can manifest itself in *active* violence. As for Black's evident lack of remorse, Logan optimistically diagnoses it as a further symptom of ASPD, and it is this false diagnosis which stays his hand while Black is still within his reach.

It is only once Black is beyond his reach that Logan reconsiders the case and realises with tragic timing that Black's communicative rationality – his ability to empathise with others, take their perspectives, and reciprocate their intentions – is severely compromised. Time and again, Black had noticeable difficulties in understanding the intended meaning of what people said to him. In the above murder scene, for instance, Black killed his attacker despite having already neutralised the threat, so Logan asked, "Why?" Yet even though the context made it perfectly obvious that Logan was asking why Black had used such excessive force, Black had difficulty understanding his question and asked, "What do you mean?"[306] Despite having just killed a defenceless human being in cold blood, he could neither empathise with his victim, nor take his questioner's perspective and reciprocate his intentions. And despite having witnessed all of this at close range, Logan could neither diagnose this severely compromised communicative rationality as a symptom of psychopathy nor could he intervene in time to save Black's latest victim and stop him from getting away with murder, again. So, as the novel closes on this bitter realisation, all he can do is accept that serial killer cases are rarely resolved with the killer's capture or death, unless, of course, you live in a world of fiction. As Logan repeatedly reminds us, though, he lives in the real world, and in the real world an open-ended resolution is often the only one left to those who have been taken in by the calculated hypocrisy of a psychopathological mind – the resolution never again to forget that anybody might be a psychopath.

James Oswald – *Natural Causes*

Now, as most of us who do not suffer from paranoia will agree, this resolution goes way beyond the novel's initial premise that the odd person may be capable of untold evil. Yet as James Oswald proves in *Natural Causes*, published in 2012, some of the most thought-provoking serial killer fiction goes even further in exploring this premise, be it by playing on the insecurities of the paranoid or by posing the question whether those who believe that there is evil out there do so because they have come into contact with the paranormal.

Asking himself that very question is Detective Inspector Tony McLean, an educated man whose instinctive scepticism is in rude health when Edinburgh suddenly plays host to a bloodbath which seems to be out of this world. Seemingly life-affirming citizens suddenly start committing very public and very violent suicide, spreading ignorant horror through the city like a lethal virus. Initially, McLean disagrees with the city's gutter press, which pruriently reports that the poor folk committing these suicides are possessed by something dark and different, but when he discovers that they all killed themselves in front of a seemingly innocent stranger who soon thereafter ended up dead with a seemingly inexplicable medical history, he does start wondering about the ill-effects of demonic possession. Soon, he is looking at evidence of a more than 60 year old satanic ritual and a very angry paranormal serial killer, or so it seems.

Oswald handles the paranormal stuff with care, always leaving enough room for an alternative, rational explanation, which goes roughly like this: First, the mutilated corpse of a girl is found after Satanists seem to have killed her more than 60 years ago. Then five octogenarian gentlemen, who knew each other from their time in the army, are found dead with no sign of foul play other than the fact that each man is found with one of his organs surgically removed and forced into his mouth. Then five suicide victims, who suffered from unrelated terminal diseases, are found to have killed the old men just before they killed themselves. And McLean explains all of these macabre coincidences rationally by finding a link between all three types of murder. First, he links the five gentlemen to the ritual killing when he finds out that personal items of theirs were interred at the girl's resting place. Then he links their deaths to hers when he finds out that several of her organs were sealed up with those personal items. And then he links the suicide killers to a mysterious serial killer when he finds out that all of them were indirectly connected to one another in that each of them killed a man who had a secret history of violence in common with the other four victims. Hence, McLean concludes, somebody with a grievance against those old men must have manipulated people who were about to die of natural causes, because by making these eerily related people murder their victims with an eerily related MO, this hidden puppet master would divert attention from what otherwise seems to be a straightforward revenge motive. Is this explanation rational? Yes. Is it reasonable? Perhaps, but McLean cannot quite convince himself that this is really how it all happened.

Hence, he considers an alternative, paranormal explanation, which goes roughly like this: More than 60 years ago, five old men raised a demon to steal its power. They trapped it in a girl, raped her, and took parts of the demon's power in the form of the girl's organs. As McLean points out, "They'd all been fabulously wealthy and successful, and none of them had died of natural causes."[307] More recently, however, construction work had disturbed the girl's resting place and somehow freed the trapped demon. Since then, this demon had been going berserk, possessing random hosts to kill the old men before one of them could trap it in another virgin. Lending credence to this theory, at least in the eyes of an increasingly gullible McLean, is the fact that none of these murderers had been diagnosed with terminal diseases prior to their post mortems, which McLean concedes may be seen as a sign that an evil spirit fed on their life force and corrupted their bodies before commanding them to commit suicide so it could pass into a fresh host. And as if to forestall any concern that this explanation seems a bit far out, McLean cautions that, "just because demons don't exist, it doesn't mean someone can't believe in them enough to kill."[308] Ultimately, then, it makes no difference whether this serial killer is a demon, a deluded maniac who somehow disguises human crimes as the acts of a demon, or a master manipulator who drives others to murder because of some dark desire for revenge. Either way, we are led to believe that evil goes far beyond what most of us want to consider.

One convincing way in which Oswald leads us to believe this is by showing that, in the final analysis, even the sceptical McLean does not want to consider the implication of there being, in this case, no identifiable human culprit for the serial killings. As McLean concludes, the implication would be that there is a darker force at work here, one which might consume him as it seems to have consumed others who let it get into their heads. So when the paranormal explanation gains traction in his cohort of esoteric misfits, he tries to distance himself from it and decides that the best thing to do is not to think about how far evil can go. Yet convincing as it may be to show us an educated sceptic arrive at this conclusion, there is a far more convincing way of demonstrating that there is an extent of evil which most of us do not care to consider. Publish two versions of the same book, show evidence of extreme evil in one but not in the other, and see which one the reviewers prefer.

With *Natural Causes*, Oswald has done just that. In the original e-book edition, self-published in 2011, the story opened with a graphic flashback to the ritual killing discussed above, yet for the subsequent edition, published by Penguin in 2012, this chapter was cut. Hundreds of readers had by then reviewed the novel online and agreed that it had made them uncomfortable to see such horrific proof of the human potential for evil, especially, as many emphasised, because Oswald had portrayed it from the victim's point of view. Many other reviewers had added to this negative feedback by admitting that they had been so horrified by the approximately 450 words of this opening scene that they had decided not to read the rest of the novel, approximately 450 pages which, ironically, are all far more restrained in their depiction of violence. So, to avoid the risk of alienating further readers, Oswald made the relatively small creative sacrifice of cutting this controversial opening scene and reverting to the less horrifying one he had written for the first print edition of *Natural Causes*, a short story published in *Spinetingler* magazine in 2006.

However, to let readers "see what all the fuss was about,"[309] he has preserved this controversial opening scene in a postscript of the

Penguin text, and in doing so, he has drawn attention to an unease among readers of crime fiction which is rarely articulated, the unease surrounding "violation and violent death," as the cultural critic Woody Haut puts it. This unease, Haut adds, "is often left unarticulated, subsumed by literary preoccupations and sociological discussions regarding crime as a means of gaining autonomy or climbing the social ladder."[310] Oswald, of course, did the same thing when he cut the satanic ritual from the novel's opening pages. By cutting this scene, he ensured that the following murders are anchored not in a paranormal context but in the genre-typical context of a police investigation. Hence, rather than read them as acts of demonic retribution, most of us are likely to read them as a means of gaining autonomy or climbing the social ladder, given that the victims are all prosperous and prominent members of their communities.

After creating this familiar first impression, however, Oswald gradually creates enough room for a lasting sense of unease. First, he introduces paranormal overtones which strongly suggest that these murders are committed by something barely – or indeed not at all – human, something so evil it goes far beyond what most of us want to consider. And as though that were not disconcerting enough, he concludes the story with a postscript about the elided ritual scene, which not only spells out the often unarticulated unease surrounding violation and violent death but also leaves us with an uneasy afterthought. Even if the old men were killed by an evil spirit, their own crimes must go even further than the evil of this fantasy creature, because whatever unspeakable crimes this creature has committed, the fact that Oswald tells us about them proves that he has not received a lot of reader complaints about them, or surely he would have cut them, as he did the controversial opening scene. Since he has not cut them, the crimes of the evil spirit do not seem to go beyond what most of us want to consider, whereas the crimes of the old men do just that, for as the elision of their ritual rape and murder scene subtly suggests, their crimes are *literally* unspeakable.

In short, Oswald makes mere humans seem like greater monsters than the evil spirit which seems to be killing them, and in doing so he breaks the principal genre convention of serial killer fiction. Ever since Hannibal Lecter, it has been genre-typical to present serial killers as monsters and make them, as Professor of Criminal Justice Richard Gray observes, "appear as we do and walk among us with the appearance of respectable citizens."[311] To that extent, Oswald is certainly in compliance with genre convention. Regardless of whether you prefer the paranormal explanation that a power-oriented demon is possessing respectable citizens to do its evil bidding, or the rational explanation that a number of human killers are committing a series of monstrous murders in the service of some evil vision, in each scenario Oswald is presenting his killer as a monster which somehow manages to walk among us with the appearance of a respectable citizen. At the same time, however, and almost uniquely among serial killer novelists, Oswald breaks with convention by presenting not just his killer as a monster but also his victims. All of them appear as we do, all of them walk among us with the appearance of respectable citizens, and all of them turn out to be as bad as their killer, or indeed worse. So at least those of us who have read far enough to reach these unsettling revelations are likely to finish the book with a sense of unease equal to the one created by that much-deplored ritual murder – a sense of unease surrounding the dark implication that, at any moment, anyone might turn out to be a monster.

THE ROUNDUP

I f the last thing you have read is *Natural Causes* – or even just my analysis of it – you might agree that "What the average… serial killer seeks above all is power and the will to power."[312] In that case, however, you might be surprised to find that you are agreeing with the Moors Murderer Ian Brady. After killing five children between 1963 and 1965, for which he was sentenced to life imprisonment in 1966, Brady wrote a highly controversial book in 2001, titled *The Gates of Janus: Serial Killing and its Analysis*, and it is in this book – part murder confession, part philosophical treatise on serial killing – that Brady drew on extensive personal experience as well as decades' worth of professional research – or so he claimed – to make the above generalisation. Hence, you might be even more surprised to find that, despite his expertise, his generalisation is not true, not in the case of Scotland's fictional serial killers anyway.

Of course, the fact that Brady was born in Glasgow does not make him an ambassador to Scottish serial killers, nor indeed to their fictional counterparts. He is, however, articulating a popular assumption, one created and propagated by such influential opinion makers as Hannibal Lecter and Brady himself. So if you were expecting to find the likes of these power-oriented serial killers in the previous pages, you will have been either disappointed or relieved, depending on your mental health. Either way, you are likely to have been surprised by the time you got to the last of the ten novels discussed in these pages, for even if you found *Natural Causes* to be a good example of Brady's average type, you will have found it to be the *only* example of a power-oriented serial killer, and one out of ten is hardly average.

One out of ten is a negligible minority, especially in view of the fact that this single example sits on the paranormal fringe of serial killer fiction. See, in that regard, too, Oswald's novel is exceptional.

Despite the diversity of Scottish serial killer fiction, demon killers are few and far between in this literature. In fact, the average Scottish serial killer novel goes nowhere near the paranormal, just like the average Scottish serial killer, at least the fictional kind, goes nowhere near Brady's Nietzschean philosophy. Sure, some of the serial killers in this chapter aspire to greatness, but, as I hope to have shown, only Oswald's demon has Nietzsche's will to power, and even this superhuman monster fails to achieve it, fails because – just like its human compatriots, and unlike Nietzsche's Übermensch – it has neither the vision nor the discipline to rise above good and evil.

This, then, brings us to the most significant deviation from Brady's average. Not a single one of the serial killers discussed in this chapter follows Nietzsche's lead to transcend his or her entrenched notions of good and evil, not even those who seem to transcend their will to power by turning into moral crusaders, like Brookmyre's and Kerr's killers who only turn to violence in order to set their societies onto a better, more wholesome course. Yet since neither of them quits his killing campaign when conscientious objectors point out the heavy moral losses which their societies have suffered on account of those campaigns, it is obvious that not even these supposedly righteous killers accept the principle of Nietzsche's Übermensch that the goodness or badness of an action is determined by the value of the outcome. Instead, they retreat behind the serial killer's two typical intellectual bulwarks: sophistry and self-aggrandisement.

In other words, the Nietzschean qualities of determination and perseverance under discipline, where apparent, are put in the service of other ambitions than the will to power, which is to say that the average serial killer in Scottish literature is either hedonistic or mission-oriented. With Brookmyre, Anderson, Moffat, and Douglas Lindsay, four out of ten Scottish serial killer novelists write about hedonists. And with Kerr, Armstrong, Rankin, Robertson, and Frederic Lindsay, five out of ten write about mission-oriented serial killers. So not only is Oswald the only one to write about a power-oriented serial killer. If you favour the rational explanation outlined in the previous pages, he is also the only one to write about the visionary type. And these proportions remain much the same if you include Val McDermid and Stuart MacBride, as I hope to show in the final section of this chapter by cross-examining their perhaps most iconic serial killers, one of whom represents the hedonistic type, the other the mission-oriented type.

Before I do so, however, I ought to clarify that this preference for two types of serial killer does not necessarily constitute more than a superficial mainstream – or two – in the Scottish serial killer novel. Although, for those who wish to see such a mainstream, I might as well point out that the vast majority of these serial killer narratives are put in the form of the police novel. In fact, with the exception of Frederic Lindsay, who puts his in the form of the PI novel, they all do. So the vast majority of these novels reflect an international trend among serial killer novels which has been growing for over three decades, as Lee Horsley, an expert in the history of crime fiction, reminds us in her essay 'From Sherlock Holmes to Present,' where she notes that serial killers "have, post-1970s, been increasingly incorporated into investigative narratives in what is often a fairly formulaic way, reliable providers of a lurid trail of corpses, and have been a particularly useful ingredient in police procedurals."[313]

One reason for the serial killer's usefulness in this literary context is that he or she provides not just a lurid trail of corpses, i.e. a series of attention-grabbing crimes which justifies the continued involvement of a large cast of cops. Perhaps more importantly, a serial killer also provides a clear sense of unity to the many criss-crossing efforts and subplots of a multi-tasking team of investigators, and that is why serial killers make such few appearances in less populated forms of crime fiction, like the private investigator novel. Or to put it in the words of the cultural critic Leonard Cassuto, "Serial killer stories mainly take the form of procedurals because it doesn't do to have a single detective chasing a serial murderer. Even when undertaken by groups, serial killer hunting is both a complicated job and a lonely pursuit into darkness and isolation."[314]

This brings us to the other main reason for the serial killer's usefulness in police procedurals. Unlike a private investigator, a team of police investigators can conceivably hunt one serial killer after another. Whereas a private investigator is unlikely ever to be hired to hunt a serial killer – and lucky to survive the first encounter without the backup of other investigators – a team of police investigators is not only extremely likely to be put in charge of such a hunt but just as likely to emerge from the experience with the necessary expertise to lead the hunt on the next serial killer. So a police novelist who specialises his or her investigators in serial killer hunting can construct an entire series around this one literary device, and there are few things a writer of (serial killer) police fiction loves more than a series. If this sounds like speculation, it is borne out by the fact that – with the exception of Frederic Lindsay, who alone stages a serial killer hunt in a standalone PI novel, and Kerr, who alone stages a serial killer hunt in a standalone police novel – every writer in this chapter incorporates his or her serial killer in a police novel which is itself part of a series.

As I hope to have shown, however, this does not mean that they incorporate their serial killers in 'a fairly formulaic way', as Horsley noted above when talking about an international trend in serial killer fiction. Far from it, every one of the Scottish writers investigated here accommodates his or her serial killer in a mainstream-defying multitude of genre niches. Kerr's serial killer novel can also be read as a techno-philosophical thought experiment, Rankin's as a gothic frontier narrative, Douglas Lindsay's as a genre satire of a barbershop noir death junky thriller, Armstrong's as a mystery of temperament and attribution bias, Brookmyre's as a literary hate crime on 21st century celebrity culture, Robertson's as an amoral journal of obsession, Anderson's as a CSI murder mystery, Moffat's as an international adventure story, and Frederic Lindsay's as a feminist rewriting of the Jack the Ripper case or an existential novel about last year's man and his alienation in fin de siècle Glasgow. Multifaceted – not formulaic – is the word to describe the ways in which Scottish writers have incorporated serial killers into investigative narratives.

Perhaps surprisingly, it is also the word to describe their representation of victimhood. Rather than make their serial killers in the image of Scottish bogeymen such as Christy Cleek and Sawney

Bean, the writers in this chapter all distance themselves from these medieval forefathers and national stereotypes of murderous anti-Englishness. Not one of their serial killers is some territorial Scot who kills trespassing Englishmen in the nationalist folklore tradition. In fact, not one of them kills *anyone* just because the victim is English. Not one of them has a suspiciously high tally of English victims, and, as if to completely disown the heritage of anti-English bigotry personified by the above bogeymen, not one of the serial killers in this chapter is some monstrous Englishman who victimises innocent Scots. Far from it, in eight out of ten cases, Scots kill Scots, and the only reason for the two exceptions, it seems, is realism. Kerr's story is set in England, so his killer and most of his victims are English, while Moffat's backstory is set in the United States of America, so his killer and victims, as far as they are known, are American.

Speaking of realism, not one of the writers in this chapter peddles the fiction that serial killing is about insane men killing innocent women. That is to say, not one of them is guilty of the casual gender stereotyping which is so often propagated in serial killer fiction, at times even as subtly as above in my use of the word fore*fathers*. Male serial killers do feature in two thirds of the novels in this chapter, but not one of them kills only women. Likewise, in the other cases not one of the female serial killers focuses on women. So, unlike many of their American contemporaries, not one of these Scottish writers relies solely on what Cassuto calls "the aesthetic value of adult female victims as vehicles of sympathetic identification."[315] And half of them do not even go for the gendered sympathy vote at all, since they make their killers target male victims only.

As for the emotionally perhaps most powerful genre convention – the late relief triggered by the killer's last-minute death – nine out of ten writers in this chapter do not let their killers die just to reassure their readers that the uncomfortable world in which the killers' crimes are set does not exist beyond their stories' conclusion. Sure, two thirds of the killers do die, but in nine out of ten cases the story has a rather discomforting diegetic afterlife in the mind of the reader, because at least one protagonist is left feeling guilty. And as long as at least one protagonist arrives at the official end of a story feeling guilty, chances are that readers will be curious enough about this protagonist's guilt to keep thinking about what led to the story's escalation of violence – or at least about where the protagonist with the haunting sense of guilt went wrong.

In Scottish serial killer fiction, this protagonist is usually the lead investigator, and he or she is usually left feeling guilty for having been morally corrupted by the killer – or for having made the critical mistake which led to the killer's escape. Alternatively, the one left feeling guilty is the killer. As both Robertson and Douglas Lindsay illustrate, the memory of having committed a capital crime, and having repeated it multiple times, can lead to a sense of guilt which for some is the only truly inescapable punishment, and in both cases this is likely to make not just the protagonist think about his crime beyond its commission. Yet perhaps even more discomforting than this extended reflection on the killer's guilt is the fact that – in Brookmyre and Kerr – two of Scotland's most successful writers demonstrate that the person who is left feeling guilty can also be the reader. After all, even a reader who does not object to the methods of these serial killers might dwell on their motives with a discomforting sense of guilt at living placidly in a society which produces, if not deserves, such violent moral guardians. As for readers who do object to violence, I hope to have shown that you are still likely to read a Scottish serial killer novel with at least a sense of moral discomfort, and that this discomfort is unlikely to end with the killer's death.

In stark contrast, an American serial killer novel is far more likely to end on a note of reassurance, even though its representation of violence and victimhood is far more sexually charged. There, the serial killer is usually a sexual deviant who stalks women from all-American families and deprives them of their purity when he defiles their nubile bodies in death, either by savagely mutilating their sex organs or by sadistically committing necrophilic obscenities. So it is fair to say that the average American serial killer novel portrays, with considerable prurience as Cassuto observes, "an imaginary murderer who ferociously attacks an imaginary family of exaggerated warmth, cohesion, and security." And since the serial killer represents "what we're afraid of,"[316] it follows that the average American audience is most afraid of sex crimes. More to the point, however, from the fact that the sex killer is usually caught or killed in the end, whereupon moral purity is restored, it follows that the average American author sees the individual, not society, as the problem. Figuratively speaking, then, in the average American serial killer novel, serial murder is a social sickness which starts with the individual sicko/psycho – a man who is typically the personification of a lethal sex pest – and with his detention or death this social sickness ends, as does all consideration of its causes.

Meanwhile, in the Scottish cases investigated in this chapter, only one half of the serial killers is dangerously psychopathic, only one third of them is sexually perverted, and only one tenth of them is written off as terminally evil. Of course, as I hope to have shown, this does not necessarily mean that, in nine out of ten Scottish cases, we are asked to see killers as victims, side with them, forgive them for their killings, or feel that we, too, may be capable of their crimes, though those are all possible responses in Robertson's, Brookmyre's, Kerr's, and Frederic Lindsay's cases. What it generally means is that – with the exception of Anderson who treats her serial killer as an evil aberration of nature rather than nurture – all the writers I have examined in the previous pages treat serial killers as symptoms of a greater social malady, whether or not they portray them as mentally sick.

To one extent or another, nine out of ten Scottish serial killer novelists ask their readers to consider whether those of us who ignore the real world's cycles of violence might be partially responsible, not for other people's genetic predispositions to violent crime, but for letting the sick live in communities in which such predispositions can develop and destroy countless lives because they go undiagnosed and undiscussed. As for readers who are immune to such authorial challenges, they, too, are likely to think about the killer's case beyond novel's end, for it raises another uncomfortably open question, and this one concerns all of us: if it took such a lot of good investigating, and typically such a lot of good luck, just to detect this one specimen, how many as yet undetected serial killers are still out there?

So, when we look at the bigger picture, an interesting and perhaps surprising commonality becomes evident among Scottish serial killer novelists. In stark contrast to their American contemporaries, who have largely defined the literature's reputation and development over the past 60 odd years, and who mostly seem to suggest that in the end all is well because it – the killer – is caught or killed, most Scots suggest that it – the problem – is still out there. And this stark contrast brings me to an important qualification, which is why I have taken McDermid and MacBride out of the above picture. Looking side by side at the two most famous Scottish serial killer novelists of their generation, I hope that two rarely noted facts, which I may inadvertently have further obscured by throwing these writers in with the rest of their contemporaries, will become obvious. One, there are internationally renowned Scots who write the American type of serial killer novel, and two, the American and Scottish types can be similarly successful in spite of their differences.

In the final section of this chapter, then, I will look at McDermid's arguably most representative novel as a representation of the classic American type and MacBride's as one of the classic Scottish type. Before I do so, however, I wish to reiterate a point which I have repeatedly made in previous chapters and hope to have done so implicitly in this one, too. National typology rarely does justice to any one novel or novelist. What I hope it does here, instead, is offer a cumulative definition, for as the examples in this chapter should show, the problem of defining the Scottish serial killer novel is bigger than one word, even if that word is 'Scottish'. The problem is that *any* one word would imply the existence of a single mainstream in this literature, when in fact the many genre crossovers which I have tried to chart in the examples above show that this would be a superficial mainstream at best.

At worst, it would be a false generalisation. To guard against this in any case, but especially in that of the country's two most commonly associated exponents of serial killer fiction, I will try to show in the following pages that there is in this form no widespread positive identification with any one literary tradition, just like there is no widespread negative identification with any unifying anti-foreign aesthetic. Much like their contemporaries working in detective and police fiction, Scottish serial killer novelists, by and large, are not at work on any joint genre-building project. Instead, they tend to pick and mix their topics as well as their techniques. So, while there are certainly those whose significant commercial or critical success can create the first impression of a definitive mainstream, even McDermid's and MacBride's combined success has not unified the multidirectional course of the Scottish serial killer novel.

THE FINAL CROSS-EXAMINATION: VAL MCDERMID & STUART MACBRIDE – *THE MERMAIDS SINGING & FLESH HOUSE*

etween them, Val McDermid and Stuart MacBride seem to define the Scottish serial killer novel. McDermid's best-known series has now run for 20 years, MacBride's for 10, and in this time both have made their authors household names at home and abroad, so it seems fair to say that their reputations precede them wherever they or their books go. According to said reputations, they both see violence in the dramatisation of vice as a literary virtue. They both rely heavily on horror, disgust, and a clear division between good and bad. And they both specialise in investigative narratives which hinge on the abnormally normal actions and appearances of psychopathic serial killers. So, it is not surprising that they have often been associated with one another, both at home, abroad, and in a lot of airport book shops in between.

What *is* surprising, given these shared reputations, is that their similarities go only as far as their mutual embrace of these basic genre conventions. As I hope to show in the following cross-examination of their most representative novels – McDermid's *The Mermaids Singing* (1995) and MacBride's *Flesh House* (2008) – Scotland's most celebrated exponents of serial killer fiction sit on opposite sides of the fence with regard to almost all the intricate ethics and aesthetics which set novels like theirs apart from the literature's legion of anti-intellectual, cliché-driven, and trend-chasing would-be page-turners. Before I discuss all these differences, though, I should define what I mean by 'most representative'. Not only do these two novels represent the definitive characteristics of their respective series, but more than anything else published by either McDermid or MacBride, these two novels also represent their authors' literary identities, their narrative strategies and recurrent themes as well as their individual styles and aesthetic foibles.

Indeed, *The Mermaids Singing* is not only the most representative of McDermid's many serial killer novels because it introduces her serial protagonist, clinical psychologist and profiler Dr Tony Hill, and signals her intent to spend the rest of the series focusing on personal dramas which will, as in this case, slow down her team's hunt for hedonistic serial killers. *The Mermaids Singing* is also McDermid's most representative piece of writing because it gives a particularly clear impression of her characteristic fondness for a multi-plotted nonlinear narration which relies heavily on expositional devices such as interior monologues. In contrast, *Flesh House* is not only the most representative of MacBride's many serial killer novels because it demonstrates his characteristic fondness for dramatic dialogue and briefly uses it to dramatise the key fragment of his serial protagonist's backstory when Detective Sergeant Logan McRae finally has his long-awaited run-in with the serial killer who once, briefly, killed him. *Flesh House* is also MacBride's most representative piece of writing because it gives a particularly clear impression of his disorientatingly kaleidoscopic shifts in perspective and his sparing use of expository devices, a narrative strategy which, as usual, speeds up his team's hunt for a mission-oriented serial killer.

Both of these novels, then, can be read as representations of the authors' larger contributions to the literature. Yet they can also be read as representations of two different types of serial killer novel, the American and the Scottish. In this reading, *The Mermaids Singing* represents the classic American serial killer novel, as it tells of a sex killer who sadistically stalks, rapes, maims, and kills innocent people, yet in the end all is well because it – the killer – is caught and killed. In contrast, *Flesh House* represents the classic Scottish serial killer novel, as it tells of an asexual killer who kills enough people with impunity to cause concern that the world might be full of serial killers who somehow avoid suspicion, and in the end it – the problem – is not contained. Objectification is key in both cases, but as I intend to demonstrate in this comparative reading, McDermid dramatises its effects on individuals, MacBride those on society.

This essential difference is perhaps most evident in their opposite approaches to sex, even though these approaches may at first seem identical, seeing as both authors resist genre convention to cast a woman in the role of the killer, and neither of them reveals this until the very end. Yet long before this commonality is revealed, the objectification of these women takes opposite dramatic effects. McDermid focuses on her killer's modus operandi, "a bizarre parody of love."[317] And as Elizabeth and Harold Schechter observe in their essay 'Killing with Kindness: Nature, Nurture, and the Female Serial Killer', in such cases "we see a dark, grotesquely distorted version of traits that have been traditionally associated with women: fatal care-taking, lethal nurturing, depraved romantic devotion."[318] All of these are on full display in the detailed interior monologues of McDermid's serial killer and the graphic post-mortem descriptions of her victims, so there are signs of the killer's unstable sexual identity long before we are told that, when she selectively targets gay men, she does so to convert these objects of her desire to her 'straight' love, and when she violently kills them, she does so because she herself felt violated and objectified prior to her sex change, back when she "was a gay man who couldn't cope with his sexuality because of cultural and family conditioning."[319]

Prior to this late psychoanalysis, however, McDermid is less interested in such gender politics than she is in the domestic dramas played out in the private lives of the killer and her main adversaries, Detective Inspector Carol Jordan and psychological profiler Dr Tony Hill. Carol and Tony analyse everyone, but most of all themselves and increasingly each other, so even though a serial killer is on the loose, their self-absorption soon leads to a distracting romantic tension in their professional relationship. To relieve said tension, Carol regularly discusses her feelings with Nelson, the other male figure in her life, so we soon learn that "the ending of her last relationship had dealt her self-esteem too seriously a blow for her to enter on another one lightly... Carol wasn't about to risk her heart again."[320] And yet this is exactly what she ends up doing, though not because Nelson recommends it. Nelson does not recommend anything, be it because – like most of the people in Carol's life – Nelson does not care about her emotional needs, or because Nelson is a cat, and cats cannot talk.

Either way, Carol has no one to talk her out of her romantic daydreams, so she ends up risking her heart again as soon as she has managed to convince herself that Tony is a good catch. If this seems surprising, given the previous heart-to-heart with her cat, it must be even more surprising for readers who can remember that Carol is meant to be a seasoned investigator trained in psychoanalysis, and how could we not remember? McDermid reminds us of these fine qualities whenever Carol stands up to one of the story's many misogynists in positions of power, and Carol does so in almost every chapter. So, for reasons of character consistency as well as professional competency, she should be well able to see that Tony is standoffish around her, not because he is secretly in love with her or because he is in a secret relationship with another woman, but because he cannot reciprocate any romantic feelings. Yet for it to be even remotely credible that their romantic sub-plot should run the length of the entire novel, Carol has to discredit McDermid's praise of her emotional intelligence and see Tony as a potential lover, despite the many signs that Tony sees himself as a "sexual and emotional cripple."[321] And that is what he sees himself as on a good day. On a bad day, he sees himself as a potential serial killer, as he tells the real killer in one of their many imaginary conversations, "I'm the poacher turned gamekeeper. It's only hunting you that keeps me from being you."[322]

In between such faintly masochistic self-flagellation sessions, we learn from the killer's journal that she is just as obsessively concerned about her compromised sexuality as Tony is about his. Thus, when she turns both herself and Tony into sex objects by repeatedly calling him to have anonymous phone sex, we know that she is doing so in a gendered protest against the profiler's objectification of her. Yet it is only due to her irregular journal transcripts, in which she tries to rationalise this hidden agenda, and the parallel narrative strand, in which the investigators try to make sense of it, that the romantic sub-plot does not steer the entire novel into Mills & Boon territory. Seemingly unsure of which way to go, it sits at a genre intersection, where parts of it are pushing in the direction of feminist literature, such as the repeatedly stalling cross-departmental investigation which Carol and Tony are struggling to coordinate while also having to contend with the endemic machismo of a police force which is only belatedly and rather reluctantly entering the era of gender equality.

The parts with greater narrative momentum, however, are pushing towards mystery and romance. Before long, these parts command most of the main protagonists' attention, and presumably that of most readers. First, there are the above-mentioned phone sex scenes, and even before Tony is aware of the caller's identity, he is uncomfortably preoccupied with the idea that sex can be used aggressively as a weapon to gain control over both one's object of desire and one's rampant sense of inadequacy. Then, there are the increasingly hot-tempered interior monologues in which Tony repeatedly interrogates himself on his motives for obeying the caller's orders to objectify her, only to arrive at the uncomfortable conclusion that he is doing so in the vain hope that it may cure his impotence. And then there are the uncomfortable complications when Carol finds out about Tony's little secret and carries her confused personal grievances about being reduced to an object in a man's power game into their increasingly strained professional relationship.

Given this focus on individuals, on how they experience the many discomforts of objectification, and on the idea that all of these discomforts can be contained when the responsible individual is held to account, it should come as no surprise that the serial killer's capture is demanded by the media and pursued by the police as though the general risk of random murder could be contained in the shape of an individual killer. At the same time, however, it should come as no surprise that this intensely debated murder inquiry gradually loses focus and its suspense moves towards nil. After all, despite the many intense debates, there is barely any dramatic development on the police front, and this leaves a hole at the centre of the novel which is gradually filled by the above outlined gender dance of a sexually frustrated woman chasing a sexually frustrated man chasing a sexually frustrated woman in seemingly never-ending cycles of melodramatic romance, masochistic auto-eroticism, and morbid rape fantasies.

In *Flesh House*, meanwhile, MacBride focuses on how a case of serial murder can affect a wider community and how rapidly it – be it the case or the community – can spin out of control. While making his police team investigate a series of similarly gruesome murders, he explores the discomforting idea that all it takes to incite mass panic and civil disobedience is for an individual to be turned into an object of terror, a serial killer who has no clear victim profile, a subhuman monster which might murder anyone anywhere at any time. To illustrate aspects of this mass panic and civil disobedience, MacBride focuses less on the cops' sex lives and the killer's murder motive than on the public's sense of vulnerability at a time of faceless violence. Rather than let his investigators sublimate their stress in sex dramas or spend most of their time speculating about the killer's secret desires, he lets an unusually large number of witnesses and suspects articulate their anxieties for themselves, and they do so with a credibility rarely found in serial killer fiction – the credibility of unintended comedy – as when a particularly anxious citizen witnesses his female neighbour being attacked by a home intruder, contacts emergency services, and alerts them that the intruder is wearing a Margaret Thatcher Halloween mask, just like the serial killer is said to wear, yet when the police arrive at the potential crime scene, that mask is all the intruder is wearing as he climbs off the prone woman and anxiously explains that, far from preying on an innocent woman, he is playing a serial killer sex game with his wife.

What makes this sense of false alarm even more acute is that MacBride also illustrates how sneakily it can spread through the wider community. One particularly unconventional way of illustrating this is his use of double page collages of fictional newspaper clippings. Spliced between chapters, these collages provide an up to date overview of the case's media coverage. So, as we turn the pages, we can see even in a brief glance at these clippings how sensational headlines and alarmist rhetoric can sneak a barely containable alarm into people's perception of a serial killer. Two facts rarely acknowledged in serial killer fiction are thus instantly apparent. One, some degree of exposure to such crass reportage is almost inevitable. Two, any exposure will have a negative effect, even on those who do not wish to follow the case yet hear or read about it in passing and cannot help but worry that their community may be under serious threat. In this case, that worry turns into alarm when one journalist's spurious claim is confirmed by several others and everyone suddenly seems to be convinced that their community is being threatened by "the most notorious serial killer in Scottish history."[323] So due to these interspersed newspaper clippings, there is a palpable sense of how rapidly alarm can escalate to a level where the police have to spend as much time trying to convince the public that the threat is under control as they spend trying to actually bring it under control.

At the same time, of course, they have to try to contain the collateral damage, and in this case, that becomes ever more difficult as the papers report that human meat may have entered the food chain. First, alarm turns into hysteria, and when a body part is found in a butcher shop, even a policeman starts spreading panic by shouting: "PEOPLE HAVE BEEN EATING IT!"[324] Then, the murder weapon is identified and disgust turns into despair after an Environmental Health Officer explains the potential implications: "If he's used a pithing cane there's a risk of variant CJD. Then there's HIV. And Hepatitis C doesn't die unless you cook it at one hundred and sixty degrees, for about three-quarters of an hour… There's going to be a lot of people wanting blood tests."[325] Amid the ensuing panic, crime statistics soon soar to the point at which the afore-quoted policeman can only despair, "Muggings, rapes, assaults, shoplifting, vandalism, extortion… The whole city's going to hell."[326] And as if to demonstrate that no one is safe from such collateral damage, this policeman suffers the worst of it himself.

His name is DI David Insch, and his tragedy is that, when the serial killer first surfaced 20 years ago, Insch beat a confession out of the wrong suspect. Now, this suspect has been released from prison and taken his violent revenge, an attack systematically targeted at everything Insch held dear, so Insch's "house's been trashed, his dog's been put to sleep, he's got two traumatised kids, his wife's in hospital with a breakdown, and his daughter's dead."[327] Yet rather than focus on this individual case, MacBride contextualises it in several other examples of what can happen when human beings reduce one another to mere objects in a bid to pursue their personal satisfaction. These examples range from moments of dark humour – as when the afore-mentioned police raid abruptly ends in awkward small-talk about a nude couple's fetish for fake serial killer sex – to moments of serious horror – as when the real killer whispers the story of her childhood abuse to one of her victims.

What contextualises all of this objectification is that, all along, a TV crew is filming a documentary about the police investigation. So every time a cop interacts with the crew to request that the cameras be turned off or bits of the footage be cut, we are reminded that every story is the object of editing, whether it be edited by somebody in the media, as in the case of TV and newspaper reporting, or by some trick of the memory, as in the killer's case. Either way, we are repeatedly reminded that everything we read in *Flesh House*, and everything its protagonists experience, is heavily mediated by various attempts at perception management. So it is easy to see how the idea of The Serial Killer can become much bigger and more terrifying than the impression which the sad little person responsible for the killings would make if outed in public.

Of course, the idea of the serial killer is also artificially inflated in *The Mermaids Singing*. In both cases, after all, the killers are publicly objectified with nicknames which make them seem more like archetypes of horror than the mentally ill individuals they really are. McDermid's is nicknamed 'The Queer Killer', MacBride's 'The Flesher', and both of these nicknames – with their definite articles and capital letters – suggest that an individual thus objectified is best thought of in a categorical sense, because according to the semantic logic of such nicknames, each killer is first and foremost a behavioural type, a thing which is objectively knowable, not a person with subjective traits which make him or her unique. That, however, is as far as the similarities go, because unlike MacBride, McDermid barely looks beyond the effect this dehumanisation has on individuals. For instance, after Tony gives a press interview in which he categorises the killer as the mission-oriented type which, in this case, kills closet homosexuals in some perverse crusade to purify society, McDermid focuses less on the anxieties which this persecution theory creates in the gay community – and even less on the wider social ramifications of such violent attacks on minority groups – than she does on the killer's personal issues and petulant response to being falsely categorised: "He had insulted me. He had poured scorn on me, refusing to acknowledge the extent of my achievements. I couldn't help but see his disposal as a challenge."[328]

Of course, the man to whom she is referring here is Tony, and of course the killer spends the rest of the novel trying to outsmart him. This is, after all, the long awaited cartoon showdown between the nifty superhero and the narcissistic supervillain, so it comes as no surprise when Tony reveals that he only let the press categorise the killer as a sad little homophobe in order to provoke a careless reaction which would lead to her capture. Meanwhile, we learn that the killer is a hedonist who set out to find a husband but instead found an unexpected pleasure in killing unsuitable candidates. That, and an unexpected rage at Tony's provocation, so she decides to capture, torture, and kill him, which, of course, is exactly the type of behaviour Tony expected, so again it comes as no surprise when he acts on his resolution that "It was a battle of wits now, his insight against the killer's stockade. Somewhere in the pattern of these crimes there lay a labyrinthine path straight to a murderer's heart. Somehow, Tony had to tread that path, wary of misleading shadows, careful to avoid straying into treacherous undergrowth."[329] Against the background of this recurrent hunting theme, not even such flowery language can hide the truth about Tony. What he says about the killer – when he still thinks that the killer is a man – could equally be said about himself: "He's desperate to be the best… He just doesn't go for the easy option."[330]

As if to be expected, this competitive egomania sets the two of them on a collision course, so once again it goes to show that, in McDermid's book, serial killing and its investigation is all about individuals. This impression is further reinforced when it turns out that the hedonistic killer is also a list murderer, for as the cultural critic Cassuto observes, "List murderers look like scarily random serial murderers until the pattern, usually based on revenge, shows up." As in most cases, such a pattern only shows up in *The Mermaids Singing* "after the members of the worlds within and outside the book… get a chance to contemplate the disturbing possibility of random murder."[331] The disturbing possibility in this case is that The Queer Killer could be killing gay men at random, yet before the members of the worlds within and outside the book get any real chance to contemplate just how disturbing this possibility is, Tony shows us the killer's pattern and thus reassures us that she is only interested in specific individuals: men she might want to marry – and Tony.

Since all of this is discussed at length long before it happens, none of it comes as a surprise, nor is any of it lastingly disturbing, since Tony not only narrows down the list of potential victims but also reassures us that the killer is an exceptionally evil case, i.e. that only this particular individual is capable of such disturbing crimes. Hence, we need not worry that similar crimes have been or will be committed elsewhere, and the idea that more of them might be committed by this particular killer is laid to rest at her eventual death – which of course is another foregone conclusion, given that we know from her interior monologues and journal entries that she intends to fight Tony to the death, and we already know from the fact that Tony will return in the next book of the series that he will survive this death match.

In contrast, MacBride offers no reassurance whatsoever. By focusing not on the individual but on the idea of the serial killer, he shows what can happen when a community alarmed by amateur psychoanalysis starts suspecting anyone who even remotely fits the type. What happens is that the public suspect the wrong people and the police waste valuable time and resources on chasing up false leads, as when the press – having already turned the killer into a larger than life caricature of evil by nicknaming it The Flesher and dining out on the fact that this Flesher has been seen wearing a butcher's apron and a Margaret Thatcher Halloween mask – alert the public that all the killer's victims have been overweight. As this idea of the killer being "a chubby chaser"[332] gains traction, both the police and the public fixate on the afore-mentioned false suspect, a certain Ken Wiseman, because Wiseman has just been released from prison after serving a sentence for killing several weight watchers, and the afore-mentioned revenge, which he soon takes on DI Insch because the senior policeman falsely typecast him as a prime suspect in a prior case, serves as a sobering reminder of the dangers of letting one's idea of a criminal eclipse individual suspects.

Another example of this danger is what happens when Logan follows up on the 'chubby chaser' lead. In typical MacBride manner, this other example balances the tragic escalation of violence in Insch's case with a sudden swerve into emotional territory rarely accessed by writers of serial killer fiction – comic relief. Upon learning that another convicted serial killer wants to share vital information about Wiseman after getting to know the man in prison, Logan decides to interview this questionable source, even though it is none other than Angus Robertson, also known as the Mastrick Monster, and also known to readers of earlier books in the series as the man who stabbed Logan 23 times and left him for dead. That was three years ago and Logan has long since been resuscitated, as has his career, but now he is willing to risk the latter by using force to extract whatever information Robertson has when he starts playing power games and requests: "Quid pro quo, Sergeant McRae…" Yet rather than pursue the promised information by flattering his informant's evident vanity and joining in the role play which the man clearly has in mind, Logan signals his willingness to resort to violence by telling Robertson in no uncertain terms that he can see through his bullshit: "You're not Hannibal Bloody Lecter: you're a nasty wee shite from Milltimber."[333] And with this reference to Lecter – the prototype of the fictional serial killer – MacBride illustrates what a risky business typology can be.

When a type of criminal behaviour becomes iconic, there is a risk that a 'nasty wee shite' like Angus Robertson will model himself on this type, and chances are that said type behaves in ways for which he himself would have neither the natural instinct nor the creative imagination. What is more, when opinion-makers like the media further inflate our idea of this type, they run the risk of handing over even more power to a 'nasty wee shite' like Angus Robertson, because chances are that by giving new dramatic life to said type, it will command even more authority than it already did – and a lot more than a 'nasty wee shite' like Angus Robertson ever could command as an individual. As a result, more people commit copycat killings, more people mislead investigators, and – while the police, press, and public are distracted by the grim antics of false suspects – more people die.

At the same time, vital clues are missed, so most of us will wrongly expect the killer to be a man, despite the Thatcher mask. And when this mask is lifted to reveal a harmless looking woman, most of us will wrongly expect her to be the visionary type of serial killer, since her irrational talk of imaginary siblings sounds like proof that she is killing in the service of some imagined voice or vision. There is, after all, an infamous precedent for this type of criminal behaviour in *Psycho*, which most of us will know either from having read the 1959 novel by Robert Bloch or from having seen the 1960 movie adaptation by Alfred Hitchcock, or indeed from any number of references to what has since become an iconic story.

In it, to be brief, the central protagonist kills his victims while channelling his dead mother, and something similar seems to be happening in *Flesh House*. Here, too, the killer seems to be slipping in and out of the murderous persona of a family member whom no one suspects, until we eventually learn from a social worker that this family member – a man called 'Jimmy' – is actually a figment of her imagination. "Kelley Elizabeth Souter was a very disturbed young lady when we took her into care, Sergeant. I understand she named 'Jimmy' after her father. Any time she did anything wrong it was always Jimmy's fault."[334] This time, Jimmy is killing people, but as one of his/her brainwashed victims explains, "Jimmy's only doing it to make us pure."[335] And as we eventually learn, Kelley Elizabeth Souter, aka The Flesher, did not start killing people because 'Jimmy' told her to do so, but because she set out on a mission to purify people. Only when the need to deflect blame arose did she resort to the old 'Jimmy' lie. So, for two reasons the ethics of *Flesh House* differ considerably from those of *The Mermaids Singing*: one, MacBride's killer is a mission-oriented serial killer, not a hedonist, which means that she kills for a purpose greater than her own gratification. And two – at this point you should skip to the final paragraph if you do not wish to find out how her story ends – MacBride's killer is not caught, so the disturbing thought of a serial killer being on the loose is ultimately not contained.

On the contrary, the thought leads to an even more disturbing after-thought. Even though The Flesher abandoned her final victim in a bone mill and caused her severe injuries when she made her getaway, this final victim developed Stockholm syndrome – a form of traumatised capture-bonding – during her time in captivity. And since she also seems to be suffering from a severe form of post-traumatic stress disorder as the novel draws to a close, it comes as no surprise when she believes The Flesher's claim that somebody else bears the responsibility for her criminal behaviour because that somebody corrupted her in her formative years. According to The Flesher, that somebody "was my father... Mum died when I was six. And he... he said he had needs."[336] Yet affecting as this history of abuse may be, it does come as a surprise – and as a deeply disturbing one at that – when MacBride revisits this victim in the novel's epilogue and reveals that she is now living alone in a boarded up house where, safe in her reputation as a PTSD sufferer, no one suspects her of completing or indeed continuing The Flesher's mission, yet as we soon find out, that is exactly what she is doing, and doing with gusto. Having tracked down The Flesher's father, she kills him and eats his heart. So, rather than end the novel with the killer's capture, MacBride creates a second killer in her image and thus implies that the consequences of abuse can be as fatal as they are far-reaching.

The premise of *Flesh House*, then, is disturbing both in itself and in the fact that it can have no positive resolution: hurt people hurt people. And nowhere in the novel is this repetition compulsion as visible as it is in its violence. Contrary to that in *The Mermaids Singing* – which is sadistic, elaborate, and protracted – the violence in *Flesh House* is dispassionate, efficient, and short. Whereas The Queer Killer enjoys it, calls her torture dungeon "the pleasure dome," and admires those who "examined the human body so intimately that they could engineer such exquisite and finely calibrated suffering,"[337] The Flesher brings a labourer's coldblooded efficiency to what, for her, has simply become a job. Trained in butchery, she kills not with arcane torture instruments but with an agricultural pithing cane. "Bolt gun shoots a metal rod through the skull… you take a flexible metal rod and shove it in the hole through the brainstem and down into the spine… Then you slit the animal's throat."[338] For The Flesher, then, murder is but a means to an end, not an end in itself. She kills people like cattle because, at the age when we learn how to treat others, she was taught that the personal needs of those with power trump the human rights of those with none. Ever since, she has seen no reason to respect anybody's needs but her own. Focused purely on her mission, she has been trying to purify people whose appearance in the papers made them figures of authority to her. In short, she has been trying – repeatedly and compulsively – to purify the ultimate figure of authority – her father – by proxy.

Meanwhile, The Queer Killer started out as a more easily recognisable type of serial killer, the power-oriented type which most of us will have encountered in any number of American serial killer novels and movies. As the psychoanalyst Carl Goldberg says in his study, *Speaking with the Devil*, most of these power-oriented serial killers are "searching for an apocalyptic sexual orgasm that will compensate – by giving them a sense of power, importance, and superiority – for all the abuse they have suffered."[339] And like these power-oriented killers, The Queer Killer starts her killing campaign with Goldberg's motive in mind. However, after her first murder stimulates a voracious appetite for the sadomasochistic thrill of torturing her victims to death, she focuses more on satiating that appetite than she does on her reasons for selecting her victims – perceived insults to her surgically enhanced femininity, which in her mind aggravate the abuse she suffered as a transgender teenager. So, while there is a commonality between The Flesher and The Queer Killer in the fact that they both reconcile their killings with the feeling of being the abuse*d* – rather than the abuse*r* – only McDermid's hedonist enjoys the role reversal.

In the end, then, The Queer Killer's violent death – delivered by a figure of state authority – can be read as a form of capital punishment, not only for her capital crimes, but also for the perverse pleasure she took in committing them. Thus, despite a few critical comments on the struggle for gender equality in the workplace, *The Mermaids Singing* is ultimately a conservative novel. Meanwhile, The Flesher's unharmed escape, both from the police and from lawful punishment, suggests that *Flesh House* is best read as a subversive novel – a novel which raises questions, not only about the efficacy of law enforcement, but also about the causes of violent crime. And it is one such subversive question which delivers final proof that *The Mermaids Singing* can be read as a representative of the classic American type of serial killer novel, whereas *Flesh House* can be read as a representative of the classic Scottish type.

This question, answered at length in both novels, is perhaps most succinctly phrased in the words of Manuel Vargas, a professor of philosophy and law: "Does madness mean no badness?"[340] In McDermid's case, the answer is a clear no. Though The Queer Killer is diagnosed as suffering from dangerous psychopathy, she defies conventional morality, not only in perverse enjoyment of her impulsive violence, but also in full knowledge of the difference between good and bad. As we know from her journal, she knows that acting on her impulse is bad because her own pleasure comes at the price of other people's pain, and we also know that she can control said impulse well enough to instrumentalise violence in her power game with the investigators, and yet she repeatedly chooses not to control it because she values her own lust more than other people's lives, and for this she is punished.

In MacBride's case, on the other hand, the answer is far less clear. Though The Flesher knows the words 'good' and 'bad', she does not know the moral distinction which sane people take for granted, and at this distance from conventional morality, badness is an intellectual model not remotely relevant. However, by ending his novel with an epilogue which tells a cautionary tale about the vicious cycle of abuse, MacBride rejects the literature's typical, categorical condemnation of the criminal and turns its central question of moral relativism over to us. And rather than make it easy to answer that question, as McDermid does by concentrating on her killer's MO and analysing it as an attempt to replicate a fantasy scheme designed for self-gratification, MacBride makes it hard to judge anyone, or indeed any one concept of morality. As I hope to have shown, he does so by concentrating on a less obvious source of controversy, the collateral damage suffered by a community when a child in foster care – for whom all the typical attachment and maturation changes of adolescence are especially difficult – is so neglected that it deals with developmental stressors by developing a dangerously uncontrollable fantasy life.

The key difference between these two novels, then, is that while *The Mermaids Singing* and *Flesh House* can both be read as case studies of psychopathy, McDermid's diagnostic focus is on the individuals immediately affected by it, whereas MacBride's is expansive enough to take in those individuals as well as the less obvious social and psychological symptoms which are felt in the surrounding community of the novel's real-life setting, Aberdeen. In contrast, McDermid's fictional Bradfield plays no significant part in the story, and since its only distinguishing feature is its cosmopolitanism, predicated on its large and vibrant gay scene, the city might be more at home in the West of the United States than it seems in the North of England. Admittedly, Tony is adamant that "we're not like the Americans… We still have a society where more than ninety per cent of murders are committed by family members or people known to the victims."[341] But as *we*, the readers, already know, in this case the killer represents the other ten per cent – the stranger who strikes out of the blue – and McDermid focuses most of her attention – far more than MacBride does, and indeed far more than most of her compatriots do – on developing this rare type of bogeywoman and exploiting her dramatic potential. As a result, she is rather sketchy on the discomforting fact that the structural healthcare problem which created this killer – or at least allowed the escalation of her violent behaviour to go unnoticed until several innocent people had been killed – cannot be contained by the capture of an individual, much as the investigators' commitment to that capture may be foregrounded for reasons of narrative tension and the promise of a happy end. Hence, with regard to the novels' aesthetics, as with regard to their ethics, *The Mermaids Singing* represents the classic American type of serial killer novel, whereas *Flesh House* defies most of that type's genre conventions. In doing so, as I hope to have shown in this chapter, *Flesh House* typifies the core principles of the Scottish serial killer novel.

CHAPTER FOUR –
THE NOIR NOVEL

Typically, the noir novel avoids both length and judgment as it tells the story of an outsider with little or no agency who is – or soon will be – alone, afraid, angry, amoral, and alienating. The author of such a novel typically tells his or her story with little exposition and no resolution, but with a lot of fragmentation and disorientation, and thus breaks up any residual sense of cause and consequence with a non-linear narrative, the narrator's limited perspective, and his or her questionable reliability.

Stereotypically, the noir novel focuses on how the five attributes listed above lead to the disintegration of the outsider's sense of self as he – for the noir protagonist is stereotypically a man – doggedly makes his way through a dark world that has been the ruin of many a poor man, a world of jive-talking cynics, wise-cracking criminals, and tired salesmen still trying to sell non-noir futures under neon signs advertising 24-hour liquor stores as silent strangers form faceless night-time crowds in silhouetted asphalt jungles forever obscured by clouds and rain, jungles in which anonymous men float in and out of late-night bars wreathed in thick cigarette smoke, vainly hoping to bed some sultry femme fatale sheathed in a thin cocktail dress which will later inevitably be discarded among another man's sweaty bed sheets while down in the dimly lit streets of this eternal purgatory shots ring out and broken human beings die like vermin – pointlessly, instantly forgotten, and never to be mourned.

What *is* mourned is a past which never was, and what that soon leads to is existential dread, inarticulate resentment, radical disengagement, desperate self-annihilation, and rapacious eroticism, none of which in turn leads anywhere near a happy end. That, of course, should come as no surprise, since the noir novel with a happy end has never been written, nor can it be, because it is about life's losers – people who lose, lose repeatedly, and lose big. Some do so because their authors decide to defeat their best efforts by setting their stories in a negatively predetermined universe, others because they make their own decisions yet are denied either the intelligence or the independence they would need to make good ones, and since they are all driven by an ever-increasing desperation, they make one bad decision after another in a life which is little more than a struggle for survival. In both cases, then, things start bad and end worse.

Now, if this quick run-through of noir stereotypes seems as well-worn as a highlight reel of Hollywood pictures from the mid-20th century, it does so for an interesting reason. Literary noir has a shared history with film noir, and though these days the two art forms have little more in common than their name, over the years enough writers have filled their pages with the clichés developed on screen to create a superficial association even in the minds of otherwise educated audiences. This goes back as far as the 1940s, when a fertile, cross-Atlantic discourse started which was to span several decades. As the preeminent scholar of film noir, James Naremore, recaps, "The discourse on American film noir was initiated by two generations of Parisian intellectuals, most of whom declared the form extinct soon after they invented it… Eventually, as old movies became increasingly available on television or in retrospectives, a European image of America was internalised by the Americans themselves. By the 1990s, noir had acquired the aura of art and had evolved into what Dennis Hopper describes as 'every director's favourite genre'."[342] In the meantime, enough writers had borrowed from the dramatic motifs and narrative techniques of those directors for literary noir to be both re-popularised – and in many places re-marketed en masse – as a literary version of film noir, its very own brain child to which it had given birth all those years ago by providing material for movie adaptations.

As a result of this retrospective focus on the halcyon days of film noir, countless cinematic images have been projected on to the term 'noir', so much so that two historical facts have often been overlooked:

one, as indicated above, most literary noir looks nothing like those cinematic images, and two, most of the material which was eventually adapted and re-adapted in noir's cross-fertilisation process was created a long way from the silver screen. As the author and critic Barry Graham points out, "Even while Arthur Conan Doyle was writing his Sherlock Holmes cozies in the 19th Century... his brother-in-law, E.W. Hornung, was writing the dark tales of Raffles, Victorian gentleman and cricket star who moonlights as a burglar. Raffles seems to be a gentleman of leisure, but it's all about surface appearance and desperate avoidance of losing his upper crust status... he is always one theft away from destitution."[343] This border state – noir's raison d'être, its belief that those worth writing about are only ever one step away from the abyss – has become both a popular aesthetic attitude and a counter-cultural space for the most subversive of minds.

Buoyed by the surge of sensational American pulp fiction – which was primarily addressed to working-class men and popularised in the 1920s – and buoyed further by the surge of the literary crime novel – which was promoted by middle-class book clubs and popularised in the 1930s – tough guy writers like Carroll John Daly and Dashiell Hammett pioneered a prose style in those early decades of the 20th century which soon became known as 'hard-boiled'. Throughout the remainder of that century, this heightened passion for literary toughness was channelled into books and screenplays about the lowest reaches of human nature by such notable writers as James M. Cain, Horace McCoy, W.R. Burnett, Cornell Woolrich, Erskine Caldwell, Day Keene, Dorothy B. Hughes, Jim Thompson, James Hadley Chase, Chester Himes, Charles Williams, John D. MacDonald, David Goodis, Charles Willeford, Patricia Highsmith, Peter Rabe, Gil Brewer, James McKimmey, Elmore Leonard, Derek Raymond, Donald E. Westlake, Lawrence Block, Ted Lewis, and James Ellroy. Together, these noirists paved the way for 21st century noir by processing a growing awareness of violence in the period around World War II, a return to consumer economies, a rise in crime rates, the ideological tensions of both the Red Scare and the Cold War, and a widespread popularisation of psychoanalysis.

Before I go on, however, I ought to clarify something. Though it is occasionally useful for reference purposes, and often inevitable for practical reasons, it is also potentially misleading to discuss noir as though it was a specific cycle of films or fictions associated with a particular aesthetic period or national tradition, i.e. one readily defined and easily agreed creative and critical concept. In truth, the only thing which is *not* debatable about noir is that it is the French word for 'black'. Everything else, from its chief influences to its generic conventions, has been debated ad nauseam, often with the laudable intention of saving arguably underrated work from obscurity, but just as often with a lamentable tendency towards antiquarianism. The problem, as Naremore explains, is this: "a concept that was generated ex post facto has become part of a worldwide mass memory."[344] So, as the noir writer Joe Lansdale concludes, "You can't point at noir and call it one thing."[345]

This, of course, does not mean that the term should not be used to describe or discuss art which is identifiably noir. It simply means that we need to think of noir in broader terms. "*Noir*," as Naremore reminds us, "functions rather like big words such as *romantic* or *classic*. An ideological concept with a history all its own, it can be used to describe a period, a movement, and a recurrent style."[346] And as this broadening of the term suggests, the on-going discussions about how to define such 'big words' arises from an old confusion about the way in which all generic concepts are formed. To be clear, people do not form them by grouping things objectively. They create extensive networks of relationship between things which are often produced in different periods and places by using their subjective forms of association. Thus, over time, several more or less authoritative definitions enter our cultural discourse.

In the case of noir, there may seem to be no room for this democratic process, seeing as something is either black or not, and yet endless debates have been held about how *much* black has to be in something for it to be noir. With no end in sight, it seems that we are unlikely ever to have 'the right' definition of noir, only a number of more or less interesting uses of the term. The challenge, then, is to find the most interesting and informative of these uses, which I hope to do in these pages, not by distilling the work of the afore-mentioned noirists into some abstract formula, but by deferring to noir's unique metaphysics. In noir, after all, more than in any other form of narrative art, character precedes plot. Not only do internal developments take precedence over external events. They also radically change the way in which we read those events as they reconstruct the narrator. Thus, while the noir plot is typically simple enough, the telling of it is not. Typically, it is complicated by five attributes – the noir protagonist's tendency to be alone, afraid, angry, amoral, and alienating.

Perhaps the first of these '5 As' to catch the reader's attention – and certainly the first one to catch the noir protagonist's attention – is that he is typically born alone. Then, he typically struggles alone, and if it comes to it, he typically dies alone. I say 'he' because the noir protagonist is typically a man, and as such he is alone both individually and universally, for as he tries in vain to understand – let alone assert – his masculinity, the woman in his life will typically remind him not only of his personal loneliness but also of man's general failure to share his loneliness with other men. To make his life even lonelier, there is typically someone to exploit this failure, the so-called femme fatale who, as Naremore says, "gets her name from France; her most important ancestors can be found in the pornographic fantasies of the Marquis de Sade and in the novels of Emile Zola and the naturalists."[347] Like these worldly ancestors, today's femme fatale embodies not just sexual availability but also sexual empowerment, for not only does she break the man's heart by sharing or threatening to share with other men the intimacy she once let him believe was uniquely theirs. She also breaks his spirit by letting him feel his impotence to hold on to her, his failure to be enough of a man to be worthy of her love. And to let him feel the full force of this emotionally and psychologically crippling loneliness, she typically does so post-coitus.

So much for the man's hurt in noir's losing game of love. There is, of course, another side to it. As the noir writer and critic Damien Seaman points out, "Maleness, the idea of it and the reality of it, dominates noir fiction more than any other genre I can think of. Because of this, the treatment of women in noir can be unsettling. At best it betrays a range of psycho-sexual obsessions, at worst unthinking misogyny. Far from being a stereotype, the femme fatale is the key to understanding a woman's place in the noir world. If she's not the instigator of the crime, the spider in her web, then she's a victim of male brutality or abuse." And what makes these extremes even more unsettling is that, as Seaman adds, "Behind the sexy femme fatale image lies the male's cry that woman is the cause of all his grief."[348] In other words, noir women are typically written by male authors or resented by male protagonist of such low emotional intelligence that they are beyond the reach of these men – not their physical reach, but the reach of their ability to make a connection which is not either abusive or fraught with anxiety. Hence, the complexity of aggression found in most noir differs significantly from that found in most crime fiction. In noir, it typically comes from the individual's irremediable sense of exclusion, so it has less to do with narrative than with ethical complexity.

Likewise, as Lee Horsley points out in her seminal study, *The Noir Thriller*, the general plot predicament of the noir narrative typically has "less to do with a desperate search for some way out of an economic impasse than with an irremediable sense of exclusion."[349] So, what the suspense of most noir narratives comes down to is just how alone the protagonist can bear to feel – how lonely in love, how disconnected from work, how separate from the social order, how out of touch with normality, and how excluded from the model of emotional and economic prosperity which seems to work so well for a privileged class which is ever so tantalisingly beyond his grasp, but not beyond his sight – without making a bad decision which will make his bad situation even worse. Yet wherever this point of maximum endurance lies, the noir protagonist is eventually pushed beyond it, so he makes that bad decision, and once the dam is broken he follows through with several more in a desperate race to correct the dangerous course upon which he has set himself, a one-way road to self-destruction via social exclusion. It is somewhere along this road that the feeling of being an outsider turns into the feeling of being an outcast.

At this turning point in the noir protagonist's self-perception, he typically becomes afraid – afraid of the man he has become, afraid of being alone with that man, afraid of trusting anyone else, afraid of dying because of his bad decisions, and yet afraid of surviving, as that would condemn him to a life of fear. Nowhere is he more afraid than in the psycho thriller, for in this variation of the noir novel, which typically focuses on the protagonist's psychopathology, his mind gradually but inexorably turns in on itself, until he is afraid that he might not even be able to trust himself, let alone anyone else. In this existential crisis, two changes come over the noir protagonist as he gradually degenerates into a neurotic or, to coin a phrase, a 'noirotic'. One, he becomes convinced that whatever his identity is, the social institution which is trying to assimilate or exterminate him is both its opposite and its enemy. And two, he feels that to be at odds with any social institution means that, in the end, the world will always break your heart.

By dramatising this, as the cultural critic Philip Simpson notes, "noir and the psycho thriller critique the deleterious impact of social institutions upon psychological development."[350] They show that, while the noir protagonist typically brings his misfortune upon himself, he does so less by acting on some malevolent impulse than by *re*acting to an institutional malaise which has infected him with the afore-mentioned irremediable sense of exclusion or convinced him that his fundamental human needs are impaired. So, when he resorts to direct violence, it is typically in reaction to this structural violence or to somebody who has threatened him with direct violence of their own, typically because their psychological development has been deleteriously affected by some social institution. The latter scenario is played out in most psycho thrillers, where it is often illustrated with scenes of graphic violence and sadistic death, and that is why this form of noir also falls within the genre boundaries of horror fiction – unless its narrative focus is on analysis or the protagonist's fear of direct violence is superseded by a more general fear, a fear of the future.

In that case, the novel's affective disposition is noir, because a protagonist who is preoccupied by a general fear of misfortune moves into the future either looking backwards or focusing on what is happening around him right now. Hence, whatever misfortune may strike, it tends to go by in a blur, which is less horrifying than it is disorienting. If the protagonist ever sees it clearly at all, then only when it has already happened to him, at which point it will still affect him negatively but, rather than induce the horror which comes with specific prospects of violence, it will induce the existential Angst which comes with too many bad memories. And given that this Angst is the noir protagonist's default state of mind, it affects the novel's entire atmosphere. As the film critic and director Paul Schrader observes with regard to the protagonists of film noir – most of whom share this Angst though for obvious reasons it is mediated very differently – they "dread to look ahead, but instead try to survive by the day, and if unsuccessful at that, they retreat into the past. Thus film noir's techniques emphasize loss, nostalgia, lack of clear priorities, and insecurity, then submerge these doubts into mannerism and style."[351]

Literary noir has the narrative advantage that it is not limited to such film techniques of submerging the protagonist's doubts into mannerism and style. It is not even limited to such popular film tricks as staging therapy sessions or expositional dialogues in which the protagonist can articulate his conscious thoughts and feelings for the edification of a spectator, who would otherwise have only limited access to them via the afore-mentioned techniques of mannerism and style. Instead, literary noir can let us read the protagonist's mind, so it can take this psychological striptease a lot further. Literary noir can let us deduce from the protagonist's thought patterns that he is drawing on an expansive gallery of fears, and this is possible even in the many noir scenarios in which the protagonist is not aware enough of his thoughts and feelings to articulate them all in filmable dialogue. For instance, even when he is not aware of his reasons for being afraid of the femme fatale in his life, his private thought patterns let us see whether he fears her for being a destabilising force in the workplace, a moral threat to the family, a danger to his ideal of romance, or any other hazard only he can see.

Typically, all this Angst eventually makes the noir protagonist angry about his lack of agency, the fact that he cannot choose the world in which he lives. A lot of the time, he cannot even choose the way in which he lives in it, and when he does make his own choices, they inevitably bring him into conflict with some social institution or powerful individual which ultimately punishes his lofty ambitions and sends him crashing down to the bottom of the pack, so it seems to make sense that noir is often called 'working class tragedy'. For two reasons, however, this is a misnomer. Neither is noir exclusive to the working class nor can it be subsumed into tragedy. As the noir writer and critic Ray Banks points out, "While the traditional audience for noir fiction in the pulps was more than likely working class, in noir the upper and middle classes have just as much of a voice as the working poor and underclass."[352] Hence, Naremore concludes by way of dismissing the attempt to define noir as working class tragedy, "It certainly isn't a proletarian art."[353]

Admittedly, it often seems that way because a lot of its protagonists struggle financially, but they typically struggle as loners and outsiders, not in the spirit of class solidarity, and others struggle even though they are not the least bit stuck in an economic impasse. So, while they all, as Graham points out, "shatter the mainstream fantasy of what is 'normal', and depict the ordinary madness of life, the third world hidden inside the first,"[354] not all of them are born into this third world or barred from leaving it. Some of them have a good education, financial security, and extensive social networks in the first world but bring such destruction upon themselves that they soon fall through the cracks, and this brings us to the second problem of defining noir as 'working class tragedy': the implication that noir is a form of tragedy. It is not.

For one, there are no tragic heroes in noir. In fact, there are no heroes at all in noir, just protagonists. As for their self-destruction – which may seem to resemble that of tragic heroes – in perhaps the definitive text on this issue, *On the Art of Poetry*, Aristotle made the discriminating point that the tragic hero brings his misfortune upon himself, "not by vice and depravity, but by some error of judgement."[355] The noir protagonist, meanwhile, is far less discriminating. Typically, he makes not one but several errors of judgment, and most of them reflect a high degree of vice or depravity. So the closest he ever comes to tragic heroism is when he makes these errors of judgment in what the noir writer and critic David Corbett calls "the belief, often born of desperation, that a criminal act can redeem one's pitiless luck." Yet even in these cases, the desperation which drives the protagonist to criminality typically leads to an even deeper desperation when he realises that no redemption is forthcoming. There are, of course, exceptions, but they owe less to any supposedly tragic sensibilities in noir's affective disposition than to the fact that, as Corbett concludes, "There was nowhere else for a tragic vision to go but noir... noir has had to shoulder an artistic burden it was never meant to carry. And the strain shows."[356] Indeed, some borderline noir is now trying to accommodate partial redemption by compromising what has always been most *un*compromising about the form – its unhappy end.

In uncompromised noir, however, the protagonist still ends up unhappy, because even when he successfully defies his destruction, he fails to redeem himself. Typically, this is the result of yet another failure, his failure to let go of his anger and move towards acceptance. By holding on to it, he typically reaches the point at which he embraces his amorality, whereupon his behaviour becomes transgressive. Alternatively, as the crime critic Peter Messent observes, "individuals' motivations and/or desires lack connection with the social values of their larger group, and lead accordingly to transgressive action."[357] Thus, while the causes may differ, the effect is the same – transgression – and so it seems to make sense that noir is often called 'transgressor fiction'. Once again, however, this is a misnomer. After all, when a reader is sold a piece of noir writing as transgressor fiction, he or she may reasonably expect its writer to focus on the transgressive action itself, not on the many ambiguous readings and restraints associated with it, yet it is precisely on these latter aspects – which are potentially obscured by the genre label 'transgressor fiction' – that noirists typically focus.

The reader in question may therefore be surprised to discover that in noir fiction, as Horsley points out, "The transgressions represented can be a mirror, the damaged self as an image of the society that caused the deformation or the unbalanced mind as a metaphor for society's lunacy. They can also be a protest, an attack on corruptions or injustices in the wider community."[358] Typically, at least one of Horsley's readings is made possible – and indeed encouraged – by noir's close relationship with restraint. This might come as a surprise, given noir's well-documented relationship with violence, vice, and depravity, but it is only because of its restraint that its depiction of extremes can elevate us above the numbing excess of a slaughterhouse documentary. And it is only because noir protagonists spend a lot of time holding back that we have enough time to realise why they eventually do act amorally – in reaction to the individuals or institutions which make them feel alone, afraid, and angry – and what such transgressions signify – serious criticisms of said individuals or institutions.

This difference is perhaps most noticeable in the literature's afore-mentioned affective disposition. As Banks points out, if its violence, vice, and depravity were not restrained by compassion, noir would ultimately just be bleak, not black. "As the most marginal of sub-genres, so it deals with the most marginal of people and, without compassion, their stories would be nothing more than a series of unfortunate events. It's the reason why pessimists can't write decent noir – they lack compassion, or they avoid it because compassion may throw up something that contradicts the relentless cynicism that informs their worldview. It's also difficult for a pessimist to fully commit to an optimistic protagonist. And noir protagonists, despite their bluster and moan, are the most optimistic protagonists in fiction. They have to be. If they weren't, we wouldn't have a story."[359] Indeed, if noir protagonists were not optimistic, they would have no drive to defy the forces of destruction. They would consider the odds and quit. It is only because they believe in the infinitesimal possibility of beating those overwhelming odds that they struggle on, and it is only because they are this optimistic that they have the necessary energy to seek redemption, even when they feel most alone, afraid, and angry.

Typically, of course, redemption does not come into the noir protagonist's sight, never mind his reach, and as he is hit by the realisation that he cannot make things better, he again embraces his amorality, then feels angry because he only makes things worse, afraid because he antagonises the wrong people, and alone because his actions are alienating. The noir protagonist's life, then, is a vicious cycle, and while different authors will focus on different stages of it, most protagonists will run through all of them without ever changing this behavioural pattern simply because, as the publisher and editor Otto Penzler puts it, "noir is about losers. The characters in these existential, nihilistic tales are doomed. They may not die, but they probably should, as the life that awaits them is certain to be so ugly, so lost and lonely, that they'd be better off just curling up and getting it over with. And, let's face it, they deserve it."[360] Admittedly, in most cases they probably do, and yet the fact that they somehow manage to survive their self-destructive behaviour for as long as they do – even though they are at odds with powerful individuals or entire institutions – can make them oddly sympathetic protagonists for readers, and highly worthy subjects for artists.

Corbett explains this dark fascination by pointing out that "Noir responds to a desire for the truth that the prevailing culture is desperately trying to drown out with consumerist pep talks, invincible heroes, feel-good schmaltz, and bad slapstick."[361] The truth as noir typically presents it is that culpability, far from being reducible to the individual criminal, is written into the social contract. And the way in which it typically presents this truth is by addressing, to put it in the words of cultural critic Slavoj Žižek, "not only direct physical violence, but also the more subtle forms of coercion that sustain relations of domination and exploitation."[362] In doing so, noirists attack the delusion that suffering leads to moral nobility, a delusion commonly found in working class tragedy where it lets us sidestep the question of culpability. In the real world, so noirists tend to agree, suffering just leads to more suffering, and in noir, there is no escaping this, not into sentimentality, not into the whitewash that comes with a happy end, and not into the easy condemnation of some black sheep, because "Even in the darkest reaches of noir," as the crime critic Charles J. Rzepka rightly points out, "identification with the criminal protagonist remains intact."[363] And since this is rarely true of either working class tragedy, transgressor fiction, or the psycho thriller, it is perhaps not surprising that none of the many terms used to describe noir have stuck – although, as I have tried to show, there may be another reason for that. As Naremore puts it, "noir is not merely a descriptive term, but a name for a critical tendency… an antigenre."[364]

THE SCOTTISH NOIR NOVEL

In Scotland, rather confusingly, the noir novel did not start, nor did it reach its pinnacle, with 'the King of Tartan Noir', Ian Rankin. Saying so, I hasten to add, betrays neither a literary value judgment nor an attempt to court controversy. It is simply a statement of fact, and one I have already tried to substantiate in Chapter Two of this book. So it is only for the sake of the odd reader who may have skipped straight to this chapter on Scottish Noir in the expectation of finding 'the King of Tartan Noir' here – and with apologies to anyone who remembers my reasoning – that I shall briefly repeat why Rankin does not write noir, not Tartan, not Scottish, not any.

Rankin writes police novels based on the far from noir premise that the legal, political, and social systems which govern Scotland are, ultimately, worth defending. So, although his cops have to bend or break the occasional law to preserve order, preserve it they do, and although they have the odd minor flaw, they manage it like the heroes they are. If Rankin wrote noir novels, his cops would not be bending or breaking any laws to preserve order, because there would be no order. If Rankin wrote noir novels, his heroes would not have any flaws, because he would have no heroes, just protagonists. And finally, if Rankin wrote noir novels, his protagonists would not care anywhere near as much about laws or flaws. They would be far too preoccupied with their noir fate of being alone, afraid, angry, amoral, and alienating.

So, how has somebody who does not even write noir come to be known as the King of Tartan Noir? As Rankin was happy to explain when I asked him that very question, he was given this unofficial title by James Ellroy, the notorious American noirist, before Ellroy had even read any of his writing:

"I met him at a crime fiction convention in Nottingham many years ago and I wanted to get him to sign a book for me. I was explaining to him that I was a crime writer as well, and wrote about Edinburgh and the darker side of Scottish life. I said, 'You could call it Tartan Noir.' He laughed and signed the book to 'the King of Tartan Noir'. So then I pretended that he'd invented it. But in fact, I told him and then he wrote it down."[365]

After Rankin told a version of this story in public – minus the final admission, which he added only recently – people started parroting Ellroy and using his authority to lend credibility to a literary movement which Rankin had invented in jest, 'Tartan Noir'.

Within a few years, Rankin had become the form's internationally recognised figurehead, and this has had some rather long-lasting consequences. On the one hand, it has moved some actual noir from the margins of Scottish literature to the mainstream, because, along with Rankin's popularity, the demand for Tartan Noir has risen dramatically. In response, the market has been flooded with literature promoted as such, and this has included some actual noir. On the other hand, however, it has also included some falsely labelled literature, the kind which merely gets labelled noir because it is a bit dark, not because it is noir in the aesthetic meaning of the word. Rankin's false promotion as a noirist is one such example. Other examples – similarly famous and similarly false – are the likes of Arthur Conan Doyle and George Douglas Brown, whose occasionally dark-ish detective fiction and social realism is often cited in an attempt at locating the earliest – or worthiest – starting point of noir in Scottish literature. Yet while this may seem like a harmless vanity project, such false genre genealogies can have unfortunate consequences. Whenever they remain uncontested, they offer muddled minds models for even more mislabelling, so it is time to look at a few examples of actual, Scottish Noir.

Alexander Trocchi – *Young Adam*

One of the first noir novels to come out of Scotland was *Young Adam*, written by Alexander Trocchi, first published in 1954, and long ignored before his voice of dissent was to echo through Scottish Noir. For decades, Trocchi's writing was so far beyond the pale of conventional ethics and aesthetics that the literary establishment deemed it to be juvenile delinquency, and unworthy of serious consideration, so for quite a while it was in some danger of being consigned to permanent exile. According to literary critic John Pringle, however, "the danger has passed."[366] Pringle declared this in 1996, when he introduced the 1966 version of *Young Adam*, the version Trocchi had authorised as "the definitive text,"[367] and almost two decades later, Pringle is still right. *Young Adam* is still demonstrating the longevity of the noir ethos which inspired it, the ethos of *The Outsider* by Albert Camus.

Like Meursault, the enigmatic narrator of *The Outsider*, Joe, the enigmatic narrator of *Young Adam*, tells the story of his two lives, one of which ended with his involvement in a suspicious death, the other of which started that very instant. The two key differences are that Joe claims the death was an accident and that he reverses the order in which Meursault tells this double story. When we first meet him, Joe is working for a bargeman somewhere on the Edinburgh-Glasgow canal. Within moments, we know such personal details about him as that he is easily bored and that he is the kind of man whose mind is always watching itself, as when he sees the corpse of a woman in the water and only fishes her out after several detached observations about his own reaction to this morbid sight. Yet only much later do we see the bigger picture and realise that he was previously involved with this woman, Cathie. What is more, he was also involved with her suspicious death, yet before he even mentions her by name, never mind the fact that he knew her, and knew her intimately just before he watched her die, he spends the first half of the novel talking at quite a leisurely pace, and in quite some detail, about what he did after her death. He went to the pub, manned the barge, and seduced his boss's wife, Ella. Then he proceeds just as callously: "I wanted to talk about Ella… For that reason, and not to complicate the issue, I said nothing about Cathie."[368]

What he also neglected to mention is how she died. When he finally does get around to mentioning this detail, he is quick to add that it was an accident. She was pregnant and threatening marriage, so he walked away, and when she ran after him, she tripped and fell into the River Clyde, where, unable to swim, she soon drowned. Unfortunately, he muses, "there was only my word for it that it was an accident. Or was it an accident? I suppose it was. It had never occurred to me to kill her."[369] Since his is indeed the only word for it that Cathie's death was an accident, and since he himself seems rather uncertain of that scenario, everything about him and his way of telling the story suddenly seems suspicious, most of all perhaps the fact that, as he admits with his general lack of compassion, he made no attempt to rescue her.

Then there is the lateness of his confession that, as the last person to have seen her alive, he withheld vital information from the police; the element of doubt in his own mind that it may not have been an accident after all; and the incriminating circumstantial evidence that, as he himself points out, "The furtive sexuality of the situation would tend to make it appear criminal."[370] Perhaps most suspicious, however, is that when a man is prosecuted for Cathie's murder and Joe is the only one who knows for certain that this man is innocent, he again makes no rescue attempt. Instead, he makes the ultimate empty gesture. He sends the judge an anonymous letter proclaiming the suspect's innocence. This, of course, is ignored in court, as Joe anticipated, and the man is promptly sentenced to death, again as Joe anticipated. Yet despite such alienating amorality, an alternative reading makes Joe hard to judge.

As we learn in one of the later flashbacks to his courtship with Cathie, Joe has literary ambitions and a realist's writing philosophy: "I'm not interested in all the usual paraphernalia. Don't you understand? That's literature, false. I've got to start with the here and now."[371] If *Young Adam*, as its episodic structure and first-person limited narration suggest, is meant to be read as Joe's journal, then we may have to concede that he had an innocent reason for not telling us any sooner that he could identify the corpse. He had to start with 'the here and now'. And if he is indeed trying to tell the story without the usual paraphernalia of literature – such as the false pretence of character consistency – then we may have to concede that the novel's psychological and moral fragmentation can be read as evidence, not only of his caprice and selfishness, but also of his candour and sincerity. Even though he is telling the story in hindsight and could therefore edit any suspicious inconsistencies, he chooses not to pretend that he was consistent in his responses to inarguably unusual and often challenging situations.

Accordingly, it is possible to read him in two different ways: either as a pseudo-intellectual criminal who is making a questionable excuse for his amorality, or as a serious-minded outsider who is making a conscientious objection to the institutions he opposes: the court of law and the court of public opinion. In the latter reading, his refusal to assist the police in their inquiry indicates not a lack of compassion for Cathie – who posthumously suffers a drawn-out character assassination in both of those courts for the supposed moral crimes of non-marital conception and entrapment – but a lack of respect for the inquiry. To assist the police in it, as he puts it, "would have been an indirect but very fundamental way to affirm the validity of the particular social structure I wished to deny."[372] What he most wishes to deny about this social structure becomes clear in the trial, in which the notion that Cathie's death may have been an accident is never even entertained. Instead, there is a lot of puritanical speculation about the suspect's motive: his family status as a husband and father, his probable entrapment by an unmarried pregnant woman, and his presumed willingness to protect the former with premeditated murder of the latter. Soon, the cries of moral outrage silence the voice of reason and the official guardians of a society which supposedly respects civil liberties and democratic principles "condemn a living creature in deference to the system."[373]

Meanwhile, Joe is morally disgusted that, just because Cathie's body was found naked, they conclude that it must have been murder. He is even more disgusted that, just because they have convinced themselves that there has been a crime, they have jumped to the conclusion that there must also be a culprit. Yet what he is most disgusted at is the moral righteousness which they betray when they deliver their guilty verdict and prove that, if there is a sex crime, any culprit will do. In this deep disgust, Joe argues that the other man's arrest "was no more absurd than the position which would be thrust upon me by an unintelligent society perennially bent on its moral purification: 'What! She didn't have her knickers on!'"[374] And while this argument may not allay every reader's suspicion that his true reason for refusing to take the suspect's place in the dock is simply that he is afraid and once again callously puts his own interests first – as when he slept with Cathie and Ella only to ignore their need once they had satisfied his desire – the argument that he has a deeper motivation for defying expectation is nonetheless attractive and thus raises an interesting point about the complexity of noir's affective disposition.

Joe can be deeply alienating in his anger, in his amorality, and perhaps most of all in his assertion of what the crime critic Bran Nicol calls "the destructive power of individual desire." And yet Joe can also be deeply affecting, at times perhaps even attractive, in his attack on our sensibilities, since it repeatedly and insistently asks, as Nicol puts it, just "how fragile and inconsequential are the moral codes that structure liberal-democratic society."[375] Read in this subversive spirit, even Joe's sexual exploits are not only indulgences of his instinctive hedonism but also revolts against his society's repressive moral codes, and while such a double reading may not repudiate the charge of callousness, it certainly proves that Trocchi's writing – like sex – is rarely simple and rarer still pure.

Instead, most of it is noir, but in the interest of brevity I shall only make one observation about his next novel to make a final point about his general 'noirness'. The title of this next novel is *Cain's Book*, so it seems fair to say that *Young Adam* also refers to the Bible, specifically to 'Old Adam' who, in Genesis, refuses to act in the biblical spirit of self-negation and thus represents man in his unredeemed state. The same, as I have tried to show in these pages, can be said of Joe, who would seem to be Trocchi's younger version of Old Adam. So the title, like the story, suggests that Joe is not just beyond redemption as the novel draws to a close, but that he will remain so for the rest of his life. That is about as noir as literature gets, be it in Scotland or anywhere else.

Hugh C. Rae – *Skinner*

Yet despite the cult status which this pioneering exploration of the noir universe has reached in Scotland, the country's subsequent noirists have not collectively followed the same trend as Trocchi. As the huge diversity of Scottish Noir indicates, he has been succeeded by subversive individualists like himself. Take Hugh C. Rae. By the time *Skinner*, his debut novel, was published in 1965, Trocchi's favourite topic, the transgression of sexual-moral boundaries, had become one of the counter-culture's most talked and written about preoccupations. Yet while *Skinner* may initially make it appear as though Rae, too, mines this rich seam, he is in fact digging for darker treasures in the noir psyche.

The reason it may not immediately appear that way is that his main protagonist, Arnold Skinner, also preys on women. He even kills several of them savagely, but not because he is revolting against repressive sexual mores, "not even," as his sister Rosemary says, "because he couldn't stop himself, because his sex is too strong for him, but because he wanted to."[376] Rae is not interested in the intellectual experience and explanation of transgression, not in Skinner's anyway. He is interested in the animal instinct that can turn a man into a predator, that and the changes which take place even within civilised people once Skinner gets into their heads. So perhaps the best way to read *Skinner* – the novel as well as the man – is as an exploration of how something which lies beneath language, something which would seem to be an animalistic instinct, can manifest itself not only in a man's actions but also in the effects which his aura has on his environment.

Of course, it is through language that Rae has to illustrate this sub-intellectual instinct and the subtle effects it has on other people, and this brings us to the novel's unusual, polyphonic narrative strategy. As the title suggests, there would be no story without Skinner, yet none of it is told by him. Instead, it is told by eleven people who all know parts of the story because they all know parts of Skinner. They are either family members, work mates, casual acquaintances, criminal accomplices, police detectives, or people bereaved by Skinner, and they all take turns to tell their parts of the story, one at a time, like in court. Since this structure is further formalised in that each part is marked with its narrator's name in place of a chapter heading, the narrative soon reads like a court transcript of witness testimonies. In time, this subtly reinforces the impression that Skinner is about to yield to his dark urges and commit a violent crime.

This impression is further reinforced by what each narrator says and thinks about Skinner, as none of it bodes well and none of it is easily dismissed. On the contrary, what the narrators notice about Skinner and his behaviour becomes ever more interesting, since the man does not narrate any part of the story himself, nor say much in the company of those who do, which is to say that we know little about what he will do and less about why he will do it. At the same time, everything the narrators say and think about Skinner, along with the increasingly nervous ways in which they do so, lets us see how deviously he gets into their heads and how disturbingly this changes them. For instance, just before he rapes Ruby, a long-time admirer of his, he utterly demoralises her, so much so that she is reduced to despair when she recounts the brutal rape: "I didn't have the guts left to even be full of fear or enough of the stuff of life to want to crawl away."[377]

When he shrugs off the charge that he routinely reduces the people around him to such despair, it makes even Booth, a reputedly stoic detective, admit to himself, "I hated him because he was not human enough to be afraid of us, or the law, or of himself... He killed because he wanted to kill, for self-glorification, and for the love of blood, and that exempted him from any sympathy I might have had left to give."[378] So, when Skinner finally gets caught and faces death by hanging, even Booth's partner Muirhead, a seasoned humanitarian, is reduced to the nasty thought: "I only long to pull the lever of the trap myself."[379] And it is in such moments of brutal honesty that we can gauge the deeply disturbing power of *Skinner*, because these words are not spoken by somebody who shares Skinner's unquenchable blood thirst. They are spoken by a man of proven compassion who hears himself utter them with genuine surprise and profound self-disgust.

In other words, Rae does more than just record the signs of Skinner's predatory nature. He also reveals how the man affects those around him on an animal level, as when Muirhead explains his aggressive impulse. Just before he surprises and disgusts himself with his sudden longing 'to pull the lever of the trap myself', he is sitting across from Skinner after a six month police investigation and accuses him of multiple murders, when, "I suddenly ceased to be affected by any of it: the moment of triumph or of truth. I lost it." Skinner, he suddenly realises, will "talk, cooking his perverted lies in braggart and evasion, spinning out over the months through all due process of law his foul defeat, reducing it at last, in time, to an arid pattern of ritual justice... Right to the moment when the boards tilt and shoot him into total darkness, some part of him too will go on snapping and squirming for life."[380] And when Skinner interrupts these troubling thoughts to ask, not for repentance, but for a cigarette, Muirhead loses his composure along with his compassion.

As far as final thoughts go, this one is doubly disturbing. For one, Rae puts it in the head of his most identifiable character, so most readers are likely to relate when this usually so benign man is disturbed to the point of renouncing his treasured humanitarian principles and fantasises about ending another human being's life. And what makes this thought even more disturbing is that it strikes Muirhead long after he has seen the extreme savagery of Skinner's crimes. Of course, he was disgusted at that, too, but not nearly as much as at the man's mind when Skinner reveals it to him in that final encounter and lets him see in what low regard he holds human life, be it that of other people or his own. In that moment, it becomes disturbingly obvious that Skinner sees human beings as things which serve the single purpose of indulging his animal cravings, something on a par with a cigarette, which is all he thinks about even as Muirhead tells him that he is certain to get the death penalty.

Anyone who does not find this deeply disturbing may wish to consider the novel's historical background. As most readers would have known at the time of its publication, *Skinner* is a fictionalisation of the infamous Peter Manuel case, an American-born serial killer who was executed in 1958 for the murder of seven people across the South of Scotland. So, in the Skinner case, there is little relief in the thought that the killer's actions and attitude are not real. Of course, they are a work of fiction, but they are also a real attempt at portraying a real-life serial killer, and the fact that Rae does not let Skinner/Manuel tell his own story – i.e. that he does not create a false narrative to explain away the mysteries of a psychopathic mind – means that Rae's account of the case seems disturbingly real and, more disturbingly still, the psychopath's mind remains a mystery.

As the many more or less insightful narrators take their turns at trying to understand Skinner, all we can do to solve the mystery of his violent behaviour is join them in their efforts. There is no single, authoritative truth, only the many subjective truths of experience as people from all walks of life relate their stories of how their mental or physical health was ruined when Skinner came into their life. Thus, attention is focused on the contrasts and commonalities between their stories, and these eventually reveal a final, disturbing fact. The casually inhumane attitude which Skinner displays in the closing scene with Muirhead cannot be mistaken for provocative defiance. As a trusted friend remembers, he has had it all along, even in a much earlier scene when he made the following, casually inhumane confession in a rather convivial atmosphere: "'I did do them,' he says in the same voice he might tell me he liked draught better'n bottle, quiet and casual like. 'I did them all.'"[381]

What he is confessing here is a series of brutal murders, and as his own sister agrees, he has always been casual and inhumane enough "To shoot a child in the face because he wanted to: not because he was afraid. He had never been afraid in all his long life."[382] Indeed, unlike most noir protagonists, Skinner is disturbingly aggressive, not because he is afraid, but because he actively nurtures his animalistic nature, and thus his serial killing is more than a disturbing crime. It is also a deeply disturbing denial of the basic humanism with which we expect human beings to treat one another. Yet what may well be the most disturbing thing about this violent animalism is that it soon became the strongest trend in Scottish Noir.

Gordon Williams – *The Siege of Trencher's Farm*

For instance, in *The Siege of Trencher's Farm*, published only four years later in 1969, Gordon Williams followed this trend by illustrating how the animal side of man, when enlarged, can turn him into a dangerous predator. Sure, the novel also points back to an earlier tradition, and in doing so, it bridges the gap between Rae and Trocchi. On one level, after all, Williams sticks close to Rae's narrative strategy as he follows the animalisation of his main protagonist step for step. Yet on another level, he tries to overtake this immediate experience with a view to intellectualising it, thus connecting with a noir tradition which Trocchi had only recently imported from France. And on a third level, he goes back to the deepest roots of noir – Europe's male fascination with the instinctive – by writing about the dark places to which instinct can take men when their masculinity is in crisis.

One of those dark places is the fictional Dando Monachorum, a tiny village stuck in the deepest countryside of Cornwall, England. Another one of those dark places is the mind of the main protagonist, George Magruder, who is stuck in the deepest winter of his life. Having recently left the United States and moved with wife and daughter to Dando, this effete academic had hoped that his new home, an idyllic farmhouse called Trencher's Farm, would let him find the ideal peace of mind to finish his book on Branksheer, a fictional 18th century British diarist. Instead, he soon finds his mind invaded by more pressing concerns, and before he knows it, this sheltered mind of his has turned into a fiercely contested battleground over which the forces of idealism and animalism fight their grimly impersonal campaigns.

Eventually, as the set-up suggests, this *in*ternal battle turns into an *ex*ternal one, but before it does so, Magruder rehearses each strike and counterstrike in his increasingly claustrophobic mind. Though at first he seems rather confident in his intellect and liberalism, he soon fears, and rightly so, that his wife has tired of his flagging libido and stepped outside their marriage, so he starts berating himself with increasing insecurity and self-loathing, as when he asks himself, "What good did it do a man to know he had brains? How could academic knowledge make up for loss of *maleness*? This was what had attracted him to Branksheer in the first place, that drunken old pox-ridden lecher, at home with Ovid or a London whore, a *complete* man."[383] Soon, Magruder's thoughts and actions are driven entirely by his desire to become and – perhaps more importantly still – to be remembered as a complete man, a broad man of the world who is symmetrical in his development, not a stunted ascetic who is so busy channelling his energy into a single, narrow area of expertise – in this case some obscure 18th century British diarist – that the other branches of his being wither and die.

What Magruder yearns to prove to both himself and his increasingly disrespectful wife is that he is both servant of a tender conscience and master of his own house. So, after he goes out in a snow storm, accidentally drives into a stranger, brings the hurt man home, calls a doctor, learns that the stranger is an infamous child killer as well as a fugitive from the local asylum, learns further that a young girl fitting the killer's victim profile has gone missing and that several local men, upon discovering that he is harbouring the main suspect, have formed a mob to lay siege to the farm, Magruder finally sees his chance to become that complete man. Hence, in spite of the escalating hysteria triggered by a home invasion and a domestic drama, he decides to defend *his* people along with *his* principles in the belief that, "Tomorrow morning he'd be the man who had done the right thing."[384]

In the meantime, however, his abstract belief in doing the *right* thing leads to a very real dilemma in which he repeatedly does the *wrong* thing. First, he insults the local men. Instead of respecting their legitimate concerns that the fugitive he is harbouring in his home may have harmed the missing girl, and instead of explaining that the man could not possibly have done so because he was unconscious at the time she went missing, Magruder takes the moral high ground as the self-declared defender of the weak and talks down to the locals for hunting the poor man like an animal. To make things worse, he triggers their social envy as he lectures them from within a farm house none of them can afford, and although he only ignores this volatile class issue because he is forever preoccupied with his private insecurities, the clannish locals at his door do not appreciate this irony. Instead, they are incensed that some arrogant incomer should interfere in what, to them, is a local issue, so the stand-off escalates as they swiftly turn against the outsider and lay siege to his home, whereupon Magruder just as swiftly shifts from arrogant insensitivity to animal instinct.

Feeling both alone and afraid in a place beyond laws, he starts acting out the adolescent fantasy of maleness which he has been rehearsing ever since he started suspecting his wife of infidelity. The way he sees it, this is his chance to channel the aggression he has built up *in*side his home into an attack on the men *out*side it. So, when they try to break in, he lashes out, and in that long-anticipated moment he loses not just his life-long civility and habitual self-control but also any sense of proportion in the violent pursuit of some frontier justice. Until then, he was proud that "All his life he'd fought against violence, signed petitions, written letters, taken unpopular lines in discussions. Violence was an obscenity."[385] Yet when he eventually breaks with this long history of conscientious objection, he breaks with it like a wild animal, not a wise academic, and this stark contrast is visually captured in the novel's climactic scene.

Night has fallen, the men laying siege to the farm have cut off its electricity supply, and Magruder is running around in the dark, desperately trying to keep them all out, when suddenly one of them gets in and bears down on him with a lethal weapon while others set fire to various parts of the house. So it is amid elemental forces that Magruder grapples with the violent intruder, and as he excitedly takes in his surroundings, he cares not a jot that his carefully compiled notes on Branksheer have been trampled on the floor and left to burn like effigies of his former ideal self. Later, when Magruder has won the fight and order seems to have returned to Trencher's farm in the shape of a policeman, his wife reports that "They were like lions fighting in a dark cage."[386] Yet in her simile, as much as in the scene itself, it is unclear whether they were fighting for supremacy or for survival.

Perhaps the best way to clarify this ambiguity is to contrast *The Siege of Trencher's Farm* with *Straw Dogs*, the movie adaptation of 1971 directed by Sam Peckinpah. In the movie, Magruder certainly goes to violent lengths, but he does so in the spirit of self-preservation, whereas in the novel, Magruder goes as far as killing a man, and after he crosses that moral line, he goes far beyond self-preservation. Having found that violence can be an end in itself, he starts fighting men like animals which "had to be destroyed."[387] And with this newfound machismo, he wins not just the fight but also his estranged wife's admiration and a new virility. As his wife assures him, "I don't deserve you, George, it's true, I don't, I don't."[388] And as he assures himself when he reviews this wild night, "It was the first time in his life that he was able to make love to a woman with the light on. He didn't have room in his head for *thoughts*. He had won."[389]

Yet clear and confident as Magruder's declaration may sound, it is not necessarily the final verdict. Certainly, by his definition he has won, and not just in the sense of beating off a bunch of home intruders, but also in the grander sense of finally becoming 'a complete man'. But the conclusion – six lives lost or ruined – suggests another reading. The fact that he has risen to this dated ideal of masculinity on the stepping stones of other people's mental and physical suffering suggests that he has not just won the respect of a simpleminded woman. Along the way, he has also become a lesser man, morally. So, in true noir manner, *The Siege of Trencher's Farm* shows that enlarging a man's animal side might make him feel whole, but it does not make him wholesome.

William McIlvanney – *The Papers of Tony Veitch*

This noir way of looking at life – the unblinking gaze at the whole of it, not just its wholesome parts – has since been popularised in a trilogy by William McIlvanney which started in 1977. Not that this explains the man's recent increase in popularity, let alone his unofficial title, 'Godfather of Tartan Noir'. As I hope to have shown in the previous pages, Scots were writing noir before McIlvanney turned his hand to it, and as I hope to show in the following pages, they have since drawn as much on the traditions of this earlier Scottish Noir as they have drawn on his. So, why is McIlvanney now commonly accorded literary paternity ahead of his noir elders, writers like Trocchi, Rae, and Williams?

As ever, this kind of question is about more than books. McIlvanney was arguably the first Scot to lift the crime novel out of the genre ghetto. Having won, among others, the notable Geoffrey Faber Memorial Prize for *Remedy is None* and the even more distinguished Whitbread Award for *Docherty*, McIlvanney had established an international reputation for artistic credibility with his work in 'proper literature' by the time he started writing crime fiction. Sure, this was a time when the genre was deemed trivial, more trivial even than it is deemed by many to this day, so his crime novels – a Glasgow-set trilogy featuring Detective Inspector Jack Laidlaw – did not have the immediate impact his current popularity would suggest. But since most critics soon agreed that his writing had not become any less credible for focusing on criminals – nor any less 'literary' – word got around that McIlvanney is temperamentally incapable of writing bad prose, whatever the genre, and a quick 35 years after the publication of his first crime novel, *Laidlaw*, the literary establishment awarded him the unofficial title, 'Godfather of Tartan Noir'.

Now, you may ask, given that versions of the term had been making the rounds among noir fans for quite a while, why did the literary establishment take so long to champion McIlvanney as a pioneer of 'Tartan Noir'? And what might have been the sudden motivation, given that his last noir novel had been published over 20 years ago in 1991? Well, the answer is anyone's guess, but for what it is worth, here is mine. The loudest voices to start using the title in public, all these years after McIlvanney had quietly made his mark on Scotland's noir scene, were other so-called 'Tartan Noirists'. This was around the time of the first Bloody Scotland crime writing festival in 2012, where this late image campaign was spearheaded by world-famous writers like Ian Rankin and Val McDermid, quickly supported by many of their lesser known compatriots, and soon publicised to great effect in most of the country's papers and bookshops, whereupon the Laidlaw novels, along with all of McIlvanney's non-noir novels, were republished the following year.

The first thing to note, then, is that there is an historical aptness – some might even say poetic justice – in the fact that this coming-of-age moment of Scottish crime fiction, its confident self-assertion as a national literature independent of the country's 'proper literature' and worthy of its own literary festival, coincided with the rediscovery and celebration of perhaps it most influential writer. Yet it also seems worth noting, even at the risk of appearing churlish, that such a revival has a pleasant side-effect. When a writer of McIlvanney's exceptional literary merit is known as the 'Godfather of Tartan Noir', any generic crime novel marketed as 'Tartan Noir' stands the chance of receiving more critical – and commercial – attention on the basis that it, too, may turn out to be a literary classic. After all, McIlvanney has written three novels which have recently been described as 'Tartan Noir', they were all initially read as genre fiction, and all of them are now recognised as literary classics.

Whether this popularity by proxy played on anyone's mind in those heady days of literary celebration is, of course, impossible to know, and irrelevant to boot. What matters is that McIlvanney has found new readers along with some long overdue recognition, and while some of those new readers doubtlessly came to him by recommendation of other writers and critics, his recognition as the 'Godfather of Tartan Noir' did not come and go with this sudden image campaign. It has sustained him at many a literary festival since, and like an unexpected pension of esteem it promises to keep doing so. The simple reason for this benign prospect is that more and more readers are finally recognising that McIlvanney did something in each of his three Laidlaws which – in noir as in any other literature – is extremely rare. He wrote about familiar types – cops and criminals – in ways which were both highly original and deeply affecting, so much so that several of his innovations have led to no end of imitation, at least, it would seem, among his compatriots.

In his 1977 noir debut *Laidlaw*, for instance, he set a national precedent by making his main protagonist a man who just so happens to be a policeman, rather than a policeman who just so happens to be a man. In *Strange Loyalties*, which was published in 1991 as Laidlaw's last case to date, he set another national precedent by making his policeman investigate a capital crime only to discover that it was no crime at all. And in *The Papers of Tony Veitch*, published in 1983 as the trilogy's middle-child – the darkest and least talked about – McIlvanney set yet another national precedent and probably his most underrated. In this story of murder, betrayal, and retribution, he made it clear that a story does not have to be excessively violent or erratically told to be unsettling. On the contrary, it can be far more unsettling when the creeping realisation that this is a dirty story is accompanied by the inescapable sense that, as Laidlaw puts it, "Most of them are. Some folk just tell them nice."[390]

At the risk of stating the obvious, Laidlaw is not suggesting that most stories are dirty in the sense that they are offensive to common decency. He is using the word dirty in its figurative meaning of morally unclean to suggest that this story, like most noir stories, is dirty because it tells of a society which treats the weak like inconvenient rodents. The weak, in this case, are represented by Eck Adamson, one of Glasgow's countless vagrants, and the society in question – ours – treats him like an inconvenient rodent in the sense that some let him live and die in squalor while others make sure he does just that. So desperate are the circumstances, and so disaffected the people in Eck's life, that Laidlaw is the only one who can be bothered to find out that the man was poisoned like a rat because he knew too much – and that many of his social betters are happy to collude with Eck's poisoner because it is the simplest way of suppressing his knowledge that a seam of corruption runs from his final resting place at the very bottom of this broken social system to its supposed model citizens at the very top.

Yet lest this one-man crusade for truth and justice sound too much like heroism, it is worth pointing out that this is a noir novel and Laidlaw no hero. When he decides to investigate Eck's death and unravel this seam of corruption, he does so only because Eck placed his faith in him personally by putting the end of that seam in his hand. He did this through a cryptic message just moments before he died, and Laidlaw is too embarrassed by a dying man's faith in him not to, as he puts it, "accept the need to face what you would rather not see."[391] What he means by this need is not a hero's need to fight the good fight but an embarrassed man's need to face himself in the mirror. Looking at Eck, he feels complicit for living in a society which in too many cases of similar immiseration 'would rather not see', and while his decision to end his complicity might also qualify as heroic, he is far too aware of his inability to end his other embarrassments to think of himself as a hero. And since he frequently voices his thoughts about these embarrassments – his ever-lengthening litany of failures as a husband, father, and human being – so are we.

Of course, none of this is new. He had the same flaws and articulate self-awareness in *Laidlaw*. What is new, though, and noir to the core, is that Laidlaw's decision to act on his best intentions leads to more deaths, including that of the student Tony Veitch whose private papers contain a series of dark and dangerous clues to all those deaths. Yet what may be even more disturbing is the moral discourse for which these papers contain a series of dark and dangerous cues, for when Laidlaw draws a number of people with personal experience of criminality, corruption, and complicity into a series of highly charged conversations, he encounters disaffection all around him, until it near enough drives him to despair. And what gets to him most is that he encounters the worst of it, not among the big bosses or the little skivvies, but among the discreet beneficiaries of Glasgow's far-ranging criminal industries – people like Tony's father – whose financial wealth insulates them against Laidlaw's social conscience, since all they have found in life is financial success, not the self-doubt which examines the terms of such success.

Deeply disturbed by this casual declaration of moral bankruptcy, Laidlaw – much like McIlvanney – dedicates far less thought and effort to the regeneration of the flawed man who solves this murder mystery than to the degeneration of the humanitarian ideal which he witnesses both in and around himself. And yet despite the timelessness of such metaphysical noir – and despite the pioneering reputation of its author – it has not become the main focus of Scottish Noir. Most of McIlvanney's successors, after all, have gone back to its earlier focus: the male fascination with the instinctive.

Iain Banks – *The Wasp Factory*

A good example of this is Frank Cauldhame, the hyper-macho protagonist of Iain Banks's 1984 debut, *The Wasp Factory*. Not only is Frank's struggle to become 'a complete man' a study in the biology of adolescence. It is also a story about the psychology of masculinity in crisis. At 16, Frank is approaching the age of manhood, yet much to his frustration his body is nowhere near his idea of what a man should look like. That much is clear early on, as he spends most of his time either complaining about his lack of height, beard, and genital growth or compensating for these perceived deficiencies. Yet what is not clear until the end of his journey to manhood is the reason for his effeminacy, because ever since he received the sketchy and uncorroborated explanation from his father that their family dog bit off most of his genitals when he was a boy, Frank has retreated from the world of adults and avoided the issue.

Ever since this violent castration, he has lived on a small island off the West Coast of Scotland, literally and figuratively 'cut off' from society in a moated fortress he shares with his largely absent father, a childishly eccentric man incapable of looking after either himself or Frank. There, he has lived all of his life in ultimate emasculation, or as he puts it, with "no birth certificate, no National Insurance Number, nothing to say I'm alive or have ever existed... for my own good reasons; fear – oh, yes, I admit it – and a need for reassurance and safety in a world which just so happened to treat me very cruelly at an age before I had any real chance of affecting it."[392] And in the spirit of this 'frankness' – which seems doubly appropriate in view of his name and the fact that he is happy to reveal some deeply disturbing memories in his many dark flashbacks – he admits that he has spent the intervening years doing his very best – or worst – to give himself that 'real chance of affecting it'.

For instance, to avenge himself on the natural world and make his mark on it, he has bombed the island, killed its wildlife in the triple digits, and filled a bunker with the severed heads of sacrificed animals. As for the social world, he has killed three of his relatives. "That's my score to date. Three. I haven't killed anybody for years, and don't intend to ever again. It was just a stage I was going through."[393] So, even before the novel's dramatic action sets in, Banks signals that, as the crime critic Lee Horsley puts it, "The noir preoccupation with the undermining of identity and with the communication of a marginalised character's narrative is central." And once the action does set in, "The 'marginal man' theme is turned into an even more explicit examination of prejudice and exclusion."[394] What triggers this examination is a phone call from his older brother, who calls to inform Frank of his escape from a mental hospital, so Frank spends the remainder of the novel in anxious anticipation of his arrival, fearing a power shift, flashing back to his past crimes, and fortifying the island's defences along with his sense of exclusion, all of which, ironically, exposes him to the crippling criticism, repeatedly implied by his father, that he does not really understand masculinity. To Frank, it is all about the survival of the nastiest, and with no alternative model on offer, he cannot tell the difference between masculinity and misanthropy, so he quashes his insecurities by remodelling himself on a barely recognisable image of the warrior king, an image he first derived from fragments of pop culture and has since further distorted through the prism of his paranoid pubescent mind.

Soon, this double negation – the denial of everything in his nature which does not conform to his image and the destruction of everything around him which might anchor him in his nature – as the literary theorist Carl Malmgren observes, "calls in question ideas of innate goodness or the essential Self and invites readers to experience vicariously various forms of psychopathology."[395] More specifically, Banks invites us to experience a spirit of malevolence which is so strong that it survives its practical exertion. By letting Frank share and even rationalise his view of his transgressive behaviour – both past and present – Banks makes sure that no authorial judgment distorts our perception of his protagonist while three of his psychological oddities become disturbingly obvious: one, Frank has found lasting pleasure in his hatred. Two, far from having exhausted it, he is energised by it. And three, he sees no wrong in any of the above.

In that regard, then, Frank is rather like the famous 19th century essayist and provocateur William Hazlitt. Indeed, had he been born around 160 years earlier, it might seem as though he had inspired Hazlitt's pronouncement "that there is a secret affinity, a hankering after evil in the human mind, and that it takes a perverse, but a fortunate delight in mischief, since it is a never-failing source of satisfaction."[396] Yet if it seems like a cruel accident of birth to have missed your obvious soulmate by several generations, consider this: throughout his lonely life, Frank has treated human beings in general, and women in particular, with a mystic horror and superstitious hatred which most sane people reserve for snakes and spiders, but for all his diverting torture games and lord-of-the-flies-megalomania, Frank's story has, ultimately, always been about coming to terms with the *cause* of his crisis, rather than the crisis itself, and this cause turns out to be an even crueller accident of birth than the one above. As Frank, the frustrated misogynist, eventually discovers – please skip to the next section if you do not wish to share in this life-changing discovery here – he was not born Francis, but Frances.

His male sex turns out to be a lie concocted by his manipulative father who has secretly been treating him with male hormones, and doing so not to compensate for his supposed castration, but because that castration story is a lie, too. Frank was born female but has lived his conscious life as an unwitting experiment in gender reassignment. When she was a baby and thus too young to remember, her unstable mother deserted the family and left her at the mercy of her even more unstable father, who promptly projected his resentment of his wife on to all women and decided to banish all femininity from the island, including that of his new baby. To do so, he made up the story about the dog and turned his daughter into a son, both medically and mentally. Thus, having been abandoned by her mother at birth and raised in a male protectorate, Frances became Francis and eventually internalised his father's misogyny along with his machismo.

What Frank has not become, however, is a 'complete' man. As he is only too aware, he has not even become a grown man, though where exactly that leaves him he does not know. Having never had his birth officially registered, he has never attended school, and having developed an entrenched reluctance to leave his comfort zone – the island – he has spent hardly any time with his peers, so in addition to his weak biological markers, he has had few social markers to track his development.

Yet it is not only highly contradictory that, despite his lifelong pursuit of masculinity, he has not taken advantage of what little opportunity he has had to seek the company and competition of other men, it is also deeply ironic that he has created a perpetual cycle of maturity rituals and rites of passage to escape his life of perpetual childhood – i.e. built and burst countless dams in an unconscious cycle of protest against repression – yet when his 16th birthday offers him the opportunity to end this cycle by moving out, he voluntarily exposes himself to more repression by choosing to remain at the centre of his father's sphere of influence, his moated fortress. There, he uneasily tries to reconcile this contradiction and simultaneously retreat from his father's influence by living in his head as the "unchallenged lord of the island and the lands about it."[397]

Perhaps more ironic still, though, is the fact that he was offered an easy way out long before he manoeuvred himself into this dead end, and it was his father of all people who offered it to him. Several years ago he gave Frank a pile of novels which, though seemingly unrelated, contain valuable guidance for those on the margins. Some of these novels focus on the margins of society, others on those of sanity, yet one of them navigates the lot with an unerring moral compass, so if Frank had only read this one novel, *The Tin Drum* by Günter Grass, he may have steered clear of his own predicament by studying that of the novel's main protagonist, the man-child Oskar Matzerath whose refusal to mature eventually leads to violence. Yet like Oskar, Frank has always rejected adult guidance along with mental maturity, so he has not read the book, and in his self-imposed ignorance, his physical complex has ruined his moral conduct. Having looked at himself and his place in the world until he was full of irrepressible resentment, and having only ever seen one 'real chance of affecting it' – violence – he has murdered three children before either of them had the chance to be the one thing he can never be: an adult.

Yet if it seems ironic for three – or indeed four – lives to be ruined because of a stubbornly refused reading assignment, consider this: having grown fond of the childish primitivism his father has failed to curb – a primitivism which is given daunting shape in the titular wasp factory, i.e. a homemade oracle-cum-torture chamber for the kind of creepy-crawlies on which young boys enjoy experimenting – Frank loses himself in puerile soldier games to the point at which he confuses machismo with manliness. Hence, he acts like a macho, not a man, when he kills weak relatives, alienates his surviving family members, and orchestrates the emasculating defeat of both his father's and his brother's sense of self, only to realise when he sees them as broken men that, unmanned, he has tried all his life to out-man all those around him, "a small image of the ruthless soldier-hero almost all I've ever seen or read seems to pay strict homage to... talk about penis envy."[398]

Barry Graham – *The Book of Man*

Despite the predominance of hate, however, of broken men with twisted minds who destroy themselves and others, noir can also be about the opposite – love. In fact, as Barry Graham demonstrates in *The Book of Man*, published in 1995, it is not only possible for a noir novel to be a love story, but the potential to be alone, afraid, angry, amoral, and alienating is far greater in love than it is in hate.

This is the story of Michael Illingworth, a Glaswegian underground writer who has just died unexpectedly at the age of 35, or so Kevin Previn, the story's narrator, assumes when he returns to his native Glasgow to research a documentary about his old friend. Yet as Kevin revisits their shared past to look beyond Mike's obituary – a few impersonal lines which fail to reveal the human being behind the literary reputation because they only cover his writing and the fact that "His best and most original work was the despairing novel *The Book of Man*, with its harrowing accounts of drug abuse and urban alienation"[399] – Kevin comes to see that this is really his own story. It is the story of Kevin's long struggle to deal with having needed Mike to find himself, then having needed to leave Mike behind so as not to erase himself in the service of his friend's needs, and finally having needed to come back to Mike so as to face the fearful boy inside himself after years of running from his childhood. In short, this is a story about the difference between need and love.

Researching the last years of Mike's life among the forlorn and forgotten inhabitants of the city's third world districts, Kevin suddenly sees this difference everywhere. Nowhere, however, does it hit him as hard as when he revisits his friendship with Mike and his courtship with Helene, because in each case doing so brings back the memory that they both needed heroin more than they loved him. Reviewing the many highs and lows of these relationships, Kevin observes that "Watching someone fix is like watching someone wank."[400] Perhaps transfixing at first, it can soon leave the observer feeling self-conscious, sordid, and sad. Eventually, he remembers, he could no longer take the loneliness of living among the permanently self-absorbed, but because he could not leave them either, he had a mental breakdown. Facing these facts now, he is fully aware of their many failings, such as the depressing fact that neither of them even noticed his breakdown until he sought professional help, and yet it is he who feels guilty.

If this seems like a confused perception of a clear case of emotional neglect, there is a specific reason for Kevin's guilt. While he nursed his mental health in a psychiatric hospital, he left his partner Helene – a woman suffering from chronic depression as well as heroin addiction – in sole charge of their infant son, David. As he remembers ruefully, "What model parents for David we must have been – Helene out of it on junk most of the time, me almost as much of a child as he was."[401] And as far as Mike is concerned, there is another, more general reason for Kevin's guilt. When Kevin left Glasgow all those years ago, he did so because he prioritised his son and his sanity, and in doing so he felt he did the right thing as a father. Yet now that Mike has died, and seems to have done so because he was deserted by his only friend when he was most in need of one, Kevin feels that in leaving Glasgow he did not do the right thing after all, at least not as a friend. Thus, his research trip turns not only into a journey of self-discovery but also into a penitential pilgrimage during which he seeks in so many ways to tell his old friend, "Mike, I am so sorry."[402]

In the end, however, when Kevin feels that he has finally done his penance, he realises that his story has also been something else entirely. However wrong or wronged he may have been at its various stages, at heart it has always been a love story, given that the lives of the most important people in it have all been defined by the decisions he made in love. Yet as you may have gathered by now, and as Kevin himself is sorely aware, his love story is a far cry from the kind found in Mills & Boon romances. Sure, he has made his life-defining decisions in love, but they could hardly have led to disappointment, despair, and death any faster had he made them all in hate. Counter-intuitive as it may seem, then, this story of pining, pain, and penance is best read as a noir love story.

As for all those bad decisions Kevin makes for the best of reasons, here are just a few examples: when he first became Mike's friend and confidant, he decided to read, discuss, and reread the aspiring author's writing so as to help him find happiness by channelling his self-destructive energy, yet in doing so he encouraged his friend's obsessiveness, exhausted himself, and ended up worn-out to the point of neglecting his responsibilities as a family man. Later, he decided to cut himself off from Mike so as to stem his obsessiveness – and thus the heroin which fuelled it – yet in doing so he neither helped

Mike fight his addiction nor did he force him into making better decisions in the absence of his enabler. He just made him feel alone, afraid, angry, amoral, and alienating, so when Mike dies of some AIDS related illness, Kevin has to assume that he contracted the virus because he no longer cared to take precautions, be it in his communal drug use or in his casual sex.

The bitter irony of Mike's death is that, as Kevin puts it, all he "ever felt for him was unmitigated love,"[403] yet it seems to have been a perceived withdrawal of love, not an abuse of heroin, that killed him. Much as Kevin regrets it, once he had tried everything to resist the pernicious influence of his environment, yet nonetheless failed to take care of his child, he had "to get out of this scene, this whole context"[404] to become a functional father. As the title suggests, he had to close the book on his own childhood and start acting like a man. Yet what may be even more unusual for a noir protagonist than this move towards maturity is his understanding of masculinity. To Kevin, it is about doing what he knows is for the best, not about what makes him feel good.

Perhaps the best example of this mature understanding comes, appropriately enough, at the end of *The Book of Man*. Having avoided confrontation with his parents ever since they made him feel unwanted as a child and gave him his life-long complex of being unworthy of love, he finally goes in search of compensation at his family home, yet what he finds instead, much to his surprise, is closure. Finding them not just reduced but severely diminished – his mother has passed away and his father has gone blind – Kevin suddenly finds that he no longer needs apologies from them. He no longer needs anything from them. All he needs now is the love of his son and the forgiveness of the frightened little boy inside his mind whom he never allowed to leave his fears behind. When he admits this to himself, a vision of the boy comes to him, holds him crying in his arms, and finally releases him from his guilt. So, while *The Book of Man* by Michael Illingworth concludes that "Life is only varying degrees of suffering,"[405] there is no need for that 'only' in *The Book of Man* by Barry Graham. As Kevin's journey illustrates, life in Graham's book is certainly varying degrees of suffering, but for those who face their vulnerability, there is sometimes a light at the end of the tunnel, faint though it may be and far the distance to travel for a protagonist with a history of taking one step forward, ten steps back. Yet whether or not he ever gets there, the prospect that he *might* do – if only at some unspecified point in the far off future, and if only he can hold off a relapse into self-destructive behaviour for long enough to out-manoeuvre the combined forces of his nature and nurture – this faint prospect is the closest that noir ever gets to a happy end.

Duncan McLean – *Bunker Man*

In most noir cases, however, that light turns out to be an oncoming train. As Duncan McLean shows in *Bunker Man*, published in 1995, the typical noir protagonist does not face his vulnerability. He is afraid of it, and for good reason, as it typically ends in *de*generation, not *re*generation. The noir protagonist in question is Rob Catto, a man who hits that unhappy end hard and fast, and then keeps going as though determined to find out just how degenerate a man can become without going to prison or dying in the process, neither of which, by the way, is he keen to avoid for anything as life-affirming as love, but for the deeply disturbing fact that he gets a hell of a kick out of racing to the bottom of that downward spiral.

Part of what makes this so disturbing is that, when we first meet Rob, he seems rather settled, both in his married life and in his new job as head janitor of a school in the North East of Scotland. Yet this seemingly stable sense of self dissolves inexorably, rather like his name does when his wife, Karen, writes it in the sand on a romantic walk along the beach and he watches the tide wash it away. Soon, he starts reacting to his self-destructive impulses as though they, too, were natural forces beyond his control, and from hereon in, there is no stopping the erosion of his life. In his private life, he becomes increasingly distressed by his suspicion that Karen "had things on her mind he didn't know about, he couldn't control,"[406] and his instinctive response to this suspicion is to feel and do precisely what he will later falsely believe Karen to be feeling and doing. So, what he says about his wife, he really ought to be saying about himself, namely that "She wants to have you, to control you, she wants to rule your life. And if she can't do that, she's going to wreck it instead."[407] That, after all, is precisely what happens when, having realised he cannot control Karen's life, he insults her friends, demeans her parents, and eventually even goads someone into raping her.

Meanwhile, his emotional and physical violence is escalating at a similar rate in his professional life. First, the report of a strange man trespassing on the school grounds triggers some serious control issues. Then, a porn magazine which is traced back to a 14-year-old pupil arouses his moral outrage, and after he channels that arousal into a blowjob from the same girl – set, rather symbolically, in a broom closet – it turns into a full-blown affair the very next day. Soon, he is taking full advantage of the girl's need for affection to act out his most depraved sexual fantasies, of which McLean provides in-depth physical descriptions. In doing so, he focuses attention on his protagonists' physical performances and keeps their feelings sketchy, which forces the reader, as the writer and critic Gore Vidal puts it, "to draw upon personal experience in order to fill in the details, thereby achieving one of the ends of all literary art, that of making the reader collaborator."[408] As a result of this imaginary involvement, readers who do not share Rob's fetishes may experience two forms of disgust: one, a visceral disgust, as when he asks his mistress to push a Mars bar into her anus so he can "lie there, gobbling it up, chewing it inch by inch, eating every last bit as it slides out your arsehole."[409] And two, a moral disgust, as when he forces her to comply with his requests by reminding her of their power dynamic: "You've a reputation, Sandra Burnett. Me, I've got a flawless record, twelve years' worth at two schools. Nobody would believe your lies."[410]

At this point, most readers will find Rob rather alienating, be it because they condemn violence on principle or because, as Mark Alfano, an expert in moral psychology, notes, "when people feel the emotion of disgust they are more inclined to describe someone's actions as blameworthy or punishable."[411] Yet lest we rush to any self-righteous moral judgment and miss McLean's subtle critique of all hasty condemnations – be they made by Rob or by his readers – it is worth pausing for a moment's reflection on the novel's historical context. Only two years prior to the publication of *Bunker Man*, John Major, the incumbent Prime Minister of the UK, had famously proclaimed that "Society needs to condemn a little more and understand a little less."[412] McLean makes Rob paraphrase this conservative attitude on several occasions, as when Rob, with tears of righteousness in his eyes, proclaims that feminists, lesbians, drug pushers, and perverts alike merit our condemnation: "We can't pussyfoot around trying to see their point of view, to understand their sad fucking emotional problems. Look at the bastards. Judge them right or wrong. Give them a fair trial, then fucking condemn them. Stamp on them. Wipe them out! It's the only answer. Rid the planet of the cunts." Yet rather than point out Rob's outrageous double standard, his wife answers with compassion, telling him "You need help."[413] And those who can appreciate that Rob's abusive behaviour and right-wing rhetoric are symptoms of Major's public moralism, and that they would only be further encouraged by more condemnation, are likely to agree with her.

As Rob's example demonstrates, the public moralist's stated love of virtue does not always denote a wish to address, never mind amend, personal faults. At least in this case – and the fact that his twisted mind goes unrecognised for years begs the question how often this is also the case in the real world – the public moralist atones for his obstinate adherence to his personal faults with the most virulent intolerance of other people's human frailties. And the only reason this intolerance eventually seems suspicious, at least to his wife, is that he focuses his increasing ill-will on her, though even then it is still too much of a common experience in this Majorite condemnation society for Karen to develop a clear understanding out of her vague sense that "Something nasty's got into you, you never used to be like that."[414] If she could understand the changes in her husband more clearly, she would know that the reason he has become 'like that' – a nasty hypocrite – is that Rob has for a long time now been demonising others for the degenerate tendencies he most detests in himself, and this psychological transference has started to noticeably affect his behaviour. Hence, Karen was beginning to feel he needed help, and "Rob was beginning to feel guilty. He didn't like the feeling."

Unfortunately, Karen does *not* understand her husband better, so she does not see that she, too, might soon need help. She does not see that Rob's moralism is becoming radical because his guilt is becoming impossible to contain after living for so long in the closet, as indeed the novel's title has been suggesting all along. She does not see that he is channelling his guilt for his own secret affair into a violent fantasy that she, too, has a secret lover. She does not see that he is at the dangerous point of daydreaming that, if he "ever found out who it was he'd kill the cunt, he'd smash his head in! Aye, and be proud of it: that kind of cheating dirty cunt deserved everything he got! As for Karen, well, she would deserve everything she got too."[415] And so she does not see that Rob is about to finish his race down that long spiral of degeneration, that he is planning for her to be there when he hits rock bottom, and that, in a quintessentially noir closing scene – which you should read before you read the rest of this paragraph – he is about to bully the titular 'Bunker Man' – a naïve recluse whom he has carefully groomed for the part – into beating and raping her, just so he can act out his revenge fantasy and smash the man's head in. Aye, and be proud of it.

Irvine Welsh – *Filth*

What this type of noir comes down to is man's defeat by the very urges he most detests about himself, and in *Bunker Man* McLean probably took this type of noir far enough for most of us to be deeply disturbed. Yet to those familiar with any of Irvine Welsh's work, it will come as no surprise that in the aptly titled *Filth*, published in 1998, Welsh took it even further. This is the story of a degenerate who becomes so controlled by his self-hatred that he ends up killing himself, yet what may be even more disturbing than this dark development, or the fact that his death is inevitable all along and seems more deserved with every page, is that when this morbid end finally arrives, it is unexpectedly moving, as it comes at just the moment when he no longer seems worth hating.

When we first meet this man, an Edinburgh policeman by name of Bruce Robertson, he is breaking just about every professional and civil code of conduct he knows, along with quite a few of which he seems never to have even heard. When he is not abusing his authority to extract illegal substances or sexual favours from suspects, he is abusing himself or his friends with a reckless abandon that verges on a death wish and a range of emotional violence that eventually terrifies even him. As he repeatedly admits to himself, and surely to no reader's surprise, "I'm consumed by an overwhelming urge to be cruel... The impulse to hurt and control, in order to try and fill the void inside."[416] As he further admits to himself, and again surely to no reader's surprise, he cannot see this ever changing, since "We hate ourselves for being unable to be other than what we are. Unable to be better."[417]

What may come as a surprise though – to Bruce as well as to his readers – is that there are several ways of reading this seemingly straight-forward expression of universal self-loathing. One way to read it, and one way to explain why Bruce often sounds a bit grand, is that he thinks of himself in the royal 'we'. If such a reading seems far-fetched in view of his far from regal manners, it may be worth remembering just how reminiscent the name Bruce Robertson is of Robert the Bruce, also known as Robert I who famously reigned over an internally divided Scotland from 1306 to 1329. In an extension of this reading, there is something of note in the fact that Bruce is elected the local Police Union Representative and proud to hold this office as the people's champion. After all, he is also an aggressive schizophrenic who represents "the guiding principle of destroying without overtly making enemies. The corporate way."[418] So, the fact that this hypocritical careerist has the support of his colleagues suggests that in modern-day Scotland, much like in the early 14th century, the statement 'we hate ourselves for being unable to be other than what we are' can be read as: we hate ourselves for being unable to be other than internally divided by hypocrites with foreign agendas. Unable to be better, nationally.

Then again, this would not be an Irvine Welsh novel if such grand critique were not accompanied by some tongue-in-cheek satire. As we soon discover, Bruce, the parasite of the Scottish police, has his own parasite. He has a talking tapeworm which serves up choice pieces of background information, all of which Bruce has spent years repressing. Yet Bruce only discovers that he even has a tapeworm when it has hollowed out a good bit of his stomach, and the fact that it has also been hollowing out his machismo escapes his notice entirely. He has no idea that his tapeworm can talk, nor that it has been talking over him all along, both figuratively and literally. While Bruce has been presenting us with his hyper-macho view of the world, his tapeworm has repeatedly 'talked over' him in the sense that it has delivered several of its own monologues. And in a visually striking display of macho satire, these increasingly authoritative worm monologues blot out large sections of Bruce's first-person narrative, as they are superimposed on the text in speech bubbles which slither down the centre of the page in the shape of a fat worm.

One way to read these worm monologues is as a guttural voiceover, a running commentary which reveals how Bruce really feels – deep down inside, as it were – and why he feels that way. It does so by probing into Bruce's sub-conscious, where the man has buried the many traumas he suffered in his formative years, and the deeper his worm probes, the more it fills what Bruce calls 'the void inside' – and the more frequently Bruce uses the pronoun 'we' when talking about himself. So the 'we' in the above statement – 'we hate ourselves for being unable to be other than what we are' – may well refer to Bruce and his tapeworm, in which case their perception of one another takes on a new significance. In that case, it is significant that Bruce perceives his tapeworm in the same way as he perceives the working class – as a parasite – and that he makes similarly aggressive attempts at distancing himself from both, because once the worm has dug through enough layers of repression, it eventually reveals that Bruce himself is a member of said class. He was raised in a mining community and, despite having long since climbed the social ladder, its traumas have done irreparable damage to his worldview, because they have stuck with him as tenaciously as his tapeworm – that other part of him which he perceives as a parasite yet simply cannot flush out of his system. So, when Bruce says 'we hate ourselves for being unable to be other than what we are,' perhaps what he means is that we – those who have tried in vain to rise above traumatic experience as it gradually eats away at them – hate ourselves for being unable to be other than the product of our traumas. Unable to be better, psychologically.

Yet before we get to the many traumas of Bruce Robertson, and the way in which they eventually consume him, it is worth noting that there is another way of reading his tapeworm. It may also symbolise the aggressive lad culture which is at risk of destroying the police service from within. Remember, Bruce is in charge of a high-profile murder investigation, yet for the most part this is all too easy to forget, given that, when he is not busy pranking his supposed friends, poaching his colleagues' wives, or partying with confiscated drugs, he is playing what he calls 'the games' to improve his chances of promotion to Detective Inspector, and these protracted games, which mainly consist of hurtful jokes about minorities and spiteful sabotage of the competition, distract both him and his team from the case. So, perhaps his tapeworm is articulating the true motive of this lad culture when he admits that concealed aggression "is the only real way I can interact with the environment I am in."[419]

In any case, far from objecting to his laddish behaviour, the institutional chauvinism and latent racism are so strong in this almost exclusively white male environment that most of his friends and colleagues approve of it, at least unofficially, and all the more so in this case, since the victim is black. Once this ethnic detail is established, it further weakens their already feeble commitment to serve and protect the public from criminals, most of whom they quite happily abide, at times even aid and abet, since "their antics mean newspaper headlines, which means big-time OT and a cry for extra polis resources. That's the way it works."[420] In the spirit of this unofficial pragmatism, Bruce and his boys do make the odd routine inquiry for the sake of appearances, but so as not to risk accidentally closing the case, and thus capping their overtime pay, they invest as little energy as possible into following up several leads on a mysterious woman who is alleged to have been with the victim at the time of his death. The rest of their energy, and there are considerable reserves left after so little work, is invested into competing with each other by doing drink, drugs, and most depravities known to man, until the book reads like one big penis measuring contest, first metaphorically and then literally. After setting each of his colleagues up for a humiliating fall in one macho dare or another, Bruce finally has them all photocopy their penises for an office party game, and as if to capture his life philosophy in a single image, he secretly uses the enlarge function on the photocopier to win by any means necessary.

In case that image is not explicit enough, though, Bruce also states his life philosophy explicitly. As far as he is concerned, "Life is one big competition."[421] And since his society strikes him as being so tolerant of attacks on its meritocracy that it has lowered standards in the spirit of equal treatment, he believes that the able and ambitious simply have to practice ruthlessness. Hence, he neither makes apologies nor does he hold himself to account for being both a bigot and a bully. Yet rather than judge him for this, Welsh sends in the tapeworm. Thus, we learn that...

This is where I must ask you to skip to the next section or accept my apologies for revealing major plot points in the hope of showing how the death of such a lowlife can leave anyone as highly conflicted as I suggested in the introduction.

... Bruce is the son of a man he only calls 'The Beast', a currently imprisoned sex offender who raped Bruce's mother and bequeathed him a genetic time bomb of mental health problems, including schizophrenia, bipolar disorder, and anxiety attacks. We learn that this made Bruce an outsider in the mining community of his childhood, that he has tried to bury his traumatic memories ever since he accidentally got his stepbrother killed in a mine, and that his failure to move on has made him feel like an outcast for life. We learn that his first girlfriend died in another lethal accident he caused, that his philandering is a release valve for his many unprocessed emotions, and that his wife and daughter have recently left him, both making accusations of domestic abuse. And when it seems as though his situation could not possibly become any more depressing, we learn that he has since been role-playing to sustain the illusion of familial happiness, that, when dressed as a woman, he murdered a man whom he falsely suspected of cuckolding him, and that, in doing so, he became the mysterious woman he and his team should have been investigating all along.

So, when he eventually commits suicide, the darkest hour of his life coincides with the most noir moment of the novel, and this, perhaps surprisingly for those who have not read the novel, has rather little to do with suicide being the superlative of noir. It has far more to do with the fact that Bruce ends his life at the very moment when two deeply disturbing impressions are suspended in a highly conflicting tension. On the one hand, there is the impression that some form of punishment, perhaps even death, has seemed more deserved every time he has opened his mouth – or fly – to abuse his environment with a seemingly endless outpouring of toxic waste. On the other hand, however, there is an equally strong impression which has gradually crept up on us in the shape of his increasingly empathetic tapeworm – the impression that Bruce has suffered as much abuse in his short life as he has made others suffer in return. So, when he ends his own life because it is the only thing he can do to ensure that those in it will no longer be terrorised by the dark urges he so detests in himself, it suddenly seems that there may be yet another way of reading the novel's central statement: 'we hate ourselves for being unable to be other than what we are.' In that moment of utter despair and ultimate defeat, it seems that what he has been trying to say all along is that we, those who cannot ask for help, hate ourselves for being unable to be other than alone, afraid, angry, amoral, and alienating in a society which all too often treats mental illness as personal weakness. Unable to be better, socially.

Ray Banks – *Beast of Burden*

When such a last-minute realisation concludes a life-long process of (self-) destruction, something profound can change in the way we read the noir protagonist's death. The prior conviction that his death will not be mourned, steadily reinforced until just a moment ago, now seems heartless, and as we appreciate the human potential for change through the renunciation of one's dark nature, most of us will come to see the departed in a much warmer light, perhaps even empathise with him. As in the case above, this works especially well when disillusionment and death are not delivered by some deus ex machina but arrive unexpectedly with what, in hindsight, turns out to be psychological necessity, as when the protagonist's long-lost conscience finally catches up with him, and in Scotland, no one does this better than Irvine Welsh – apart perhaps from Ray Banks, the dark horse of Scottish Noir.

Having first made his name by ploughing a lone furrow on the shared ground between noir and PI fiction, Banks has over the past decade advanced to cult status on the fringe of the Scottish literary scene. Along the way, he has earned a reputation for writing with near enough unparalleled emotional integrity, or as he puts it, "That bloody emotional integrity thing's going to follow me to the grave, isn't it? Alright, I do actively strive towards truth of character, so there's no moral judgment in my books, and I think the key to art is empathy, which is why I write in the first person, but it's difficult to maintain your characters' emotional integrity as they change throughout a series. That's been my aim, but I don't know if I've been wholly successful."[422]

Perhaps the best measure of this success is *Beast of Burden*, published in 2009 as the last of four novels about long-suffering PI Callum Innes. Originally from Edinburgh, Cal started and soon stalled his car crash of a career in Manchester. Newly out of prison, and entirely out of his depth in the world of his client, gang lord Morris Tiernan, Cal made a horrible mess of unlicensed private investigation in his debut, the 2006 novel *Saturday's Child*, so even back then Cal was what the crime critic Lee Horsley calls "the antithesis of the iconic private eye – morally deficient, lacking in all effective agency and representing traumatized masculinity at its most vulnerable."[423] Yet as he comes full circle in *Beast of Burden*, where he once again works for Tiernan, Cal is even more unlike the iconic private eye in that he is obviously, and with great difficulty, carrying the burden of his past.

Having suffered a stroke, he limps along on a cane with his face set in a partial but permanent smirk, so he can neither wise-crack his way out of a fight nor fight his way out of his predatory environment. To stay one step ahead anyway, Cal has to hustle, much like most PIs do, yet unlike the moral compromises of his fictional colleagues, his are far from attractive. Cal, after all, is nothing like the genre-typical, boozed and sexed up private dick. He is an impotent cripple, a broken man who was raped in prison and has since become addicted to painkillers. And while his physical infirmity sets him apart from most private investigators, the emotional integrity of Banks's writing sets him apart from most protagonists in any genre.

Banks writes close up, always. In Cal's case, this means not only that he writes in the first person and in the present tense but also that he lets us see how Cal feels in the way he talks, in his mood sensitive speech rhythm. To put it in the words of the noir critic James Naremore, "This rhythm is meant to seem more instinctive than eloquent. It is a transparent language, of the sort that wants to cut through the crap and get down to truths so basic to the culture that they seem like natural laws."[424] In *Beast of Burden*, this instinctive rhythm beats behind the plot like a walking bass line in a blues song.

Meanwhile, the plot reinforces this blues rhythm as it, too, follows a cyclical pattern of repetition with variation. Like in his first case, Cal is hired by Morris Tiernan and ends up in trouble because of Tiernan's son, Mo. Only this time, Cal does not get into trouble with Tiernan Senior because Mo gets in the way of his investigation. This time, Mo goes missing, but Cal gets into trouble with Tiernan Sr. nonetheless, because the gang lord finds out that Cal did not take the case for money, as he had claimed, but for payback. His vulnerable brother had re-entered his life, as he had done in his first case, to ask for help kicking his drug habit, only this time his brother dies and Cal blames his dealers, the Tiernans, so he only agrees to work for them as a freelance PI because the job looks like his best chance to ruin their family business – or just their family. Cal has never been one to quibble, and in this case, as he puts it in his 'transparent language', "These people fucked my life. They deserve everything they get."[425]

Unfortunately, Cal has never been in a worse position to take the fight to a social institution like the Tiernan crime syndicate. So, although things initially look like they did in his first case, where his increasingly desperate attempts to retain control at least met with partial success, he eventually loses control of this case entirely, and then he loses control of himself. In his attempt to overcome the Tiernans, he becomes ever more like them as he is gradually consumed by his own violence, and Banks charts this degeneration all the way to its deeply disturbing but psychologically sound and dramatically necessary conclusion. As Horsley explains, "The revenge plot, with its central action of exposing and scourging, requires a protagonist who strips off the civilised part of himself and accepts a reduction to a primitive or existential state in which he is capable of the violence required to bring down or reduce the transgressor."[426] Being that pared-back protagonist, and being written with unflinching character consistency even in his ugliest moments, Cal is soon on the ropes and hopelessly punch-drunk, so when he eventually finds Mo dead, he thinks that beating up the corpse is a risk worth taking to make it look like the man was killed by his resentful sister, yet since this is a noir novel, his last-ditch attempt to trigger a family feud backfires. Tiernan Sr. sees it coming and focuses the full force of his mighty pride and violent temperament on the now down and out would-be avenger.

Yet before Banks finally lets Cal roll over and die, he suspends him – and his readers – in an uneasy uncertainty about the consequences of his risk-taking. As in Cal's first case, Banks challenges the PI's typical sense of individual autonomy, objectivity, and authority by splitting the novel's narrative perspective between two first-person points of view. Only this time, the second narrator is not Mo, so there is no certainty about whether Cal indirectly had a hand in his death. Instead, there is reason to believe that he will get done over whether or not he was involved in the death, and whether or not Tiernan Sr. thinks so, because the second narrator is Detective Iain Donkin, also known as 'Donkey', and this long-time nemesis is not only unwavering in his conviction that Cal is guilty. He is also uncompromising in his method of getting Cal a conviction, be it in or preferably outside of a courtroom. So he pursues Cal long after he has been suspended from duty on a charge of police brutality, and although the two of them would fiercely contest the point, this die-hard perseverance proves just how close they are to one another psychologically.

Although they strenuously deny it on several occasions, neither of them is really after the truth. In contrast to typical PI fiction in which, as the literary historian Maurizio Ascari puts it, "the quest for 'truth' and for a 'transcendental meaning' is still a prime motive,"[427] Cal and Donkey are both driven by a dark and desperate need to convince everybody that their story, and their story alone, is the truth. As their conflicting accounts of one another – and of the case on which they are both working – steadily increases the uncertainty whether their respective risk-taking will pay off, the two slowly but surely become more alike, first because they both behave like the titular beast of burden, and ultimately because they both back their way into a dramatic moment of disillusionment.

The only difference is that, when Donkey suddenly discovers that he was wrong to suspect Cal of murder and that his vigilantism in the pursuit of an innocent has got him kicked off the force, he seeks solace in cynicism. When Cal suddenly discovers that he was wrong to underestimate Tiernan Sr. and that he will not get away with his bad decision to seek revenge, he realises with similar surprise that his long-lost conscience has finally caught up with him, so he gives up on revenge and instead seeks redemption. For once, he tries to make a good decision, one which will not perpetuate the cycle of violence which his life up until this point has been, but end it once and for all. In the certain knowledge that Mo's real murderer, if discovered, will be murdered in turn, Cal decides to protect him with a false confession because he still sees hope for the man, because although this man has turned to violence, much like he himself has done time and again, Cal knows that, unlike himself, the man has not been ruined by it yet. So, even though his self-sacrifice comes at the highest price – his life – Cal confesses to Mo's murder, which is to say he demonstrates that, even in noir, there is real potential for change through the renunciation of one's dark nature. Alas, in *Beast of Burden*, it leads not to noir's version of a happy end – disaster deferred, relapse implied – but to a death as disturbing and conflicting as the life it destroys.

Liam McIlvanney – *All the Colours of the Town*

Further evidence of this grim prospect, though with a more intellectual than emotional focus, comes in the misleadingly titled novel *All the Colours of the Town*. Published in 2009, this is the debut of Liam McIlvanney, son of the celebrated William McIlvanney, and thus perhaps by rights the 'Godson of Tartan Noir'. The latter title, of course, is a flight of fancy, but should it, or a variation of it, ever gain traction in Scotland's literary landscape, chances are it would not be a privilege of birth as much as a distinction conferred on merit. As McIlvanney Junior shows in *All the Colours of the Town*, he not only has the vision and skill to create a convincing scenario in which a noir protagonist embarks upon a journey of self-destruction and yet manages to rise above his dark instincts, love another more than he hates himself, and demonstrate this transformation by way of self-sacrifice. He also has the unsettling knack to make disagreeable protagonists likeable, and in this case he uses it to full effect by sending two of them on a long journey of redemption only to show that, in the end, not even a redeemed noir protagonist has a bright future.

In *All the Colours of the Town*, he shows this with regard to two protagonists, one on either side of the law. Gerry Conway has just about made his name as one of Glasgow's leading political journalists when he gets an anonymous tipoff that Peter Lyons, now the Justice Minister of Scotland, had connections to loyalist paramilitaries in the early 1980s. This, of course, was a long time ago, and the two have since developed a friendly, mutually beneficial relationship, so at first Conway is conflicted about digging up dirt on Lyons. For one thing, he knows that Lyons is the First Minister in waiting and intends to make him his Director of Communications. What is more, he knows that Lyons, whether or not he was bad in the past, has been good for Scotland. As he puts it, "To hear some of his acolytes talk, he had saved the new Parliament from dying of embarrassment."[428]

So, not only has Lyons already been good for the country, but he promises to be even better for Conway in the future, and yet, in the short-term, a politician with a paramilitary past might just be best for copy. Fact is, Conway knows, "In this part of Scotland, sectarianism sold. It was better than sex."[429] His conflict, then, comes down to the question whether to act against his journalistic instinct by ignoring the tipoff or whether to act against his country's establishment – and indeed against his own long-term interests – by investigating Lyons on the off chance that the tipoff should turn out to be true, and it is in his resolution of this conflict that Conway proves himself to be a rather uncommon noir protagonist. Sure, he makes his decision on a subversive impulse, which is common enough in noir, but the decision itself, and the fact that he follows through on it, express a spirit of idealism which is rare indeed: "I wanted to know if a fact, properly primed and planted, could still make a difference."[430]

Thus, he follows the story to Northern Ireland, where his encounter with the country's sectarianism, both past and present, soon makes him self-consciously explore Scotland's part in 'The Troubles'. Reviewing the status quo with his own shameful memories in mind, memories of growing up sheltered yet posturing as one of the oppressed, he realises that, "Across the West of Scotland, in the clubs and lodges, the stadiums and bars, people missed the Troubles... There is something narcotic in watching a war unfold on your doorstep, knowing all the while it can't harm you."[431] At the thought that men like Lyons and, he is ashamed to admit, men like him hijacked an historical cause without suffering the consequences, he is emboldened to make a high-profile example of Lyons. Yet as he does so on the payroll of a newspaper which will only print his story because such scandalous exposés titillate a lot of readers and thus increase circulation, he feels increasingly ambivalent about his role in reducing sectarian violence to a spectator sport, all the more so when he realises that his colleagues in Northern Ireland cannot afford to match his paper's enthusiasm for whistleblowers, because those who live there still risk their lives when they report the truth about the lasting repercussions of The Troubles. As one of them puts it, "That's what they do here… They shoot people dead for telling the truth."[432] Sobered by these realisations, Conway starts taking his lead from the locals, and soon he, too, is risking his life by scratching the cosmopolitan surface of Belfast, "the foreign city with its repertoire of hurt,"[433] all the more so since he is a Catholic in enemy territory.

Thus, McIlvanney not only takes his protagonist a long way out of his comfort zone. He also locates his journey of enlightenment in the larger context of what the noir critic Naremore calls "the Dark City, a literary topos inherited from the nineteenth century."[434] In this dark city, Conway captures his impressions of 21st century Northern Ireland – including its ancient heirlooms of tribal violence which lie scattered among the country's current affairs like unexploded ordnance – with a sharp eye for the telling details of political allegiance and a sensitive ear for the coded messages of the pathologically suspicious. Yet the most accurate measure of the mess left in this not so distant corner of the British Empire is that, despite his considerable sensitivity, Conway's account of his visit reads like a late-19th century travelogue of a virgin adventurer who cannot escape the disturbing impression that he has gone off the map. What appeared to be a familiar culture, back when he looked at it from across the water, turns out to be wildly different and disorienting as he rapidly loses his way among hordes of unpredictable strangers and dangerous savages who seem to be accosting him from a time and place far, far away. Soon, one local confirms this impression by asking him, "Aren't you a little, *delicate* for your line of work, Mr Conway?"[435] And after he gets on the wrong side of another one, he has to admit, "The beating had discomposed me. I was no longer a unit but a rackety assemblage, a jerry-built contraption of a man."[436]

The fact, though, that he can feel this far out at sea in his neighbouring country, and in this day and age, has less to do with the delicate state of his nerves than it does with the delicate state of Northern Ireland, a country which despite the peace process has remained deeply divided. As Conway charts its moral and political fault lines, he traces its present division back to its many unresolved legacy issues, such as the grievous economic disparities between those who paid for the privilege of living in NI with the lives of family members and those who are now paid EU development money to lay off their murderous trade. Making it even more difficult to navigate this minefield of historical grievance and international interference is the ever more frustrating fact that Conway fears he cannot trust anyone to be straight with him. While some object strongly to UK imperialism, and others just as strongly to EU incentives, no one will give him the full story, and as his probing questions are answered with silence, suspicion, and subterfuge, Conway gets the uneasy feeling that The Troubles are far from over.

So, while Belfast initially strikes him as reminiscent of "an older Glasgow, a darker, truer city before the stone-cleaning and the logos, Princes Square and the City of Culture," he eventually realises that, "For all the city's hard-man swagger, its razor kings and ice-cream murders, Glasgow wasn't Belfast. A life meant something in Glasgow, a death mattered, in a way it didn't here."[437] And it is when he fully understands this contrast that Conway finally understands his case. He understands how someone like Lyons could have been attracted to the darker, truer sectarianism of an Irish paramilitary group like the Ulster Volunteer Force. He understands that Lyons is a terror tourist, that he is not the kind to sign up for life, but that he enjoyed playing a bit part in their armed campaign. And he understands why Lyons walked away from the UVF. He understands that, for all his hard-man swagger, Lyons walked away because association with terrorism in Ireland is career suicide for those with political ambition in Scotland.

Yet before Conway finally links Lyons to The Troubles, McIlvanney first lingers on Conway's family troubles. To readers of political thrillers, this may come as a surprise, and since the novel's domestic scenes are noticeably slower paced than its investigative plot, they may seem like unnecessarily retarding elements, the artistic indulgence perhaps of a young father and debut author. Yet *All the Colours of the Town* is far more than a political thriller. It is also a noir novel, and by re-enacting the political drama on a private stage – by showing how a failed marriage and an unresolved custody battle can make a man doubt his judgment along with his fitness to serve as a role model – these domestic scenes allow for a much fuller appreciation of the novel's central theme: the cross-generational and compromise-based Realpolitik that is reshaping Europe's Western Front at the beginning of the 21st century. Indeed, by revealing that idealists like Conway can, in their own ways, be as compromised and wanting as ideologues like Lyons, these scenes subtly suggest that most Realpolitik is determined by people who are as compromised and wanting as the nations for which they fight.

And for a truly noir ending…

Please skip the end of this section if you do not wish to read here how the novel ends, or read on, duly forewarned that I am about to tell you in the hope of showing just how fast things can fall apart in noir.

… McIlvanney radically rewrites the bright future for which both men seemed destined. Lyons is imprisoned after Conway's exposé is published, and Conway himself discovers only too late that he has unwittingly abetted a criminal conspiracy to remove the Justice Minister, so he is fired. In the end, then, the two men who tried to do so much to make Scotland a better place – one by risking his life in search of the truth, the other by consigning the worst of himself to the past in the service of the country's future – both have to realise that they have been played, that they have lost big, and that they have been handed a piss-poor consolation prize: the bitter knowledge that they have not only failed to make Scotland a better place, but in the process made themselves living examples of the noir fact that, in the end, it hardly matters who is in government. Criminals are in power.

THE ROUNDUP

This, then, is Scottish Noir, or at least a representative sample of its many conventions and contrasts. It is a literature which frequently disrespects genre boundaries and crosses over into such literary traditions as mystery, tragedy, and horror, so perhaps the only thing which can be said about it in summary is that it is as highly diverse as it is deeply disturbing. Yet as I hope to have shown in this and the previous three chapters, and as I hope even those will agree who have not found their personal favourites in these pages, it is ultimately a literature which has rather little in common with so-called 'Tartan Noir' – the world-famous brand of dark-ish but rather conservative Scottish crime fiction – so I will try to summarise in counterpoint.

Point number one: the Tartan Noir brand has largely been defined by the man who invented it, Ian Rankin, and the likes of Val McDermid and Stuart MacBride who, like Rankin, are internationally bestselling authors with well-established reputations for writing about police detectives. Yet out of the ten writers in this chapter, only four write about cops, and not one of them respects the police novel's central genre convention, the hassled but heroic cop. And their subversion goes even further. Not one of them agrees with Rankin – who has nonetheless been feted as the 'King of Tartan Noir' – that the legal, political, and social systems which govern Scotland are, ultimately, worth defending, so the cops in Scottish Noir are in many ways unlike those in Tartan Noir.

This, of course, is not to say that the latter do not break or at least bend a few laws to preserve order. They do, hence the popular belief that their stories are noir. But in real noir, that is not what cops do. As the sample above indicates, noir cops do not break the law, nor do they even bend it, to preserve order, because there is no order for them to preserve, at least not the public order which they are paid to preserve. In those stories, as Ray Banks indicates by writing about a rogue cop who tries to play the system but is overwhelmed by its many ever-shifting hierarchies of more or less visible centres of unofficial power, there is only a criminal order and it does not respect police authority. What makes this situation even more overwhelming is that, unlike their colleagues in Tartan Noir, who typically have some minor flaws but manage them heroically, cops in Scottish Noir have major flaws which they cannot manage at all, and the reason for this, too, is simple. As William McIlvanney indicates by writing about a cop who causes several preventable deaths because he is as flawed as the system which he is meant to serve and protect, there are no heroes in Scottish Noir, just protagonists.

As I hope to have shown, however, the greatest difference between the cops in Tartan Noir and those in Scottish Noir is that the latter rarely care about laws or flaws, never mind the solution of some criminal mystery, because none of that can command their attention for very long. As Irvine Welsh indicates by writing about a cop who spends as little time examining criminals as he spends examining his conscience, cops in Scottish Noir tend to spend most of their time grappling with the unintended consequence of somebody's ceaseless struggle against the feeling of being alone, afraid, angry, amoral, and alienating – and usually this struggle is their own. As for the few occasions upon which cops are not themselves struggling – as when Hugh C. Rae writes about two who seem fairly stable as they arrest a man who is clearly not – there is no happy end here either, no conservative notion that all is well now that order has finally been restored, because what is revealed about human nature along the way is so deeply disturbing that the capture of one criminal seems rather insignificant.

Point number two: Tartan Noir is reputed to be dark and gritty, but as every novel discussed in this chapter shows, 'dark and gritty' means something very different in Scottish Noir. In Tartan Noir, as I have tried to show in the previous three chapters, it typically denotes a social and psychological realism which is, to a varying but significant extent, sanitised for public consumption. Some of its protagonists do struggle, but ultimately even their worst struggles are nowhere near as deeply disturbing as those dramatised in Scottish Noir, where protagonists typically live beyond the reach of our social and emotional support systems and can rarely even afford the hope, never mind the prospect, of being rehabilitated by novel's end. What is more, most of them also live beyond our sight – and thus in many cases beyond our understanding – because their lives are confined to the third world which lies in the shadow of the first, and they take for granted depths of desperation and depravity which most readers are bound to consider dreadful. Scottish Noir, then, is not just darker and grittier than Tartan Noir. It is also more extreme, because it shows the world as it is, not as it has to be for the hero's flaws to be contained by the system, for the system to seem strained but serviceable, and for the status quo to seem worthy of service, strain, and sacrifice.

Yet lest this should create the false impression that Scottish Noir is written by anarchists, it is worth noting that not even those with strong anti-establishment agendas – writers like Alexander Trocchi, Irvine Welsh, Barry Graham, and Ray Banks – oppose the conservative ideology of mainstream crime fiction simply by bringing down the system. They do something far more subversive. They say that the system cannot be brought down, at least not by those who suffer most under it. They say that when such an individual goes up against an institution, the institution wins, every time. And perhaps more subversive still, they tell the truth about those who live on the wrong side of the tracks, about their ordinary madness of life, which is to say that they shatter the mainstream notion of what is normal. They say that the overwhelming majority of those who are forced to suffer will either pass on their suffering or fall apart, and sometimes both, because in the real world, suffering rarely produces saints. In the real world, suffering generally just produces more suffering, and for readers of Scottish Noir there is no escaping this, not into the moral whitewash of a happy end, not into the scapegoating of a black sheep, and not into Tartan Noir's often implicit promise that, the plot notwithstanding, no likeable protagonist was lastingly damaged in the making of this novel.

Point number three: while the main protagonists of Tartan Noir typically escape countless dramatic scrapes with barely a mark on them, and with even fewer psychological scars, those of Scottish Noir have to live with the health- and often soul-destroying consequences of their bad decisions. And we have to live with the thought that they live among us. Few of them, after all, are arrested for their actions, injurious to personal and public safety though they typically are, and it is almost as rare that they are otherwise prevented from future acts of (self-) destruction. Besides, even Alexander Trocchi, Hugh C. Rae, Gordon Williams, and Liam McIlvanney, who do have characters arrested for their crimes, do not ultimately reassure their readers that the system works, seeing as their conclusions suggest that the police can only contain criminal behaviour to a disturbingly insignificant extent. In each case, a lot of other crime goes unpunished, and what is revealed about the immense human capacity for crime is so deeply disturbing that, once again, the capture of one criminal seems rather insignificant.

William McIlvanney makes the same point, suggesting that criminal behaviour can only be contained to a disturbingly insignificant extent, but he does not even let the police contain it to said disturbingly insignificant extent by arresting the criminal. Instead, he lets other criminals take the law into their own hands by executing one of their own, so in his case the conclusion is even more disturbing, as it suggests that crime is so deeply ingrained in our social system that it has layers which the state can neither probe nor police. This, incidentally, may well be where his philosophy is closest to that of his son, Liam McIlvanney, who suggests the same deeply ingrained power dynamic on the afore-mentioned second level of his conclusion. As for the only other writer in this sample who eventually prevents his protagonist from future acts of (self-) destruction, Irvine Welsh is perhaps the most radical in that he enforces this preventive measure, not by any external means such as arrest or execution, but by the ultimate internal form of punishment, suicide. His protagonist's only external punishment is demotion, but such punishment is laughable considering what he does to himself afterwards and what his prior treatment of others suggests about the police at large, namely that there must be other cops as depraved as him on the force. After all, despite the fact that his conduct is more reprehensible than that of the criminals he is paid to arrest, he is neither arrested himself nor even sacked. He is merely put back into uniform and let loose on the public.

Point number four: while most 'baddies' are eventually stopped and punished in Tartan Noir, and while most protagonists of Scottish Noir behave much worse than those 'baddies', most of the latter are too complex to have such a morally simplistic label affixed to them, and most of them get away with it – 'it' being all manner of morally and legally transgressive behaviour. Even Duncan McLean's protagonist, who is caught in the act by his wife, transgresses with impunity, for by the end of the novel neither the police nor the public have become aware of his crimes, and, judging by his past ruthlessness, he is not the kind of man who will let another person, least of all a woman, get in the way of future thoughts and acts of transgressive self-gratification, never mind his feverish self-destruction.

Similarly, Ray Banks lets his main criminal act with impunity despite the existence of a witness who might testify against him, and in his case, this is more than just implicit in the previous actions of the criminal and the charged atmosphere of an open end. It is made explicit in the novel's merciless conclusion, when the criminal casually has the witness killed and cleverly avoids police suspicion. With no one left to testify against him, he can rest assured that he has got away with his past crimes, and with no one suspecting him of this one, he can take it for granted that no punishment will get in the way of future transgressions – something, incidentally, which is also true in Liam McIlvanney's case. Not only does his main criminal have a persona non grata removed by letting others do the dirty work, but he, too, can take it for granted that he will get away with it – and future ploys like it – so much routine does he have in transgressing with impunity.

Point number five: when it comes to predatory rule breaking, Tartan Noir tends to focus on clues and containment strategies, Scottish Noir on the animal instincts which turn ordinary people into orgiastic predators. This, of course, does not mean that Tartan

Noirists do not mention such instincts. They do. But real noirists, as I hope to have shown, do a lot more than just mention them or structure the kind of mystery around them which focuses on how such instincts affect other people in the form of crime. Real noirists focus most of their and their protagonists' attention on how the animal side of a person can become enlarged to the point at which it controls and defines him, and how that person can then act as a predator and still get away with breaking society's rules, if for no other reason than that, whatever rules he might break, he respects at least one: the rule of the jungle. Take, for instance, the transgressors of Barry Graham, Gordon Williams, Alexander Trocchi, and Iain Banks. Different though they are emotionally, psychologically, philosophically, and sexually, they all put self-interest first. They all ruthlessly take what they want, be it hard drugs or harder actions, another man's wife or another man's life.

To those who had not read, nor even read about, any real noir from Scotland prior to reading this chapter, but had been led to believe otherwise because Tartan Noir had been sold to them as the real deal, this will have come as some surprise. And as I hope to have shown by separating the respective literary traditions, Scottish Noir has little to nothing in common with the detective, police, and serial killer fiction collectively known as Tartan Noir. It is altogether darker and more disturbing, which brings me to a final observation which may be of interest even to those who, prior to reading this book, had not connected the term with any Scottish crime fiction but had instead thought of 'Tartan Noir' more loosely, be it as a type of tartan or as a label for a literature which somehow meets the conflicting demands of being at once black and colourful. So, at the risk of stating the obvious at the end of this dark chapter, it may be worth noting that, apart from its country of origin, Scottish Noir has nothing in common with a tartan, not even a dark one.

First of all, since only three of the writers in this chapter – William McIlvanney, Iain Banks, and Irvine Welsh – have spent any length of time in the limelight of the Scottish literary scene, and since even their collected noir writings would hardly fill a single shelf, never mind an entire window display in a high street bookshop, it seems fair to generalise that Scotland's noirists are neither as common a sight nor as commodified as the country's world-famous tartans. And just about as obvious as this difference in visibility is the difference in design. Tartans are patterns made by criss-crossed horizontal and vertical bands in multiple colours, patterns which – unlike any of the novels discussed in this chapter – are designed with a very limited number of elements in an instantly recognisable fashion and an easily discernible layout, because even the darkest tartan has at least two colours. Thus, a noir – i.e. black – tartan is chromatically impossible and the term 'Tartan Noir' an oxymoron.

So much for the literal problem. As for the term's figurative meaning, that, too, is misleading, as it creates the false impression that the literature, like the pattern which is worn on kilts, wraps, hats, and all manner of accessories by men and women alike, is unisex, i.e. that it is written in similar numbers by men and women about men and women. Perhaps just as misleadingly, it suggests that the literature, like the pattern, is defined by clear contrasts between light and dark, i.e. that it offers clear distinctions between right and wrong alongside clear-cut categories of guilt and innocence. Typically, however, the Scottish noirist is male, focuses mainly on male protagonist and male issues, and, as the noir critic Naremore observes, does not write about "guilt and innocence, or even about professional ethics, but about what he regards as a bewildering, predatory struggle beneath civilisation."[438]

That, in a sentence, is Scottish Noir's most defining trend. So, while the tartan label, at least in its figurative meaning, is well suited to some of the more colourful writing discussed in previous chapters – the kind which conforms both to easily discernible genre conventions and to clear-cut moral categories – it ill befits the country's noir. Now, is that a result of me over-analysing a clichéd moniker which, some will say, is no more than a meaningless, one-size-fits-all marketing label? Perhaps so, but since this moniker has also been used as a collective literary label in countless book reviews and critical discussions without there being a general consensus on what exactly the term means and which ethics or aesthetics are likely to be found in a text thus labelled, the term 'Tartan Noir' has always been a vague and falsely homogenising umbrella term, which is to say that it has never fitted a literature as clearly distinct from mainstream crime fiction as Scottish Noir. So, if only to ensure that critics no longer perpetuate this confusion, and that readers no longer pick up a piece of Scotland's mainstream crime fiction in the expectation that they are about to read some of the country's noir – or vice versa – I suggest that we finally start distinguishing between Tartan Noir and Scottish Noir.

THE FINAL CROSS-EXAMINATION: HELEN FITZGERALD & ALLAN GUTHRIE – *BLOODY WOMEN & SLAMMER*

Anyone who still remains uncertain whether Scottish Noir really differs from Tartan Noir – or has yet to be convinced of how diverse a literature it really is – might be relieved to learn that I have kept the two best examples until last. Anyone else may close this book now and express their certainty in an appropriately glowing review, ideally published online and quoted repeatedly in conversation with anyone from family members to impressionable friends and approachable strangers. Judging by the immense popularity of the literature discussed in these pages, people just love reading about crime from Scotland, and they will love *you* just as much for telling them about this book. You're welcome.

In the meantime, I will try to remove any lingering doubts and – for anyone who has just joined us in the expectation of finding all their questions answered in the final section of this book – briefly summarise how they could have arisen in the first place. Allow me, then, to refer back to a phenomenon which I mentioned earlier with regard to Ian Rankin, the so-called 'King of Tartan Noir', namely that he has become well-known without being known well, that his reputation has become larger than life, that it now seems like a friendly caricature, and that it hides his writing like a disguise. I repeat this here because the same can be said of Tartan Noir at large. Since so much has been labelled 'Tartan Noir' simply because it is a bit dark-ish, it is by no means safe to assume that, underneath the Tartan Noir label, a piece of writing is indeed noir. In writing this book, I have therefore tried to peel off the label so as to offer a glimpse of the unsuspected noir I so vividly have in mind, a literature not to be described wholly or even mainly by the familiar adjectives – gritty, dark, and violent – but rather as one combining the traits literary criticism notes in the most deeply disturbing of books, books about outsiders who are alone, afraid, angry, amoral, and alienating enough to shatter the mainstream notion of what is normal.

As I hope to show in these final pages, this literature is currently best represented in the writing of Helen FitzGerald and Allan Guthrie, two noirists whose relative obscurity, at least according to one of them, is further proof of their extraordinary quality. As Guthrie puts it, "The better you are at writing noir, the more you'll put people off reading your work. The best noir writer in the world is the writer who has no readers cause he's driven them all away with his relentlessly bleak and grim view of humanity and his constant obsession with death and the fact that we're all fucked, no matter what."[439] So, perhaps FitzGerald and Guthrie are not the best noir writers in the world, perhaps not even the best in Scotland, since they have amassed at least enough readers to have remained in print for over a decade now. Yet in all this time, they have not been borne aloft to fame and fortune on the ever rising tide of Tartan Noir, despite the extraordinarily high quality of their work and some extraordinarily early endorsements which have publically testified to said quality.

In 2004, for instance, none other than Ian Rankin, who had by then already gained his world-wide reputation as the 'King of Tartan Noir', urged his audience at the Edinburgh International Book Festival to read Guthrie's debut with the propitious words, "You should seek him out and buy his book."[440] Seven years later, Brian Lindenmuth, an influential critic and reviewer of crime fiction, extended this endorsement to FitzGerald, when he made the rather memorable if slightly crass comparison that one of her books was "like an Allan Guthrie novel with ovaries."[441] And as I hope to show below, this comparison is not just memorable, or even memorably crass, but also fitting, and deeply so, seeing as its anatomical image draws attention to the writers' shared focus on sexual desires and other basic instincts which drive the vast majority of human behaviour in the vast majority of Scottish Noir, and nowhere is this more intimately and disturbingly examined than in *Bloody Women* by Helen FitzGerald and *Slammer* by Allan Guthrie.

Perhaps coincidentally, both of these novels were published in 2009. What is surely more than a coincidence, though, and also more meaningful a commonality, is the fact that they are both pervaded by the fear which most defines the protagonists of Scottish Noir. This is a fear of a particularly dreaded moment which one of the literature's main pioneers, William McIlvanney, has encapsulated in an anecdote about a Scottish football player and the country's arguably worst moment in the World Cup of 1974: "When Billy Bremner failed to score and take us to the next level, he was down on his knees with his face buried in his hands, and Alan [Sharp] said: 'I know that moment. It's a Scottish moment – the moment you're found out.'"[442] To be clear, Sharp did not mean that Bremner's failure to score had been a deliberate act of sabotage and that the player's prostration could be read as a sign of his fear that his rule breaking had been found out. Instead, so McIlvanney suggests, the player was struck down by the sudden realisation that, "This time, *this* time they're going to see the emperor is bollock naked here."[443]

Bremner's 'Scottish moment', then, was not about the discovery of guilt, much like the protagonists of Scottish Noir have typically not been afraid of being found out for mere legal transgressions. Unlike most law breakers of crime fiction, they are far less preoccupied by such specific fears than they are by the sneaking, self-deprecating, and at times even superstitious fear that they will be found out for being frauds, that there will inevitably come a moment of reckoning when the world will see that they, like the infamous Bremner, have been playing above their league. That it is not just Scottish football players who can relate to this fixation on the inevitability of being 'found out' should be obvious to anyone who has read such Scottish classics as James Hogg and Robert Louis Stevenson, two celebrated 19th-century writers in whose seminal works of Gothic horror, *The Private Memoirs and Confessions of a Justified Sinner* (1824) and the *Strange Case of Dr Jekyll and Mr Hyde* (1886), the central protagonists spend relatively little time in fear of being found out for their transgressions.

Increasingly, they live in fear that their darkest secret – the disturbing cause of their deplorable actions – will be found out, and that they will sooner or later have to face the animal side of their personality which they so struggle to control and fear will finally consume them.

So, perhaps the most important impact Scottish Gothic has had on Scottish Noir is not its famous focus on people with split personalities, though both FitzGerald and Guthrie – and indeed a number of their better known contemporaries – write about protagonists with this rare mental condition, now known as dissociative identity disorder. Yet even more important seems to have been that writers like Hogg and Stevenson proved that it was possible to convince readers that the fear of being 'found out' can be greater than that of being outed as a criminal, particularly when it is exacerbated by an illness like dissociative identity disorder, because when a part of yourself is unknown even to you, it carries a far greater risk of shameful revelation. This, after all, is the premise of both *Bloody Women* and *Slammer*, yet whereas their Gothic ancestors built this atmosphere of Angst largely on their characters' and readers' belief in the supernatural, FitzGerald and Guthrie have shifted their focus to psychopathology, removed the supernatural element along with the safe distance it so often creates, and showed how the suppressed decline of a person's mental health can be just as full of drama – and perhaps even more deeply disturbing – than the grand spectacle of Doppelgänger, diabolism, and the decay of the soul, which is perhaps a rather roundabout way of saying that FitzGerald and Guthrie have shown more clearly than any of their contemporaries just how far Scottish Noir has come from its origin in Gothic.

Against this historical background, it is only appropriate, then, that both authors take quite a while to develop their dramas because they take this shift from supernatural to psychopathological so far. When we meet their main protagonists, they have both laboured under a life-long sense of misfortune which has been exacerbated by severe mental illness, psychological trauma, and memory loss. Soon, it seems as though they should trust neither their perception of others nor that of themselves, and as they are increasingly afraid of being 'found out', it will come as no surprise that they treat the depths of their own minds as something too dangerous and disturbing to be divulged to anyone, including themselves. What *will* come as a surprise, though, at least to readers unfamiliar with noir, is that both writers let these symptoms of mental illness manifest themselves in their storytelling, even though doing so delays the drama considerably. Both limit our insight into the thoughts and feelings of their main protagonists to the little they themselves reveal in conversation, be it in the odd dialogue with others or their ever more frequent and frenzied internal monologues. In either case, though, both habitually forget, repress, or distort key memories, so for a long time, we, like they themselves, see neither the full extent of their illnesses nor how their symptoms affect their perception of events, not until they finally get into so much trouble that an intervention is staged to make them face reality.

In *Bloody Women*, the initially reluctant beneficiary of this intervention is a certain Cat Marsden. The interveners are her mother, her best friend, and her biographer. And with Cat's late cooperation, it is at least a partial success. In *Slammer*, the increasingly reluctant beneficiary is a certain Nick Glass. The only one to intervene is his psychotherapist. And without Glass's cooperation, it is an unmitigated failure. Yet prior to these opposite conclusions, which are no less dramatic for being psychologically inevitable, both writers offer several conflicting versions of events in a tightly compacted sequence of flashbacks. So each of these stories soon turns out to be, as the literary theorist Carl Malmgren puts it, "more a subject to be experienced, less an object to be known," and as Malmgren rightly concludes, "that experience is decidedly disturbing, disquieting, even disorienting."[444] Both protagonists allow us to appreciate not only *that* they fear their own minds but also *why* and *how* they do so. And in addition to letting their thought patterns speak for themselves, they frequently articulate their fears in their afore-mentioned internal monologues, as when Cat observes, "It looks like I did it and I can't say for sure I didn't... Since my teens I'd had a tendency to black out in stressful situations, as well as a tendency to assume my own guilt."[445] Hence, she repeatedly asks herself the very question which Glass cannot get out of his head: "Why did he keep imagining the worst?"[446]

Aside from amnesia, low self-esteem, and manic depression, the answer in both cases is that there is strong external evidence of their guilt. That and the fact that both of them fear that there may be even stronger internal evidence of this guilt buried in their sub-conscious, so they redirect, side-track, or even lock down their thoughts whenever they stray into dangerous territory – such as raw memories of heartbreak, lethal weapons, or deaths in the family – and every time they police their thoughts, they become a little more convinced that they have every reason to 'keep imagining the worst'. Inevitably, this soon makes them more desperate to police their thoughts, then more suspicious, then again more desperate, and so on and so forth. As Cat tells herself, "I needed to stop the flashbacks, or perhaps not the past, just dreams, perhaps... just nonsense... burning their way into my grey matter."[447] Yet the more ardently she tells herself off for having negative thoughts, the more anxious she becomes to correct them, until doing so becomes a nervous reflex to just about every external stimulus, whereupon she watches her mind ever more closely, until her occasional memory-editing process becomes habitual and all she is aware of are negative thoughts – much like Glass, who spends more and more time watching his mind "while time passed and things happened in his head and he forgot them and then they happened again and he changed what happened because what he saw in his head wasn't right, couldn't be right, wasn't going to be right, hadn't been right."[448]

In both cases, this surrealist atmosphere of delusion and confusion is intensified by the circumstance that large sections of the stories unfold on the margins of dreams and hallucinations. So, for a long time there is little sense of coherence, and what little there is seems unreliable, since it is the result of dubious rationalisation strategies. FitzGerald repeatedly interrupts Cat's account of her life to let her biographer provide her own views in several extracts from the biography which she is writing in between interviews with Cat. Similarly, Guthrie provides an outside perspective by repeatedly interrupting Glass's scattered thoughts and letting his psychotherapist interpret them in what turns out to be a series of therapy sessions. And since both Cat's biographer and Glass's psychotherapist blank out what they believe to be irrational babble, these rationalisation strategies have the same effect as a stencil placed on a chaotic mind map. In those scenes, we only see what shows through the gaps of a thought pattern created for the benefit of a third party, and the more complicated these thought patterns become in other scenes, the less reliable this stencil method seems.

Eventually, it becomes apparent that, at least in Cat's case, it is not the least bit reliable, even though she offers almost full disclosure. When she unexpectedly finds herself in prison, awaiting trial for the murder of three ex-boyfriends, none of whom she remembers killing, she decides that "Janet was my lifeline. She would help me remember. She would help me hate myself a little less."[449] Unfortunately for Cat, Janet is a false friend who claims she wants to "help get your side across"[450] by writing a true crime book about Cat's life leading up to her imprisonment, yet what she is writing instead is a series of assumptions about Cat's murder motive, titled *Cat Marsden, Portrait of a Serial Monogamist*. As she says in the introduction, "This book will attempt to explain why. It will offer some insight into the mind of an obsessive, man-hating, violent, crazed killer."[451] And since Cat is deeply impressed by both the confidence and the coherence of Janet's narrative – and compulsively critical of herself – she fears that not even the factual errors which seem to abound in her biography make a difference in the grand scheme of things, so afraid is she that the composite image created of her in those pages is nonetheless the truth.

If this seems counter-intuitive, it is worth remembering that, as the crime critic David Schmid puts it, "the truth of true crime means getting to the heart of the matter; emotional truth is prized far more than literal truth."[452] It is this emotional truth which Cat fears may be at the heart of her biography – until, that is, she eventually stops hating herself and starts rebuilding her self-worth. That this belief should seem credible in the first place – and soon become a near certainty even in the mind of an innocent suspect – is the result of Janet's conspiratorial methodology, the genre-typical reverse engineering found in most so-called 'true crime' literature. Like most authors who write about factual, rather than fictional, criminals, Janet foster her readers' gullibility by going to Cat's childhood, not to offer a fair appraisal of her formative years, but to focus on a few incidents of childish insubordination, imply their almost daily occurrence, and sensationalise them in such a way as to suggest that Cat is not just evil but has shrewdly disguised this fact ever since her deviant childhood. Indeed, Janet says, "Catriona's primary school years were littered with incidents that could have warned the world."[453] With this incriminating backstory in mind, her guilt is a foregone conclusion – rather like that of Amanda Knox, the American student publically demonised and falsely convicted of murdering a friend, or Lindy Chamberlain, the Australian mother publically demonised and falsely convicted of murdering her daughter – even though all she had done to confirm public suspicion is that she "had accidentally smiled once" after her arrest. Unfortunately, "once was enough for the gawkers with mobiles to snap the 'smirk of evil'."[454]

This, of course, is not to say that the stencil of suspicion is always applied externally. As I said earlier, to the considerable extent to which Cat fears her suppressed memories, she herself blanks out information which would allow her, people like Janet, and the public at large to see the full picture, contextualise details, and judge her fairly. Yet as her case shows, when the full picture is partially obscured by the suspect herself, the mean-spirited misinterpretation of a third party can be an especially effective tool in predisposing people to a negative view of said suspect. And as Glass's case shows, when the suspect blanks out enough information, there is no need even for the mean-spirited misinterpretation of a third party. In that case, an *in*ternal stencil can distort perception just as much as an *ex*ternal one, and it can do just as much damage to a person's prospect of being regarded with sympathy, rather than suspicion.

Glass's guilt appears to be just as much of a foregone conclusion as Cat's, even though his psychotherapist only rarely suggests that what Glass says by way of self-defence is false. In general, the man seems fair, fastidious, and friendly as he tries to create a coherent narrative from Glass's fractured memories, so the fact that Glass seems guilty from the get-go has rather little to do with how the person to whom he opens up represents him, and rather a lot with how he opens up to that person, or rather how he does not open up. As early as in their first conversation about his new job as a prison guard, we see Glass filter everything he tells his therapist. This conversation is set in 1992, when he has only been in the job for six weeks, yet already it is clear that he is caught up in lies. He is hyper-sensitive about both his wife and his daughter, and he is obviously afraid of several prisoners, so when one of them makes threats against his family, he quickly caves in under their pressure and starts working for them as a drug courier. Yet when he gets his chance to relieve his troubled conscience and seek guidance in a confidential conversation with a non-judgmental therapist, he dissembles, distorts, and denies everything.

Soon, he feels that the moment for confessions, even confessions of this gentle kind, has long come and gone. After only a few weeks in the job, he reviews his professional performance and realises with a mixture of disbelief and despair that "The last few weeks he'd muled smack, coke, speed, acid, poppers, Es, tranx, anti-psychotics, anti-convulsants, painkillers. Each time, he put a little aside for himself."[455] And each time he does so, he realises how much power he is letting his blackmailer gain over him, the thought of which makes him so stressed that he takes more and more of the man's drugs to medicate his anxiety issues, only to become even more stressed at the thought that his blackmailer is sure to notice his theft and use every bit of the power he has given him. So he takes more drugs, and gets more stressed, and takes more drugs, and so on and so forth, until his thoughts and actions become dangerously and undeniably erratic. At that point, he wakes up after a particularly rough night, not just without his right index finger, but also without any memory of how he lost it. What he does remember, though, is seeing the scar of an injury at a time when he had yet to sustain it, and thus he starts messing up the timeline of his memories.

Soon thereafter – or perhaps long before then – he starts presenting multiple versions of events, which not only reinforces the impression of his guilt but also makes it seem like the entire novel is Glass's schizophrenically fragmented interior monologue. That or a series of therapy sessions, all of which might be set in the same year as the end of the story, 2009, when Glass reviews the events leading up to his mental breakdown and subsequent – or prior – hospitalisation. Either way, the coherence which seems to be created by his therapist's structured questioning is by no means reliable, since for all we know it is all happening in Glass's head. After all, when once again he offers two versions of the same events, his therapist's voice asks "'WHICH IS IT?'... in Glass's head."[456] So, even though his therapist is ultimately convinced that Glass is a delusional murderer, we can never be certain of his guilt. There is always the possibility that Glass is either so deluded that the entire story, not just his attempts at editing it, is happening in his head, or that he is not deluded at all, only made to look that way. His therapist does have a rather leading way of phrasing his questions, as when he asks, "'You ever wondered why you made up a story about a guy who killed his wife and kid and... this guy not only has someone cover up for him but he can't even remember he's done it. You see a parallel?' 'No,' Glass said. '*You* see a parallel.'"[457]

In their separate ways, then, both Cat and Glass illustrate the subtle workings of attribution biases, why they can be attractive, and how they can be dangerous. As the moral psychologist Mark Alfano explains, most of us are hardly objective when we determine whether someone is guilty of a crime, especially when that crime is murder: "In addition to biases that influence judgments of intentionality, agency, and good and bad, people are affected by biases when assessing who performed an action."[458] In Cat's case, the general public assumes that she is guilty of murdering three men despite the absence of the murder weapon or any witnesses, and the average reader is likely to agree, not because we are all professional psychotherapists, but because, like her biographer, most of us are likely to suspect that her amnesia is perhaps a little too convenient. At least the general public does so, and when they see her 'smirk of evil', they take the biased view that someone with her lack of propriety simply must be guilty, all the more so when she causes further offense to public decency.

Having been asked to identify one of the corpses by nothing other than its penis, she has what appears to be the impertinence, and indeed the heartlessness, to laugh. Little allowance is made for the stressful incongruity of the situation or the inadvertent visual comedy of a solemn identification scene in which an apprehensive woman, who has just been informed of the grievous murder of her former partner, is scrutinised for signs of guilt by a quiet group of strange men as one of them slowly draws back a sheet from the remains of the deceased and, with the dramatic timing of a stage illusionist, reveals a severed penis. Given her own timing when she responds to this surprising sight with an 'involuntary chortle', Cat is convinced that she has made herself an easy target for a damning attribution bias. As she puts it, "I'm sure my involuntary chortle at the sheet-covered knob was partly why they decided to arrest me two days later, why I was no longer viewed as the bereaved ex-lover of three men, but was accused of shagging, mutilating and murdering them, not necessarily in that order."[459]

If, at this point, she still sounds impervious to such perceptual errors in the evaluation of her behaviour, it is a further demonstration of how powerful attribution biases can be that even this strong woman eventually succumbs to as many as four of them. As Cat reads a draft of her biography while awaiting trial in prison, she realises that her judge and jury are likely to take the same negative view as her biographer, and that she herself has already taken it, simply because "I was sounding crazy. But I was crazy. Things had started ram-raiding my head."[460] One of those things ram-raiding her head is the attribution bias that she must be guilty of all the crazy behaviour attributed to her in her biography just because it seems suspiciously convenient that she suffers from partial amnesia; another is the attribution bias that she must be guilty of the amorality and aggression attributed to her just because she was capable of chortling at a severed penis. And the longer she considers the implications of this 'involuntary chortle', the more she shares her biographer's attribution bias that she must have been just as capable – and just as guilty – of killing the owner of said penis.

Yet it is the fourth of Cat's attribution biases which most clearly shows how immensely powerful their allure and insidious their effect can be, as this fourth one sneaks up on her when she seems to be least at risk and hurts her where she is most vulnerable. Cat has only just started believing that she did not kill those three men after all, now that her best friend has finally got through to her with her insistent claim that Cat "always blamed herself for things that were not her fault."[461] Yet rather than enjoy the reassurance of having a true friend offer her unconditional support, or the relief of having the burden of guilt lifted off her at long last, Cat starts obsessively searching her mind for clues as to who might have framed her for those three murders, and when her memory starts confusing her with conflicting versions of formative experiences in her childhood, she abruptly attributes responsibility to her mother. Remembering all those 'accidents' which her mother seemed to have orchestrated for her – and which conveniently ensured her the reputation of a struggling parent along with the sympathy of the entire community – Cat suspects that her mother must have set her up once again because she still suffers from Münchausen Syndrome by Proxy. As it turns out, though, it was neither Cat nor her mother who mutilated and murdered those three men. It was a jealous, manipulative misogynist, but due to the above biases he almost escapes suspicion.

Now, if this scenario seems disconcerting – demonstrating as it does that it is all too easy to attribute blame to an innocent person even when the charge is as serious as multiple homicide – the novel's potential to disturb is nevertheless limited by a late containment strategy. Right at the end, the seemingly untameable animal aggression – which has manifested itself in each of the three murders and threatened to haunt Cat beyond the novel's conclusion – is finally given human shape, explained, and tamed as the serial killer is identified, psychoanalysed, and killed. Much to Cat's relief, and presumably to that of most readers, she turns out not be the serial killer, so she was wrong to be afraid that she may be capable of committing such atrocities and then forgetting everything about them. Letting Cat – and the novel – come to this conclusion, FitzGerald contains the prior unease that anyone may have an unknowable and untameable animal side, and when she lets the actual serial killer die in circumstances which prove that he is fully aware of his psychopathic personality disorder, she firmly closes the lid on this unease by implying that such disorders do not run wild without their owners' knowledge. At the same time, she reassures us that Cat is neither a feral wild cat nor a moral wild card. The woman was simply falsely suspected, and when she joins her biographer, along with everyone else, in accepting the truth about herself and those whom she has trusted, her earlier wish comes true. While her mind may still be a dark and disturbing place, she at least hates herself a little less.

To such 'noir light', Guthrie provides a disturbing contrast. In Glass's case, a psychotherapist assumes that he is guilty of murdering three men in addition to his wife and daughter, and the average reader is likely to agree, not because we are all professional psychotherapists, but because, like Glass, most of us are likely to sense his lack of conviction when he reassures himself that there was "No way he could take a human life, no matter how despicable that human was. He just wasn't a killer."[462] Like Glass, most of us are likely to sense that he might lose control at any moment, because he is permanently and dangerously out of his depth among convicted murderers. As he himself admits, "Any sign of weakness and these predators would rip him apart... They were animals. But so what? He was an animal too."[463] And though this may sound like bravado, his self-assessment turns out to be true. In fact, it is only his therapist's suspicion which is ultimately impossible to verify, because, as I suggested above, it is impossible to say whether he is guilty of murder, whether he lost control of his animal side so completely that he killed all those people in a frenzy which he later forgot – or whether the entire story, including all of his crimes, only happened in his head.

If, by the time of the novel's conclusion, it seems almost certain that he did kill all those people, this assessment is still no more than an attribution bias, blame being attributed to Glass on the biased assumption that a schizophrenic must surely be too unstable for his denial to stand up in court, that his amnesia must surely be too convenient to be credible, or that his capacity for animal violence must surely be too great for him to remain at large. Either way, though, and regardless of how guilty Glass may seem, blame cannot be attributed to him on the basis of any incontrovertible evidence. He does spend the final scenes in a closed psychiatric hospital where he accepts his detention without the slightest protest, even though imaginary witnesses repeatedly try to convince him of his innocence, but none of this is proof that he committed the many crimes he so inconsistently and unreliably discusses. He may have fantasised about them, he may have been in hospital all along, and he may have accepted his detention merely due to his therapist's subtle persuasion that, with his severe mental illness, life outside a hospital is a serious personal and public health risk. So, while it seems almost certain that he either has or soon will be 'found out', there is, in his case, always room for doubt whether he is actually guilty or just theoretically capable of acting like an animal.

As opposed to *Bloody Women*, then, *Slammer* does not contain the unease it creates, the unease that anyone may have an unknowable and untameable animal side. Yet despite this difference, the fear of being 'found out' is equally haunting for both main protagonists, and this commonality is at its clearest in a shared piece of symbolism. Both Cat, with her feline ability to bounce back, and Glass, with his fragile inability to do just that, are so afraid of seeing who or what they really are that they both try to smash a mirror. And what makes these mirror scenes even more revealing is that they reflect not only their shared fear but also their main contrast: where Glass succeeds, Cat fails. In fact, Glass succeeds twice, and the only reason he is not successful on a third occasion is that he smashed the second one in hospital, whereupon his doctor diagnosed him with a fear of mirrors and removed the rest of them from his environment. In a symbolic sense, then, Glass is actively prevented from ever having to look into another mirror and face the risk of seeing who or what he really is, so great is his fear of being 'found out' and the danger that he may damage himself to prevent it.

In contrast, Cat tries time and again to smash the safety mirror in her prison cell, yet she fails on every occasion and by the time she is finally released from prison, she is no longer at risk of trying to smash any mirrors, because she has learned to look at herself again, literally as well as figuratively. So clearly does she now see herself that she realises that her fear of being 'found out' was exacerbated by her partial amnesia, that she was unreasonably afraid of a shameful revelation because a reputedly dark part of herself was unknown to her. Yet although she now sees that the animal side of her personality was never at risk of consuming her, she still suffers from a genetic predisposition to stress-related blackouts and a lifelong habit of self-deprecation, so her fear of being 'found out', unreasonable thought it may be, is unlikely to ever stop haunting her.

Despite the fact, then, that their paths ultimately point in opposite directions – Cat is released from prison, whereas Glass ends up in a closed hospital – both live in a deeply noir world, a world which, as the cultural critic Philip Simpson observes, is "both existential and deterministic. Arbitrary chance may strike down the most virtuous of characters for no good reason whatsoever, but the essence of a character also usually determines his or her ultimate destiny..."[464] As I hope to have shown in the previous pages, though, FitzGerald and Guthrie are like most Scottish noirists in that they are less interested in their characters' ultimate destiny than in their fear of being 'found out' and their efforts to control that fear before it controls them. Besides, since both authors dwell at length on their characters' bad habits and worse luck, that ultimate destiny seems almost certain anyway. In the knowledge that they have merely learned to curb their animal instincts and keep their overt actions within the bounds of humanity, not however to subdue their thoughts and feelings to the same mild tone, it is with a sense of foreboding, a sense that they are almost certain to be 'found out' sooner or later, that we take our leave from them at novel's end.

CONCLUSION

So, what is Tartan Noir?

Well, since you might have taken one glance at a long conclusion and expected it to settle the issue, and since I do not wish to mislead you after trying to answer this question as honestly and comprehensively as possible in the previous pages, I should like to say only this. In writing this book, I hope to have shown that Tartan Noir will not do as a synonym for Scottish Noir, but that it has its use as an Ersatz genre label for a mêlée of literary styles and subjects which can roughly be divided into the four main sub-genres discussed in the previous pages.

Should you desire a more detailed distinction between Tartan Noir and Scottish Noir, or perhaps a more detailed discussion of the respective sub-genres, I kindly suggest that you try reading the rest of this book, rather than expect the conclusion to answer all your questions. By 'you' I mean students. I was one of you for long enough to know how you read. As for those of you who have already read the rest of this book yet still want to know more about Tartan Noir, I sincerely hope that you will accept my appreciation of your enthusiasm along with my humble apology that it has been beyond the scope of this book to say everything there is to say about a literature as diverse and dynamic as Tartan, or indeed Scottish, Noir.

As the literature has changed dramatically in the course of the last century, and as it looks set to keep doing so in the next one, I should like to think that in avoiding generalisation I have acted in the best interests of both its writers and its readers. For what my personal opinion is worth, I have come to believe that to discuss this literature is to create a sense of fragmentation, because it is neither the coordinated effort of some genre building project nor that of a single school of art, working on a shared syllabus or drawing on shared influences. Most of it is not even that 'tartany', which is to say that it is not in any stereotypical sense Scottish. The label 'Tartan Noir', however, is unlikely to yield to the more suitable yet rather prosaic 'dark contemporary Scottish crime fiction', too marketable is its evocation of Franco-Gaelic exoticism. So, to answer my opening question, 'What is Tartan Noir?', I have discussed the books which have most influenced either the literature's reputation or its identity, and it is my hope that in doing so I have – if not demystified Tartan Noir – then at least defined the term and refined its use. And there I shall leave it, for my express purpose in writing this book has been to start a conversation, not to have the last word.

ACKNOWLEDGMENTS

I n both the researching and the writing of this book, I have been indebted to the department of Literatures, Languages, and Cultures at the University of Edinburgh for endowing me with a generous scholarship. For this, and for the even more generous support I have received from the people within, I wish to thank the department.

Personally, I wish to thank Professor Terry Dolan for paying me the 'compliment' – upon which I have drawn like a blank cheque in times of doubt – that I have just the right mix of intelligence and masochism to write a book as ambitious as the one in your hands. And since it would not be in your hands without the much appreciated contributions of several other brainy masochists, I wish to extend my gratitude to Dr Carole Jones for her benign aggression in ripping apart my early efforts, Dr Lee Horsley for her tough love in helping me put together a new and improved plan, Dr Bob Irvine for his judicious comments in supervising the rewrite, and Al Guthrie, alter Seelenschänder, for sharing with me his supreme expertise and uncanny delight in all things noir to make sure that another, final rewrite would turn what was still a PhD thesis into a publishable book.

Yet most of all, I wish to thank my parents, my parents-in-law, my wife, and my son for holding my hand – and the puke bucket – as I struggled through all of the above.

BIBLIOGRAPHY

Alfano, Mark. "The Situation of the Jury: Attribution Bias in the Trials of Accused Serial Killers." *Serial Killers: Being and Killing.* Ed. S. Waller. Oxford: Wiley-Blackwell, 2010.

Amper, Susan. "Dexter's Dark World: The Serial Killer as Superhero." *Serial Killers: Being and Killing.* Ed. S. Waller. Oxford: Wiley-Blackwell, 2010.

Anderson, Lin. *Picture Her Dead.* London: Hodder & Stoughton, 2011.

Anderson, Patrick. *The Triumph of the Thriller: How Cops, Crooks, and Cannibals Captured Popular Fiction.* New York: Random House, 2007.

Aristotle. *On the Art of Poetry.* Boston: IndyPublish, 2004.

Aristotle. *Politics.* Oxford: Oxford University Press, 2009.

Armstrong, Campbell. *Butcher* (2006). London: Allison & Busby, 2007.

Ascari, Maurizio. *A Counter-History of Crime Fiction: Supernatural, Gothic, Sensational.* Basingstoke: Palgrave Macmillan, 2007.

Babener, Liahna K. "Raymond Chandler's City of Lies." *Los Angeles in Fiction: A Collection of Essays.* Ed. David Fine. Albuquerque: University of New Mexico Press, 1995.

Banks, Iain. *The Wasp Factory* (1984). London: Abacus, 1992.

Banks, Ray. *Saturday's Child* (2006). Edinburgh: Polygon, 2007.

Banks, Ray. *Beast of Burden.* Edinburgh: Polygon, 2009.

Banks, Ray. "The French Word for Bleak." 31. Dec 2011. <http://www.thecrimefactory.com/2011/11/the-french-word-for-bleak/>.

Banks, Ray. "Ray Banks." *The Crime Interviews: Volume Two.* Ed. Len Wanner. Glasgow: Blasted Heath, 2012.

Barzun, Jacques. *The Culture We Deserve.* Middletown: Wesleyan University Press, 1989.

Beaton, M.C. *Death of a Gossip* (1985). London: Constable & Robinson, 2008.

Binyon, T.J. *Murder Will Out: The Detective in Fiction.* Oxford: Oxford University Press, 1990.

Black, Tony. *Paying For It* (2008). London: Preface Publishing, 2009.

Brady, Ian. *The Gates of Janus: Serial Killing and its Analysis.* Los Angeles: Feral House, 2001.

Brookmyre, Christopher. *A Snowball in Hell* (2008). London: Abacus, 2009.

Brookmyre, Christopher. *Quite Ugly One Morning* (1996). London: Abacus, 2009.

Cameron, Deborah and Frazer, Elizabeth. *The Lust to Kill: A Feminist Investigation of Sexual Murder*. Cambridge: Polity Press, 1987.

Campbell, Karen. *Proof of Life* (2011). London: Hodder and Stoughton, 2012.

Cassuto, Leonard. *Hard-Boiled Sentimentality: The Secret History of American Crime Stories*. New York: Columbia University Press, 2009.

Cawelti, John G. *Adventure, Mystery, and Romance*. Chicago: The University of Chicago Press, 1977.

Chabon, Michael. *Maps & Legends: Reading and Writing along the Borderlands*. New York: Harper Perennial, 2009.

Chandler, Raymond. *The Simple Art of Murder* (1950). 1st Vintage Books Edition. New York: Random House, 1988.

Cohen, Josh. "James Ellroy, Los Angeles and the Spectacular Crisis of Masculinity." *Criminal Proceedings: The Contemporary American Crime Novel*. Ed. Peter Messent. London: Pluto Press, 1997, pp. 168-186.

Corbett, David. "Insulting Your Intelligence ('Just gimme some noiriness')." 28. Oct 2010. <http://www.mulhollandbooks.com/2010/10/28/insulting-your-intelligence-just-gimme-some-noiriness>.

Deal, William E. "The Serial Killer Was (Cognitively) Framed." *Serial Killers: Being and Killing*. Ed. S. Waller. Oxford: Wiley-Blackwell, 2010.

Dietrich, Eric and Fox Hall, Tara. "The Allure of the Serial Killer." *Serial Killers: Being and Killing*. Ed. S. Waller. Oxford: Wiley-Blackwell, 2010.

Diemert, Brian. "Ian Rankin and the God of the Scots." *Race and Religion in the Postcolonial British Detective Story: Ten Essays*. Ed. Julie H. Kim. London: McFarland & Company, 2005.

Doyle, Arthur Conan. *Memories and Adventures*. London: Hodder & Stoughton, 1924.

Ferris, Gordon. *The Hanging Shed* (2010). London: Corvus, 2011.

FitzGerald, Helen. *Bloody Women*. Edinburgh: Polygon, 2009.

Friedman, Richard A. "Revising the Script on Mental Illness and Violence." *New York Times*. 4th of March 2003.

Gavin, Adrienne E. "Feminist Crime Fiction and Female Sleuths." *A Companion to Crime Fiction*. Ed. Charles J. Rzepka and Lee Horsley. Oxford: John Wiley & Sons, 2010.

Goldberg, Carl. *Speaking with the Devil.* New York: Penguin, 1997.

Gormley, Jr., William T. "Moralists, Pragmatists, and Rogues: Bureaucrats in Modern Mysteries." *Public Administration Review*, Vol. 61, No. 2 (Mar.-Apr., 2001), pp. 184-193. JSTOR. Blackwell Publishing. 20. Feb. 2009. <http://www/jstor.org>.

Graham, Barry. *The Book of Man* (1995). New York: Cracked Sidewalk Press, 2011.

Graham, Barry. "Noir: The Marxist Art Form." 14. May 2013. <http://www.thebigclickmag.com/noir-the-marxist-art-form>.

Gray, Alex. *A Pound of Flesh.* London: Sphere, 2012.

Gray, Richard M. "Psychopathy and Will to Power: Ted Bundy and Dennis Rader." *Serial Killers: Being and Killing.* Ed. S. Waller. Oxford: Wiley-Blackwell, 2010.

Grella, George. "The Hard-Boiled Detective Novel." *Detective Fiction.* Ed. Robin W. Winks. Woodstock: The Countryman Press, 1988.

Guthrie, Allan. *Slammer.* Edinburgh: Polygon, 2009.

Guthrie. Allan. "Allan Guthrie's Ten Rules to Write Noir." <http://www.deadendfollies.com/2011/07/allan-guthries-ten-rules-to-write-noir.html>.

Harvey, John. "The Last Good Place; James Crumley, the West and the Detective Novel." *Criminal Proceedings: The Contemporary American Crime Novel.* Ed. Peter Messent. London: Pluto Press, 1997.

Haut, Woody. *Neon Noir.* London: Serpent's Tail, 1999.

Hazlitt, William. *Selected Writings.* Harmondsworth: Penguin, 1970.

Hodgson, John A. "Arthur Conan Doyle." *A Companion to Crime Fiction.* Ed. Charles J. Rzepka and Lee Horsley. Oxford: John Wiley & Sons, 2010.

Horsley, Lee. *Twentieth-Century Crime Fiction.* Oxford: Oxford University Press, 2005.

Horsley, Lee. *The Noir Thriller.* Basingstoke: Palgrave Macmillan, 2009.

Horsley, Lee. "From Sherlock Holmes to Present." *A Companion to Crime Fiction.* Ed. Charles J. Rzepka and Lee Horsley. Oxford: John Wiley & Sons, 2010.

Jameson, Fredric. "On Raymond Chandler." *The Poetics of Murder: Detective Fiction and Literary Theory.* Ed. Glenn W. Most & William W. Stowe. New York: Harcourt Brace Jovanovich, 1983. 122-149.

Jardine, Quintin. *A Rush of Blood.* London: Headline, 2010.

Johnston, Paul. *Body Politic*. London: Hodder and Stoughton, 1998.

Kant, Immanuel. *Philosophy of Law* (1796). Trans. William Hastie. Edinburgh: T & T Clarke, 1887.

Keegan, Chris. "It Puts the Lotion in the Basket." *Serial Killers: Being and Killing*. Ed. S. Waller. Oxford: Wiley-Blackwell, 2010.

Kerr, Philip. *A Philosophical Investigation* (1992). London: Vintage, 1996.

Kerr, Philip. *March Violets* (1989) in *Berlin Noir*. London: Penguin Books, 1993.

Lansdale, Joe R. *Darkness in the East*. 12. Feb. 2010. <http://www.mulhollandbooks.com/2010/11/12/darkness-in-the-east>.

Lindenmuth, Brian. "Bloody Women by Helen FitzGerald." *Spinetingler Magazine*. 13. Jan. 2011. <http://www.spinetinglermag.com/2011/01/13/bloody-women-by-helen-fitzgerald-review/>.

Lindsay, Douglas. *The Long Midnight of Barney Thomson* (1999). Inverness: Long Midnight Publishing, 2008.

Lindsay, Frederic. *Jill Rips* (1987). London: Corgi, 1988.

MacBride, Stuart. *Cold Granite*. London: HarperCollins, 2005.

MacBride, Stuart. *Flesh House* (2008). London: HarperCollins, 2009.

Macdonald, Ross. "The Writer As Detective Hero." *Detective Fiction*. Ed. Robin W. Winks. Woodstock: The Countryman Press, 1988. 179-188.

Major, John. Quoted in "Major on Crime." *The Independent* (1993). 27. Oct. 2013. <http://www.independent.co.uk/news/major-on-crime-condemn-more-understand-less-1474470.html>

Malmgren, Carl. "Anatomy of Murder: Mystery, Detective, and Crime Fiction." *Journal of Popular Culture*, Volume 30, Issue 4, pages 115–135, Spring 1997.

Mansel, H. L. "Sensation Novels." *Quarterly Review*. 113: 226 (April 1863), pp. 488-499.

May, Peter. *The Blackhouse*. London: Quercus, 2011.

McDermid, Val. *The Mermaids Singing*. London: HarperCollins, 1995.

McDermid, Val. *The Wire in the Blood* (1997). London: Harper, 2010.

McIlvanney, Liam. *All the Colours of the Town* (2009). London: Faber and Faber, 2010.

McIlvanney, William. *Laidlaw* (1977). London: Sceptre, 1996.

McIlvanney, William. *The Papers of Tony Veitch* (1983). London: Sceptre, 1992.

McIlvanney, William. *Strange Loyalties* (1991). London: Sceptre, 1992.

McIlvanney, William. "William McIlvanney." *The Crime Interviews: Volume Two*. Ed. Len Wanner. Glasgow: Blasted Heath, 2012.

McLean, Duncan. *Bunker Man* (1995). New York: W. W. Norton, 1997.

Messent, Peter. "Introduction: From Private Eye to Police Procedural – The Logic of Contemporary Crime Fiction." *Criminal Proceedings: The Contemporary American Crime Novel*. Ed. Peter Messent. London: Pluto Press, 1997.

Messent, Peter. "The Police Novel." *A Companion to Crime Fiction*. Ed. Charles J. Rzepka and Lee Horsley. Oxford: John Wiley & Sons, 2010.

Messent, Peter. *The Crime Fiction Handbook*. Oxford: John Wiley & Sons, 2013.

Mina, Denise. *The Field of Blood* (2004). London: Bantam Books, 2006.

Mina, Denise. *Gods and Beasts*. London: Orion, 2012.

Moffat, GJ. *Protection*. London: Headline, 2012.

Naremore, James. "Dashiell Hammett and the Poetics of Hard-Boiled Detection." *Art in Crime Writing*. Ed. Bernard Benstock. New York: St. Martin's Press, 1983, pp. 49-73.

Naremore, James. *More than Night: Film Noir in its Contexts*. Berkeley and Los Angeles: University of California Press, 2008.

Newton, Michael. *The Encyclopedia of Serial Killers* (2000). 2nd Ed. New York: Facts On File, 2006.

Nicol, Bran. "Patricia Highsmith." A Companion to Crime Fiction. Ed. Charles J. Rzepka and Lee Horsley. Oxford: John Wiley & Sons, 2010.

Oswald, James. Natural Causes (2012). London: Penguin, 2013.

Paglia, Camille. Sexual Personae: Art and Decadence from Nefertiti to Emily Dickinson. New Haven: Yale University Press, 1991.

Panek, LeRoy Lad. "The Police Novel." Death by Pen: The Longman Anthology of Detective Fiction From Poe to Paretsky. Ed. Deane Mansfield-Kelley & Lois A. Marchino. New York: Pearson Longman, 2007.

Penzler, Otto. "Noir Fiction Is About Losers, Not Private Eyes." 24. Jul 2011. <http://www.huffingtonpost.com/otto-penzler/noir-fiction-is-about-los_b_676200.html>.

Pepper, Andrew. "The 'Hard-Boiled' Genre." A Companion to Crime Fiction. Ed. Charles J. Rzepka and Lee Horsley. Oxford: John Wiley & Sons, 2010.

Piven, Jerry. "The Thread of Death, or the Compulsion to Kill." Serial Killers: Being and Killing. Ed. S. Waller. Oxford: Wiley-Blackwell, 2010.

Plain, Gill. Ian Rankin's Black and Blue. London: Continuum International Publishing Group, 2002.

Priestman, Martin. Crime Fiction: From Poe to the Present. Plymouth: Northcote House Publishers, 1998.

Priestman, Martin. "Post-War British Crime Fiction." The Cambridge Companion to Crime Fiction. Ed. Martin Priestman. Cambridge: Cambridge University Press, 2008. 173-191.

Pringle, John. "Introduction." Young Adam (1966). Edinburgh: Rebel Inc., 1996.

Rae, Hugh C. Skinner (1965). Glasgow: Richard Drew Publishing, 1988.

Ramsay, Caro. Dark Water. London: Penguin, 2010.

Rankin, Ian. Knots and Crosses (1987). London: Orion, 2008.

Rankin, Ian. Black & Blue (1997). London: Orion, 2008.

Rankin, Ian. Resurrection Men (2001). London: Orion, 2008.

Rankin, Ian. Quoted in The Scotsman. "Crime Writer does it by the Books." 30. Aug. 2004. <http://www.scotsman.com/news/crime-writer-does-it-by-the-books-1-1023543>.

Rankin, Ian. The Complaints (2009). London: Orion, 2010.

Rankin, Ian. "Ian Rankin." Dead Sharp: Scottish Crime Writers on Country and Craft. Ed. Len Wanner. Isle of Lewis: Two Ravens Press, 2011.

Robertson, Craig. Random (2010). London: Simon & Schuster, 2011.

Rowland, Susan. "The 'Classical' Model of the Golden Age." A Companion to Crime Fiction. Ed. Charles J. Rzepka and Lee Horsley. Oxford: John Wiley & Sons, 2010.

Russell, Craig. Blood Eagle. London: Arrow, 2006.

Russell, Craig. Lennox (2009). London: Quercus, 2010.

Rzepka, Charles J. "Introduction: What is Crime Fiction?" A Companion to Crime Fiction. Ed. Charles J. Rzepka and Lee Horsley. Oxford: John Wiley & Sons, 2010.

Scaggs, John. Crime Fiction. Abingdon: Routledge, 2005.

Schechter, Elizabeth and Schechter, Harold. "Killing with Kindness: Nature, Nurture, and the Female Serial Killer." Serial Killers: Being and Killing. Ed. S. Waller. Oxford: Wiley-Blackwell, 2010.

Schmid, David. "A Philosophy of Serial Killing: Sade, Nietzsche, and Brady at the Gates of Janus." Serial Killers: Being and Killing. Ed. S. Waller. Oxford: Wiley-Blackwell, 2010.

Schmid, David. "David Goodis." A Companion to Crime Fiction. Ed. Charles J. Rzepka and Lee Horsley. Oxford: John Wiley & Sons, 2010.

Schrader, Paul. "Notes on Film Noir." Film Noir Reader. Ed. Alain Silver and James Ursini. New York: Limelight Editions, 1996.

Seaman, Damien. "Femme Fatale: Women, Sex and Guilt in Noir Fiction." 23. Jan. 2012. <http://www.allanguthrie.co.uk/pages/noir_zine/articles/femme_fatale.php>.

Seltzer, Mark. Serial Killers: Death and Life in America's Wound Culture. New York: Routledge, 1998.

Simpson, Philip. "Noir and the Psycho Thriller." A Companion to Crime Fiction. Ed. Charles J. Rzepka and Lee Horsley. Oxford: John Wiley & Sons, 2010.

Symons, Julian. Bloody Murder, From the Detective Story to the Crime Novel. 3rd rev. ed. New York: The Mysterious Press, 1993.

Terjesen, Andrew. "Are Serial Killers Cold-Blooded Killers?" Serial Killers: Being and Killing. Ed. S. Waller. Oxford: Wiley-Blackwell, 2010.

Trocchi, Alexander. Young Adam (1966). Edinburgh: Rebel Inc., 1996.

Vargas, Manuel. "Are Psychopathic Serial Killers Evil? Are They Blameworthy for What They Do?"

Serial Killers: Being and Killing. Ed. S. Waller. Oxford: Wiley-Blackwell, 2010.

Vidal, Gore. Selected Essays. Ed. Jay Parini. London: Abacus, 2007.

Welsh, Irvine. Filth (1998). London: Vintage, 1999.

Welsh, Louise. The Cutting Room (2002). Edinburgh: Canongate, 2003.

Willet, Ralph. Hard-Boiled Detective Fiction. Staffordshire: British Association for American Studies, 1992.

Williams, Gordon. The Siege of Trencher's Farm (1969). London: Titan Books, 2011.

Žižek, Slavoj. Violence. London: Profile

Books LTD, 2009.

ENDNOTES

01 Rankin, Ian. "Ian Rankin." *Dead Sharp: Scottish Crime Writers on Country and Craft*. Ed. Len Wanner. Isle of Lewis: Two Ravens Press, 2011, pp. 3-4.

02 Symons, Julian. *Bloody Murder, From the Detective Story to the Crime Novel*. 3rd rev. ed. New York: The Mysterious Press, 1993, p. 29.

03 Hodgson, John A. "Arthur Conan Doyle." *A Companion to Crime Fiction*. Ed. Charles J. Rzepka and Lee Horsley. Oxford: John Wiley & Sons, 2010, p. 390.

04 Horsley, Lee. "From Sherlock Holmes to Present." *A Companion to Crime Fiction*. Ed. Charles J. Rzepka and Lee Horsley. Oxford: John Wiley & Sons, 2010, p. 29.

05 Symons, Julian. *Bloody Murder, From the Detective Story to the Crime Novel*. 3rd rev. ed. New York: The Mysterious Press, 1993, pp. 68/9.

06 Priestman, Martin. *Crime Fiction: From Poe to the Present*. Plymouth: Northcote House Publishers, 1998, p. 14.

07 Doyle, Arthur Conan. *Memories and Adventures*. London: Hodder & Stoughton, 1924, p. 95.

08 Priestman, Martin. *Crime Fiction: From Poe to the Present*. Plymouth: Northcote House Publishers, 1998, p. 10.

09 Messent, Peter. "Introduction: From Private Eye to Police Procedural – The Logic of Contemporary Crime Fiction." *Criminal Proceedings: The Contemporary American Crime Novel*. Ed. Peter Messent. London: Pluto Press, 1997, p. 7.

10 Willet, Ralph. *Hard-Boiled Detective Fiction*. Staffordshire: British Association for American Studies, 1992, p. 6.

11 Horsley, Lee. "From Sherlock Holmes to Present." *A Companion to Crime Fiction*. Ed. Charles J. Rzepka and Lee Horsley. Oxford: John Wiley & Sons, 2010, pp. 32-33.

12 Chandler, Raymond. *The Simple Art of Murder* (1950). 1st Vintage Books Edition. New York: Random House, 1988, p. 14.

13 Binyon, T.J. *Murder Will Out: The Detective in Fiction*. Oxford: Oxford University Press, 1990, p. 38.

14 Horsley, Lee. "From Sherlock Holmes to Present." *A Companion to Crime Fiction*. Ed. Charles J. Rzepka and Lee Horsley. Oxford: John Wiley & Sons, 2010, p. 32 .

15 Panek, LeRoy Lad. "Raymond Chandler." *A Companion to Crime Fiction*. Ed. Charles J. Rzepka and Lee Horsley. Oxford: John Wiley & Sons, 2010, pp. 407/408.

16 Ibid, p. 410.

17 Cassuto, Leonard. *Hard-Boiled Sentimentality: The Secret History of American Crime Stories*. New York: Columbia University Press, 2009, p. 82.

18 Chandler, Raymond. *The Simple Art of Murder* (1950). 1st Vintage

Books Edition. New York: Random House, 1988, p. 18.

19 Harvey, John. "The Last Good Place; James Crumley, the West and the Detective Novel." *Criminal Proceedings: The Contemporary American Crime Novel.* Ed. Peter Messent. London: Pluto Press, 1997, p. 150.

20 Scaggs, John. *Crime Fiction.* Abingdon: Routledge, 2005, p. 58.

21 Simpson, Philip. "Noir and the Psycho Thriller." *A Companion to Crime Fiction.* Ed. Charles J. Rzepka and Lee Horsley. Oxford: John Wiley & Sons, 2010, p. 190.

22 Rankin, Ian. "Ian Rankin." *Dead Sharp: Scottish Crime Writers on Country and Craft.* Ed. Len Wanner. Isle of Lewis: Two Ravens Press, 2011, p. 19.

23 Pepper, Andrew. "The 'Hard-Boiled' Genre." *A Companion to Crime Fiction.* Ed. Charles J. Rzepka and Lee Horsley. Oxford: John Wiley & Sons, 2010, p. 142.

24 McIlvanney, William. *Laidlaw* (1977). London: Sceptre, 1996, p. 183.

25 Ibid, p. 230.

26 Ibid, p. 40.

27 Grella, George. "The Hard-Boiled Detective Novel." *Detective Fiction.* Ed. Robin W. Winks. Woodstock: The Countryman Press, 1988, pp. 107/9.

28 McIlvanney, William. *Laidlaw* (1977). London: Sceptre, 1996, p. 31.

29 Ibid, p. 1.

30 Ibid, p. 5.

31 Ibid, p. 274.

32 Ibid, p. 84.

33 Cohen, Josh. "James Ellroy, Los Angeles and the Spectacular Crisis of Masculinity." *Criminal Proceedings: The Contemporary American Crime Novel.* Ed. Peter Messent. London: Pluto Press, 1997, p. 169.

34 Diemert, Brian. "Ian Rankin and the God of the Scots." *Race and Religion in the Postcolonial British Detective Story: Ten Essays.* Ed. Julie H. Kim. London: McFarland & Company, 2005, p. 172.

35 Rankin, Ian. *Knots and Crosses* (1987). London: Orion, 2008, pp. 16/67.

36 Ibid, p. 183.

37 Ibid, p. 21.

38 Ibid, p. 25.

39 Plain, Gill. *Ian Rankin's Black and Blue.* London: Continuum International Publishing Group, 2002, p. 26.

40 Rankin, Ian. *Knots and Crosses* (1987). London: Orion, 2008, p. 177.

41 Ibid, p. 193.

42 Ibid, p. 28 .

43 Ibid, p. 164.

44 Pepper, Andrew. "The 'Hard-Boiled' Genre." *A Companion to Crime Fiction.* Ed. Charles J. Rzepka and Lee Horsley. Oxford: John Wiley & Sons, 2010, p. 147.

45 Kerr, Philip. *March Violets* (1989) in *Berlin Noir.* London: Penguin Books, 1993, p. 28.

46 Ibid, p. 19.

47 Ibid, p. 242.

48 Ibid, p. 11.

49 Ibid, p. 174.

50 Ibid, p. 118.

51 Ibid, p. 59.

52 Rowland, Susan. "The 'Classical' Model of the Golden Age." *A Companion to Crime Fiction*. Ed. Charles J. Rzepka and Lee Horsley. Oxford: John Wiley & Sons, 2010, p. 122.

53 Kerr, Philip. *March Violets* (1989) in *Berlin Noir*. London: Penguin Books, 1993, p. 37.

54 Ibid, p. 50.

55 Horsley, Lee. *The Noir Thriller*. Basingstoke: Palgrave Macmillan, 2009, p. 226.

56 Brookmyre, Christopher. *Quite Ugly One Morning* (1996). London: Abacus, 2009, p. 249.

57 Horsley, Lee. *The Noir Thriller*. Basingstoke: Palgrave Macmillan, 2009, pp. 193/226.

58 Brookmyre, Christopher. *Quite Ugly One Morning* (1996). London: Abacus, 2009, p. 25.

59 Ibid, p. 157.

60 Chabon, Michael. *Maps & Legends: Reading and Writing along the Borderlands*. New York: Harper Perennial, 2009, p. 93.

61 Pepper, Andrew. "The 'Hard-Boiled' Genre." *A Companion to Crime Fiction*. Ed. Charles J. Rzepka and Lee Horsley. Oxford: John Wiley & Sons, 2010, p. 151.

62 Žižek, Slavoj. *Violence*. London: Profile Books LTD, 2009, p. 64 .

63 Horsley, Lee. *The Noir Thriller*. Basingstoke: Palgrave Macmillan, 2009, p. 250.

64 Ibid, p. 256.

65 Johnston, Paul. *Body Politic* (1997). London: Hodder and Stoughton, 1998, p. 172.

66 Pepper, Andrew. "The 'Hard-Boiled' Genre." *A Companion to Crime Fiction*. Ed. Charles J. Rzepka and Lee Horsley. Oxford: John Wiley & Sons, 2010, p. 144.

67 Jameson, Fredric. "On Raymond Chandler." *The Poetics of Murder: Detective Fiction and Literary Theory*. Ed. Glenn W. Most & William W. Stowe. New York: Harcourt Brace Jovanovich, 1983, p. 131.

68 Welsh, Louise. *The Cutting Room* (2002). Edinburgh: Canongate, 2003, p. 27.

69 Ibid, p. 2.

70 Naremore, James. "Dashiell Hammett and the Poetics of Hard-Boiled Detection." *Art in Crime Writing*. Ed. Bernard Benstock. New York: St. Martin's Press, 1983, p. 51.

71 Welsh, Louise. *The Cutting Room* (2002). Edinburgh: Canongate, 2003, p. 153.

72 Ibid, p. 104.

73 Mina, Denise. *The Field of Blood* (2004). London: Bantam Books, 2006, p. 340.

74 Messent, Peter. "Introduction: From Private Eye to Police Procedural – The Logic of Contemporary Crime Fiction." *Criminal Proceedings: The Contemporary American Crime Novel*. Ed. Peter Messent. London: Pluto Press, 1997, p. 2.

75 Scaggs, John. *Crime Fiction*.

Abingdon: Routledge, 2005, p. 82.

76   Cawelti, John G. *Adventure, Mystery, and Romance*. Chicago: The University of Chicago Press, 1977, pp. 142/3.

77   Banks, Ray. *Saturday's Child* (2006). Edinburgh: Polygon, 2007, p. 147.

78   Ibid, p. 141.

79   Ibid, p. 40.

80   Messent, Peter. "Introduction: From Private Eye to Police Procedural – The Logic of Contemporary Crime Fiction." *Criminal Proceedings: The Contemporary American Crime Novel*. Ed. Peter Messent. London: Pluto Press, 1997, p. 17.

81   Pepper, Andrew. "The 'Hard-Boiled' Genre." *A Companion to Crime Fiction*. Ed. Charles J. Rzepka and Lee Horsley. Oxford: John Wiley & Sons, 2010, p. 142.

82   Banks, Ray. *Saturday's Child* (2006). Edinburgh: Polygon, 2007, p. 226.

83   Black, Tony. *Paying For It* (2008). London: Preface Publishing, 2009, p. 27.

84   Ibid, p. 57.

85   Ibid, p. 78.

86   Horsley, Lee. *The Noir Thriller*. Basingstoke: Palgrave Macmillan, 2009, p. 40.

87   Chabon, Michael. *Maps & Legends: Reading and Writing along the Borderlands*. New York: Harper Perennial, 2009, p. 76.

88   Black, Tony. *Paying For It* (2008). London: Preface Publishing, 2009, p. 137.

89   Ibid, p. 10.

90   Cawelti, John G. *Adventure, Mystery, and Romance*. Chicago: The University of Chicago Press, 1977, p. 161.

91   Black, Tony. *Paying For It* (2008). London: Preface Publishing, 2009, pp. 135/226.

92   Ibid, p. 31.

93   Ibid, p. 210.

94   Horsley, Lee. *The Noir Thriller*. Basingstoke: Palgrave Macmillan, 2009, p. 105.

95   May, Peter. *The Blackhouse*. London: Quercus, 2011, p. 47.

96   Ibid, p. 458.

97   Jameson, Fredric. "On Raymond Chandler." *The Poetics of Murder: Detective Fiction and Literary Theory*. Ed. Glenn W. Most & William W. Stowe. New York: Harcourt Brace Jovanovich, 1983, p. 131.

98   May, Peter. *The Blackhouse*. London: Quercus, 2011, pp. 459-460.

99   Macdonald, Ross. "The Writer As Detective Hero." *Detective Fiction*. Ed. Robin W. Winks. Woodstock: The Countryman Press, 1988, pp. 185-186.

100   Horsley, Lee. *The Noir Thriller*. Basingstoke: Palgrave Macmillan, 2009, p. 188.

101   Simpson, Philip. "Noir and the Psycho Thriller." *A Companion to Crime Fiction*. Ed. Charles J. Rzepka and Lee Horsley. Oxford: John Wiley & Sons, 2010, p. 191.

102   Macdonald, Ross. "The Writer As Detective Hero." *Detective Fiction*. Ed. Robin W. Winks. Woodstock: The

Countryman Press, 1988, p. 183.

103 Ferris, Gordon. *The Hanging Shed*
(2010). London: Corvus, 2011, p. 327.

104 Russell, Craig. *Lennox* (2009).
London: Quercus, 2010, p. 354.

105 Ibid, p. 175 .

106 Ferris, Gordon. *The Hanging Shed*
(2010). London: Corvus, 2011, p. 176.

107 Ibid, pp. 292-293/308/314/316.

108 Russell, Craig. *Lennox* (2009).
London: Quercus, 2010, p. 175.

109 Ibid, p. 391.

110 Ferris, Gordon. *The Hanging Shed*
(2010). London: Corvus, 2011, p. 350.

111 Russell, Craig. *Lennox* (2009).
London: Quercus, 2010, p. 313.

112 Ibid, p. 97.

113 Ferris, Gordon. *The Hanging Shed*
(2010). London: Corvus, 2011, p. 249.

114 Horsley, Lee. *The Noir Thriller*.
Basingstoke: Palgrave Macmillan,
2009, p. 188.

115 Russell, Craig. *Lennox* (2009).
London: Quercus, 2010, p. 37.

116 Ferris, Gordon. *The Hanging Shed*
(2010). London: Corvus, 2011, p. 215.

117 Ibid, p. 215.

118 Russell, Craig. *Lennox* (2009).
London: Quercus, 2010, p. 100.

119 Ferris, Gordon. *The Hanging Shed*
(2010). London: Corvus, 2011,
pp. 12/206.

120 Ibid, p. 249.

121 Cassuto, Leonard. *Hard-Boiled
Sentimentality: The Secret History
of American Crime Stories*. New
York: Columbia University Press,
2009, p. 112.

122 Russell, Craig. *Lennox* (2009).
London: Quercus, 2010, p. 192.

123 Ibid, p. 4.

124 Ibid, p. 4.

125 Ferris, Gordon. *The Hanging Shed*
(2010). London: Corvus, 2011, p. 382.

126 Russell, Craig. *Lennox* (2009).
London: Quercus, 2010, p. 123.

127 Ibid, p. 14.

128 Ferris, Gordon. *The Hanging Shed*
(2010). London: Corvus, 2011, p. 382.

129 Russell, Craig. *Lennox* (2009).
London: Quercus, 2010, p. 2.

130 Ferris, Gordon. *The Hanging Shed*
(2010). London: Corvus, 2011, p. 6.

131 Babener, Liahna K. "Raymond
Chandler's City of Lies." *Los
Angeles in Fiction: A Collection
of Essays*. Ed. David Fine.
Albuquerque: University of New
Mexico Press, 1995, p. 128.

132 Messent, Peter. *The Crime Fiction
Handbook*. Oxford: John Wiley &
Sons, 2013, p. 41.

133 Ibid, p. 43.

134 Binyon, T.J. *Murder Will Out: The
Detective in Fiction*. Oxford: Oxford
University Press, 1990, p. 133.

135 Panek, LeRoy Lad. "The Police
Novel." *Death by Pen: The
Longman Anthology of Detective
Fiction From Poe to Paretsky*. Ed.
Deane Mansfield-Kelley & Lois
A. Marchino. New York: Pearson
Longman, 2007, p. 343.

136 Horsley, Lee. "From Sherlock
Holmes to Present." *A Companion
to Crime Fiction*. Ed. Charles J.
Rzepka and Lee Horsley. Oxford:
John Wiley & Sons, 2010, p. 34.

137 Priestman, Martin. "Post-War
British Crime Fiction." *The
Cambridge Companion to Crime
Fiction*. Ed. Martin Priestman.

Cambridge: Cambridge University Press, 2008, p. 5.

138 Cohen, Josh. "James Ellroy, Los Angeles and the Spectacular Crisis of Masculinity." *Criminal Proceedings: The Contemporary American Crime Novel.* Ed. Peter Messent. London: Pluto Press, 1997, p. 169.

139 Simpson, Philip. "Noir and the Psycho Thriller." *A Companion to Crime Fiction.* Ed. Charles J. Rzepka and Lee Horsley. Oxford: John Wiley & Sons, 2010, p. 192 .

140 Panek, LeRoy Lad. "The Police Novel." *Death by Pen: The Longman Anthology of Detective Fiction From Poe to Paretsky.* Ed. Deane Mansfield-Kelley & Lois A. Marchino. New York: Pearson Longman, 2007, p. 349.

141 Ibid, p. 347.

142 Messent, Peter. *The Crime Fiction Handbook.* Oxford: John Wiley & Sons, 2013, pp. 45/43.

143 Messent, Peter. "Introduction: From Private Eye to Police Procedural – The Logic of Contemporary Crime Fiction." *Criminal Proceedings: The Contemporary American Crime Novel.* Ed. Peter Messent. London: Pluto Press, 1997, p. 12.

144 Messent, Peter. *The Crime Fiction Handbook.* Oxford: John Wiley & Sons, 2013, p. 44.

145 Rzepka, Charles J. "Introduction: What is Crime Fiction?" *A Companion to Crime Fiction.* Ed. Charles J. Rzepka and Lee Horsley. Oxford: John Wiley & Sons, 2010, p. 7.

146 Messent, Peter. "Introduction: From Private Eye to Police Procedural – The Logic of Contemporary Crime Fiction." *Criminal Proceedings: The Contemporary American Crime Novel.* Ed. Peter Messent. London: Pluto Press, 1997, p. 12.

147 Gormley, Jr., William T. "Moralists, Pragmatists, and Rogues: Bureaucrats in Modern Mysteries." *Public Administration Review,* Vol. 61, No. 2 (Mar.-Apr., 2001), pp. 184-193. JSTOR. Blackwell Publishing. 20. Feb. 2009. <http://www/jstor.org>, p. 191.

148 Beaton, M.C. *Death of a Gossip* (1985). London: Constable & Robinson, 2008, p. 7.

149 Ibid, p. 117.

150 Ibid, p. 96.

151 Ibid, p. 147.

152 Ibid, pp. 166-167.

153 McIlvanney, William. *Strange Loyalties* (1991). London: Sceptre, 1992, p. 8.

154 Messent, Peter. "The Police Novel." *A Companion to Crime Fiction.* Ed. Charles J. Rzepka and Lee Horsley. Oxford: John Wiley & Sons, 2010, p. 185.

155 McIlvanney, William. *Strange Loyalties* (1991). London: Sceptre, 1992, p. 18.

156 Ibid, p. 89.

157 Ibid, p. 181.

158 Ibid, p. 238.

159 Ibid, p. 201.

160 Ibid, p. 351.

161 Ibid, pp. 359/360.

162 McDermid, Val. *The Wire in the Blood* (1997). London: Harper, 2010, p. 16.

163 Simpson, Philip. "Noir and the

Psycho Thriller." *A Companion to Crime Fiction*. Ed. Charles J. Rzepka and Lee Horsley. Oxford: John Wiley & Sons, 2010, p. 187.

164 McDermid, Val. *The Wire in the Blood* (1997). London: Harper, 2010, p. 481.

165 Ibid, p. 481.

166 Gavin, Adrienne E. "Feminist Crime Fiction and Female Sleuths." *A Companion to Crime Fiction*. Ed. Charles J. Rzepka and Lee Horsley. Oxford: John Wiley & Sons, 2010, p. 268.

167 McDermid, Val. *The Wire in the Blood* (1997). London: Harper, 2010, p. 79.

168 Messent, Peter. "The Police Novel." *A Companion to Crime Fiction*. Ed. Charles J. Rzepka and Lee Horsley. Oxford: John Wiley & Sons, 2010, p. 185.

169 MacBride, Stuart. *Cold Granite*. London: HarperCollins, 2005, p. 9.

170 Ibid, p. 309.

171 Ibid, p. 575.

172 Panek, LeRoy Lad. "The Police Novel." *Death by Pen: The Longman Anthology of Detective Fiction From Poe to Paretsky*. Ed. Deane Mansfield-Kelley & Lois A. Marchino. New York: Pearson Longman, 2007, p. 346.

173 MacBride, Stuart. *Cold Granite*. London: HarperCollins, 2005, p. 42.

174 Ibid, p. 42.

175 Russell, Craig. *Blood Eagle*. London: Arrow, 2006, p. 2.

176 Ibid, p. 451.

177 Ibid, p. 126/127.

178 Ibid, p. 126.

179 Ibid, pp, 346/347.

180 Ibid, p, 450.

181 Ramsay, Caro. *Dark Water*. London: Penguin, 2010, p. 141.

182 Ibid, p. 453.

183 Messent, Peter. "Introduction: From Private Eye to Police Procedural – The Logic of Contemporary Crime Fiction." *Criminal Proceedings: The Contemporary American Crime Novel*. Ed. Peter Messent. London: Pluto Press, 1997, p. 16.

184 Žižek, Slavoj. *Violence*. London: Profile Books LTD, 2009, p. 174.

185 Jardine, Quintin. *A Rush of Blood*. London: Headline, 2010, pp. 6/10.

186 Ibid, p. 433.

187 Ibid, p. 10.

188 Messent, Peter. "The Police Novel." *A Companion to Crime Fiction*. Ed. Charles J. Rzepka and Lee Horsley. Oxford: John Wiley & Sons, 2010, p. 180.

189 Ibid, p. 181.

190 Panek, LeRoy Lad. "The Police Novel." *Death by Pen: The Longman Anthology of Detective Fiction From Poe to Paretsky*. Ed. Deane Mansfield-Kelley & Lois A. Marchino. New York: Pearson Longman, 2007, p. 349.

191 Campbell, Karen. *Proof of Life* (2011). London: Hodder and Stoughton, 2012, pp. 2-3.

192 Ibid, p. 246.

193 Ibid, p. 242.

194 Gavin, Adrienne E. "Feminist Crime Fiction and Female Sleuths." *A Companion to Crime Fiction*. Ed. Charles J. Rzepka and Lee Horsley. Oxford: John Wiley & Sons, 2010, p. 267.

195 Gray, Alex. *A Pound of Flesh*. London: Sphere, 2012, pp. 160/195/126/238.

196 Cassuto, Leonard. *Hard-Boiled Sentimentality: The Secret History of American Crime Stories*. New York: Columbia University Press, 2009, pp. 19/112.

197 Gray, Alex. *A Pound of Flesh*. London: Sphere, 2012, pp. 279/317.

198 Ibid, p. 158.

199 Ibid, p. 63.

200 Ibid, p. 239.

201 Ibid, p. 239.

202 Messent, Peter. "Introduction: From Private Eye to Police Procedural – The Logic of Contemporary Crime Fiction." *Criminal Proceedings: The Contemporary American Crime Novel*. Ed. Peter Messent. London: Pluto Press, 1997, p. 15.

203 Aristotle. *Politics*. Oxford: Oxford University Press, 2009, Book I, 1253.a27.

204 Mina, Denise. *Gods and Beasts*. London: Orion, 2012, p. 211.

205 Ibid, pp. 118/177.

206 Ibid, p. 162.

207 Ibid, p. 128.

208 Ibid, p. 127.

209 Rankin, Ian. Quoted in *Dead Sharp: Scottish Crime Writers on Country and Craft*. Ed. Len Wanner. Isle of Lewis: Two Ravens Press, 2011, p. 3.

210 Anderson, Patrick. *The Triumph of the Thriller: How Cops, Crooks, and Cannibals Captured Popular Fiction*. New York: Random House, 2007, p. 223.

211 Messent, Peter. "The Police Novel." *A Companion to Crime Fiction*. Ed. Charles J. Rzepka and Lee Horsley. Oxford: John Wiley & Sons, 2010, p. 183.

212 Rankin, Ian. *The Complaints* (2009). London: Orion, 2010, p. 10.

213 Ibid, pp. 375-376.

214 Gormley, Jr., William T. "Moralists, Pragmatists, and Rogues: Bureaucrats in Modern Mysteries." *Public Administration Review*, Vol. 61, No. 2 (Mar.-Apr., 2001), pp. 184-193. JSTOR. Blackwell Publishing. 20. Feb. 2009. <http://www/jstor.org>, p. 187.

215 Rankin, Ian. *Resurrection Men* (2001). London: Orion, 2008, p. 304.

216 Ibid, p. 395.

217 Rankin, Ian. *The Complaints* (2009). London: Orion, 2010, p. 227.

218 Ibid, p. 3.

219 Rankin, Ian. *Resurrection Men* (2001). London: Orion, 2008, p. 94.

220 Ibid, p. 326.

221 Ibid, p. 470.

222 Ibid, p. 140.

223 Ibid, p. 392.

224 Rankin, Ian. *The Complaints* (2009). London: Orion, 2010, p. 359.

225 Rankin, Ian. *Resurrection Men* (2001). London: Orion, 2008, p. 135.

226 Ibid, p. 135.

227 Ibid, p. 287.

228 Rankin, Ian. *The Complaints* (2009). London: Orion, 2010, p. 276.

229 Cohen, Josh. "James Ellroy, Los Angeles and the Spectacular Crisis of Masculinity." *Criminal Proceedings: The Contemporary American Crime Novel*. Ed. Peter

Messent. London: Pluto Press, 1997, p. 168.

230 Rankin, Ian. *The Complaints* (2009). London: Orion, 2010, p. 372.

231 Plain, Gill. *Ian Rankin's Black and Blue*. London: Continuum International Publishing Group, 2002, p. 46.

232 Waller and Deal 2010: 3

233 Priestman, Martin. *Crime Fiction: From Poe to the Present*. Plymouth: Northcote House Publishers, 1998, p. 33.

234 Seltzer, Mark. *Serial Killers: Death and Life in America's Wound Culture*. New York: Routledge, 1998, p. 1.

235 Cassuto, Leonard. *Hard-Boiled Sentimentality: The Secret History of American Crime Stories*. New York: Columbia University Press, 2009, p. 262.

236 Ibid, p. 259.

237 Friedman, Richard A. "Revising the Script on Mental Illness and Violence." *New York Times*. 4th of March 2003, p. 6.

238 Dietrich, Eric and Fox Hall, Tara. "The Allure of the Serial Killer." *Serial Killers: Being and Killing*. Ed. S. Waller. Oxford: Wiley-Blackwell, 2010, pp. 94-95.

239 Priestman, Martin. *Crime Fiction: From Poe to the Present*. Plymouth: Northcote House Publishers, 1998, p. 30.

240 Horsley, Lee. "From Sherlock Holmes to Present." *A Companion to Crime Fiction*. Ed. Charles J. Rzepka and Lee Horsley. Oxford: John Wiley & Sons, 2010, p. 40.

241 Cassuto, Leonard. *Hard-Boiled Sentimentality: The Secret History of American Crime Stories*. New York: Columbia University Press, 2009, p. 242.

242 Gray, Richard M. "Psychopathy and Will to Power: Ted Bundy and Dennis Rader." *Serial Killers: Being and Killing*. Ed. S. Waller. Oxford: Wiley-Blackwell, 2010, pp. 196/192/195.

243 Deal, William E. "The Serial Killer Was (Cognitively) Framed." *Serial Killers: Being and Killing*. Ed. S. Waller. Oxford: Wiley-Blackwell, 2010, pp. 164-165.

244 Cassuto, Leonard. *Hard-Boiled Sentimentality: The Secret History of American Crime Stories*. New York: Columbia University Press, 2009, p. 267.

245 Mansel, H. L. "Sensation Novels." *Quarterly Review*. 113: 226 (April 1863), p. 499.

246 Barzun, Jacques. *The Culture We Deserve*. Middletown: Wesleyan University Press, 1989, p. 176.

247 Anderson, Patrick. *The Triumph of the Thriller: How Cops, Crooks, and Cannibals Captured Popular Fiction*. New York: Random House, 2007, p. 219.

248 Lindsay, Frederic. *Jill Rips* (1987). London: Corgi, 1988, p. 85.

249 Cameron, Deborah and Frazer, Elizabeth. *The Lust to Kill: A Feminist Investigation of Sexual Murder*. Cambridge: Polity Press, 1987, p. 22.

250 Schechter, Elizabeth and Schechter, Harold. "Killing with Kindness: Nature, Nurture, and the Female Serial Killer." *Serial Killers: Being*

and Killing. Ed. S. Waller. Oxford: Wiley-Blackwell, 2010, pp. 118/124.

251 Paglia, Camille. *Sexual Personae: Art and Decadence from Nefertiti to Emily Dickinson.* New Haven: Yale University Press, 1991, p. 247.

252 Lindsay, Frederic. *Jill Rips* (1987). London: Corgi, 1988, p. 225.

253 Ibid, p. 225.

254 Ibid, p. 131.

255 Kerr, Philip. *A Philosophical Investigation* (1992). London: Vintage, 1996, p. 145.

256 Ibid, p. 49.

257 Ibid, p. 227.

258 Ibid, p. 337.

259 Kant, Immanuel. *Philosophy of Law* (1796). Trans. William Hastie. Edinburgh: T & T Clarke, 1887, p. 198.

260 Rankin, Ian. *Black & Blue* (1997). London: Orion, 2008, p. 26.

261 Plain, Gill. *Ian Rankin's Black and Blue.* London: Continuum International Publishing Group, 2002, p. 41.

262 Rankin, Ian. *Black & Blue* (1997). London: Orion, 2008, p. 111.

263 Plain, Gill. *Ian Rankin's Black and Blue.* London: Continuum International Publishing Group, 2002, p. 40.

264 Ibid, p. 29.

265 Rankin, Ian. *Black & Blue* (1997). London: Orion, 2008, p. 399.

266 Lindsay, Douglas. *The Long Midnight of Barney Thomson* (1999). Inverness: Long Midnight Publishing, 2008, p. 31.

267 Alfano, Mark. "The Situation of the Jury: Attribution Bias in the Trials of Accused Serial Killers." *Serial Killers: Being and Killing.* Ed. S. Waller. Oxford: Wiley-Blackwell, 2010, p. 47.

268 Lindsay, Douglas. *The Long Midnight of Barney Thomson* (1999). Inverness: Long Midnight Publishing, 2008, p. 144.

269 Ibid, p. 154.

270 Ibid, p. 3.

271 Keegan, Chris. "It Puts the Lotion in the Basket." *Serial Killers: Being and Killing.* Ed. S. Waller. Oxford: Wiley-Blackwell, 2010, p. 133.

272 Armstrong, Campbell. *Butcher* (2006). London: Allison & Busby, 2007, p. 381.

273 Ibid, p. 495.

274 Keegan, Chris. "It Puts the Lotion in the Basket." *Serial Killers: Being and Killing.* Ed. S. Waller. Oxford: Wiley-Blackwell, 2010, p. 130.

275 Piven, Jerry. "The Thread of Death, or the Compulsion to Kill." *Serial Killers: Being and Killing.* Ed. S. Waller. Oxford: Wiley-Blackwell, 2010, p. 212.

276 Armstrong, Campbell. *Butcher* (2006). London: Allison & Busby, 2007, p. 155.

277 Ibid, p. 248.

278 Piven, Jerry. "The Thread of Death, or the Compulsion to Kill." *Serial Killers: Being and Killing.* Ed. S. Waller. Oxford: Wiley-Blackwell, 2010, p. 207.

279 Brookmyre, Christopher. *A Snowball in Hell* (2008). London: Abacus, 2009, p. 5.

280 Ibid, p. 4.

281 Terjesen, Andrew. "Are Serial Killers Cold-Blooded Killers?" *Serial Killers: Being and Killing.*

282 Brookmyre, Christopher. *A Snowball in Hell* (2008). London: Abacus, 2009, p. 17.

283 Ibid, p. 100.

284 Ibid, pp. 7/13.

285 Ibid, p. 210.

286 Schmid, David. "A Philosophy of Serial Killing: Sade, Nietzsche, and Brady at the Gates of Janus." *Serial Killers: Being and Killing.* Ed. S. Waller. Oxford: Wiley-Blackwell, 2010, p. 35.

287 Robertson, Craig. *Random* (2010). London: Simon & Schuster, 2011, p. 293.

288 Ibid, p. 37.

289 Piven, Jerry. "The Thread of Death, or the Compulsion to Kill." *Serial Killers: Being and Killing.* Ed. S. Waller. Oxford: Wiley-Blackwell, 2010, p. 211.

290 Robertson, Craig. *Random* (2010). London: Simon & Schuster, 2011, p. 334.

291 Ibid, p. 113.

292 Ibid, p. 218.

293 Ibid, p. 321.

294 Amper, Susan. "Dexter's Dark World: The Serial Killer as Superhero." *Serial Killers: Being and Killing.* Ed. S. Waller. Oxford: Wiley-Blackwell, 2010, p. 112.

295 Cassuto, Leonard. *Hard-Boiled Sentimentality: The Secret History of American Crime Stories.* New York: Columbia University Press, 2009, p. 241.

296 Anderson, Lin. *Picture Her Dead.* London: Hodder & Stoughton, 2011, p. 185.

297 Ibid, p. 436.

298 Ibid, p. 219.

299 Messent, Peter. "Introduction: From Private Eye to Police Procedural – The Logic of Contemporary Crime Fiction." *Criminal Proceedings: The Contemporary American Crime Novel.* Ed. Peter Messent. London: Pluto Press, 1997, p. 16.

300 Piven, Jerry. "The Thread of Death, or the Compulsion to Kill." *Serial Killers: Being and Killing.* Ed. S. Waller. Oxford: Wiley-Blackwell, 2010, p. 216.

301 Anderson, Lin. *Picture Her Dead.* London: Hodder & Stoughton, 2011, p. 307.

302 Moffat, GJ. *Protection.* London: Headline, 2012, pp. 66/145.

303 Ibid, p. 300.

304 Gray, Richard M. "Psychopathy and Will to Power: Ted Bundy and Dennis Rader." *Serial Killers: Being and Killing.* Ed. S. Waller. Oxford: Wiley-Blackwell, 2010, p. 197.

305 Moffat, GJ. *Protection.* London: Headline, 2012, p. 372.

306 Ibid, p. 369.

307 Oswald, James. *Natural Causes* (2012). London: Penguin, 2013, p. 359.

308 Ibid, p. 113.

309 Ibid, p. 446.

310 Haut, Woody. *Neon Noir.* London: Serpent's Tail, 1999, p. 207.

311 Gray, Richard M. "Psychopathy and Will to Power: Ted Bundy and Dennis Rader." *Serial Killers: Being and Killing.* Ed. S. Waller. Oxford: Wiley-Blackwell, 2010, p. 192.

312   Brady, Ian. *The Gates of Janus: Serial Killing and its Analysis.* Los Angeles: Feral House, 2001, p. 86.

313   Horsley, Lee. "From Sherlock Holmes to Present." *A Companion to Crime Fiction.* Ed. Charles J. Rzepka and Lee Horsley. Oxford: John Wiley & Sons, 2010, p. 40.

314   Cassuto, Leonard. *Hard-Boiled Sentimentality: The Secret History of American Crime Stories.* New York: Columbia University Press, 2009, p. 241.

315   Ibid, p. 244.

316   Ibid, pp. 270/271.

317   McDermid, Val. *The Mermaids Singing.* London: HarperCollins, 1995, p. 87.

318   Schechter, Elizabeth and Schechter, Harold. "Killing with Kindness: Nature, Nurture, and the Female Serial Killer." *Serial Killers: Being and Killing.* Ed. S. Waller. Oxford: Wiley-Blackwell, 2010, p. 124.

319   McDermid, Val. *The Mermaids Singing.* London: HarperCollins, 1995, p. 399.

320   Ibid, p. 58.

321   Ibid, p. 110.

322   Ibid, p. 193.

323   MacBride, Stuart. *Flesh House* (2008). London: HarperCollins, 2009, p. 136.

324   Ibid, p. 39.

325   Ibid, p. 359.

326   Ibid, p. 367.

327   Ibid, p. 258.

328   McDermid, Val. *The Mermaids Singing.* London: HarperCollins, 1995, p. 310.

329   Ibid, pp. 45-46.

330   Ibid, p. 152.

331   Cassuto, Leonard. *Hard-Boiled Sentimentality: The Secret History of American Crime Stories.* New York: Columbia University Press, 2009, pp. 246/247.

332   MacBride, Stuart. *Flesh House* (2008). London: HarperCollins, 2009, p. 275.

333   Ibid, p. 145.

334   Ibid, p. 565.

335   Ibid, p. 586.

336   Ibid, p. 403.

337   McDermid, Val. *The Mermaids Singing.* London: HarperCollins, 1995, pp. 96/3.

338   MacBride, Stuart. *Flesh House* (2008). London: HarperCollins, 2009, p. 357.

339   Goldberg, Carl. *Speaking with the Devil.* New York: Penguin, 1997, p. 32.

340   Vargas, Manuel. "Are Psychopathic Serial Killers Evil? Are They Blameworthy for What They Do?" *Serial Killers: Being and Killing.* Ed. S. Waller. Oxford: Wiley-Blackwell, 2010, p. 67.

341   McDermid, Val. *The Mermaids Singing.* London: HarperCollins, 1995, p. 13.

342   Naremore, James. *More than Night: Film Noir in its Contexts.* Berkeley and Los Angeles: University of California Press, 2008, pp. 27/28.

343   Graham, Barry. "Noir: The Marxist Art Form." 14. May 2013. <http://www.thebigclickmag.com/noir-the-marxist-art-form>, p. 1.

344   Naremore, James. *More than Night: Film Noir in its Contexts.* Berkeley and Los Angeles: University of California Press, 2008, p. 39.

345 Lansdale, Joe R. *Darkness in the East*. 12. Feb. 2010. <http://www.mulhollandbooks.com/2010/11/12/darkness-in-the-east>, p. 1.

346 Naremore, James. *More than Night: Film Noir in its Contexts*. Berkeley and Los Angeles: University of California Press, 2008, p. 6.

347 Ibid, p. 279.

348 Seaman, Damien. "Femme Fatale: Women, Sex and Guilt in Noir Fiction." 23. Jan. 2012. <http://www.allanguthrie.co.uk/pages/noir_zine/articles/femme_fatale.php>, p. 1.

349 Horsley, Lee. *The Noir Thriller*. Basingstoke: Palgrave Macmillan, 2009, p. 154.

350 Simpson, Philip. "Noir and the Psycho Thriller." *A Companion to Crime Fiction*. Ed. Charles J. Rzepka and Lee Horsley. Oxford: John Wiley & Sons, 2010, p. 197.

351 Schrader, Paul. "Notes on Film Noir." *Film Noir Reader*. Ed. Alain Silver and James Ursini. New York: Limelight Editions, 1996, p. 58.

352 Banks, Ray. "The French Word for Bleak." 31. Dec 2011. <http://www.thecrimefactory.com/2011/11/the-french-word-for-bleak/>, p. 1.

353 Naremore, James. *More than Night: Film Noir in its Contexts*. Berkeley and Los Angeles: University of California Press, 2008, p. 298.

354 Graham, Barry. "Noir: The Marxist Art Form." 14. May 2013. <http://www.thebigclickmag.com/noir-the-marxist-art-form>, p. 1.

355 Aristotle. *On the Art of Poetry*. Boston: IndyPublish, 2004, p. XIII.

356 Corbett 2010: 1

357 Messent, Peter. *The Crime Fiction Handbook*. Oxford: John Wiley & Sons, 2013, p. 51.

358 Horsley, Lee. *The Noir Thriller*. Basingstoke: Palgrave Macmillan, 2009, p. 13.

359 Banks, Ray. "The French Word for Bleak." 31. Dec 2011. <http://www.thecrimefactory.com/2011/11/the-french-word-for-bleak/>, p. 1.

360 Penzler, Otto. "Noir Fiction Is About Losers, Not Private Eyes." 24. Jul 2011. <http://www.huffingtonpost.com/otto-penzler/noir-fiction-is-about-los_b_676200.html>, p. 1.

361 Corbett, David. "Insulting Your Intelligence ('Just gimme some noiriness')." 28. Oct 2010. <http://www.mulhollandbooks.com/2010/10/28/insulting-your-intelligence-just-gimme-some-noiriness>, p. 1.

362 Žižek, Slavoj. *Violence*. London: Profile Books LTD, 2009, p. 8.

363 Rzepka, Charles J. "Introduction: What is Crime Fiction?" *A Companion to Crime Fiction*. Ed. Charles J. Rzepka and Lee Horsley. Oxford: John Wiley & Sons, 2010, p. 6.

364 Naremore, James. *More than Night: Film Noir in its Contexts*. Berkeley and Los Angeles: University of California Press, 2008, p. 22.

365 Rankin, Ian. "Ian Rankin." *Dead Sharp: Scottish Crime Writers*

on Country and Craft. Ed. Len
Wanner. Isle of Lewis: Two
Ravens Press, 2011, p. 3.

366 Pringle, John. "Introduction."
Young Adam (1966). Edinburgh:
Rebel Inc., 1996, p. v.

367 Trocchi, Alexander. Young Adam
(1966). Edinburgh: Rebel Inc.,
1996, p. xi.

368 Ibid, p. 77.

369 Ibid, p. 81.

370 Ibid, p. 83.

371 Ibid, p. 125.

372 Ibid, p. 146.

373 Ibid, p. 150.

374 Ibid, p. 90.

375 Nicol, Bran. "Patricia
Highsmith." A Companion to
Crime Fiction. Ed. Charles J.
Rzepka and Lee Horsley.
Oxford: John Wiley & Sons,
2010, p. 504.

376 Rae, Hugh C. Skinner (1965).
Glasgow: Richard Drew
Publishing, 1988, p. 278.

377 Ibid, p. 171.

378 Ibid, p. 149.

379 Ibid, p. 286.

380 Ibid, pp. 284/285/286.

381 Ibid, p. 205.

382 Ibid, p. 279.

383 Williams, Gordon. The Siege of
Trencher's Farm (1969). London:
Titan Books, 2011, p. 47.

384 Ibid, p. 185.

385 Ibid, p. 146.

386 Ibid, p. 216.

387 Ibid, p. 218.

388 Ibid, p. 223.

389 Ibid, p. 223.

390 McIlvanney, William. The Papers
of Tony Veitch (1983). London:
Sceptre, 1992, p. 203.

391 Ibid, p. 21.

392 Banks, Iain. The Wasp Factory
(1984). London: Abacus, 1992,
pp. 13-14/136.

393 Ibid, p. 42.

394 Horsley, Lee. The Noir Thriller.
Basingstoke: Palgrave Macmillan,
2009, p. 171.

395 Malmgren, Carl. "Anatomy of
Murder: Mystery, Detective, and
Crime Fiction." Journal of Popular
Culture, Volume 30, Issue 4, pages
115–135, Spring 1997, p. 131.

396 Hazlitt, William. Selected
Writings (1826). Harmondsworth:
Penguin, 1970, p. 398.

397 Banks, Iain. The Wasp Factory (1984).
London: Abacus, 1992, p. 139.

398 Ibid, p. 183.

399 Graham, Barry. The Book of
Man (1995). New York: Cracked
Sidewalk Press, 2011, p. 7.

400 Ibid, p. 27.

401 Ibid, p. 129.

402 Ibid, p. 79.

403 Ibid, p. 6.

404 Ibid, p. 143.

405 Ibid, p. 28.

406 McLean, Duncan. Bunker Man
(1995). New York: W. W. Norton,
1997, p. 91.

407 Ibid, p. 288.

408 Vidal, Gore. Selected Essays. Ed. Jay
Parini. London: Abacus, 2007, p. 330.

409 McLean, Duncan. Bunker Man
(1995). New York: W. W. Norton,
1997, p. 153.

410 Ibid, p. 77.

411 Alfano, Mark. "The Situation of the

Jury: Attribution Bias in the Trials of Accused Serial Killers." *Serial Killers: Being and Killing.* Ed. S. Waller. Oxford: Wiley-Blackwell, 2010, p. 47.

412 Major, John. Quoted in "Major on Crime." *The Independent* (1993). 27. Oct. 2013. <http://www. independent.co.uk/news/major-on-crime-condemn-more-understand-less-1474470.html>, p. 1.

413 McLean, Duncan. *Bunker Man* (1995). New York: W. W. Norton, 1997, p. 248.

414 Ibid, p. 181.

415 Ibid, pp. 211/49.

416 Welsh, Irvine. *Filth* (1998). London: Vintage, 1999, pp. 118/389.

417 Ibid, p. 392.

418 Ibid, p. 221.

419 Ibid, p. 70.

420 Ibid, p. 76.

421 Ibid, p. 195.

422 Banks, Ray. "Ray Banks." *The Crime Interviews: Volume Two.* Ed. Len Wanner. Glasgow: Blasted Heath, 2012, p. 1.

423 Horsley, Lee. "From Sherlock Holmes to Present." *A Companion to Crime Fiction.* Ed. Charles J. Rzepka and Lee Horsley. Oxford: John Wiley & Sons, 2010, p. 39.

424 Naremore, James. "Dashiell Hammett and the Poetics of Hard-Boiled Detection." *Art in Crime Writing.* Ed. Bernard Benstock. New York: St. Martin's Press, 1983, p. 50.

425 Banks, Ray. *Beast of Burden.* Edinburgh: Polygon, 2009, p. 253.

426 Horsley, Lee. *The Noir Thriller.*

Basingstoke: Palgrave Macmillan, 2009, p. 112.

427 Ascari, Maurizio. *A Counter-History of Crime Fiction: Supernatural, Gothic, Sensational.* Basingstoke: Palgrave Macmillan, 2007, p. 12.

428 McIlvanney, Liam. *All the Colours of the Town* (2009). London: Faber and Faber, 2010, p. 81.

429 Ibid, p. 79.

430 Ibid, p. 128.

431 Ibid, p. 131.

432 Ibid, p. 153.

433 Ibid, p. 200.

434 Naremore, James. *More than Night: Film Noir in its Contexts.* Berkeley and Los Angeles: University of California Press, 2008, p. 44.

435 McIlvanney, Liam. *All the Colours of the Town* (2009). London: Faber and Faber, 2010, p. 179.

436 Ibid, p. 199.

437 Ibid, pp. 33/122.

438 Naremore, James. "Dashiell Hammett and the Poetics of Hard-Boiled Detection." *Art in Crime Writing.* Ed. Bernard Benstock. New York: St. Martin's Press, 1983, p. 64.

439 Guthrie. Allan. "Allan Guthrie's Ten Rules to Write Noir." <http://www.deadendfollies. com/2011/07/allan-guthries-ten-rules-to-write-noir.html>, p. 1.

440 Rankin, Ian. Quoted in *The Scotsman.* "Crime Writer does it by the Books." 30. Aug. 2004. <http://www.scotsman.com/news/crime-writer-does-it-by-the-books-1-1023543>, p. 1.

441 Lindenmuth, Brian. "Bloody Women by Helen FitzGerald." *Spinetingler Magazine.* 13. Jan. 2011. <http://www.spinetinglermag.com/2011/01/13/bloody-women-by-helen-fitzgerald-review/>, p. 1.

442 McIlvanney, William. "William McIlvanney." *The Crime Interviews: Volume Two.* Ed. Len Wanner. Glasgow: Blasted Heath, 2012, p. 1.

443 Ibid, p. 1.

444 Malmgren, Carl. "Anatomy of Murder: Mystery, Detective, and Crime Fiction." *Journal of Popular Culture*, Volume 30, Issue 4, pages 115–135, Spring 1997, p. 131.

445 FitzGerald, Helen. *Bloody Women.* Edinburgh: Polygon, 2009, p. 10.

446 Guthrie, Allan. *Slammer.* Edinburgh: Polygon, 2009, p. 169.

447 FitzGerald, Helen. *Bloody Women.* Edinburgh: Polygon, 2009, p. 53.

448 Guthrie, Allan. *Slammer.* Edinburgh: Polygon, 2009, p. 147.

449 FitzGerald, Helen. *Bloody Women.* Edinburgh: Polygon, 2009, p. 14.

450 Ibid, p. 7.

451 Ibid, p. 20.

452 Schmid, David. "David Goodis." *A Companion to Crime Fiction.* Ed. Charles J. Rzepka and Lee Horsley. Oxford: John Wiley & Sons, 2010, p. 205.

453 FitzGerald, Helen. *Bloody Women.* Edinburgh: Polygon, 2009, 29.

454 Ibid, p. 8.

455 Guthrie, Allan. *Slammer.* Edinburgh: Polygon, 2009, p. 93.

456 Ibid, p. 156.

457 Ibid, pp. 246-247.

458 Alfano, Mark. "The Situation of the Jury: Attribution Bias in the Trials of Accused Serial Killers." *Serial Killers: Being and Killing.* Ed. S. Waller. Oxford: Wiley-Blackwell, 2010, p. 48.

459 FitzGerald, Helen. *Bloody Women.* Edinburgh: Polygon, 2009, p. 4.

460 Ibid, p. 49.

461 Ibid, p. 124.

462 Guthrie, Allan. *Slammer.* Edinburgh: Polygon, 2009, p. 55.

463 Ibid, pp. 13/22.

464 Simpson, Philip. "Noir and the Psycho Thriller." *A Companion to Crime Fiction.* Ed. Charles J. Rzepka and Lee Horsley. Oxford: John Wiley & Sons, 2010, p. 197.